M000315619

Prisoner Reentry

Stan Stojkovic
Editor

Prisoner Reentry

Critical Issues and Policy Directions

Editor
Stan Stojkovic
Helen Bader School of Social Welfare
University of Wisconsin-Milwaukee
Milwaukee, Wisconsin, USA

ISBN 978-1-137-57928-7   ISBN 978-1-137-57929-4 (eBook)
DOI 10.1057/978-1-137-57929-4

Library of Congress Control Number: 2016949464

Cover illustration © Myron Jay Dorf, © baona / Getty Images

Printed on acid-free paper

This Palgrave Macmillan imprint is published by Springer Nature
The registered company is Nature America Inc.
The registered company address is: 1 New York Plaza, New York, NY 10004, U.S.A.

Acknowledgments

I would like to thank the authors of the chapters in this volume. Their expertise and commitment to understanding the prisoner reentry process is unparalleled. I believe their contributions to this volume will have a profound impact on how we understand and conceptualize prisoner reentry and how we should proceed to make sure prisoner reentry efforts are rooted in the best scientific evidence available.

I dedicate this book to the memory of my brother – Milan Stojkovic – a police officer for 31 years with the Milwaukee Police Department, Milwaukee, Wisconsin, USA.

I wish to extend my gratitude to Ms. Stephanie Carey for her support and probing queries. I am sure the book is a much better product due to her diligence and efforts.

Contents

List of Tables

Introduction

Stan Stojkovic

No other issue facing the criminal justice system is more pressing than the prisoner reentry issue (Petersilia 2004). At a time when prison populations have stabilized and many states have either reduced prison commitments or have been forced to reduce prison populations (e.g., California), we have seen unprecedented growth in returning offender populations (Bureau of Justice Statistics 2015; Zimring 2016). Additionally, there have been concerns on how best to deal with offenders once they are released from prison (Council on State Governments 2010; see Council on State Governments' Justice Center reports on prisoner reentry initiatives across the country). These concerns have spawned many discussions and debates both at the federal level and at the state level about how to address burgeoning prisoner reentry populations. Offenders are leaving prisons and now need to be managed within communities (Schrag 2013; Crow and Smykla 2014).

S. Stojkovic (✉)
Helen Bader School of Social Welfare, University of Wisconsin-Milwaukee, Milwaukee, Wisconsin, USA
e-mail: stojkovi@uwm.edu

© The Author(s) 2017   1
S. Stojkovic (ed.), *Prisoner Reentry*,
DOI 10.1057/978-1-137-57929-4_1

In the history of the country, we have never seen the numbers of offenders that now need to be managed in the community like we are seeing in 2016 and beyond (Lofstrom and Raphael 2016). States are under enormous pressure to address the concerns of offenders returning from prison in large numbers, but their budgets are meager at best to manage the primary concerns of returning offenders: homelessness; joblessness; massive personal debt; strained familial relationships; adjustment problems, especially for unique offender populations, such as sex offenders; offender program veracity and implementation issues; and finally, a sufficient number of quality agencies providing offender services within communities.

Governments have tried to address these concerns by first examining the issues with data collection efforts (Rhine and Thompson 2011). The federal government, for example, wanted to know more about prisoner reentry programs, offender participants, and difficulties in managing offenders in the community since 2000. The Serious and Violent Offender Reentry Initiative (SVORI) was one of the first federally funded programs that sought to examine ways in which states attempted to address the needs of offenders returning home. As suspected, research on the effectiveness of SVORI regarding recidivism among program participants has been lacking. As is true with many criminal justice research efforts, the studies are not all measuring the same thing or examining the issues faced by returning offenders the same way. The product is an amalgam of conflicting studies and limited findings for communities to use going forward in the management of returning offenders (Petersilia 2003).

What is needed is some general first principles (evidence based) of effective prisoner reentry and how they can be implemented across varying offender populations within communities. We have had over 15 years of offender populations returning to communities across the country under the rubric of prisoner reentry. What do we really know about these returning offender populations? What do we know about what works and does not work for returning offenders? What do we know about critical elements of offender lives or communities that enable effective prisoner reentry to occur? What do we know about especially problematic offenders (e.g., sex offenders) and prisoner reentry? What do we know about the role families play in the reentry process for offenders? What do we know about effective offender reentry from the perspective of service providers? What do we know about the employment problem and retraining offenders? What do we know about offender views regarding their reentry into communities?

All of these questions raise the question of public policy choices within the realm of prisoner reentry. The purpose of this book is to generate some answers on how best to conceive, implement, and evaluate prisoner reentry initiatives such that we can answer the questions listed above. To that end, this volume was created with a public policy mindset, focused on answering hard questions based in what we know from research evidence. No current volume has been able to answer difficult questions because most reentry monologues focus on the descriptive nature of prisoner reentry efforts. Such descriptions are crucial to our understanding of effective prisoner reentry efforts, but they do not go far enough. We need more analysis of the prisoner reentry phenomenon, and we need more integration of what we know about various prisoner reentry topics with what is actually being practiced in the prisoner reentry service world (Visher and Travis 2011).

This small volume has chosen to fill the public policy void regarding prisoner reentry with lengthy chapters on not only what is needed to have an effective prisoner reentry program but also, more importantly, how we apply these effective practices to specific issues we see as germane and central to effective prisoner reentry. As noted in Chapter 5, effective prisoner reentry programs must be understood as having diverse foci and the services they provide will be varied, given the nature of offender populations. We recognize this as a given in examining the prisoner reentry topic, but we do feel there are some issues that warrant further attention and detail than what has been traditionally covered in scholarly pieces on prisoner reentry. These topics tend to stick out as issues that require more examination and discussion among criminal justice professionals, politicians, and the general citizenry.

As we are in favor of offering an assessment of evidence-based initiatives regarding prisoner reentry programming, we offer in Chapter 5 a review of the evidence concerning what works in prisoner reentry programming. Ndrecka, Listwan, and Latessa provide some answers in the fifth chapter to this volume. They offer an exhaustive review of the literature what we need to know about prisoner reentry and what works with differing offender populations. Based on work that has been generated over the past 30 years, they offer a direction that suggest regardless of reentry program, there must be attention paid to the principles of *risk*, *need*, and *responsivity*. Extant research has shown how paying attention to these principles pays huge dividends when constructing and implementing an effective prisoner reentry program (Latessa 2012). Applying these principles to prisoner reentry programs increases the chances that they will reduce offender recidivism in the long run, and as suggested by Petersilia (2004), we need to answer which programs should communities invest in for returning offenders, given the best evidence available. Chapter 5 of this volume attempts to answer this question by reviewing the most recent prisoner reentry literature and coming up with solid answers to the hard questions posed earlier.

One issue that deserves attention is the role families play in the reentry efforts of offenders. Most extant research on family dynamics and prisoner reentry is fairly limited and is highly descriptive: Families are affected by prisoners coming back home, but how are they affected? What do we know about family dynamics and effective prisoner reentry? Do families matter in the reentry process, and if they do, how do they matter?

Chapter 3 by Begun, Hodge, and Early begin to ask and answer questions posed when examining family dynamics and prisoner reentry. The prisoner reentry literature is replete with references to the importance of families to effective prisoner reentry (Hairston et al. 2004), yet very little is documented on *what elements* of the family dynamic are crucial to effective prisoner reentry, and what do we really know about family dynamics and how such an understanding sheds light on how best we can promote effective prisoner reentry. Begun, Hodge, and Early provide some fascinating insights that previous research has either neglected or simply dismissed the importance of family dynamics, that is, how family roles shape offender responses to daily situations and the prisoner reentry process. In the words of the authors, " . . . families are profoundly affected by a member's incarceration, so too are they powerfully affected by the reentry process."

Chapter 3 provides an exhaustive overview of why family systems are so critical to effective prisoner reentry efforts. Moreover, the chapter introduces us to the importance of social policies that reinforce strengthening families. Much extant research on prisoner reentry addresses family dynamics in almost a superficial way, appealing to an intuitive understanding of families in the reentry process, with very little in-depth understanding of family dynamics and the crucial role it plays in reducing offender recidivism. Additionally, the authors highlight the importance of prison visitation to effective prisoner reentry.

There has been much research on prison visitation and its role in assisting staff to maintain prison order, as well as promote positive outcomes once offenders are released from prison (Sharp 2003). Begun, Hodge, and Early provide an effective roadmap for prisoner reentry success based on their extensive research done on prisoners and their families. They remind us that the incarceration of a family member does not mean the family ceases to exist, and even though the hardships placed on the family when a family member is incarcerated are significant, they can be overcome and families can potentially thrive. As noted by these authors, however, the challenges facing families of the incarcerated are significant in degree and numerous in number, yet families do survive.

As a society, we have to ask how much are we willing to have families suffer due to the criminal actions of their loved ones, and how does excessive incarceration not only potentially damage offenders but also does irreparable harm to their families. The authors note the resilience of families as they experience incarceration alongside their family members, yet the collateral consequences of protracted incarceration on families is not only demonstrable but in some cases is also devastating. As we work toward more effective prisoner reentry policies and practices, we must consider what impact, either positive or negative, they have on the returning offender and their families.

Similarly, we need to examine how we address prisoner reentry in the context of employment opportunities for released offenders. Pogrebin, West-Smith, Walker, and Unnithan in Chapter 7 address an issue that raises the question of employment for ex-offenders, but also introduces the larger question: Is employment enough for the formerly incarcerated to survive in the community once released from prison? Does employment, in effect, really impact the adjustment of former offenders? The authors offer a rather sober response to this question based on their research findings.

For many, it seems quite intuitive to view employment as a key factor in the reentry process, but as suggested by the authors in Chapter 7, when is employment just not enough to carry the day for the typical offender? Utilizing a qualitative research design, the authors ask former offenders directed questions on how they survive post-incarceration. The answers are somewhat revealing, and more importantly, begin to raise questions about employment efficacy within the context of a myriad of problems that offenders face when released from prison.

What Pogrebin, West-Smith, Walker, and Unnithan provide is a trenchant analysis of "getting by" when employment does not pay the bills. What they reveal is an intricate web of financial obligations that do not portend success for offenders. In other words, many offenders have accumulated so much debt—prior to incarceration, during incarceration, and subsequent to release—that employment only makes a small dent in what they owe. Does this make employment almost meaningless to many offenders? What about offenders who still get by financially with a job? Is there a resilience factor among some offenders, and what makes them resilient? Answers to these questions are important, but the authors make it clear: Employment by itself is not a panacea solution to the problems offenders face when released from prison. There is no doubt that stable employment for former prisoners is important to their long-term stability in their communities, yet employment most be understood within the context of a number of competing demands, for example, familial demands, correctional supervision demands, educational demands, treatment demands, and limited time and resources to address them.

Chapter 4 by Jacobs, Katcher, Krummenacher, and Tonnesen examines how one agency in the state of California manages offenders released from prison. "Root & Rebound" is a legal resource center that " . . . combines direct services, education, and policy advocacy to achieve its mission: to increase access to justice and opportunity for people in reentry from prison and jail, and to educate and empower those who support them, fundamentally advancing and strengthening the reentry infrastructure across the State of California." With this mission in mind, Root & Rebound is a rare entity, one committed to the myriad of problems and prospects of prisoner reentry. It is the type of agency that has to address and answer the many questions posed earlier in this introduction. Fundamentally, these authors describe the reentry process in the largest state in the Union and propose a sequencing of tasks and obligations that make prisoner reentry difficult. In their words, there is a painful recognition that offenders have multiple needs upon release from prison, and society has limited and scarce resources to address these concerns.

The authors not only provide a roadmap for how prisoner reentry works but also the obstacles and barriers that must be overcome in order for successful prisoner reentry to occur. The chapter offers an inside look on how one agency pursues prisoner reentry. Often times in the research literature, there are assessments and evaluations of how agencies perform on some measure(s) of offender adjustment in the community, for example, recidivism of program participants. Yet, what is of greater value is what agencies actually do in the provision of services and supports to former prisoners. This type of *process evaluation* is extremely important to providing some general and specific rules and actions in the delivery of reentry services, whether they be direct services, education, and/or policy advocacy. Although not a process evaluation per se, Chapter 4 serves as a model for what are the key issues and constraints faced by service providers within the prisoner reentry realm. The authors are the "feet on the ground" in the prisoner reentry arena. What they have to offer is both practical and demonstrative of a commitment to assisting prisoners once they have been released from prison. Both practice and level of commitment required to make prisoner reentry a successful endeavor have been minimally studied by academics. Jacobs, Katcher, Krummenacher, and Tonnesen offer us a beginning roadmap that can be useful to both academicians and policymakers.

Chapter 1 by Farkas and Yoder tackles one of the most difficult offender reentry issues: How do we manage sex offenders in the community? There is probably no other offender group that receives the most attention by politicians and citizens than sex offenders. The imagery of the sex offender in the "bushes" has guided our collective understanding and engendered some of the most draconian and questionable policies and practices within communities: residence restrictions, movement restrictions, housing restrictions, to mention a few. This restrictive approach has raised many questions regarding best practices in the management of sex offenders in the community.

Farkas and Yoder provide an insightful analysis on what we know and don't know about sex offending and the management and supervision of offenders in communities. Much of what is known about sex offenders is not part of the public discussion and debate on how best to manage these types of offenders once released from jails or prisons. Farkas and Yoder begin the discussion by defining how sex offenders fit into the larger context of prisoner reentry, and as a unique population, they " . . . do not fit well with the reentry paradigm of individual return and adjustment, development of autonomy and community acceptance and support." As a unique offending population, the country has responded in rather uneven way to sex offenders, yet the general practice has been premised on many assumptions about sex offending and sex offender management that are simply unverifiable from an empirical point of view. Farkas and Yoder move the analysis forward by initially dispelling the many myths that surround sex offenders.

The most telling myth is that all sex offenders are similar and a strategy for their treatment and supervision in the community can only be based on a containment approach. As a model of management accepted by many supervising agencies in both the criminal justice system and the social service arena, Farkas and Yoder note that this is not the only model of sex offender management available and used across the country. There are many models and there is no one best model. The variations of sex offending are so wide and diverse that one best model or method of community supervision just does not exist. Farkas and Yoder note the difficulty of supervising sex offenders in the community, but they also state the importance of making sure not all sex offenders are viewed as the same and that we appreciate sex offending differences as a basis for the appropriate supervision model employed.

Additionally, Farkas and Yoder note the consequences of laws and policies that do not recognize the variation in sex offending and the consequences of such laws on sex offenders, their families, and the communities they reside. These consequences are very serious and often times offer no or limited hope and a strategy for successfully transitioning from prison or jail to the community once released. In fact, many of the consequences are so dire and have such a lasting negative impact on the lives of sex offenders that their chances of success while supervised in the community are minimal. These adverse consequences affect not only the sex offender but also his/her family and the community they live. An interesting irony of many current attempts to manage sex offenders through a restrictions rubric has been less effectiveness for sex offenders and higher probabilities of re-offending, something all of us do not want to see.

In Chapter 6, Lebel, Richie, and Maruna offer a different type of analysis of prisoner reentry. This chapter begins with an examination of prisoner reentry from the perspective of the returning offender. They suggest that any effective model of prisoner reentry must include the perspectives offered by offenders themselves. Offenders, through their individual and collective experiences, can offer much to both academicians and correctional professionals who supervise them subsequent to their release from jail or prison. The offender provides the firsthand account of what successful reentry means from their perspective as the persons being supervised. Interestingly, Chapter 6 examines former offenders' views on the "American Dream." This chapter, along with Chapter 4, incorporates the views and perceptions of former offenders on how they experience the reentry process and what they ultimately aspire to when released back into the community. Additionally, Chapters 6 and 7 are actual pieces of research and practice that highlight some relevant and important issues associated with both success and failure among offenders released back into communities.

What Lebel, Richie, and Maruna show is that the formerly incarcerated aspire to the same ideals that most Americans hold dearly: economic success, happiness, spiritual fulfillment, and living life to its fullest. One of the messages received by this chapter is that former prisoners, in many instances, believe in the old adage that if you work hard you can succeed in America. Although the attitudes held toward the American Dream are not uniform across all offenders, there are a constellation of factors that seem to provide support for the American Dream among the formerly incarcerated according to these authors. Most importantly, there are also psychological and sociological factors that make acceptance of the American Dream more likely. These findings are in contrast with some research that suggests former prisoners view their chances of post-prison success as being very limited and society has it in for them (Anderson 2001).

Again, the uniformity of this one view is challenged by Lebel, Richie, and Maruna in this chapter, and these authors found divergent points of view, yet general acceptance of the American Dream ideal among their sampled former inmates. Noting there may be some limitations to their study, they nevertheless offer a convincing argument that many offenders still hold positive attitudes toward American society and believe their chances for a full life are still possible. Hope springs eternal, yet hope is not a methodology! So, we need more research regarding released offenders to determine if and why they ascribe to traditional views and values in spite of their incarceration experience and under what conditions or what strategies are the most successful for those trying to readjust back to their communities once released from jail or prison.

When finished reading these chapters, the reader should have a thorough understanding of the complexities and problems associated with prisoner reentry as both a *concept* but also as a *practice*. Prisoner reentry initiatives are here to stay. Governments at both the federal and state levels have invested hundreds of millions of dollars in trying to make sure prisoners successfully adjust to their communities upon release from jail or prison. What is needed now is more rigorous science and research in what works for the various types of offending populations. If anything is certain, it is the complexity of post-prison adjustment among offenders is not uniform and the federal government and state governments operate under different mandates, different laws, and differential levels of funding. In addition, prisoner reentry programs are no different than any other governmental expenditure: too few resources with unlimited expectations.

The primary purpose of this volume is to provide both some conceptual clarity as well as clear and convincing advice to politicians, correctional professionals, reentry offenders, and the general citizenry regarding the importance of prisoner reentry, and most important, clarity on what seems to work with offending populations and how best to proceed forward. The future of prisoner reentry is not totally uncertain, but it can be unpredictable: Political views concerning crime change, and as such, policies regarding released offenders may change as well. I hope we have provided a rough "roadmap" on how best to proceed forward with prisoner reentry efforts based on the best science and analysis of the most salient and current issues. If we have accomplished this objective, we have contributed to both our understanding of the prisoner reentry issue as well as provided direction and advice to those who offer reentry services to the formerly incarcerated.

References

Anderson, E. (2001). Going straight: The story of a young inner-city ex-convict. *Punishment & Society, 3*(1), 135–152.

Bureau of Justice Statistics. (2015). *Prisoners in 2013*. Washington, DC: Department of Justice.

Crow, M., & Smykla, J.O. (Eds.) (2014). *Offender reentry: Rethinking criminology and criminal justice.* Massachusetts: Jones & Bartlett Learning.

Council on State Governments. (2010). *A new era in inmate reentry.* Washington, DC: The Justice Center.

Hairston, C.F., Rollins, J., Jo, H. (2004). Family connections during imprisonment and prisoners' community reentry. Jane Adams Center for Social Policy and Research, Jane Addams College of Social Work, University of Illinois at Chicago.

Latessa, E. (2012). Why work is important, and how to improve the effectiveness of correctional reentry programs that target employment. *Criminology & Public Policy, 11,* 87–91.

Lofstrom, M., & Raphael, S. (2016). Incarceration and crime: Evidence from California's public safety realignment reform. *Annals, AAPSS, 664,* 196–220. California: Sage Publishing.

Petersilia, J. (2003). *When prisoners come home: Parole and prisoner reentry.* New York: Oxford University Press.

Petersilia, J. (2004). What works in prisoner reentry: Reviewing and questioning the evidence. *Federal Probation, 68,* 4–10.

Rhine, E.E., & Thompson, A.C. (2011). The reentry movement in corrections: Resiliency, fragility, and prospects. *Criminal Law Bulletin, 47,* 177–209.

Schrag, M. (2013). *Rethinking the reentry paradigm: A blueprint for action.* North Carolina: Carolina Academic Press.

Sharp, S.F. (2003). Mothers in prison: Issues in parent-child contact. In R. Muraskin (Ed.) & S.F. Sharp (Vol. Ed.), *Prentice-Hall's women in criminal justice series. The incarcerated woman: Rehabilitative programming in women's prisons* (pp. 151–166). New Jersey: Prentice-Hall.

Visher, C., & Travis, L. (2011). Life on the outside: Returning home after incarceration. *The Prison Journal, 91,* 102S–119S.

Zimring, F. (2016). Measuring the impact of complex penal change—A consumer's guide. *Annals, AAPSS, 664,* 304–307.

Stan Stojkovic is Dean and Professor of Criminal Justice in the Helen Bader School of Social Welfare at the University of Wisconsin-Milwaukee (UWM). He received his M.S. and Ph.D. from Michigan State University. He has been at UWM for 34 years. He has published extensively in the areas of criminal justice administration and corrections. He is author, co-author, and co-editor of 8 books, over 50 academic publications, and dozens of professional publications, as well as writing many editorials on criminal justice related matters for newspapers across the country, including the New York Times. He is a frequent guest on National Public Radio and has done numerous radio and television interviews. He co-directed the California Leadership Institute for the California Department of Corrections from 1994-2004 and currently works with aspiring police commanders in California to address prisoner reentry issues post the landmark case of Brown v. Plata (2011). He currently coordinates the Executive Leadership Institute for the California Department of Corrections and Rehabilitation.

Unique Challenges of Reentry for Convicted Sex Offenders

Jamie Yoder and Mary Ann Farkas

Introduction

Reentry has its roots in the rehabilitative era in correctional history. Reentry or reintegration is a series of transitions and changes that occur during the process of the prisoner becoming an ex-offender, and ultimately, a free resident or citizen. These transitions and changes accompany challenges surrounding the most competent and prepared way to leave prison and to integrate into their communities. Reentry can also be viewed as a process, a process of six linked experiences: arrest, prosecution and conviction, incarceration, release under supervision, and release. Each experience has its own obstacles to overcome until one is fully prepared for release and to move forward (Pew Center on the States 2011).

J. Yoder (✉)
Ohio State University, College of Social Work, Columbus, USA

M.A. Farkas
Criminology and Law Studies, Marquette University, Milwaukee, USA

© The Author(s) 2017
S. Stojkovic (ed.), *Prisoner Reentry*,
DOI 10.1057/978-1-137-57929-4_2

13

The medical model was the underlying theory of sex offending and the offender was regarded as psychologically sick and/or beset with problems that caused their criminal behavior (Travis 2005). The focus was on diagnosing, treating, and resolving their problems with the goal of a smooth reintegration into society. Prison programs and services were developed with an eye to a successful transition to the community. Many clinicians and other professionals working within corrections believed the importance of release planning was to reduce sex offender recidivism (Willis 2010). A stable residence post-release with oversight was the preferred option. Halfway houses were popular during this period as a way to help inmates transition between prison and the community. The halfway houses provided structure, supervision, job preparation, and treatment.

In the past few decades, corrections is realizing the need to have a comprehensive, cohesive approach to reentry. This approach is to develop reentry programs for offenders, especially sex offenders, that will provide housing, employment, and psychological and social support. Pre-release programs must also be considered to assist inmates with pre-release preparation for reentry. The reentry literature espouses the overarching goal of reentry as the return to society of an individual who has discharged his or her legal obligation to society by serving his or her time and demonstrated an ability to follow societal rules (Travis 2001). In other words, the offender has earned a place in society. Unfortunately, this philosophy of helping offenders successfully reintegrate into society does not comport with the assistance to special classes of criminal offenders processed in our contemporary criminal justice system. Sex offenders do not fit well with the reentry paradigm of individual return and adjustment, development of autonomy, and community acceptance and support. Public sentiments of fear, mistrust, and abhorrence buttresses their belief that sex offenders cannot change.

According to law professor Jonathan Simon (2012), the criminal justice system has undergone a marked change in priorities. The priority of the individual, his or her characteristics, and progress has been usurped by a focus on special groups, categories, and classes. The language of actuarial risk assessment, risk management, and statistical prediction of recidivism becomes familiar. With this type of approach, attitudes toward prison reentry and reintegration are not evenhanded nor uniform for all returning offenders. Sex offenders are perceived as high-risk subjects who pose a serious risk to the public and are in need of incapacitation and management with special laws, policies, and procedures. Little or nothing can be done to rehabilitate and transform this category of offenders. Moreover, the populist push for more punishment generated by this approach has prompted politicians and lawmakers to propose and enact draconian, exclusive restrictions that register, track, notify and monitor, and incapacitate sex offenders in prisons and special facilities and in the community through the use of technology. DNA data banks also store the genetic profile collected from convicted sex offenders (Petrunik 2002).

Prison reentry has been affected by the large numbers of inmates in prison and especially, significant numbers of incarcerated sex offenders. The philosophical underpinnings of reentry efforts for sex offenders could be classified as a risk management, community protection approach. It is the special class of the convicted sex offender and the resultant sex offender specific laws and policies that have been activated with this approach. According to the Bureau of Justice Statistics (2011), at year-end in 2009, 67,600 inmates were sentenced for rape and another 99,400 were sentenced for sexual assault to state prisons, representing 5 % and 7.3 % of all inmates respectively (Guerino et al. 2010). The vast majority of these inmates will be released at some point in the future. In fact, most sex offenders are under supervision in the community. In 2010, there were 491,000 offenders on state sex offender registries (www.registeredoffenderlist.org). Incarcerated sex offenders convicted of rape served an average sentence of 162 months and those offenders convicted of sexual assault served an average of 98 months (Guerino et al. 2010).

The great numbers of convicted sex offenders and their lengthy prison stays hamper efforts to develop quality pre-release programs. In addition, harsher sentencing laws, including mandatory minimum sentencing, the increased time away from families and communities, and "get tough on crime" attitudes on the part of politicians, legislatures, and the public impacts reentry efforts. There are a variety of laws and policies that are activated upon a sex offender's release from confinement.

Out-of-Home Placement

With regard to juvenile sex offenders, approximately, 50,000 young offenders are incarcerated on any given day nationwide (Office of Juvenile Justice and Delinquency Prevention 2016). The types of facilities include juvenile detention centers, residential placements, group homes or halfway houses, boot camps, or juvenile correctional facilities. Although the rates of incarcerated youth have decreased 50 % since the mid-1990s, incarceration of young offenders is a serious social problem facing the United States. The United States has the largest incarceration rate in the world and institutionalizes more young offenders than any other industrialized country (Sabol et al. 2009). The incarceration rate for youth who commit sexual crimes peaked in the early 1990s and continued to grow into the early 2000s (Snyder and Sickmund 2006). It has been estimated that as of 2003, 8 % of juveniles in residential facilities around the country are sexual offenders (Snyder and Sickmund 2006). It seems that while community-based treatment centers are available, many jurisdictions are failing to fully take advantage of them (McGrath et al. 2003). So, while there remains a least restrictive care philosophy underlying the placement of juveniles (Bonhours and Daly 2007; Lundrigan 2001), it may vary in practice.

Determining the most "appropriate" placement is a complex process, particularly when youth offended against an individual living in the home or an individual with whom he or she has constant contact in his or her living environment. Placement and therapeutic care can occur synchronously or in disparate locations. For example, youth can move into a residential facility that operates as both a therapeutic community and living quarters, or they can be placed into kinship care and receive outpatient or in-home therapeutic services. In extremely rare situations, and typically in response to concurrent violent offenses, youth will be relocated to a correctional facility. In any case, placement and rehabilitative services are inextricably linked, such that one is contingent upon the other. So, when court personnel make sentencing decisions, in tandem, they are deciding the residence location of youth.

To further complicate the process, there is great variation in judicial regulations that dictate sentences and subsequent placement decisions (Bonhours and Daly 2007; Chaffin and Longo 2004; Lyons et al. 2001). Many jurisdictions have dissimilar sentencing laws pertaining to juvenile sex crimes (Chaffin 2008; Levenson and D'Amora 2007; Trivits and Reppucci 2002). Sentences are not usually handed down without deliberate and thoughtful consideration of contextual influences (Chaffin and Longo 2004; Gerdes et al. 1995). By and large, crime-level variables, including offense-severity and associated risk, are considered the most critical in court processing (Zakireh et al. 2008). Other factors include the relationship to the victim and victim safety (Chaffin and Longo 2004; Swisher et al. 2008); kinship alternatives; availability of residential, group home, or foster homes; dynamic risk level; suggested evidence-based treatment approach; financials; and educational institution (Chaffin and Longo 2004; Zakireh et al. 2008).

In some rare cases, there is a clear breach in evidence-guided decisions, as some sentencing and placement decisions are made without exhaustive consideration of research on impacts of restrictive care settings (Chaffin 2008). Sometimes, the sentencing may be overly punitive or restrictive toward youth. However, in most cases, judicial sentencing and placement is guided in a continuum-of-care approach, whereby the least restrictive placement is considered best practice (Bonhours and Daly 2007; Lundrigan 2001). This least restrictive care option yields greater uniformity and limited transitions among placement settings (Chaffin and Longo 2004). Even youth sexual offenders deemed low or moderate risk do not consistently receive community-based care (Hunter et al. 2004b; Lundrigan 2001; Swisher et al. 2008). Residential facilities are incarceration settings that are generally accredited for treating youth through a coordinated care model (Bogestad et al. 2010; Hair 2005), using consistent and regulated principles, cognitive-behavioral and relapse prevention interventions, and milieu-based programming to address inappropriate sexual behaviors (Chaffin and Longo 2004; Hair 2005; Hunter et al. 2004b; Swisher et al. 2008). Irrespective of circumstantial evidence or risk levels, these settings have been used to house and contain youth with sexual behavior problems (Chaffin and Longo 2004; Hair 2005; Hunter et al. 2004b; Swisher et al. 2008).

We are left attempting to understand implications of policy and rehabilitation research in our placement decisions (McCarney and Ireland 2010). Certainly a youth's sentence and living situation will dramatically impact his or her ability to successfully re-enter into the community. Evidence-based community-care models (MST; Letourneau et al. 2009) that provide in-home intensive treatment to youth and families are the most conducive to community (re)integration. Such models are delivered in the home, community, park, neighborhood, schools, or outpatient office to address individual and systemic contributors to sexually harmful behavior (Hunter et al. 2004b; Lundrigan 2001).

Circumventing home disruption through early and consistent community-based care may ultimately lead to better outcomes for youth, families, and communities (Hunter et al. 2004b; Thornton et al. 2008). Rehabilitative services within the confines of a youth's natural environment can support community engagement much earlier. It has been argued that such a parallel process can combat community stigma, foster early relapse prevention strategies, and coincide with ongoing safety plans (Hunter et al. 2004b; Letourneau and Borduin 2008). For example, youth may be better equipped to overcome triggers or high-risk situations when provided more supervised opportunities to engage in their natural environment in an incremental fashion.

Conversely, incarcerated settings, such as a residential facility may fail to adequately prepare youth for the exchanges they will inevitably encounter in their real-life context (Letourneau and Borduin 2008). A controlled environment with excessive restriction and regulation may insufficiently promote skills necessary to overcome problems in pragmatic contexts. Their precarious state of development can be greatly influenced by punitive or overly harsh practices within incarceration settings (Ramirez 2013). As research has robustly cited iatrogenic effects of placing high-risk offenders with lower risk offenders (Cecile and Born 2009; DeLisi et al. 2011), certainly youth developmental trajectories can be permanently modified from exposure to punitive practices. Such experiences can be associated with greater transition challenges (Tewksbury 2005). Withdrawal from natural environments can leave youth feeling insecure, ill prepared to manage sexual behavior problems, or far removed from reality. So, knowing that approximately, 50,000 young offenders are incarcerated on any given day nationwide (OJJDP 2016), and 8 % juveniles in residential facilities around the country are sexual offenders (Snyder and Sickmund 2006), we can expect a similar number of juveniles to be released back into our communities every year (Snyder and Sickmund 2006). This warrants a great concern for systematic plans for reentry for our young people who have sexually offended.

For adult and juvenile sex offenders, preparation for release to their families and communities should begin while in confinement. Prisoner reentry is a critical issue to address given the fact that most offenders will eventually return to society. The need for pre- and post-release programs, job preparation and employment skills, mental health and substance abuse treatment programs, the renewal and building of family ties, and community support efforts for returning inmates. There has also been a flurry of specialized sex offender laws and policies that have created unique challenges for reentering adult and juvenile sex offenders. Draconian laws and policies have resulted in unintended consequences that may actually undermine the goals of managing sex offenders, heightening public protection, and increasing community safety (Mercado et al. 2008).

Societal Misrepresentations

For convicted sex offenders, release from confinement and reentry to a community that is unwelcoming and exclusive, is a daunting experience. The public holds many erroneous assumptions about sex offenders. Sexual offenders and sex crimes ignite great fear and anxiety combined with feelings of condemnation and revulsion (Palermo and Farkas 2013). The labels *sex offender* and *juvenile sex offender* "may evoke strong subconscious associations with a population presumed to be: compulsive, at high risk of re-offense, and resistant to rehabilitation (Harris and Socia 2014, p. 1)." Sexual offenders are believed to be highly dangerous, especially if they are sexual offenders with child victims. The percentage of sexual assaults committed by strangers are overestimated, while assaults committed by individuals known to their victims are underestimated. The myth of "stranger danger" is the basis of many of our sex offender specific laws and policies. The reality is that young children, in particular, are much more likely to be sexually victimized by family member, friend, or acquaintance than by a stranger (Meloy et al. 2008).

Rates of recidivism are also much lower than the public presumes. This notion that sexual offenders inevitably re-offend was negated in a meta-analysis of 61 studies by Hanson and Bussiere 1998). Only a small minority of the total sample (13.4 % of 23,393 offenders) committed a new sexual offense within the average four- to –five-year follow-up period. Sex offenders were actually more likely to recidivate with non-sexual offenses when they did recidivate. In another study, Langan et al. examined the recidivism rates of 9,691 male sex offenders released from prisons in 15 states in 1994. They found a sexual recidivism rate of 5.3 % for the entire sample during the three-year follow-up period. In 2003, Sample and Bray examined the arrest recidivism of 146,918 sex offenders and found one-year, three-year, and five-year rearrest rates for a new sexual offense of 2.2 %, 4.8 %, and 6.5 % respectively.

Sex offenders are also perceived to be a homogenous group specializing in sex crimes exclusively (Palermo and Farkas 2013). Researchers have referred to this sentiment as the "myth of homogeneity," which has infiltrated public policy and the media presentation of sex offenders (Harris and Socia 2014). Many sex offenders, especially rapists, do not confine their recidivism offense to clearly sexual crimes (Harris et al. 1998). Regardless of the nature of their sex crimes (e.g., pornography or voyeurism) or the age of their victims, all sex offenders are placed under an umbrella category of "high-risk sex offenders." Sample and Bray (2006) assert that sex offenders are not equally prone to re-offending. Rapists or sex offenders with adult victims may recidivate at a higher rate than child molesters (Marquez et al. 1994). Those sex offenders in the child molestation, rape, and hebephile categories have significantly higher rates of recidivating than do those in the child pornography and pedophile categories (Sample and Bray 2003).

Still other inaccuracies are that sex offenders are untreatable, reinforcing the belief that recidivism is inevitable. Meta-analysis of treatment outcomes reveals that sex offenders who successfully complete cognitive-behavioral modification treatment protocols tend to recidivate less often and recidivate less quickly than their nontreated counterparts (Hall 1995; Hanson et al. 2002, Losel and Schmucker 2005). The outcome of this false information is a very broad categorization of adult and juvenile sex offenders.

Regarding juvenile offenders, youth who commit sexual crimes share more characteristics with non-sexually offending youth. In fact, through delineation of comparable or disparate risk, comparative research continues to explore whether sexual offending is a unique behavior problem or a subset of overall delinquency (Seto and Lalumiere 2010). Research has revealed that youth who commit sexual crimes may not specialize in sexual offending; rather, they are more versatile in their offending (France and Hudson 1993). It is well-established that youth who commit sexual crimes tend to re-offend more non-sexually than sexually (Caldwell 2010). One large meta-analysis of 63 youth data sets revealed that the mean *sexual* recidivism rate was 7.1 % and the mean *non-sexual* recidivism rate was 43.4 % (Caldwell 2010). Specifically, tracking sexual recidivism during adolescence yields higher rates than reliance on adult recidivism; youth who do sexually recidivate tend to re-offend during adolescence; there is a developmental stage discontinuity effect (Caldwell 2010), and a small percentage of youth will develop life-course patterns of sexual offending. Research has also revealed positive treatment effects in respect to low sexual recidivism, where at five years post-release, treated youth had a sexual recidivism rate of 7.37 % relative to 18.93 % for the comparison group (Reitzel and Carbonell 2006).

The propensity for long-term sexual offending trajectories is a critical public safety interest. Chronic sexually harmful behaviors can be understood through a developmental lens. Advancing the work of Moffit (1993), Seto and Barbaree (1997) proposed a dual-pathway developmental framework that explained persistent sexual criminality based on age at which antisocial behavior emerged. The scholars theorize that early onset of conduct problems, behavioral difficulties, and multiple methods of inappropriate sexual expression characterizes "persistently antisocial" youth. Those on the other pathway are "adolescence-limited youth," and considered opportunistic in perpetrating sexual crimes. These offenders often act out in response to a situation or context that triggers or disinhibits (see: Marshall and Marshall 2000) youth behaviors (Seto and Barbaree 1997).

In differentiating life-course persistent sexual offenders, Moffit's theory (1993) can extend to juveniles who commit sexual crimes; rape is a form of antisociality that is a benchmark for long-term criminality. Antisociality and sexual deviance, in particular, has been signified as critical risk factors that are associated with re-offending (McCann and Lussier 2008). The presence of callous and unemotional traits may be a distinctive subgroup of antisocial and aggressive youth in general (Frick and White 2008). Antisociality or callous unemotional traits include lack of empathy, remorse, guilt, or shame that may characterize more severe youth who are more severe in deviant or aggressive manifestations through the life course (Frick and White 2008). Antisociality paired with sexual deviance may be especially significant determinants for long-term sexual behavior problems, as a meta-analysis indicated they are cumulatively linked to sexual recidivism (McCann and Lussier 2008).

Furthermore, within-group typological distinctions continue to suggest juveniles who commit sexual crimes are a heterogeneous group (Malin et al. 2014). Juvenile sexual offenders are categorized according to various traits, including psychological traits and victim age (Glowacz and Born 2013). Typological theories have delineated sub-groups of juveniles who commit sexual crimes suggesting that they comprise a hostile masculine type, egotistical/antagonistic masculine type, a psychosocial deficit type, and a non-sexual aggression and delinquency type (Hunter et al. 2004a). These typologies are also linked with the victims such that psychosocial deficit offenders are more likely to perpetrate against younger non-peer victims (Hunter et al. 2004a). An abundance of research is also focused on exploring other factors that help categorize sub-groups of youth sexual offenders, including criminal profiles and trajectories (van Wijk et al. 2007a; van Wijk et al. 2007b). Family typologies have also begun to be established such that families fall on the spectrum of open and closed systems: They can have diffuse or even inappropriate boundaries around sexuality or they could have rigid beliefs that prohibit healthy sexual expression (Yoder et al. 2015b).

Public support is then garnered for sex offender management policies that control and incapacitate adult and juvenile sex offenders. Harris and Socia (2014) studied how the labels of adult and juvenile sex offender shape sex offender policies. The juvenile sex offender label led citizens to support policies that subjected adolescents to public Internet notification and registration and affected the beliefs about juvenile sex offenders' propensity to re-offend as adults. Thus, sex offender laws and policies appear to be based on a small subset of convicted sex offenders who fit the public's stereotypes, media misrepresentations, and the political framing of get tough on crime initiatives.

Seven broad types of sex offender laws and policies have been identified in the literature on sex crime laws and policies, including sex offender registries, community notification, residence restrictions, civil commitment, lifetime supervision with or without electronic monitoring, and castration laws (Mancini et al. 2011). This list is not exhaustive since new restrictions seem to surface at will. When all sex offenders within particular offense categories are designated equally high risk to re-offend, uniform treatment modalities and "one size fits all" laws and policies are the end result. This may have serious collateral consequences for low-risk adult and juvenile offenders, as well as undermining public safety (Shaffer and Miethe 2011). These collateral consequences not only affect convicted sex offenders but also their family members, those who work with the offenders, and the public as a whole. We will next examine the process of reentry for convicted sex offenders in the context of laws and policies designed to control, isolate, and exclude such offenders.

Offender Specific Laws and Policies

Civil Commitment Laws

Civil commitment is a form of selective incapacitation devised to address sex offender recidivism and community safety. The rise of civil commitment laws coincided with a community protection risk management approach to the management of convicted sex offenders. Of these sex offenders, none are more feared than the predatory pedophile or rapist for whom neither punishment nor treatment is considered effective

(Petrunik 2002). The move toward SVPs (Sexually Violent Person) civil commitment is an outgrowth of calls for expanded government control of "uncontrollable," sex offenders. Twenty states currently have civil commitment legislation specifically for convicted sex offenders. Arizona, California, Florida, Illinois, Iowa, Kansas, Massachusetts, Minnesota, Missouri, Nebraska, New Hampshire, New Jersey, North Dakota, Pennsylvania, South Carolina, Texas, Virginia, Washington, Wisconsin and New York. The "psychopathic personality" may also be applied to a person who committed a crime of sexual violence and who suffers from a mental abnormality or personality disorder that makes the person likely to engage in predatory acts of sexual violence (Lieb and Matson 1998). The SVP law is typically applied after the termination of a prison sentence. The law permits the state to retain custody of individuals found by a judge or jury to be at risk of committing future harmful sexual conduct by virtue of a mental abnormality or personality disorder (Harris 2009). According to Deming (2008), in most states, a single conviction for a qualifying sexual offense, combined with a diagnosable mental disorder and an assessment of likely sexual re-offense, can amount to civil commitment as an SVP.

The laws have common elements although organizational structure and operation of the facilities vary from state to state. There were 4,534 people detained under SVP Laws across the United States in 2006 (Gookin 2007). California (614 persons) and Florida (540 persons) accounted for approximately 1/3 of the total civilly committed persons (Deming 2008). Five states—California, Illinois, Minnesota, Missouri, and Washington—had civilly committed female sex offenders (five each state) (Deming 2008). Annual programs costs were estimated at a total of $454.7 million annually, whereas program costs averaged $97,000 per person per year. New admissions surpassed discharges; to date, only 494 residents were discharged (Jackson et al. 2007). There has been a steady growth of civil confinement facilities, and several states are considering passing laws to incapacitate this category of sexually violent sex offenders.

Becker et al. (2003) reported the characteristics of 120 civilly committed sex offenders at the Arizona Community Protection and Treatment Center.

Characteristics of civilly committed sex offenders from Arizona:

1. Offenders were predominantly white (69 %) with a mean age of 44.
2. Eighty-two percent (82 %) of the civilly committed sex offenders had a substance abuse problem.
3. The committed sex offenders had two sex convictions and 3.5 non-sexual convictions.
4. The most frequent Axis I disorders included pedophilia (35 %) and antisocial personality disorder (26 %).

Deming (2008) describes the similarity of the multistep civil commitment process for sex offenders. The assessment process begins during the last months of their incarceration, regardless of whether they participated in treatment or not, and may last months or years prior to the offender's release from prison (Birgden and Cucolo 2011). The incarcerated offenders are screened for the presence of risk factors. They are then referred for a face-to-face evaluation and a risk assessment conducted by a psychologist or psychiatrist. If individuals are found to meet the criteria for commitment, a prosecutor determines whether there is sufficient evidence to file a probable cause petition. If probable cause is found, a trial is held in which both the state and the sex offender (with defense attorney) present evidence that is heard by a judge or jury. In most states, once committed, the sex offender is confined indefinitely to a special facility but is regularly evaluated until he or she is no longer considered to be a danger to the community.

Nearly all states had clearly defined stages and/or phases of their programs, and offenders were mandated to participate in cognitive-behavioral group psychotherapies that focused on developing relapse prevention and risk management plans. Polygraph examinations and PPG (penile plethysmograph) were also used in assessment (Deming 2008).

The use of civil commitment laws and processes with sex offenders has met with opposition on several grounds. Such laws have encountered the constitutional *ex post facto* and double jeopardy challenges. The constitutionality of sex offender civil commitment was upheld in two U.S. Supreme Court cases, *Kansas v. Hendricks* (1997) and *Kansas v. Crane* (2002). Another concern with the commitment statute is that since violent sex offenders are not mentally ill in any "medically recognized sense," the efficacy of treatment becomes questionable. The designation of mental abnormality holds no medical or other scientific basis (Harris 2009). Labelling certain sex offenders as mentally ill does not make it so. The laws are also faulted for being punishment in the guise of treatment (Palermo and Farkas 2013). Under civil commitment, convicted sex offenders are continuing their sentence after transport to another facility to begin a "new" confinement (Farkas and Stichman 2002). The state is permitted to retain custody of individuals found by a judge or jury to present a risk of future harmful sexual conduct by virtue of a mental abnormality or personality disorder (Harris 2009). The integrity of the civil commitment process as an opportunity for rehabilitation is challenged. Even though elements of treatment are offered, the quality and value is uncertain. Other critics argue that the indefinite length of civil confinement amounts to cruel and unusual punishment. Yearly evaluations of the sex offender's progress toward release are conducted.

There are two routes to exit civil confinement for sex criminals: earned release through treatment compliance and substantive progress or a court determination, informed by expert testimony, that the behavioral and psychological factors that supported commitment are no longer present (Harris 2009). Gookin (2007) claims release through the first route is very rare. The second route also does not occur very often, but it is a little more common than the therapy route (Harris 2009). When approval for release is granted, another set of challenges occur, reentry necessitates a place of residence for the SVP. An article by Stojkovic and Farkas (2013) chronicles the experience of searching for placements for SVPs released from a civil commitment facility in the state of Wisconsin. The negative political and community response to the possibility of housing high-risk sex offenders illustrates the practical obstacles for such offenders in moving forward from civil commitment.

The Association for the Treatment of Sex Offenders (ATSA) has issued the following guidelines for the more effective implementation of civil commitment statutes:

1. Sexual predator assessments should be conducted using empirically validated risk assessment instruments, measures, and methods.

2. ATSA recommends that states provide a contemporary, properly designed prison-based treatment program to enable incarcerated offenders to receive treatment in order to promote risk-reduction and successful community reintegration. This treatment should be consistent with current research and professional standards and guidelines, and it should reflect each individual's qualifying mental disorder (s), relative risk, and criminogenic needs. Individualized treatment plans are critical and should provide for systematic measurements of the sex offender's progress in treatment.

3. If a state chooses to implement civil commitment, it should be reserved for sexual offenders who are found to pose the highest threat to public safety, and it should be viewed as only one part of a comprehensive continuum of responses to sexual offending behavior.

4. Treatment that follows the end of incarceration/criminal jurisdiction, in cases where a state elects to implement civil commitment, should also be consistent with current research and professional standards and guidelines, and reflect each individual's qualifying mental disorder(s), relative risk, and criminogenic needs. Such treatment should include a reassessment each year to evaluate progress toward treatment goals.

5. Prior to being considered for civil commitment, offenders should be offered opportunities during their regular criminal sentences to address their risk-relevant mental disorders and criminogenic needs through properly designed and competently implemented treatment.

Sexual Offender Registration and Community Notification

The passage of the Adam Walsh Child Protection and Safety Act (AWA) in 2006, established a national sex offender registry, requiring a three-tiered offense-based classification system, and enhanced state registration and notification procedures (Mercado et al. 2008). Title I of AWA—designated as the Sex Offender Registration and Notification Act (SORNA)—included the expansion of federal mandates to tribal jurisdictions and foreign convictions, extension of registration and notification to juvenile sex offenders, and the specification of how long registrants should be classified, how long registrants should remain on the registry, and the methods of public notification (Harris and Lobanov-Rostovsky 2010). SORN laws mandate that convicted sex offenders have their personal information available to law enforcement and to the public via registries (Frenzel et al. 2014). The information on the registries generally included the offender's name, demographics, home address, and a recent photograph. Information that may also be included might be the presence of tattoos, nickname, and license plate number and vehicle make, model, and color (Frenzel et al. 2014).

Community or public notification laws are grounded in the principle that citizens should be notified of information regarding the whereabouts of sex offenders, in order to take action to protect their children (Palermo and Farkas 2013). Community notification requires that the public be notified of the sex offender registrant's presence. Notification involves the release of relevant offender information about sexual offenders to law enforcement, public/private entities, and the general public for public safety purposes. Law enforcement has several options, from simply informing specific agencies, sending out flyers, door-to-door notification, community notification meetings, and/or contacting the local media.

Sex offender registration and community notification laws provided additional legal and correctional strategies for sex offenders released into the community. Sex offender registration is viewed as a way of identifying those offenders convicted or adjudicated of a sex-related offense and keeping track of these offenders and their whereabouts. The registration of sex offenders can also be a valuable law enforcement tool, providing identifiable information about sex offenders and facilitating investigation of a crime (Palermo and Farkas 2013). Sex offenders are generally required to register with local law enforcement within 10 days of their release or placement to community supervision. Registrants must provide their address, photograph, fingerprints, and vehicle license number. Most states provide some sort of penalty for knowingly failing to register or providing false information. Failing to register can also be the basis of probation or parole revocation. Sex offenders are required to register while on supervision and for *15 years* following expiration from sentence or commitment. Some sex offenders (sexually violent offenders, civil committees, and two-strike cases) are mandated to register *for life*.

Critics believe that notification laws are flawed and have negative, unanticipated consequences. Unlike other types of offenders, sex offenders are punished in the criminal justice system and the stigmatization of being posted on a registry for the public's scrutiny. This may negatively impact their reentry. Neighbors may come across the registry or be warned by community supervision agents. The registered sex offenders may be evicted or unable to live in certain neighborhood and their notoriety may prevent them from being hired for a job. The public registration process may also stigmatize their family members and friends resulting in harassment, bullying, and vigilantism. Family members have reported emotional problems due to the hardships they incurred from the registry (Frenzel et al 2014). Registered sex offenders reported the emotional pain of not being able to attend school functions with their children (Levenson and Cotter 2005; Zevitz and Farkas 2000). There appears to be widespread support and knowledge of registration and notification laws among the general public (Levenson et al. 2007).

Community notification laws have also met with numerous legal and moral challenges. Legal criticisms have focused on the *ex post facto* nature of the laws in that they retroactively apply to sex offenders convicted before the statute was enacted. Other challenges include whether the statute constitutes double jeopardy and cruel and unusual punishment because notification has exacted further punishment and resulted in financial, legal, psychological, and social consequences for their families and significant others (Zevitz and Farkas 2000; Tewksbury and Levenson 2009). Sex offenders have reported feelings of shame, vulnerability, and social isolation (Levenson and Cotter 2005; Tewksbury and Lees 2006). The unstable, stressful living and employment circumstances may actually increase the likelihood of recidivism among such offenders.

Violations of their right to privacy have also been alleged based on the public exposure of their crime, identity, and personal information. State Supreme Court rulings have been mixed regarding these statutes. In *State v. Ward* (1994), the Washington State Supreme Court upheld the notification statute. Community notification statutes have been struck down in Louisiana and Alaska; however, the New Jersey Supreme Court has ruled it is constitutional to notify a neighborhood when a sex offender moves in. Washington has been the only state where both registration and community notification have been upheld. However, the overall trend in court rulings is to elevate the rights of the community to be protected from dangerous and repeat sex offenders over the civil rights of the sex offenders.

The efficacy of sexual offender registration and community notification is also a concern. Because the laws are still relatively new, there is a lack of empirical research regarding their effects on preventing and reducing sexual violence. According to Meloy et al. (2007), such laws are not decreasing sexual victimization because the public is likely to misperceive risk by focusing on stranger assailants and to underestimate the security associated with these measures by assuming all or most sex offenders are accounted for on registration lists.

There is no evidence that community notification resulted in a decreased number of sexual assaults by strangers and little evidence that the laws had an effect on reducing intra-familial sexual abuse (Palermo and Farkas 2013). Other studies have also concluded that registration and notification laws are limited in their ability to reduce sexual victimization (Freeman and Sandler 2010). Evaluations of SORNA have been less than favorable with implementation, fiscal, and collateral public safety consequences (Freeman and Sandler 2010; Harris and Lobanov-Rostovsky 2010; Sandler et al. 2008). The reclassification of individuals into three offense-based tiers and the inclusion of certain classes of juvenile sex offenders may have a "net widening effect" for those subjected to registration and notification (Harris and Lobanov-Rostovsky 2010).

Residence Restrictions

Residence restrictions are focused on removing opportunities for sex offenders to access victims, especially child victims (Bratina 2013). Similar to other sex offender specific laws, the restrictions were enacted to protect the public from the risk of sexual victimization (Mercado et al. (2008). The statutes are designed to restrict where convicted sex offenders can live, and in some cases, work (Meloy et al. 2008). To date, about 30 states have enacted housing restrictions, prohibiting convicted sex offenders from residing in close proximity to schools, daycare centers, parks, school bus stops, and any other places where children may congregate. In addition, thousands of cities, counties, and towns have passed municipal sex offender zoning and ordinances (Levenson and D'Amora 2009). The most common distances are 1000- to 2500-foot boundaries (Levenson and Cotter 2005).

The residency restrictions have a number of far-reaching collateral consequences for sex offenders that impact their successful reentry. Due to the residency laws, sex offenders face a difficult struggle in obtaining housing and employment. Sex offenders reported residency restrictions isolated them from family and society. They pointed to increased instability and stress in their lives (Levenson and Cotter 2005). These restrictions are particularly onerous for those persons with a persistent and serious mental disease, compounding their already-complex problems in reintegrating into society (Harris et al. 2010). Some research has suggested that child safety zones or loitering zones could be used as an alternative to residency restrictions. Rather than stipulating where sex offenders may reside, such zones would circumscribe the activities of sex offenders at risk of abusing children (Zgoba et al. 2009).

Preliminary research studies are inconclusive regarding the impact that residency restrictions have on sex offender recidivism. Tewksbury and Mustaine (2008) found that a higher concentration of registered sex offenders in a neighborhood had no significant correlation with the number of sex offenses that occurred. Three studies have found that the majority of registered sex offenders with child victims were likely to reside in close proximity to places where children congregate (Grubesic et al. 2008). These results contradict a study by Walker et al. (2001) that found that a higher percentage of child sex offenders lived within 1000 ft. buffer zones around schools, daycares centers, and parks than did nonchild sex offenders. More research is needed to corroborate the value of these laws for public safety and for sex offenders (removal of opportunities).

Chemical Castration

In 1996, California became the first state to pass legislation allowing the chemical castration of convicted sex offenders (Meisenkothen 1999). Some states allow eligible offenders to choose reversible chemical castration in place of other sanctions and a handful of states allow offenders to elect surgical castration as a permanent solution (Mancini et al. 2011). Surgical castration is proposed periodically by politicians as a solution for sex offending, nonetheless it has fallen into disfavor because it is irreversible, not always effective, and other reversible medication is available (Miller 1998). Chemical castration consists of weekly intramuscular injections of 300 mg. of Depo Provera (medroxyprogesterone-MPA). MPA, is an FDA approved synthetic birth control drug, which quells the sex drive of sex offenders (Meisenkothen 1999). Pharmaceutical agents used in the treatment of sex offenders include (but are not limited to), antiandrogens. neuroleptics, antidepressants, anti-anxiety drugs, and psychotropic medications (Palermo and Farkas 2013). When used together with supportive psychotherapy, it decreases pedophilic sexual misconduct. Sexual offenders are thought to be driven to act on their urges and fantasies because of an abnormally elevated testosterone level (McConaghy 1998). Medroxyprogesterone acetate (Provera) (MPA) is used frequently in the United States to treat paraphilic behaviors. The potential side-effects of MPA include weight gain, diabetes mellitus, sweats, thrombosis, testicular atrophy, mild, irregular gallbladder functioning, lethargy, cold sweats, and hot flashes. Hypertension may also be present.

Chemical castration is also being used with sex offenders under community supervision. However, this raises problems of informed consent that may be problematic when pharmacological treatment is court ordered or when it is a requirement for parole release. Pharmaceutical agents used in treating sexual offenders include (but are not limited to) the use of antiandrogens, neuroleptics, antidepressants, and anti-anxiety and psychotropic medications. There is little substantive evidence to support the use of psychotropic medication to diminish an individual's sexual libido (Palermo and Farkas 2013). Antidepressants have been reported to be successfully used in non-paraphilic sexual addiction and paraphilias in men. Also, for some sex offenders, antidepressants were effective with treatment (Becker and Murphy 1998). One problem with antiandrogens is the need for ongoing medication compliance from the sex offender. All side-effects are reported to dissipate over time once the shots are discontinued, nonetheless, it may take up to six months for full sexual functioning to return, (Miller 1998).

The research on the impact of chemical castration are preliminary, at best. Several studies of paraphiliac offender who have undergone chemical castration have demonstrated a decrease in sexual offending as a result of this intervention (Scott and del Busto 2009). Much more research is needed to understand the potential uses and ways to enhance the use of chemical castration.

Christopher Meisenkothen (1999) suggested several provisions for the ideal chemical castration statute:

1. *Statement of Legislative Purpose*—A statute is not complete without a brief statement of the goals of the statute's purpose.
2. *Ways to Obtain Such Treatment*—The ways to obtain such treatment and the manner in which it will be carried out should be specified.
3. *Mechanism to Monitor the Paraphiliac's Process*

Chemical castration through weekly Depo Provera injections in combination with psychological therapy is a safe effective way to curb the recidivism rates of paraphiliacs (Meisenkothen 1999).

Collateral Consequences of Sex Offending

Collateral consequences are additional obstacles, penalties, or negative effects that an offender may confront resulting from his or her criminal conviction. Thus, the criminal conviction, particularly a sex crime conviction, is not the end point of the criminal process but rather the impetus for an array of obstacles that will hinder the convicted individual long beyond the conclusion of the formal sentence and throughout the reentry process (Pinard 2010). Unlike other offenders, convicted sex offenders are not only punished with criminal sanctions but also are subjected to stigmatization and a variety of legal, psychological, and social consequences. These costs may also include housing restrictions, employment difficulties, and feelings of rejection, isolation, and anguish. The possibility that sex offenders can return as productive members of society may be jeopardized. Moreover, collateral consequences may affect more than just the offenders but also their families, relatives, significant others, and their communities. For example, the stigma associated with the status of convicted sex offender can extend to his or her family members resulting in their personal shame and harassment by others. Family members experience a "courtesy stigma" (Goffman 1963) sharing the disgrace and humiliation of the registered sex offenders. Sex offender laws and policies are powerful forces in changing one's social identity and that of their family members.

Sex Offender Expectations and Accounts of Reentry

Depending on the circumstances, families and kinship can be irreparably broken, especially if there are victims in the family. Some relatives will not be welcoming to the registered sex offender. Those sex offenders who do not reunite with their families face a variety of challenges. Incarcerated sex offenders have a very limited understanding of the many obstacles that they will face upon release from prison or civil confinement. Research (Tewksbury and Copes 2012) has found that incarcerated sex offenders tended to hold positive expectations for reentry and were unprepared for the impending restrictions and sanctions as they reentered the community, including residency restrictions and public notification (community meetings, door-to-door warnings, and/or TV bulletins). A large majority of the subjects knew of only two restrictions, registration and their status on conditional release. All sex offenders in the sample knew they would be listed on the state's sex offender registry, yet almost no sex offenders were aware of other restrictions. Tewksbury and Copes (2012) assert that this overly optimistic attitude of the incarcerated sex offenders ignores the realities of life after prison and may actually heighten the problems returning sex offenders will face. Reentry programs need to educate such offenders about the legal requirements they will be subject to and the unintended consequences of these specialized sex offender laws.

Housing Restrictions and Unavailability

Stable housing post-release is critical for returning sex offenders. Housing provides the structural foundation for a successful reentry into society. Returning sex offenders face multiple hurdles in locating housing, and this is exacerbated by the fact that they must have a viable and approved housing plan before they will even be released from prison. Sex offenders with a lifetime registration requirement are ineligible for all public housing and other federally funded housing programs (Farkas and Miller 2007). Inaccessible housing and residency restrictions have been shown to increase feelings of isolation, create emotional and financial stress, and lead to general feelings of instability and uncertainty for released sex offenders (Leonard, K. 2011).

As aforementioned, sex offenders face enormous obstacles in locating housing largely due to the legal restrictions enacted to control and contain such offenders. Approximately 30 states have passed residency restrictions to minimize the potential for interaction between sex offenders and children and thereby reduce the risk of sex offense recidivism and enhance public safety (Tewksbury and Levenson 2009, Grubesic et al. 2011). Sex offenders are restricted to living a certain distance, typically 500—3,500 ft., from a school, daycare facility, playground, park, or any other place where children may congregate. Many sex offenders reported housing disruption and being unable to live with supportive or dependent family members because of the home's close proximity to a school or daycare (Levenson and Cotter 2005). This is unfortunate because family support is invaluable to successful reentry.

The restrictions surrounding housing has made it extremely difficult for the sex offenders to identify places to live. Some states have increased this difficulty by including a clause in their community notification laws that required an "actual address" for the sex offender. Alabama, as an example, added a clause in 2005 that states that within 45 days prior to release, the convicted sex offender must provide a valid, actual address. After the clause was challenged in circuit court for its constitutional vagueness, this clause was amended to the requirement that the convicted sex offender must provide an "actual physical address" within 180 days prior to his release date. Sex offenders could then be held beyond their release dates.

Reports of incarcerated sex offenders being held beyond their release dates are becoming more common (Zevitz and Farkas 2000; Goldstein 2014). For example, relative to their non-sexual offending counterparts, juveniles who commit sexual crimes spend more time in placements (McGrath et al. 2003; Snyder and Sickmund 2006). On average, youth sexual offender treatment within residential facilities lasts 18 months (McGrath et al. 2010). The long length of stay has partially been attributed to poor aftercare planning and reentry (CSOM 2016), as youth are perceived as threatening to communities. As such, the facilities may hold youth longer if there is a limited transition plan in place. Research demonstrates that the longer the youth are in placement, the more difficult it is to reintegrate (Chaffin et al. 2002; Hunter et al. 2004a). Many times, youth can be displaced from their school or family systems for an extended period.

According to Rolfe, Tewksbury, and Schroeder (2016), residence restriction laws may be the most prohibitive to the reintegration process for sex offenders since it makes living with family members stressful and unlikely. Residency restrictions are a constant reminder to convicted sex offenders that they are stigmatized, ostracized, and reviled by the general public. Moreover, the restrictions exclude most sex offenders from living in most affordable metropolitan areas, so their only option is homelessness. Combined with residency restrictions, sex offenders may be forced to move so that even if a convicted sex offender finds a residence, there is no guarantee that he can continue living at that location. One study found that housing disruption is common with 20–40 % of sex offenders reporting that they had to move from their residence because a landlord or neighbor learned about their status (Levenson and Tewksbury 2009). Higher concentrations of sex offenders are found in communities that are undesirable, socially disorganized with more concentrated economic disadvantage, more residential instability, and higher rates of robbery and child sexual abuse (Tewksbury and Mustaine 2008). With the residency restrictions, many sex offender releasees are relegated to homelessness and areas further away from employment opportunities, public transportation, access to treatment, and social support (Mustaine 2014).

Several other states are also holding such offenders beyond their release dates because of changes to their residency restriction laws. Some states with Sexually Violent Persons (SVP) laws have experienced insurmountable difficulty siting transitional housing for SVPs released from civil commitment. A siting committee in the state of Wisconsin struggled to communicate and educate political officials and citizenry about the importance of finding appropriate housing and supervision for high-risk sex offenders, but were essentially blocked at every turn by their fear and condemnation of SVPs (Stojkovic and Farkas 2013),

Homeless shelters were proposed as another potential alternative for those held beyond their release dates and homeless convicted sex offenders. However, most (71.9 %) of homeless shelters do not allow sex offenders, which may have resulted from misinformation to the public. The state of Michigan decided to experiment with the idea of emergency homeless shelters for homeless sex offenders provided two conditions were met: (1). sex offenders could sleep at the shelter, but need to leave the next morning and (2). there was no expectation of securing a shelter the next day. New York re-examined its residency restriction and determined that the majority of homeless shelters were located within 1000 ft. of areas where children gather. Thereby, only 14 of the 270 shelters are eligible to receive sex offenders and these 14 are filled to capacity. Nationwide, most homeless shelters do not grant access to sex offenders, and thus homelessness for sex offenders becomes the unavoidable reality (Rolfe et al. 2016). Restrictions from being released from prison might inadvertently increase triggers for re-offense, given the high emotion and frustration level. Again, unobtainable stable housing and tedious housing restrictions have led to increased stress and anxiety regarding when the inmates will be released and where they will live. Housing restrictions that prevent sex offenders from living in just about any area of the city and the lack of an "actual physical" address may lead to a sense of hopelessness, despair, and a heightened risk of re-offense.

Transitional housing, such as halfway houses, have become a temporary answer to the problem of inadequate housing and homelessness. Transitional housing is designed to provide a structured, supportive residence so offenders, including registered sex offenders, can locate more permanent housing. Halfway houses help to facilitate the gradual return of offenders to society and to meet the basic needs of sex offenders but also may include elements such as counseling and substance abuse treatment (Kras et al. 2016). The intent of these temporary strategies is to decrease the number of sex offenders held in prison beyond their release date, the number of indigent offenders, and the many homeless sex offenders. However, the role of transitional housing has changed over the years from more of a rehabilitative function to provide a controlled environment for offenders during the high-risk, immediate post-release period (Fontaine et al. 2012). Unfortunately, the laws only restrict housing for returning sex offenders; they do not provide housing for sex offenders released from prisons or civil commitment facilities (Evans and Cubellis 2015).

Employment and Financial Concerns

Many returning prisoners have significant employment, financial, and educational needs, roughly half lack a high school degree and depended on illegal income prior to their incarceration. Most of those released from prison, worked while incarcerated in prison or participated in job training programs while incarcerated and so they had better employment outcomes post-release (Visher et al. 2008). Family members of recently released offenders mentioned that obtaining a job or job training was the most important need for their significant other (Naser and Visher 2006). Steady employment gives convicted sex offenders financial resources, a sense of identity, and meaning to their lives. Jobs provide structure and create a routine in the lives of offenders reentering the community. Research demonstrates the rich fantasy life of many sex offenders. The opportunity to engage in sexual fantasies and subsequent criminal behavior is reduced by restricting their free time. Obtaining and keeping a job increases their self-esteem as they become a contributing member of the family and they feel more independence. Stable employment is critical for a transition into the community, however ex-prisoners tend to have statistics that make them hard to employ. Finding employment is one of the most challenging tasks that sex offenders face, yet this task is the foundation for successful reintegration.

Once released to the community, returning sex offenders have great difficulties in obtaining a job, which results in economic hardship. Many sex offenders reported their inability to get a job resulted in their spouses or significant others working multiple jobs to make ends meet (Frenzel et al. 2014). Employers are reluctant to hire felons and most importantly, felons who have committed a sex crime. Sex offenders are required to inform their employer of their sex offender status. This label may deter the employer from hiring due to a variety of factors, the employer may fear customer reaction, such as boycotting or picketing, continuous visits by law enforcement and correctional agents may be intrusive, or the employer may be unnerved or repulsed by a convicted sex offender. Some employers may also worry about being sued for negligent hiring. This type of hiring refers to the hiring of individuals who the employer knew, or should have known, were unfit for hiring.

Being publicly identified through online registries as a sex offender restricts employment in several ways. With some employers mandated to check the sex offender registry, and many others implementing the checks as part of their private business policy, many sex offenders are finding themselves unable to secure and maintain a job. Research shows that private employers are reluctant to hire sex offenders even if their offense has no bearing on the nature of the job (Kling and Weiman 2001). Offenders who tell prospective employers they are registered sex offenders are usually denied employment; those who fail to tell are eventually fired when employers find out—often through fellow employees who found the information through searching online sex offender registries.

Some state laws place employment restrictions on sex offenders, prohibiting them from working in schools, childcare centers, child-oriented non-profit organizations, and other places where they may come into regular contact with children. These laws are typically directed at individuals who committed sex crimes against children. Laws barring persons convicted of sexually abusing children from working directly with children may be reasonable. For example, the state of Virginia prohibits sex offenders convicted of sex crimes that involved children from working or volunteering at a school or daycare center. Members of the community can also react so strongly to the presence of a registered offender on the job that employers will end up firing them.

A study by Mercado et al. (2008) found that over half (52 %) of their sample lost their jobs and a smaller percentage reported having to move out of rented apartments due to community notification.

Psychological Consequences

The collateral consequences that many sex offenders report are depression, loneliness, and fear for their own safety (Levenson and Tewksbury (2009). Research examining the psychological impact of notification laws (Levenson and Cotter 2005; Mercado et al. 2008) found that 50 % or more of sex offenders reported stress, shame, hopelessness, and a loss of social supports. Sex offenders reported that community notification laws were unfair (Levenson and Cotter 2005; Tewksbury and Lees 2006). Registered sex offenders reported moderate to high stress resulting from their listing on the sex offender registry (Tewksbury and Zgoba 2010; Mercado et al. 2008).

Social Consequences

Due to the registration requirement for convicted sex offenders, these individuals face considerable stigmatization (Tewksbury and Copes 2012). Irrespective of age, individuals who have committed sexual crimes are significantly ostracized from local communities and society. Societal responses to sexual crimes are argued to be severe and harsh (Letourneau and Miner 2005; Trivits and Reppucci 2002; Quinn et al. 2004), particularly because of the perceived dangerousness and future risk associated with the criminal behavior (Zimring 2009). The perpetrators are often despised, hated, and stigmatized (McAlinden 2014). These reactions not only extend to community or neighborhoods but also families.

This phenomenon can be contextualized through the lens of Social Reaction Theory, or the consequences of the responses to criminal behaviors (Paternoster and Iovanni 1989). Social Reaction Theory focuses on the responses such that adjunct individuals (peers or family), the criminal justice system, and the community at-risk promote legislation that effectively forbids the crime, subsequently labeling the offender (Paternoster and Bachman 2013). There are two arms of this theory: (1) the status characteristics hypothesis argues that power differentials exist between those who label and those who are labeled and (2) the secondary deviance hypothesis states that negative labels produce a self-fulfilling prophecy such that individuals who are labeled have to cope with it and may lead to more criminal behaviors (Paternoster and Bachman 2013).

"Social stigma"—the "sexual predator" or the "sexually violent offender" have become umbrella labels for all convicted sex offenders. These labels, lump all sex offenders as the most dangerous or the most extreme, regardless of their low designated level or their offense conviction (Tewksbury and Lees 2006). Often, the label of "sex offender" elicits many emotions about who the individual is and what type of crime they've committed; semantics are more powerful than we otherwise assumed. When the title of "sex offender" is used participants tend to respond more harshly as opposed to when the label of "person who committed a sexual offense is used" (Harris and Socia 2015). Adult sexual offenders experience a wide range of outcomes as a result of the label.

Robber's (2008) study examined the effects of labeling, specifically disintegrative shaming—through informal and formal sanctions on sex offender reintegration. Findings revealed that the majority of sex offenders are subjected to negative treatment in communities because of their status as sex offenders, they were publicly labelled and socially shunned. Convicted sex offenders have been forced to find a method of stigma management. Isolating oneself or social withdrawal are ways that such offenders can limit their interactions and encounters with others (Winnick and Bodkin 2008). This method would keep others from learning about their registered sex offender status because they very rarely see the person. Relatedly, sex offenders can keep their status on the registry secret and hope that their neighbors or coworkers do not check the registry. Grouping, whereby registered sex offenders seek out others in similar situations for social support and denial, through which stigmatized persons disavow the sex offender label, are two additional means of stigma management (Evans and Cubellis 2015).

Registration and community notifications, while intended for adults, were unequivocally applied to juveniles (Chaffin 2008; Letourneau and Miner 2005; Letourneau et al. 2009). Such sanctions can create barriers for rehabilitation during treatment and reintegration such that young offenders and families can be further ostracized from local communities and neighborhoods (Hackett et al. 2015). Research has begun to document the influence of registration and community notification on the rehabilitative process for youth offenders. One research study indicated that registration status for juvenile sexual offenders may lead to greater surveillance by flagging additional non-sexual offending crimes (Letourneau et al. 2009). Furthermore, registration and community notification may not associate to its intended purpose of deterring sexual offenses; in South Carolina, the SORN policy was not associated with a deterrent effect of juvenile sexual offending when accounting for other legislative initiatives enacted around a similar time as SORN (Letourneau et al. 2010).

Other social responses can be directed at families. Families of youth who commit sexual crimes are often stigmatized from their communities. There is a sense of moral indignation as a result of sexual crimes committed by juveniles (Salerno et al. 2010) and often, the first ones to blame are the families (Hackett et al. 2015). Research has shown that reactions cannot only include stigmatization, social isolation, and physical property damage, but some youths and families were forcibly removed from their homes (Masson et al. 2014). Community-level risks can actually be elevated due to such responses (Masson et al. 2014).

The families of youth who commit sexual crimes relative to families of adults may be at greater risk for negative responses. Some have reported that physical attacks by family members are common when sexual offenses are disclosed (Lacombe 2008). The families may face extreme retribution and fear community and extra-familial backlash (Yoder and Brown 2015). Families of youth who commit sexual crimes can experience "courtesy stigma", or stigma that is projected onto families regardless of whether or not they support their child (Goffman 1963). Further, placing youth on the registry can exacerbate negative response effects (Masson et al. 2014). Registration requirements often highlight the location and residence of family.

As a result, families and youth become isolated or retreat to avoid negative or overly punitive reactions. Research has revealed that families avoid service engagement because of the fear of judgment and ostracism (Yoder and Brown 2015). Families have legitimate concerns the treatment provider and judicial system will blame them for the sexual crime and place additional barriers to the rehabilitative process (Yoder and Brown 2015). Families navigating through the justice system have experienced the stress related to new rules and demands placed upon them, and hesitate to engage in treatment that further restricts their parenting capacities (Yoder and Brown 2015).

Social Disorganization

Socially disorganized communities are characterized by vacant lots, litter, higher crime rates, higher rates of poverty, more vacant houses, lower housing values, and lower median incomes (Tewksbury and Mustaine 2008, Levenson and Cotter 2005). Such communities tend to have higher numbers of registered sex offenders (Tewksbury and Mustaine 2008, Mustaine and Tewksbury 2011). Mustaine and Tewksbury (2011) point to three processes that aggregate to exacerbate the residential relegation for sex offenders: legal restrictions on residential location, social cohesion of the communities, and economic factors. As aforementioned, in many jurisdictions, sex offenders are restricted to living a certain distance from a facility or location in which children routinely congregate. When sex offenders are clustered in certain areas, the property values fall (Mustaine and Tewksbury 2011). Sex offenders also may be restricted from work opportunities, or there may not be work opportunities available for sex offenders. Socially disorganized communities end up being the only residences in which sex offenders can find housing. These communities are composed of more diverse, more transient residents or renters who may not have a financial or personal stake in their residences, thereby removing or decreasing their concern over sex offenders living nearby.

Harassment, Threats, and Vigilantism

Vigilantism was fairly common. In one study of vigilantism, nearly half (48 %) of 137 sex offenders reported having been physically threatened or harassed and 11 % were actually physically assaulted or injured (Mercado et al. 2008). Many registered sex offenders described harassment and ridicule by assorted people in their lives, including neighbors, landlords, law enforcement, and even strangers (Frenzel et al. 2014). Regarding juvenile offenders who commit sexual crimes, they can be bullied by peers (Edwards and Hensley 2001), and face many of the same negative experiences as adults. Research has revealed high levels of disgust sensitivity toward juveniles who commit sexual crimes and produce greater support for placing juvenile sexual offenders on the registries (Stevenson et al. 2015). Research has also noted a contagion effect in community responses toward youth who commit sexual crimes. Punitive community reactions extended to all youth in the sample representing many different contexts. In this particular research study, these responses exacerbated youths' risk factors for re-offense (Hackett et al. 2015).

Maintaining Family Ties and Relationships with Significant Others

Family and significant other ties provides assistance and financially, emotionally, and socially serve as anchors for convicted sex offenders— once released from prison, they are referred to as releasees or returnees—to prepare them for release and to cope with the stress of transitioning back to the community. For many returning inmates, family members are their greatest support. Most family members reported that providing emotional support to returning offenders was fairly easy but that financial assistance was much more difficult (Naser and Visher 2006). However, registered sex offenders may lose the support of family and other significant others when they experience the negative consequences of their relationship to the offender (Evans and Cubellis 2015). There is always the ever present fear of being recognized as related to a "pervert" (Frenzel et al. 2014). Lengthy prison terms lead to the strain and disruption of intimate relationships and other personal relationships. Family roles and relationships may have restructured, and members have to find a way to fit in the new reconfiguration. Long periods of separation adversely impact one's ability to communicate and interact with their significant others both pre- and post-release. There is great difficulty for the registered sex offender in meeting familial and intimate other responsibilities, as well as an inability to participate in expected parental duties, such as attending a parental function (Levenson and Cotter 2005).

Berg and Huebner (2011) assert that familial relations involve three components that may affect returnees and their involvement in crime. The ties may have a controlling effect on the behavior and motivation of prison releases. Families connect reentering offenders to conventional order and impede their impulse to recidivate. For offenders, their routines and activities are organized and their associates are monitored. Family members may encourage them to follow conditions of supervision and to attend treatment and support groups. Second, returning sex offenders are afforded emotional support to cope with the stress of registration and public notification and to comply with the conditions and intrusions of community supervision and surveillance by law enforcement. Third, research finds that family relationships are fundamental components in processes of cognitive change. Family ties act as an anchor enabling offenders to construct an alternative identity (pp. 385–386). Research indicates that the family of a returning offender has a significant impact on his post-release success or failure. The emotional, financial, and other tangible support, including housing and transportation is likely to influence the success or failure of the releases (Naser and Visher 2006). These findings reaffirm the importance of family dynamics to the reentry process (See Begun, Hodge, and Early chapter in this volume).

Secondary Consequences for Family Members

Family members of convicted sex offenders feel extreme anxiety and conflicting emotions over their reentry. Some family members were primary victims, while others must cope with the reality what their significant other has done. Family members of sex offenders are also not impervious to sex offender laws and policies and report experiencing the secondary effects of stigmatization. Families who choose to accept the returning prisoner have an enormous responsibility. Released offenders rely heavily on their family members to navigate virtually every aspect of the reentry process from housing assistance to financial support to emotional comfort (Farkas and Miller 2007). Most offenders have positive expectations for their reentry because of their belief that they have familial and social resources to rely on (Tewksbury and Copes 2012). Even though stigma often extends to the family members of sex offenders, relative to the wider community, the family is more likely to view the offenders' stigma as only part of the offender's total identity (Berg and Huebner 2011). Nonetheless, families living with a registered sex offender were likely to confront threats and harassment by neighbors. They also report persistent feeling of depression, frustration and stress, a sense of isolation, shame, and fear for their safety.

Most family members related that their children were treated differently than other children. Children reported feeling sad and ashamed when their parent could not attend a school event. In a study of registered sex offenders conducted by Zeviz and Farkas (2000), one subject recounted how his daughter was taunted at school about her daddy playing sex with her. For children, the impact of the sex offender registry was evident in their behavior. They most often exhibited anger, depression, and anxiety (Levenson and Tewksbury 2009). Unfortunately, children may experience the most deleterious effects of their parent's identity as a registered sex offender (Levenson and Tewksbury 2009).

Some additional collateral consequences for juveniles, like adults include discorded relationship with family and friends. However, because youth are embedded in the family contexts, and sometimes offenses can occur between family members, many times, the pain of the sexual abuse filters through the family more severely in juvenile cases. Specifically, there are variations in family responses. Research has begun documenting some of the emotional processing families endure, and has been explained as a grief progression, where there are stages of ambiguity, denial, hurt, and acceptance (Yoder and Brown 2015). Further, the process is painful for families, as they often feel they are exposed and blamed for the criminal behavior (Yoder and Brown 2015). Other research has revealed some familial responses can fluctuate between supportive and rejection, where families are largely influenced by whether the victim was intra- or extra-familial; in many cases, parents were more accepting if the victim was extra-familial (Hackett and Phillips 2014).

Research on peers and friendships has consistently revealed that youth who commit sexual crimes are more socially isolated relative to their non-sexual offending counterparts (Miner and Munns 2005), and this has been conjectured to be a contributor to seeking out sexual gratification with children (Fagan and Wexler 1988; Marshall 1989). These theoretical positions have also been supported by research (Miner et al. 2010). Nevertheless, the authors themselves have speculated these findings as possibly effects that result from the criminal behavior themselves (Miner and Munns 2005). For example, the sexual offense could produce fear and stigma and subsequent isolation from peers, and rather than the isolation being the correlate to the sexual crime, it may be the consequence (Miner and Munss 2005).

Establishing Friendships and Dating Relations

Social relations poses a particular challenge for sex offenders released from prison, detention, or civil commitment status. The social stigma attached to a convicted sex offender is fed by special bulletin notifications sent to many facilities, schools, playgrounds, public swimming pools, libraries, and other public areas where children are likely to congregate. The returning sex offender may have great difficulty forming relationships, including friendships and romantic relationships and may suffer disintegration of their current relationships (Evans and Cubellis 2015). They may feel isolated and shunned by neighbors and former acquaintances. The type of public notification that is implemented depends on law enforcement's discretion in the particular jurisdiction. A level one (highest risk) sex offender warrants the most extensive form of public notification, which could encompass a television news bulletin, a community notification meeting at the location where the sex offender plans to live, and door-to-door flyers. This high-risk sex offender is monitored by law enforcement with neighborhood patrols and periodic visits and by community supervision agents who supervised the offenders and make unannounced stops day or night.

Community Supervision and Monitoring of Sex Offenders

The majority of adult- and juvenile-convicted sex offenders will return to the community under supervision. Therefore, a sensible reentry process must focus on the twin goals of community protection and sex offender rehabilitation. The unique challenges and risks that sex offenders present for the public requires specialized approaches to their supervision in the community. The reentry process should be graduated from more restrictive to less restrictive supervision. Risk should be closely and continually monitored through periodic risk assessment. Close collaboration and frequent information sharing among supervision agents, treatment providers, and relevant others are needed. Specialized, ongoing training for supervisory agents, specialized, smaller caseloads of convicted sex offenders. and specialized conditions of supervision are all part of sex offender community supervision and management.

Models of Community Supervision

The Containment Model

A model for promising community safety and monitoring that materializes out of the Center for Sex Offender Management (CSOM 2016) is the containment model. CSOM spearheads efforts to ensure the comprehensive approach to management and endorses a model of *Comprehensive Approaches to Sex Offender Management*. This holistic model mandates cross-system collaboration, offender accountability, rehabilitation, community management, and reentry (Calley 2007). Specifically, the multidisciplinary team approach is useful in drawing upon members of the team to supervise and monitor youth during treatment program. The containment model developed by Kim English and her team at the Colorado Division of Criminal Justice has become a popular approach in many jurisdictions to managing adult and juvenile sex offenders released to the community. The use of both internal (sex-offender-specific treatment to develop internal control over deviant thoughts) and external control measures (official supervision and polygraph monitoring to determine conformance to treatment and supervision conditions) are combined to more effectively supervise convicted sex offenders (English 1998).

The "containment model" and its five components:

1. A philosophy that values victim protection, public safety, and reparation for victims as the paramount objectives of sex offender management.
2. Implementation strategies that depend on agency coordination and multidisciplinary partnerships.
3. A containment-focused case management and risk control approach that is individualized based on each offender's characteristics.
4. Consistent multi-agency policies and protocols.
5. Quality control mechanisms, including program monitoring and evaluation.

Moreover, the model is intended to use a triangle of supervision. Treatment providers become part of a supervision network working with the internal controls of the sex offender. External controls are in place that include conditions of supervision, intensive supervision and professional collaboration with law enforcement, social workers, and correctional staff and through periodic communication with neighbors, employers, landlords, and associates of the offenders.

The Comprehensive Approach

A secondary approach called the "comprehensive approach to sex offender management" was also developed by the Center for Sex Offender Management. This framework encourages a strategic, deliberate, and integrated response to managing sex offenders and reducing recidivism. Nevertheless, this form of community risk management during treatment is only feasible for youth who are placed within a community-based care program with families willing and able to participate. The aforementioned Colorado Sex Offender Management Board evaluation indicated that 58 % of the youth in the sample received informed supervision (see: Yoder et al. 2015a). There are other forms of community supervision that may be utilized separately or in coordination with informed supervision to maintain public safety during the course of treatment.

The "Comprehensive approach" and its five components:

1. Victim-Centeredness—Ensuring that the interests of current and potential future victims remain at the forefront for those working to manage sex offenders in the community. Victim advocacy is a central component that involves establishing relationships with victims, acting as a resource for victims as they participate in the criminal justice process, and continuing to support victims after offenders are released into community.
2. Specialized knowledge and training—All of those involved with the management of sex offenders should have specialized knowledge and training about sex offenders and their victims.
3. Public education—Providing the public with accurate information about sex offending is central to successful prevention and management efforts. Accurate information will help dispel commonly held myths and equip the general public to better respond to and deal with the issue of sex offending in their community.
4. Monitoring and evaluation—Sex offender practices should be monitored and evaluated on an ongoing basis to ensure that remain current with the emerging science (evidence-based practice).
5. Collaboration—Collaboration is critically needed in response to the problem of sex offending at both the case management and policy levels.

Specialized Caseloads

Specialized caseloads promote the specialization of job duties for supervisory staff and also promote support and camaraderie among agents to reduce secondary trauma and to increase agency-wide consistency in sex offender supervision practices (CSOM 2016). Agents should have extensive supervision experience and be trained in sex offenders' issues, such as treatment, assessment, and use of the polygraph.

Risk Assessment

Structured risk assessment tools are commonly used by professionals working with sex offenders. For those who supervise sex offenders, the accurate prediction of sex offender recidivism will help the agents determine the level of community supervision needed, the number of home and work visits, and the number of collateral contacts necessary. This prediction of risk consists of using the most accurate, objective, empirically based, scientifically validated tools. However, while there has been significant advancement in the development of sex offender specific risk assessment instruments, there is certainly no single best risk assessment for all sex offenders in all situations. Three common tools of assessment for use with sex offenders include the STATIC-99, Minnesota Sex Offender Screening (MnSOST-R), and the Sex Offender Risk Appraisal Guide (SORAG). Numerous studies have examined and compared different instruments (see Hanson and Bussiere 1998; Hanson and Thornton 2000; and Langton et al. 2007).

Specialized Treatment

There are many forms of treatment that have been proposed as "the best treatment approach" for sex offenders. The research is mixed in this regard: There are aspects of each approach, such as relapse prevention. In fact, some treatment professionals recommend blending more than one model (see "How to integrate the Good Lives Model into Treatment Programs," Willis et al. 2013).

CSOM points to important aspects of sex offender specific treatment:

1. Primary focus is the protection of the community.
2. Considerable attention is directed toward understanding the harm the offender has caused his victim.
3. Sex offenders' thinking errors that contribute to their offending patterns are revealed, examined, and challenged.

4. Offenders participate in professionally facilitated group sessions; these sessions provide opportunities for offenders to challenge one another regarding their denial. distortions, and manipulations.
5. Information discussed in group is shared with supervising agents, polygraph examiners, and other stakeholders.

Cognitive-Behavioral Treatment

The support for this therapy is based on a stronger and more intensive literature than other approaches (Harris et al. 1998), and it includes a relapse prevention component and cognitive-behavioral techniques. Some of the problems with sex offender treatment in prisons and civil commitment facilities is that the quality of treatment varies, treatment can be denied or a phase postponed, and treatment staff may have varying skills and qualifications (Fitch and Hammen 2003).

Risk-Need Model

Another major approach to treating sex offenders is the risk-need model with its attendant relapse prevention model. The primary goal of this model is to help sex offenders understand their offense pattern and cope with situational and psychological factors that place them at risk for re-offending (Ward and Hudson, 554). The best way to reduce recidivism rates is to identify and reduce or eliminate an individual's array of dynamic risk factors (see Ndrecka, Listwan, and Latessa chapter in this volume). The risk-needs model presupposes the following:

1. Risk assessment should drive need assessment and the treatment process. Offenders' level of risk should determine the required intensity and duration of treatment.
2. Allocating to intervention streams on the basis of their assessed level of risk results in better outcome. Conversely, giving low-risk offenders high levels of treatment may actually *increase* their probability of re-offending.

3. Focusing treatment on criminogenic needs or dynamic risk factors will result in better outcomes by reducing or controlling risk factors and thereby reducing their influence on vulnerable individuals.
4. An offender's level of risk increases with the pressure of each additional risk factor.

Although the strengths of the risk-need model is that it is empirically guided and that it has a relapse prevention model, a limitation consists of difficulty motivating offenders. Another limitation is that the treatment strategies are outlined in negative terms, including the elimination of deviant interests, extinction of deviant sexual interests, and developing a list of people and places to avoid (relapse prevention) (Ward and Stewart 2003).

The Good Lives Model

The good lives model (GLM) is a strengths-based approach to offender rehabilitation in which the aim is to enhance individuals' capacities to live meaningful, constructive, and ultimately satisfying lives so they can desist from re-offending (Ward and Maruna 2007). The focus is on providing offenders with the skills, values, opportunities, and social support so that they meet their human needs in more adaptive and constructive ways. An offender may attempt (often implicitly) to satisfy primary goods, such as romantic relatedness, pleasure, and connectedness to others; confront obstacles; and engage in offending behaviors. The GLM is buttressed by three core ideas (Langlands et al. 2009):

1. Humans are active, goal-seeking beings who consistently attempt to construct a sense of meaning and purpose in their lives.
2. The majority of human actions reflect attempts to meet inherent human needs or primary human needs.
3. Instrumental or secondary goals provide the concrete means or strategies to pursue and achieve primary human goods.

According to the GLM model, there are a variety of problems that may be evident in an offender's ways of living and life plans. Assessment begins with understanding the weight that the offender's gives to primary goods, including inner peace, spirituality, and excellence in work (Ward and Brown 2004). Rehabilitative programs should identify obstacles and problems in the sex offender's achieving his primary goods in more constructive, socially acceptable ways. Treatment is individually tailored to assist the offender in implementing his good lives rehabilitation plan. According to McGrath et al. (2010), the GLM is the theoretical foundation successfully used by several sex offender treatment programs.

The Risk-Need and Good Lives Models

Ward and Stewart (2003) have proposed combining the risk-need and the good lives models in sex offender treatment. A treatment plan should always take into account the match between characteristics of the offender and the likely environment she or he will encounter upon release. To successfully embed the risk-need model within the good lives model means that the focus of therapy should be on instilling the necessary capabilities to achieve human goods in socially acceptable ways that are personally meaningful and satisfying. Thus, effective treatment requires the acquisition of competencies and external supports, as well as opportunities to live a different life.

Conditions of Supervision and Contacts with Supervising Agents

The goal of public safety underlies all of the conditions. Convicted sex offenders are typically assigned intensive or specialized supervision with specialized conditions. They must follow the standard conditions of supervision that all offenders released to community supervision must follow. In addition, there are a special set of conditions that they are required to abide by. Because of the large and varied types of sexual behavior, it is difficult to individualize these specialized restrictions. The special conditions typically include no contact with the victim(s), polygraph testing, sex offense specific treatment covered by a signed contract, and electronic monitoring and global positioning system. Restrictions on their movement in the community is accomplished by driving and travel limitations.

To ensure effective supervision of youthful offenders, a supervision plan ought to outline the risk level and his or her needs. The plan is typically in effect for the length of time the juvenile is in treatment. The plan delineates the frequency of contact with a supervising officer that is often contingent upon the risk level of youth (CSOM 2016). This plan takes into account the family and socioecological situations of the youth. Typically, it includes any contextual factors that could positively or negatively impact youths' ability to be safe and stable within the community. The safety of others and potential or previous victims should be the first and foremost consideration. The plan should also entail strengths and resiliencies present in the individual youth as well as his or her social situation (CSOM 2016). The probation officer is often charged with the responsibility of directly supervising youth during treatment and working in conjunction with other members of the multidisciplinary team (CSOM 2016). The probation or supervision officer provides direct oversight of youth and families. They are a liaison to the court and work alongside treatment providers to assist in making necessary determinations based on the progress of youth (CSOM 2016). In fact, in the most recent Safer Society Survey, it was reported that 97 % probation officers exchange information with caseworkers in community-based programs and 95 % in residential programs (McGrath et al. 2010). An earlier Safer Society Survey indicated over 90 % of treatment providers and probation officers share information (McGrath et al. 2003). Furthermore, probation officers are assets to the rehabilitative process, as they are familiar with specialized treatment for youth who have committed sexual crimes and are clear about the necessary milestones youth must achieve (CSOM 2016).

Conditions of supervision are designed to minimize, or eliminate, deviant thoughts, fantasies, or impulses and to eliminate opportunities to re-offend.

Post-Conviction Polygraph (PCSCOT)

In a majority of states, post-conviction polygraph or "lie detector" testing is used with convicted sex offenders. Polygraph testing is incorporated as an additional tool in a broader risk management strategy. It is also an additional tool in the surveillance of sex offenders to obtain a more thorough disclosure of past sexual offending and to determine compliance with supervisory and treatment conditions. The rationale behind polygraph examinations is that full disclosure of the deviant thoughts, fantasies, and the behaviors of sex offenders are essential for their treatment and maintenance in the community. The use of the polygraph requires the collaborative efforts of the polygraph examiner, the therapist, and the supervising criminal justice agent. The polygraph is considered an effective tool in reducing denial, eliciting admission of past and present sexual offenses, improving treatment outcomes, and improving the supervision of sex offenders (Ahlmeyer et al. 2000).

There are three types of post-conviction polygraph: a disclosure polygraph after sentencing, a specific issue and denial exam, and a maintenance polygraph administered while in treatment (English et al. 2000). With the disclosure polygraph, sex offenders are questioned about their sex offense history and history of sexually deviant behavior (Farkas and Stichman 2002). Specific issue testing is used when an individual is denying or minimizing events surrounding the offense. The maintenance polygraph is a monitoring exam to assess compliance with conditions of supervision.

There is a clear chasm in the proponents and opponents for polygraph testing for juveniles and adults. Proponents of polygraph testing argue that it is a mechanism for eliciting more detailed information about the sexual crime (Hindman and Peters 2001). This leads to a more holistic understanding of the correlates to the sexual crime, informing targeted intervention and preventative efforts (Grubin et al. 2004; Kokish et al. 2005). Others opposed the use of polygraph citing the limited research and methodological limitations along with the notion that it can be excessively coercive when used with youth (Ben-Shakhar 2008; Chaffin 2011). Researchers have argued, quite extensively, that the polygraph is a flawed procedure riddled with threats to validity and reliability (Rosky 2012).

There is limited research available on the effects of polygraph testing for juveniles who commit sexual crimes. The scant research base that is available has indicated the promise of polygraphs, when timed correctly can elicit disclosures (Emerick and Dutton 1993; Stovering et al. 2013). Another research study revealed indiscriminate differences between adults and juveniles in level of deceit (Jenson et al. 2015). In an attempt to expand upon the extant research base, one study revealed that among a sample of youth sexual offenders who received the polygraph test, youth who had significant reactions on the polygraph test had more disclosures, and non-significant reactions, inconclusive results, and more disclosures were associated with more polygraph testing. Furthermore, youth with more non-significant reactions were five times more likely to successfully complete treatment, but test results and number of tests were not associated with one-, three-, or five-year recidivism outcomes (Yoder et al. 2016a).

A model has emerged, whereby judicious use of the polygraph ought to be instituted under controlled conditions and while accounting for individual needs of youth (Yoder et al. 2016a). Furthermore, this model is now endorsed through the Colorado Sex Offender Management Board as best practice polygraph (CSOMB 2014).

As a cautionary note, polygraph findings should not be relied upon as the sole criteria in case of management decisions because of the risk of false positives or negatives (Blasingame 1998). Despite its increasing use, there is considerable debate regarding the admissibility, validity, and accuracy of polygraph result (Farkas and Stichman 2002). Blasingame (1998) has suggested four measures to enhance the validity and usefulness of the polygraph test:

a) Polygraphers, treatment providers, and probation officers should collaborate to form the questions for the exam. (b). Questions should focus on behavior rather than the intent of the sex offender. (c). Sex offenders should be given guaranteed immunity for admission of new or previous sex crimes, and (d) a system should be in place, such as refraining from obtaining details about victims, so that mandatory reported is not required.

Phallometry is used in some jurisdictions as a tool in sex offender treatment. A pressure-sensitive penile plethysmograph is placed on the penis of the sex offender to test his erectile response to an array of sexually stimulating images and auditory stimuli (Harlow and Scott 2007). The plethysmograph detects minute changes in the circumference of his penis to determine his level of attraction. There is some research to support the claim that this tool is a reliable and valid method of objectively measuring and assessing the erectile response in male sex offenders (Barker and Howell 1992). However, there is still controversy over its use in correctional assessment (Purcell et al. 2015).

Electronic Monitoring (EM) and Global Positioning

Two relatively newer conditions or strategies of sex offender supervision are electronic monitoring (EM) and global positioning systems GPS. The mandated EM of sex offenders released to the community has become a regular part of supervision or a special condition of community supervision. At present, nearly every state has implemented some form of electronic monitoring (EM). Three types of EM are used throughout the United States: passive, active, and hybrid systems (Meloy and Coleman 2009). Passive systems are used most often, and download data once daily. Active systems can immediately alert to possible violations (expensive and used less frequently) and hybrid systems regularly transmit tracking data to supervisors. National estimates of the cost of EM are $13–36 dollars a day (Budd and Mancini 2015). In 2005, the state of Florida passed the Jessica Lunsford or Jessica's law named after nine-year-old murder victim Jessica who was abducted from her home by a registered sex offender living anonymously 150 yards away. The law provided for lifetime electronic monitoring for adults who have been convicted of lewd, unchaste, or unclean acts against a victim less than 12 years old. Jessica's law also instituted a mandatory minimum sentence of 25 years in prison for the same offense.

GPS tracking monitors the offender's whereabouts 24 hours a day and sends a report to a supervising officer at predetermined reporting intervals, whereas active GPS provides continuous real-time surveillance and alerts the officer as soon as an offender travels in a prohibited zone. As stated by Levenson and D'Amora, (2007), GPS tracking provides offender accountability and community protection and is cost efficient. It allows multiple sex offenders to be supervised in the community, to be employed, to support their families, and to pay the GPS monitoring fees. It may also deter criminal behavior, given that the sex offenders are aware they are being tracked.

Studies examining the recidivism rates of sex offenders on GPS tracking, however, have provided inconclusive results, and more reliable studies are needed (Meloy and Coleman 2009). In fact, research examining the impact of GPS when used only as a punitive sanction have found that it did not lower recidivism and had little effect on it (Aos et al. 2001; Turner et al. 2000).

Driver's License Notation

Laws have been enacted in some states that require sex offenders to display a special driver's license notation identifying their sex offender registration status (Mancini et al. 2011). In Florida, for example, the drivers' license of a sex offender will indicate statute number 775 for a designated sexual predator and statute 943 for other types of convicted sex offenders. Other states stipulate a special driver's license as a supervision condition.

Electronic Devices and Internet Use are Prohibited

Offenders may not possess a camera camcorder, videocassette recorder/player without their supervising agent's permission. The use of the Internet is also controlled for registered sex offenders in several states. The intent behind this condition is to prevent the offenders from using the computer for sexual purposes, such as accessing pornography or visiting chatrooms looking for a victim. They are required to inform law enforcement and their supervising agent if they have access to the Internet at home or at their place of employment. Registered sex offenders are also required to submit to periodic, unannounced examinations of their computers and to install hardware or software that monitors their use.

Conditions of Supervision for Juvenile Offenders

Some conditions required during community supervision or the probationary period include curfew restrictions, drug testing, community service or restitution, reporting requirements, prosocial relationships with peers, or consistent school attendance and participation (CSOM 2016). Further, there are also some specialized restrictions that are contingent upon the severity and conditions of the sexual offense. These can include close observation over Internet usage, restrictions on television and video gaming, restrictions on locations, electronic monitoring, approval and monitoring of sports, clubs, or games after school, close observation of contact with previous or potential victims, and ensuring treatment follow through (CSOM 2016).

Strategies for a Successful Reentry

During the supervisory period, it is recommended that while avoidance of high-risk situations and triggers are important, offenders also ought to set "approach goals" or identify the activities or interactions that are going to promote positive growth. Such approach goals include participating in prosocial events or activities with permission, seeking out and gaining part time employment, and networking.

The contemporary political environment and public sentiment toward sex offenders is fearful. Attitudes prevail among the public that sex offenders deserve punishment and that treatment does not work. Policies and laws tend to be restrictive and exclusionary and greatly impact the reentry and reintegration of such offenders back into the community. The laws were meant to protect the community through the control and incapacitation of sex offenders. There is a price to pay for implementing these intrusive measures. Achieving the overriding goals has unexpected and far-reaching collateral consequences.

In order to ensure successful reentry and aftercare, it is critical that there is a comprehensive plan that considers all issues surrounding health and mental health, sustainability of programmatic or intervention strategies, integration and empowerment of family members, and consideration of alternative systems, including any other child serving system collaboration (CSOM 2016). In many cases, the educational needs of youth should also be infused into the aftercare planning. Research has revealed the positive protective effect of integrating school personnel and multidisciplinary team members and involving youth in extracurricular activities to mitigate against risky school-level variables and lead toward successful treatment (Yoder et al. 2016b). Similarly, career and vocational interests also ought to be a critical component of comprehensive aftercare. This includes independent skills trainings, potential career matching, workforce and community development, and identifying career strengths (CSOM 2016).

Sex Offender Reentry Courts

Sex offender reentry courts can be classified as a "specialized treatment court" or a "problem-solving court" that begins with a criminal prosecution and ends with a final discharge of the sex offender. Therapeutic jurisprudence underlies the legal concepts, court structure, and judicial practices to facilitate the rehabilitative process. As a reentry court, the focus is on assisting offenders that are released from prison so they comply with court supervision and conditions to ultimately integrate into the community. When the reentry model is applied to sex offenders, attempts are directed at managing their re-offending with close supervision and monitoring through the use of polygraph examinations. The judge assumes a more active, engaged and collaborative role, using a risk management approach and the principles of therapeutic jurisprudence. The judge's role provides stronger incentives for offender rehabilitation and risk management.

Offense histories and patterns are collected for each offender through clinical interviews and polygraph examinations (LaFond and Winick 2004). The judge has information about the previous victim (s)and so she/he can develop individualized restrictions regarding victim contact. The judge also collaborates closely with supervision agents so that the sex offenders are monitored, polygraphed, and attend treatment, using the authority of the court to monitor compliance and to apply positive reinforcement, graduated sanctions and marshal treatment. The explicit use of judicial authority helps motivate the sex offender to achieve specific, contractual short-term and long-term goals (LaFond and Winick 2004).

Circles of Support and Accountability (COSA)

The increase in the prison population over the last few decades has resulted in a significant number of individuals released to society. Incarcerated offenders typically face many obstacles upon release. Convicted sex offenders face unique barriers and challenges upon release. The management, intervention, and supervision of registered sex offenders should be conducted with the individual's risk in mind rather than a blanket approach. The COSA model originated in Ontario, Canada as a grassroot, faith-based program developed by a Mennonite pastor. The Correctional Service of Canada adopted and expanded the program. The COSA model was evaluated and found to have a significant impact on recidivism (Wilson et al. 2009). The precise implementation of the model varied but the different variations contained several key features (Fox 2017, p. 46):

1. A corrections-related, moderately high risk to the community "core member" or convicted sex offender due for release, who is in need of support and,
2. A team of appropriately screened volunteers who commit to weekly, consistent meetings for a period of twelve months.

The COSA model relies on a team approach rather than an individual mentor model to disperse responsibility and lessen the stress. The team could use each other as a sounding board for decisions and a source of unconditional support. Fox maintains that the strength of the COSA model is in the relationships that form and the unconditional support the team provides the sex offender.

The model focuses on the risk level and particularly the risk level of high-risk released sex offenders. The accountability consists of an "inner circle" of trained community volunteers who provide support for such offenders reintegrating back into society (van Rensburg 2012). The volunteers become the offender's family/peer network and support. The inner circle is not meant to replace criminal justice and therapeutic professional support and expert advice but to serve as an adjunct for the social support needs of the sex offender (Petrunik 2002). The community, essentially, assists in the management of reentering sex offenders encouraging them to be accountable and responsible. The COSA volunteers model prosocial relationships and assist with the reentry needs housing, employment, and following conditions of supervision (van Rensburg 2012).

Convicted sex offenders have reported stress, loneliness, depression, and isolation. Social isolation is particularly problematic and may have a large impact on recidivism. The social supports for registered sex offenders are typically lacking, and the sex offender feels alone and shunned by others. Community notification and residence restrictions may influence the offender's ability to relocate with their family or other significant others. The family home may be situated in a prohibited distance from a daycare, school, or playground, or family members may fear harassment or intimidation (Levenson and Cotter 2005). In research on family members of registered sex offenders, they reported being ostracized, disrespected, and being constantly watched by neighbors (Farkas and Miller 2007). Research suggests COSAs are successful in significantly reducing recidivism in high-risk sex offenders (Wilson et al. 2007). Research of both offenders and volunteers alike indicated generally high levels of satisfaction with the process, with feeling supported and accepted and community members feeling empowered and more accepting and understanding of offenders and their behavior (Wilson et al. 2007). Thus, COSAs may help released sex offenders adjust to the community and increase the involvement of citizens in monitoring and supporting returning sex offenders.

Families as Informed Supervisors and Family Reunification for Youthful Offenders

Like informed supervision with families, there are family reunification strategies that can be instituted early on to prepare youth for successful reintegration with communities and families of origin. Family reunification is a process of family service delivery where youth living in an out-of-home placement will be returning home. The families of these youth are often required to complete plans for contact with the victim, victim clarification, and steps to reintegrate the youth back into the community (Thomas 2010). A formative step of family reunification includes continuous assessment of victim safety (Thomas and Viar 2005); a hasty return back into the home or origin or contact with the victim can be harmful (CSOM 2016). The family reunification process is typically guided by measurable and attainable goals that progressively bring youth back into their home environments. This process includes a step-by-step process that begins with out-of-home placement and transitions to supervised contacts in clinical and then home settings to transition to family supervision, and ultimately back home (Thomas and Wilson 1999). This step is critical for ensuring a smooth transition between placements and ensuring family members can have sustained engagement in fostering healthy and non-abusive behavior patterns.

Programs that serve youth with sexual behavior problems, for example, report approximately 88 % involve family members or significant others in the process (McGrath et al. 2010). Whether or not youth are undergoing family reunification, family treatment can be useful, with treatment components varying from recognition of triggers to processing the pain of the sexual crime (Yoder and Ruch 2016). Consequently, family engagement in treatment can promote a sustained model of empowerment for families and youth alike (Yoder 2014). In fact, it has been strongly suggested to prioritize family therapy for successful rehabilitation and reentry (CSOM 2016) and has been demonstrated as one critical family treatment that can lead to successful treatment success (Yoder et al. 2015b) and participating in family functions (CSOM 2016).

Concluding Thoughts

Some sex offenders (adults and juveniles) pose a very serious risk to the public, and they are deserving of criminal sanction and strict monitoring, surveillance, and risk management. The tendency with the implementation of specialized sex offender laws is to apply them broadly, rather than reserve the laws for the more dangerous, high-risk sex offenders. The current response is to treat *all* sex offenders as predatory, untreatable recidivists. As we have repeatedly stated, blanket laws and policies that are applied to *all* sex offenders are counterproductive, creating emotional stress for sex offenders that may ultimately result in their re-offending.

Registered sex offenders continue to report that they are routinely exposed to collateral consequences of the sex offender laws and policies (Frenzel et al. 2014). Blanket policies, not only negatively affect sex offenders but also rouse fear and mistrust among the general public toward the offenders and a call for even more harsh policies. Moreover, the fact that the majority of sex offender laws and policies are premised on inaccurate assumptions and misinformation has resulted in a myriad of unexpected and unwelcome collateral consequences affecting sex offenders, their family members and significant others, victims, and society in general. These policies and laws need to be sensibly reevaluated for their collateral consequences, especially considering the huge numbers of adult and juvenile sex offenders returning to their communities. Pre-release and reentry programs need to develop a balanced focus on community safety and sex offender rehabilitation emphasizing community inclusion through support (such as circles of support) rather than social exclusion through control and containment (Birgden and Cucolo 2011, Palermo and Farkas 2013).

References

Adam Walsh Child Protection and Safety Act (2006).

Ahlmeyer, S., Heil, P., McKee, B., English, K. (2000). The impact of the polygraph on admissions of victims and offenses in adult sex offenders. *Sexual Abuse: A Journal of Research and Treatment, 12,*123–138.

Bonhours, B. and Daly, K. (2007), Youth sex offenders in court: An analysis of judicial sentencing remarks. *Punishment in Society, 9*(4), 372–294.

Bogestad, A.J., Kettler, R.J. and Hagan, M.P. (2010). Evaluation of a cognitive intervention program for juvenile offenders. *Journal of Offender Therapy and Comparative Criminology, 54*(4), 552–565.

Aos, S., Phipps, P., Barnoski, R., Lieb, R. (2001). *Comparative costs and benefits of programs to reduce crime.* Olympia: Washington State Policy Institute.

Barker, J. G. and Howell, R. J. (1992). The plethysmograph: A review of the recent literature. *Journal of the American Academy of Psychiatry and the Law, 20*(1), 13–25.

Becker, J. V., & Murphy, W. D. (1998). What we know and do not know about assessing and treating sex offenders? *Psychology, Public Policy and the Law, 4*(1/2), 116–137.

Becker, J. V., Stinson, J., Tromp, S., Messer, G. (2003). Characteristics of individuals petitioned for civil commitment. *International Journal of Offender Therapy and Comparative Criminology, 47,* 185–195.

Ben-Shakhar, G. (2008). The case against the use of polygraph examinations to monitor post-conviction sex offenders. *Legal and Criminological Psychology, 13,* 191–207.

Berg, M. T., & Huebner, B. M. (2011). Reentry and the ties that bind: An examination of social ties, employment, and recidivism. *Justice Quarterly, 28*(2), 382–410.

Birgden, A., & Cucolo, H. (2011). The treatment of sex offenders: Evidence, ethics and human rights. *Sexual Abuse: A Journal of Research and Treatment, 23*(3), 295–313.

Blasingame, G. D. (1998). Suggested clinical uses of polygraph in community-based sexual offender treatment programs. *Sexual Abuse: A Journal of Research and Treatment, 10,* 37–45.

Bratina, M. P. (2013). Sex offender registry requirements. An effective crime prevention strategy or a false sense of security? *International Journal of Police Science and Management, 15,* 200–218.

Bureau of Justice Statistics. (2011). *Prisoners, year end 2009.* Washington, DC: Department of Justice.

Budd, K.M. and Mancini, C. (2015). Public perceptions of GPS monitoring for convicted sex offenders: Opinions on the effectiveness of electronic monitoring to reduce sexual recidivism. *International Journal of Offender Therapy and Comparative Criminology,* doi: 10.1177/0306624X15622841

Caldwell, M. F. (2010). Study characteristics and recidivism base rates in juvenile sex offender recidivism, *International Journal of Offender Therapy and Comparative Criminology, 54*(2), 197–212.

Calley, N. (2007). Promoting an outcomes-based treatment milieau for juvenile sex offenders. A guided approach in assessment. *Journal of Mental Health Counseling, 29*(2), 121–143.

Cecile, M., and Born, M., (2009). Intervention in juvenile delinquency: Danger or iatrogenic effects? *Children and Youth Services Review, 31*(12), 1217–1221.

Center for Sex Offender Management(CSOM). (2016). The effective management of juvenile sex offenders in the community: A training curriculum. http://www.csom.org/train/juvenile/5/5_5.htm. Accessed 23 June 2016.

Chaffin, M., Letourneau, E., Silovsky, J. F. (2002). Adults, adolescents, and children who sexually abuse children: A developmental perspective. In J. E. B. Myers, L. Berliner, J. Briere, C. T. Hendrix, C. Jenny, T. A. Reid (Eds.), *The APSAC handbook on child maltreatment.* 2nd edition (pp. 205–232). Thousand Oaks, CA: Sage Publications.

Chaffin, M. (2008). Our minds are made up- don't confuse us with the facts: Commentary on policies concerning children with sexual behavior problems and juvenile sex offenders. *Child Maltreatment, 13*(2), 110–121.

Chaffin, M. (2011). The case of juvenile polygraphy as a clinical ethics dilemma. *Sexual Abuse: A Journal of Research and Treatment, 23*(3), 314–328.

Chaffin, M. and Longo, R.E (2004). Guidelines for placement within a continuum of care for adolescent sex offenders and children with sexual behavior problems. *Family Violence and Sexual Assault Bulletin, 20*(3), 5–18.

Colorado Sex Offender Management Board. (2014). *Standards and Guidelines for the Evaluation, Assessment, Treatment, and Supervision of Juveniles who have Committed Sexual Offenses.* Denver, CO: Colorado Department of Public Safety Division of Criminal Justice Office of Domestic Violence & Sex Offender Management.

DeLisi, M., Hochstetler, A., Jones-Johnson, G., Caudill, J. W., Marquart, J. W. (2011). The road to murder: The enduring criminogenic effects of juvenile confinement among a sample of adult career criminals. *Youth Violence and Juvenile Justice, 9*(3), 207–221.

Deming, A. (2008). Sex offender civil commitment programs: Current practices, characteristics, and resident demographics. *Journal of Psychiatry, 36,* 439–461.

Edwards, W., & Hensley, C. (2001). Contextualizing sex offender management legislation and policy: Evaluating the problem of latent consequences in community notification laws. *International Journal of Offender Therapy and Comparative Criminology. 45,* 83–101.

Emerick, R, L., & Dutton, W. A. (1993). The effect of polygraphy on the self-report of adolescent sex offenders: Implications for risk assessment. *Annals of Sex Research, 6*(2), 83–103.

English, K. (1998). The containment approach: An aggressive strategy for the community management of adult sex offenders. *Psychology, Public Policy and the Law, 4*(1/2), 218–235.

English, K., Jones, L., Pasini-Hill, D., Patrick, D., Cooley-Towell, S. (2000). *The value of polygraph testing in sex offender management* (pp. 32–127). Colorado Department of Public Safety: Division of Criminal Justice.

Evans, D. N., & Cubellis, M. A. (2015). Coping with stigma: How registered sex offenders manage their public identities. *American Journal of Criminal Justice, 40*(3), 593–619.

Fagan, J., & Wexler, S. (1988). Explanations of sexual assault among violent delinquents. *Journal of Adolescent Research, 3*, 363–385.

Farkas, M.A. and Stichman, A.(2002). Sex offender laws: Can treatment, punishment, incapacitation, and public safety be reconciled? *Criminal Justice Review, 27*(2), 284–300

Farkas, M.A. and Miller, G.M. (2007). Reentry and reintegration: Challenges faced by families of convicted sex offenders. *Federal Sentencing Reporter, 20*, 88–92.

Fitch, W. L., & Hammon, D. A (2003). The new generation of sex offender commitment laws: Which states have them and how do they work? In B. J. Winick & J. Q. LaFond (Eds.), *Protecting Society from Sexually Dangerous Offenders: Law, Justice & Therapy*, (pp. 27–39). Washington, DC. American Psychological Association.

Fontaine, J., Gilchrist-Scott, D., Roman, J., Taxy, S., Roman, C. (2012). *Supportive housing for returning prisoners: Outcomes and impacts of Returning home*. Ohio Pilot Project. Washington, DC: Urban Institute.

Fox, K. (2017). Contexualizing the policy and pragmatics of reintegrating sex offenders. *Sexual Abuse: Journal of Research and Treatment, 29*(1), 28–50.

France, K., & Hudson, S. (1993). The conduct disorders and the juvenile sex offenders. In H. E. Barbaree, W. L. Marshall, S. M. Hudson (Eds.), *The juvenile sex offender* (pp. 225–234). New York: Guilford Press.

Frick, P. J., & White, S. F. (2008). Research review: The importance of callous-unemotional traits for developmental models of aggressive and antisocial behavior. *Journal of Child Psychology and Psychiatry, 49*(4), 359–375.

Frenzel, E. D., Bowen, K.N, Spraitz, J. D., Bowers, J. H., Phaneuf, S. (2014). Understanding collateral consequences of registry laws: An examination of the perceptions of sex offender registrants. *Justice Policy Journal, 11*(2), 1–21.

Freeman, N.J. and Sandler, J.C. (2010). The Adam Walsh Act: A false sense of security or an effective public policy initiative? *Criminal Justice Policy Review, 21*(1), 31–49.

Gerdes, K.E., Gourley, M.M. and Cash, M.C. (1995). Assessing juvenile sex offenders to determine adequate levels of supervision. *Child Abuse and Neglect, 19*(8), 953–961.

Glowacz, F., & Born, M. (2013). Do adolescent child abusers, peer abusers, and non-sex offenders have different personality profiles? *European Child Adolescent Psychiatry, 22*(2), 117–125.

Gookin, K. (2007). *Comparison of state laws authorizing involuntary commitment of sexually violent predators: 2006 Update; Revised. (No. 2008).* Olympia: Washington State Institute for Public Policy.

Goffman, E. (1963). *Stigma: Notes on the management of spoiled identity.* Prentice-Hall: Englewood Cliffs, NJ.

Goldstein, J. (2014). Housing restrictions keep sex offenders in prison beyond release dates. *The New York Times,* 21 August 2014.

Grubin, D., Madson, L., Parsons, S., Sosnowsk D, and Warberg, B. (2004). A prospective study of the impact of polygraphy on high risk behaviors in adult sex offenders. *Sexual Abuse: Journal of Research and Treatment, 16*(3), 209–222.

Grubesic, T.H., Murray, A.T. and Mack, E.A. (2008) Sex, housing and spatial restriction zones. *GeoJournal, 73*(4), 255–269.

Grubesic, T. H., Murray, A. T., Mack, E. A. (2011). Sex offenders, residence restrictions, housing and urban morphology. *Cityscape: A Journal of Policy Development and Research, 13*(3), 7–36.

Guerino, P., Harrison, W. S., Sabol, W. J. (2010). *Prisoners in 2010.* Washington, DC: Bureau of Justice Statistics.

Hackett, S., Masson, H., Balfe, M., Phillips, J. (2015). Community reactions to young people who have sexually abused and their families: A shotgun blast, not a rifle shot. *Children & Society, 29,* 243–254.

Hackett, S., & Phillips, J. (2014). Family responses to young people who have sexually abused: Anger, ambivalence, and acceptance. *Children & Society, 28,* 128–139.

Hair, H. J. (2005). Outcomes for children and adolescents after residential treatment. A review of research from 1993–2003. *Journal of Child and Family Studies, 14*(4), 551–575.

Hall, G. (1995). Sexual offender recidivism: A meta-analysis of recent treatment studies. *Journal of Consulting and Clinical Psychology, 63*(5), 802–809.

Hanson, R. K., & Bussiere, M. T. (1998). Predicting relapse: A meta-analysis of sexual offender recidivism studies. *Journal of Consulting and Clinical Psychology, 66*(2), 348–362.

Hanson, K., & Thornton, D. (2000). Improving risk assessments for sex offenders: A comparison of three actuarial scales. *Law and Human Behavior, 24*(1), 119–136.

Harris, A. J. (2009). The civil commitment of sexual predators: A policy review. In R. W. Wright (Ed.), *Sex offender laws: Failed policies and new directions.* (pp. 339–372). New York: Springer Publishing Company.

Harris, A. J., Fisher, W., Veysey, B. M., Ragusa, J. M., Lurigio, A. J. (2010). Sex offending and serious. Mental illness. Directions for Policy. *Justice and Behavior, 37,* 596–612.

Harris, G. T., Rice, M. E., Quinsey, V. L. (1998). Appraisal and management of risk in sexual aggressors: Implications for criminal justice policy. *Psychology, Public Policy, and Law, 4*(1/2), 73–115.

Harris, A. J., & Lobanov-Rostovsky, C. (2010). Implementing the Adam Walsh Act's sex offender registration and notification provisions: A survey of the states. *Criminal Justice Policy Review, 21*(2), 202–222.

Harris, A. J., & Socia, K. M. (2014). What's in a name? Evaluating the effects of the "sex offender" label on public opinions and beliefs. *Sexual Abuse: A Journal of Research and Treatment, 26,* 1–19.

Harris, A. J., & Socia, K. M. (2015). *Advancing public opinion research on sexual violence and sex offender management policy.* Association for the Treatment of Sexual Abusers 34th Annual Conference. Quebec: Montreal, Canada.

Harlow, A. and Scott, J. (2007). Penile plethysmograph testing for convicted sex offenders. *Journal of the American Academy of Psychiatry and the Law, 35*(4), 536–537.

Hindman, J., & Peters, J. M. (2001). Polygraph testing leads to a better understanding of adult and juvenile sex offenders. *Federal Probation, 65*(3), 8–15.

Hunter, J. A., Figueredo, A. J., Malamuth, N. M., Becker, J. V. (2004a). Juvenile sex offenders: Towards the development of a typology. *Sexual Abuse: A Journal of Research and Treatment, 15*(1), 27–48.

Hunter, J., Gilbertson, S., Vedros, D., Morton, M. (2004b). Strengthening community-based programming for juvenile sexual offenders: Key concepts and paradigm shifts. *Child Maltreatment, 9*(2), 177–189.

Jackson, R., Schneider, J., and Travia, T. (2007). Surveying sex offender civil commitment programs: Program and resident characteristics. Paper presented at the annual meeting of the Association for the Treatment of Sexual Abusers (ATSA), San Diego, CA.

Jenson, T. M., Shafer, K., Roby, C. Y., Roby, J. L. (2015). Sexual history disclosure polygraph outcomes: Do juvenile and adult sex offenders differ? *Journal of Interpersonal Violence, 30*(6), 928–944.

Kansas v, Crane (2002) 534 U.S. 407.

Kansas v. Hendricks (1997) 117 S. Ct. 2072.

Kras, K. R., Pleggenkuhle, B., Huebner, B. M. (2016). A new way of doing time on the outside: Sex offenders' pathways in and out of a transitional housing facility. *International Journal of Offender Therapy and Comparative Criminology*, *60*(5), 512–534.

Koetzle Shaffer, D., & Miethe, T. D. (2011). Are similar sex offenders treated similarly? A conjunctive analysis of disparities in community notification decisions. *Journal of Research in Crime and Delinquency*, *48*(3), 448–471.

Kokish, R., Levenson, J., Blasingame, G. (2005). Post-conviction sex offender polygraph examination: Client-reported perceptions of utility and accuracy. *Sexual Abuse: A Journal of Research and Treatment*, *17*, 211–221.

Lacombe, D. (2008). Consumed with sex: The treatment of sex offenders in risk society. *British Journal of Criminology 48*, 55–74.

LaFond, J. Q., & Winick, B. J. (2004). Sex offender reentry courts: A proposal for managing the risk of returning sex offenders to the community. *Seton Hall Law Journal*, *34*, 1173–1212.

Langlands, R. L., Ward, T., Gilchrist, E. (2009). Applying the good lives model to male perpetrators of domestic violence. *Behavior Change*, *26*(2), 113–129.

Leonard, K. (2011). Home is where the park bench is: The psychological benefits and consequences of requiring homeless sex offenders to present a physical address for release from Alabama prisons, *Law and Psychiatry Review*, *35*, 209–224.

Letourneau, E. J. and Bourduin, C. M. (2008). The effective treatment of juveniles who sexually offend: An ethical imperative. *Ethics and Behavior, 18* (2–3), 286–306.

Letourneau, E. J. and Miner, M. H. (2005). Juvenile sex offenders: A case against the legal and clinical status quo. *Sexual Abuse: Journal of Research and Treatment*, *17*(3), 293–312.

Letourneau, E. J., Bandyopadhyay, D., Sinha, D., Armstrong, K. S. (2009). The influence of sex offender registration on juvenile sexual recidivism. *Criminal Justice Policy Review*, *20*(2), 136–153.

Letourneau, E. J., Bandyopadhyay, D., Armstrong, K. S., Sinha, D. (2010). Do sex offender registration and notification requirements deter juvenile sex crimes? *Criminal Justice and Behavior*, *37*(5), 553–569.

Levenson, J. S., & Cotter, L. P. (2005). The effect of Megan's law on sex offender reintegration. *Journal of Contemporary Criminal Justice*, *21*(1), 49–66.

Levenson, J. S. and D'Amora, D. A. (2007). Social policies designed to prevent sexual violence. The emperor's new clothes. *Criminal Justice Policy Review*, *18*(2), 168–199.

Levenson, J. S., & Tewksbury, R. (2009). Collateral damage: Family members of registered sex offenders. *American Journal of Criminal Justice*, *34*, 54–68.

Levenson, J. S., Brannon, Y. N., Fortney, T., Baker, J. (2007). Public perceptions about sex offenders and community protection policies. *Analyses of Social Issues and Public Policy, 7*, 137–161.

Lied, R., & Matson, S. (1998). *Sexual predator commitment laws in the United States*. Olympia, WA: Washington State Institute for Public Policy.

Losel, F., & Schmucker, M. (2005). The effectiveness of treatment for sex offenders: A comprehensive meta-analysis. *Journal of Experimental Criminology, 1*, 117–146.

Langton, C.M., Barbaree, H.E. Seto, M.C., Peacock, E.J., Harris, L., and Hansen, K.T. (2007). Actuarial assessment of risk for reoffense among adult sex offenders. Evaluating the predictive of the Static-2002 and five other instruments. *Criminal Justice and Behavior, 34*(1), 37–59.

Lundrigan, P.S. (2001). *Treating youth who sexually abuse*. New York: Hawthorne Press.

Lyons, J.S., Royce Baerger, D., Quigley, P., Erlich, J., and Griffen, E. (2001). Mental health service needs of juvenile offenders: A comparison of detention, incarceration, and treatment settings. *Journal of Children's Services. Social Policy Research and Practice, 4*(2), 69–85.

Malin, H. M., Saleh, F. M., Grudzinskas, A. J. (2014). Recent research related to juvenile sex offending: Findings and directions for further research. *Current Psychiatry Reports, 16*(4), 1–7.

Mancini, C., Barnes, J. C., Mears, D. P. (2011). It varies from state to state: An examination of sex crime laws nationally. *Criminal Justice Policy Review, 14*(2), 166–198.

Marquez, J. K., Day, D. M., Nelson, C., West, M. A. (1994). Effects of cognitive-behavioral treatment on sex offender recidivism. Preliminary results of a longitudinal study. *Criminal Justice and Behavior, 21*(1), 28–54.

Marshall, W. L. (1989). Intimacy, loneliness, and sexual offenders. *Behaviour Research and Therapy, 27*, 491–503.

Marshall, W. L., & Marshall, L. E. (2000). The origins of sexual offending. *Trauma, Violence, & Abuse: A Review Journal, 1*, 250–263.

Masson, H., Hacket, S., Phillips, J., and Balfe, M. (2014). Looking back on the long-term fostering and adoption of children with harmful sexual behaviours: Carers' reflections on their experiences. *British Journal of Social Work, 44*(8), 2200–2217.

McCarney, W. and Ireland, N. (2010). A restorative justice approach to working with children in residential care. *Law and Justice Review, 1*(1), 247–288.

McCann, K., & Lussier, P. (2008). Antisociality, sexual deviance, and sexual reoffending in juvenile sex offenders: A meta-analytical investigation. *Youth Violence and Juvenile Justice, 6*(4), 363–385.

McAlinden, A.M. (2014). Deconstructing victim and offender identities in discourses on child sexual abuse: Hierarchies blame and the good/evil dialectic. *British Journal of Criminology, 54*(2), 180–198.

McGrath, R. J., Gumming, G. E, Burchard, B. L. (2003). *Current practices and trends in sexual abuser management: The Safer Society 2002 Nationwide Survey.* Brandon, VT: Safer Society.

McConaghy, N. (1998). Arousal reduction in sex offenders of androgen hormones. Sexual abuse: *A Journal of Research and Treatment, 10,* 337–341.

McGrath, R., Cumming, G., Burchard, B., Zeoli, S., Ellerby, L. (2010). *Current practices and emerging trends in sexual abuser management: The safer society 2009 North American Survey.* Brandon, Vermont: Safer Society Press.

Meisenkothen, C. (1999). Chemical castration: Breaking the cycle of paraphilic recidivism. *Social Justice, 26*(1), 139–154.

Miner, M., & Munns, R. (2005). Isolation and normlessness: Attitudinal comparisons of adolescent sex offenders, juvenile offenders, and nondelinquents. *International Journal of Offender Therapy and Comparative Criminology, 49*(5), 491–504.

Miner, M., Robinson, B., Knight, R., Berg, D., Swinburne Romine, R., Netland, J. (2010). Understanding sexual perpetration against children: Effects of attachment style, interpersonal involvement, and hyper sexuality. *Sexual Abuse: A Journal of Research and Treatment, 22*(1), 58–77.

Moffitt, T. E. (1993). Adolescence-limited and life-course-persistent antisocial behavior: A developmental taxonomy. *Psychological Review, 100,* 674–701.

Meloy, M. L., Miller, S. L., Curtis, K. M. (2008). Making sense out of nonsense: The deconstruction of state-level sex offender residence restrictions. *American Journal of Criminal Justice, 33*(2), 209–222.

Meloy, M. L., & Coleman, S. (2009). GPS monitoring of sex offending. In R. W. Wright (Ed.), *Sex offender laws: Failed policies and new directions* (pp. 243–266). New York: Springer Publishing Company.

Meloy, M. L., Salah, Y., Wolff, N. (2007). Sex offender laws in America. Can panic driven legislation ever create safe societies? *Criminal Justice Studies, 20*(4), 423–443.

Mercado, C. C., Alvarez, S., Levenson, J. (2008). The impact of specialized sex offender legislation on community reentry. *Sexual Abuse: A Journal of Research and Treatment, 20,* 188–205.

Miller, R. D. (1998). Forced administrations of sex-drive reducing medications to sex offenders: Treatment or punishment. *Psychology, Public Policy and Law, 4*(1/2), 175–199.

Mustaine, E. E., and Tewksbury, R. (2011). Residential relegation of registered sex offenders. *American Journal of Criminal Justice, 36*(1), 44–57.

Mustaine, E. E. (2014). Sex offender residency restrictions: Successful integration or exclusion? *Criminology & Public Policy, 13*, 169–177.

Naser, R. L., & Visher, C. A. (2006). Family members' experiences with incarceration and reentry. *Western Criminology Review, 7*(2), 20–31.

Office of Juvenile Justice and Delinquency Prevention: U. S. Department of Justice. (2016). *Statistical briefing book.* http://www.ojjdp.gov/ojstatbb

Palermo, G. B., & Farkas, M. A. (2013). *The dilemma of the sexual offender.* 2nd Edition. Springfield, IL: Charles C. Thomas Publishing.

Paternoster, R., & Iovanni, L. (1989). The labeling perspective and delinquency: An elaboration of the theory and an assessment of the evidence. *Justice Quarterly, 6*(3), 359–394.

Paternoster, R., & Bachman, R. (2013). Labeling theory. *Criminology.* doi: 10.1093/OBO/9780195396607-0078

Petrunik, M. G. (2002). Managing unacceptable risk: Sex offenders, community response and social policy in the U.S. and Canada. *International Journal of Offender Therapy and Comparative Criminology, 46*, 433–511.

Pew Center on the States. (2011). *State of recidivism: The revolving door of America's prisons.* Washington, DC: Pew Charitable Trust.

Pinard, M. (2010). Reflections and perspectives on reentry and collateral consequences. *Journal of Criminal Law and Criminology, 100*(3), 1213–1224.

Purcell, M.S., Chandler, J.A. and Fedorroff, J.P. (2015). Use of phallometric evidence in Canadian criminal law. *Journal of the American Academy of Psychiatry and Law, 43*(2), 141–153.

Quinn, J.F., Forsyth, CJ, and Mullen-Quinn, C. (2004) Societal reaction to sex offenders: A review of the origins and results of the myths surrounding their crimes and treatment amenability. *Deviant Behavior, 25*(3), 215–232.

Ramirez, M. D. (2013). Punitive sentiment. *Criminology, 51*(2), 329–364.

Reitzel, L. R., & Carbonell, J. L. (2006). The effectiveness of sexual offender treatment for juveniles as measured by recidivism: A meta-analysis. *Sexual Abuse: A Journal of Research and Treatment, 18*, 401–421.

Robbers, M. (2008). Lifers on the outside: Sex offenders and disintegrative shaming. *International Journal of Offender Therapy and Comparative Criminology 53*, 5–28.

Rolfe, S. M., Tewksbury, R., Schroeder, R. D. (2016). Homeless shelters' policies on sex offenders: Is this another collateral consequences? *International Journal of Offender Therapy and Comparative Criminology, 60*, 1–17.

Rosky, J. W. (2012). The (f)utility of post-conviction polygraph testing. *Sexual Abuse: A Journal of Research and Treatment, 25*(3), 259–281.

Sabol, W. J., West, H. C., Cooper, M. (2009). Prisoners in 2008 (NCJ 228417). Washington, DC: Bureau of Justice Statistics.

Salerno, J. M., Najdowski, C. J., Stevenson, M. C., Wiley, T. R. A., Bottoms, B. L., Vaca, R. J., et al. (2010). Psychological mechanisms underlying support for juvenile sex offender registry laws: Prototypes, moral outrage, and perceived threat. *Behavioral Sciences and the Law, 28*, 58–83.

Sample, L. L., & Bray, T. M. (2003). Are sex offenders dangerous? *Criminology and Public Policy, 3*(1), 59–82.

Sample, L. L., & Bray, T. M. (2006). Are sex offenders different? An examination of rearrest patterns. *Criminal Justice Policy Review, 17*, 83–102.

Sandler, J. C., Freeman, N. J., Socia, K. M. (2008). Does a watched pot boil? A time-series analyses of New York state's registration and notification. *Psychology, Public Policy and the Law, 14*(4), 284–302.

Scott, C., & del Busto, E. (2009). Chemical and surgical castration. In R. W. Wright (Ed.), *Sex offender laws: Failed policies and new directions* (pp. 291–338). New York: Springer Publishing Company.

Seto, M. C., & Barbaree, H. E. (1997). Sexual aggression as antisocial behavior: A developmental model. In D. M. Stoff, J. Breiling, J. D. Master (Eds.), *Handbook of antisocial behavior* (pp. 524–533). New York, NY: Wiley.

Seto, M. C., & Lalumiere, M. L. (2010). What is so special about male adolescent sexual offending? A review and test of explanations through meta-analysis. *Psychological Bulletin, 136*(4), 526–575.

Simon, J. (2012). Mass incarceration: From social policy to social problem. In J. Petersilia & K. R. Reitz (Eds.), *In the Oxford handbook of sentencing and corrections* (pp. 79–109). New York: Oxford University Press.

Snyder, H. N., & Sickmund, M. (2006). Juvenile offenders and victims: 2006 national report. Office of Juvenile Justice and Delinquency Prevention. http://www.ojjdp.gov/ojstatbb/nr2006/downloads/NR2006.pdf. Access 23 June 2016.

Stevenson, M. C., Malik, S. E., Totton, R. R., Reeves, R. D. (2015). Disgust sensitivity predicts punitive treatment of juvenile sex offenders: The role of empathy, dehumanization, and fear. *Analyses of Social Issues and Public Policy, 15*(1), 177–197.

Stovering, J., Nelson, W. M., Hart, K. J. (2013). Timeline of victim disclosures by juvenile sex offenders. *The Journal of Forensic Psychiatry & Psychology, 24* (6), 728–739.

Swisher, L.M., Silovsky, J.F., Stuart, J.R.H. and Pierce, K. (2008). Children with sexual behavior problems. *Juvenile and Family Court Journal, 59*(4), 49–69.

Tewksbury, R. (2005). Collateral consequences of sex offender registration. *Journal of Contemporary Criminal Justice, 21*(1), 67–81.

Tewksbury, R., & Copes, H. (2012). Incarcerated sex offenders' expectations for reentry. *The Prison Journal, 93*(1), 102–122.

Tewksbury, R., & Lees, M. B. (2006). Perceptions of sex offender registration: Collateral consequences and community experiences. *Sociological Spectrum, 26,* 309–334.

Tewksbury, R., & Levenson, J. (2009). Stress experiences of family members of registered sex offenders. *Behavioral Sciences and the Law, 27,* 611–626.

Tewksbury, R., & Mustaine, E. E. (2008). Where registered sex offenders live. Community characteristics and proximity to possible. *Victims and Offenders, 3* (1), 86–98.

Tewksbury, R., & Zgoba, K. M. (2010). Perceptions and coping with punishment. How registered sex offenders respond to stress, internet restrictions, and the collateral consequences of registration. *Journal of Offender Therapy and Comparative Criminology, 54*(4), 537–551.

Thomas, J., & Viar, C. W. (2005). Family reunification in sibling incest: A step by step process. In M. C. Calder (Ed.), *Children and young people who sexually abuse: New theory, research and practice developments* (pp. 108–134). Dorsett: Russell House Publishing.

Thornton, J.A., Stevens, G., Grant, J., Indermaur, D., Chamarette, C., and Halse, A. (2008). Intrafamilial adolescent sex offenders: Family functioning and treatment. *Journal of Family Studies, 14*(2.3), 362–375.

Thomas, J., & Wilson, C. (1999). Family reunification where the young person has sexually abused a sibling. In M. Erooga & H. Masson (Eds.), *Children and young people who sexually abuse.* London: Taylor & Francis Books Ltd.

Thomas, J. (2010). Family therapy: a critical component in treatment of sexually abusive youth. In G. Ryan, T. Leversee, S. Lane (Eds.), *Juvenile sexual offending: causes consequences and correction* (pp. 357–379). New Jersey: Wiley.

Travis, J. (2001). But they all come back: Rethinking prisoner reentry. *Corrections Management Quarterly, 5*(3), 23–39.

Travis, J. (2005). But they all come back: Facing the challenges of prisoner reentry. Washington DC: The Urban Institute Press.

Trivits, L.C. and Reppucci, N.D. (2002). Application of Megan's Law to juveniles. *American Psychologist, 57*(9), 690–704.

Turner, B.W. Bingham, J.E. and Andrasik, F. (2000). Short-term community-based treatment for sex offenders: Enhancing effectiveness. *Sexual Addiction and Compulsivity: Journal of Treatment and Prevention, 7*(3), 211–223.

Van Rensburg, J. (2012). The dawn of circles of support and accountability in New Zealand. *Sexual Abuse in Australia and New Zealand, 4*(2), 30–35.

van Wijk, A., Mali, S. R. F., Bullens, R. A. R., Vermeiren, R. (2007a). Criminal profiles of violent juvenile sex and violent juvenile non-sex offenders. *Journal of Interpersonal Violence, 22*(10), 1340–1355.

van Wijk, A., Mali, S. R. F., Bullens, R. A. R. (2007b). Juvenile sex-only and sex-plus offenders. *International Journal of Offender Therapy and Comparative Criminology, 51*(4), 407–419.

Visher, C., Debus, S., Yahner, J. (2008). *Employment after prison: A longitudinal study of releases in three states. Research brief.* Urban Institute: Justice Policy Center.

Walker, J. T., Golden, J. W., Van Houten, A. C. (2001). Are similar sex offenders treated similarly? A conjunctive analyses of community notification decisions. *Journal of Research in Crime and Delinquency, 48,* 448–471.

Ward, T., & Maruna, S. (2007). *Rehabilitation. Beyond the Risk Paradigm.* London, UK: Routledge.

Ward, T. and Stewart, C. (2003). The treatment of sex offenders: Risk management and good lives. *Professional Psychology, Research and Practice, 34*(4), 353–360.

Ward, T. and Brown, M. (2004). The good lives model and conceptual issues in offender rehabilitation. *Psychology, 44 Crime and Law, 33,* 243–257.

Western, B., Kling, J.R. and Weiman, D.F. (2001). Labor market consequences of incarceration. *NCCD News, 47* (3), 410–427.

Willis, G. M. (2010). Back to basics: Empirical support for the importance of release planning in reducing sex offender recidivism. *Sexual Abuse in Australia and New Zealand, 2*(2), 54–57.

Wilson, R. J., Cortoni, F., Vermani, M. (2007). *Circles of support and accountability: A national replication of outcome findings.* Research report #R-185. Correctional Services of Canada.

Willis, G.M., Yates, P.M, Gannon, T.A., & Ward, T. (2013). How to integrate the Good Lives Model into treatment programs for sexual offending: An introduction and overview. *Sexual Abuse: A Journal of Research and Treatment, 25*(4), 123–142.

Wilson, R. J., Cortoni, F., McWhinnie, A. (2009). Circles of support and accountability: A Canadian national replication of outcome findings. *Sexual Abuse: A Journal of Research and Treatment, 21*, 412–430.

Winnick, T. A., & Bodkins, M. (2008). Anticipated stigma and stigma management among those to be labeled "ex con." *Deviant Behavior, 29*(4), 295–333.

Yoder, J. R. (2014). Service approaches for youths who commit sexual crimes: A call for family oriented models [Special Issue, State of the evidence in juvenile justice]. *Journal of Evidence-Based Social Work, 11*(4), 360–372. doi:10.1080/10911359.2014.897108

Yoder, J., & Brown, S. (2015). Challenges facing families of sexually abusive youth: What prevents service engagement? *Victims & Offenders: An International Journal of Evidence-Based Research, Policy, and Practice, 10*(1), 29–50. doi:10.1177/0306624X16651903

Yoder, J., Hansen, J., Lobanov-Rostovsky, C. (2016a). A framework for the judicious use of the polygraph for youth who have committed a sexual crime. Manuscript submitted for publication.

Yoder, J. R., Hansen, J., Ruch, D., Hodge, A. (2016b). The effects of school based risk and protective factors on treatment success among youth adjudicated of a sexual crime. *Journal of Child Sexual Abuse, 25*(3), 310–325. doi:10.1080/10538712.2016.1137668

Yoder, J., & Ruch, D. (2016). A qualitative investigation of treatment components for families of youth who have sexually offended. *Journal of Sexual Aggression, 22*(2), 192–205. doi:10.1080/13552600.2015.1107141

Yoder, J., Hansen, J., Lobanov-Rostovsky, C., Ruch, D. (2015a). The impact of family service involvement on treatment completion and general recidivism among male youthful sexual offenders. *Journal of Offender Rehabilitation, 54*(4), 256–277. doi:10.1080/10509674.2015.1025177

Yoder, J. R., Ruch, D., Hodge, A. (2015b). Families of youth who have sexually offended: Understanding shared experiences and moving towards a typology. *Journal of Child and Family Studies.* doi:10.1007/s10826-015-0339-8

Zakireh, B., Ronis, S. T., Knight, R. A. (2008). Individual beliefs, attitudes, and victimization histories of male juvenile sexual offenders. *Sexual Abuse: A Journal of Research and Treatment, 20*(3), 323–351.

Zevitz, R. G., & Farkas, M. A. (2000). Sex offender community notification: Managing high risk criminals exacting further vengeance? *Behavioral Sciences and the Law, 18*, 375–391.

Zgoba, K. M., Levenson, J. S., McKee, T. (2009). Examining the impact of sex offender. Restrictions on housing availability. *Criminal Justice Policy Review, 20*(1), 91–110.

Zimring, F. E. (2009). *An American tragedy: Legal responses to adolescent sexual offending* Chicago: University of Chicago Press.

Further Reading

Abel, G. G., Mittelman, M., Becker, J. V. (1985). Sex offenders: Results of assessment and recommendations for treatment. In S. Ben-Aron, S. Hucker, Et C. Webster (Eds.), *Clinical criminology: Current concepts* (pp. 191–205). Toronto, Canada: M Et M Graphics.

Abrams, L. S., Terry, D., Franke, T. M. (2011). Community-based juvenile reentry services: The effects of dosage on juvenile and adult recidivism. *Journal of Offender Rehabilitation, 50*, 492–511.

Anderson, A. L., & Sample, L. L. (2008). Public awareness and action resulting from sex offender community notification law. *Criminal Justice Policy Review, 19*(4), 371–396.

Andrade, J. T., Vincent, G. M., Saleh, F. M. (2006). Juvenile sex offenders: A complex population. *Journal of Forensic Sciences, 51*(1), 163–167.

Andrews, D. A., & Bonta, J. (2003). *The psychology of criminal conduct.* 3rd edition. Cincinnati, OH: Anderson.

Andrews, D. A., & Bonta, J. (2006). *The psychology of criminal conduct.* 4th edition. Newark, NJ: Anderson.

Andrews, D. A., Bonta, J., Hoge, R. D. (1990). Classification for effective rehabilitation: Rediscovering psychology. *Criminal Justice and Behavior, 17*, 19–52.

Barbaree, H. E., Seto, M. C., Langton, C. M., Peacock, E. J. (2001). Evaluating the predictive accuracy of six risk assessment instruments on adult sex offenders. *Criminal Justice and behavior, 28*(4), 490–521.

Barnes, J. C., Dukes, T., Tewksbury, R., De Troye, T. M. (2009). Analyzing the impact of a statewide residence restriction law on South Carolina sex offenders. *Criminal Justice, 21*, 34–54.

Bumby, K. M., Talbot, T. B., Carter, M. M. (in press). Sex offender reentry: Facilitating public safety through successful transition and community reintegration. *Criminal Justice and Behavior.*

Bumby, K., Talbot T., Carter, M. (2007). Managing the challenges of sex offender reentry. *Center for Sex Offender Management*. http://www.csom.org/pubs/reentry_brief.pdf. Accessed 3 March 2016.

Burton, D. L., Demuynck, S., Yoder, J. R. (2014). Executive dysfunction predict delinquency but not characteristics of sexual aggression amongst adolescent sexual offenders. *Sexual Abuse: A Journal of Research and Treatment*. doi: 10.1177/1079063214556357

Burton, D. L., Duty, K. J., Leibowitz, G. A. (2011). Differences between sexually victimized and non-sexually victimized male adolescent sexual abusers: Developmental antecedents. *Sexual Abuse: A Journal of Research and Treatment*. doi: 10.1080/10538712.2011.541010

Burton, D. L., & Meezan, W. (2004). Revisiting recent research on social learning theory as anetiological proposition for sexually abusive male adolescents. *Journal of Evidence-Based Social Work, 1*(1), 41–80.

Carter, M. M., & Morris, L. (2007). *Enhancing the management of adult and juvenile sex offenders. Handbook for policymakers and practitioners*. U.S. Department of Justice Programs. Washington, DC: Center for Sex Offender Management (CSOM).

Caldwell, M. (2002). What we do not know about juvenile sexual reoffense risk. *Child Maltreatment, 7*, 291–302.

Cecile, M., & Born, M. (2013). Intervention in juvenile delinquency: Danger of iatrogenic effects? *Children and Youth Services Review, 31*(12), 1217–1221.

DeLisi, M., Drury, A. J., Kosloski, A. E., Caudill, J. W., Conis, P. J., Anderson, C. A., et al. (2010). The cycle of violence behind bars: Traumatization and institutional misconduct among juvenile delinquents in confinement. *Youth Violence and Juvenile Justice, 8*(2), 107–121.

Dicataldo, F. C. (2009). *The perversion of youth: Controversies in the assessment and treatment of juvenile sex offenders*. New York: New York University Press.

Douglas, K. S., & Kropp, P. R. (2002). A prevention-based paradigm for violence risk assessment: Clinical and research applications. *Criminal Justice and Behavior, 29*, 617–658.

Fanniff, A. M., & Kimonis, E. R. (2014). Juveniles who have committed sexual offenses: A special group? *Behavioral Sciences and the Law, 32*, 240–257.

Farr, C., Brown, J., Beckett, R. (2004). Ability to empathize and masculinity levels: comparing male adolescent sex offenders with a normative sample of non-offending adolescents. *Psychology, Crime & Law, 10*,155–167.

Ferrara, M. L., & McDonald, S. (1996). *Treatment of the juvenile sex offender: Neurological and psychiatric impairments*. Northvale, NJ: Jason Aronson.

Gottfredson, S. D., & Moriarty, L. J. (2006). Statistical risk assessment: Old problems and new applications. *Crime & Delinquency, 52*(1), 178–200.

Grubin, D. (2008). The case for polygraph testing of sex offenders. *Legal and Criminological Psychology, 13*, 177–189.

Hanson, R. K., Bourgon, G., Helmus, L., Hodgson, L. (2009). The principles of effective correctional treatment also apply to sexual offenders: A meta-analysis. *Criminal Justice and Behavior, 36*, 865–891.

Hanson, R., & Morton-Bourgon, K. (2009). The accuracy of recidivism risk assessments for sexual offenders: A meta-analysis of 118 prediction studies. *Psychological Assessment, 21*, 1–21. doi:10.1037/a0014421

Jaffee, S. R., & Maikovich-Fong, A, K. (2014). Effects of chronic maltreatment and maltreatment timing on children's behavior and cognitive abilities. *Journal of Child Psychology and Psychiatry, and Allied Disciplines, 52*(2), 184–194.

Johnson, M. M., Dismukes, A. R., Vitacco, M. J., Breiman, C., Fleury, D., Shirtcliff, E. A. (2014). Psychopathy's influence on the coupling between hypothalamic-pituitary-adrenal and –gonadal axes among incarcerated adolescents. *Developmental Psychology, 56*(3), 448–458.

Knight, R. A., & Sims-Knight, J. E. (2003). Developmental antecedents of sexual coercion against women: Testing of alternative hypotheses with structural equation modeling. In R. A. Prentky, E. S. Janus, M. Seto (Eds.), *Sexual coercive behavior: Understanding and management* (pp. 72–85). New York: New York Academy of Sciences.

Langan, P., Schmidt, E., Durose, M. (2003). Recidivism of sex offenders released from prison in 1994. *Recidivism of sex offenders released from prison in 1994.* Washington, DC: Department of Justice Programs. Bureau of Justice Statistics.

Lasher, M. P., & McGrath, R. J. (2012). The impact of community notification of sex offender reintegration: A quantification review of the research literature. *International Journal of Offender Therapy and Comparative Criminology, 56*(1), 6–28.

Lindsey, R. E., Carlozzi, A. F., Eells, G. T. (2001). Differences in the dispositional empathy of juvenile sex offenders, non-sex-offending delinquent juveniles, and non-delinquent juveniles. *Journal of Interpersonal Violence, 16*, 510–521.

Longo, R. E., & Prescott, D. S. (2006). Introduction: A brief history of treating youth with sexual behavior problems. Longo, R. E., & Prescott, D. S. (Eds.) In *Current perspectives: Working with sexually aggressive youth & youth with sexual behavior problems*, (pp. 31–43). Massachusetts: NEARI Press.

Lussier, P., & Healey, J. (2010). Searching for the developmental origins of sexual violence: examining the co-occurrence of physical aggression and sexual behaviors in early childhood. *Behavioral Sciences and the Law*, *28*, 1–23.

Lussier, P. (2005). The criminal activity of sexual offenders in adulthood: Revisiting the specialization debate. *Sexual Abuse: A Journal of Research and Treatment*, *17*, 269–292.

Marshall, W. L., Hudson, S. M., Jones, R., Fernandez, Y. M. (1995). Empathy in sex offenders. *Clinical Psychology Review*, *15*(2), 99–113.

Mustaine, E. E., & Tewksbury, R. (2009). Residential relegation of registered sex offenders. *American Journal of Criminal Justice*, *36*, 44–57.

Mustaine, E. E., Tewksbury, R., Connor, D. P., Payne, B. K. (2015). Criminal justice officials' views of sex offenders, sex offender registration, community notification, and residency restrictions. *Justice System Journal*, *36*(1), 63–95.

Nellis, A. (2009). Back on track: Supporting youth reentry from out-of-home placement to the community. Prepared by the youth reentry task force of the Juvenile Justice and Delinquency Prevention Coalition. Washington, DC.

Perry, B. D., Pollard, R. A., Blakley, T. L., Baker, W. L., Vigilante, D. (1995). Childhood trauma, the neurobiology of adaptation, and "use-dependent" development of the brain: How "states" become "traits". *Infant Mental Health Journal*, *16*(4), 271–291.

Prentky, R. A., Harris, B., Frizzell, K., Righthand, S. (2004). An actuarial procedure for assessing risk with juvenile sex offenders. *Sexual Abuse: A Journal of Research and Treatment*, *12*(2), 71–93.

Prentky, R. A., & Righthand, S. (2003). Juvenile sex offender assessment protocol—II Manual. Unpublished manuscript.

Prisco, R. (2015). Parental involvement in juvenile sex offender treatment: Requiring a role as informed supervisor. *Family Court Review*, *53*(3), 487–503.

Powers-Sawyer, A. B., & Miner, M. H. (2009). Actuarial prediction of juvenile recidivism: The static variables of the juvenile sex offender assessment protocol-II (JSOAP-II). *Sex Offender Treatment*, *4*(2), no page numbers indicated.

Ryan, G. (2010b). The families of sexually abusive youth. In G. Ryan, T. Leversee, S. Lane (Eds.), *Juvenile sexual offending: Causes consequences and correction* (pp. 147–164). New Jersey: Wiley.

Sample, L. L., & Evans, M. K. (2009). Sex offender registration and community notification. In R. W. Wright (Ed.), *Sex offender laws: Failed policies and new directions* (pp. 211–242). New York: Springer Publishing Company.

Schiavone, S. K., & Jeglic, E. L. (2009). Public perceptions of sex offender social policies and the impact on sex offenders. *International Journal of Offender Therapy and Comparative Criminology*, *53*(6), 679–695.

Schneider, J. E. (2008). A review of research findings related to the civil commitment of sex offenders. *Journal of Psychiatry and Law, 36*, 463–483.

Schore, A. N. (2001). The effects of early relational trauma on right brain development, affect regulation, and infant mental health. *Infant Mental Health Journal, 22*(1–2), 201–269.

Seidler, K. (2010). Community management of sex offenders: stigma versus support. *Sexual abuse in Australia and New Zealand, 2*(2), 66–76.

Seiter, R. P., & Kadela, K. R. (2003). Prisoner reentry: What works, what does not, and what is promising. *Crime and Delinquency, 49*(3), 360–388.

Sex Offender Registration and Notification Act (SORNA) (2006).

Sipe, R., Jensen, E. L., Everett, R. S. (1998). Adolescent sexual offenders grown up. *Criminal Justice and Behavior, 25*, 109–124.

Stalans, L. J. (2004). Adult sex offenders on community supervision. A review of recent assessment strategies and treatment, *Criminal Justice and Behavior, 31*(5), 564–618.

Steinberg, L. (2007). Risk-taking in adolescence: New perspectives from brain and behavioral science. *Current Directions in Psychological Science, 16*, 55–59.

Steinberg, L. (2008). A social neuroscience perspective on adolescent risk-taking. *Developmental Review, 28*, 78–106.

Stojkovic, S., & Farkas, M. A. (2013). So you want to find a transitional house for sexually violent predators. *Criminal Justice and Behavior, 25*(6), 659–682.

Veneziano, C., & Veneziano, L. (2004). Neuropsychological executive functions of adolescent sex offenders and nonsex offenders. *Perpetual and Motor Skills, 98*, 661–674.

Viljoen, J. L., Mordell, S., Beneteau, J. L. (2012). Prediction of adolescent sexual reoffending: A meta-analysis of the JSOAP-II, ERASOR, JSORRAT-II, and Static-99. *Law & Human Behavior, 36*(5), 423–438.

Walker, J. T. (2007). Eliminate residency restrictions for sex offenses. *Criminology, and Public Policy, 6* (4), 863–870.

Ward, T., & Beech, A. R. (2004). The etiology of risk: A preliminary model. *Sexual Abuse: A Journal of Research and Treatment, 16*(4), 271–284.

Ward, T., & Stewart, C, A. (2003). The treatment of sex offenders: Risk management and good lives. *Professional Psychology, Research, and Practice, 34*(4), 353–360.

Ward, T., & Hudson, S. M. (2000). Sex offender's implicit planning: A conceptual model. *Sexual Abuse: A Journal of Research and Treatment, 12*(3), 189–202.

Willis, G. M., & Grace, R. C. (2008). The quality of community reintegration planning for child molesters. *Sex Abuse: A Journal of Research and Treatment, 20*(2), 218–240.

Winick, B. J. (2002). Therapeutic jurisprudence and problem solving courts. *Fordham Urban Law Journal, 30*(3), 1055–1103.

Winnick, T. A., & Cubellis, M. (2008). Anticipated stigma and stigma management among those to be labeled "ex-con." *Deviant Behavior, 29*(4), 295–333.

Worley, K. B., Church, J. K., Clemmons, J. C. (2011). Parents of adolescents who have committed sexual offenses: Characteristics, challenges, and interventions. *Clinical Child Psychology and Psychiatry, 17*(3), 433–448.

Worling, J., & Curwen, T. (2001). Estimate of risk of adolescent sexual offender recidivism (the ERASOR) (Version 2.1). Unpublished manuscript.

Worling, J. (2004). The estimate of risk of adolescent sexual offense recidivism (ERASOR): Preliminary psychometric data. *Sexual Abuse: A Journal of Research and Treatment, 16*(3), 235–254.

Zimring, F. E., Piquero, A. R., Jennings, W. G. (2007). Sexual delinquency in Racine: Does early sex offending predict later sex offending in youth and young adulthood? *Criminology and Public Policy, 6*, 507–534.

Jamie Yoder (PhD, University of Denver, 2013) is Assistant Professor of Social Work at the Ohio State University. Dr. Yoder has extensive practice experience working with youth offenders and victims of sexual crimes. Her research interests span etiology, prevention initiatives, and equitable and effective intervention strategies for sexually abusive youths, with a particular focus on systemic strength-based services. She has numerous publications and is currently working as a principal investigator on projects that rigorously identify risk and protective factors, study differential changes in risk and resiliency, and examine outcomes of a specified systemic treatment for youth with sexually abusive behaviors. You can access Dr. Yoder's work on twitter @JamieYoder22.

Mary Ann Farkas is Professor of Criminology and Law Studies at Marquette University. She teaches corrections, prison, probation and parole, media and urban crime, sex offenders and offenses, victimology, and women, crime and criminal justice. She has coauthored the following books: *Correctional Leadership: A Cultural Perspective* (2001) with Stan Stojkovic and *The Dilemma of the Sexual Offender* (first and second editions, 2001, 2013) with Dr. George Palermo and *A Law unto Themselves: The Media and the Criminal Justice System* with Frank Burke, 2015.

A Family Systems Perspective in Prisoner Reentry

Audrey L. Begun, Ashleigh I. Hodge, and Theresa June Early

Introduction

Numbers of individuals returning to mainstream society after being incarcerated are rising amidst concerns about overcrowding, disparities, and inequities in who becomes or remains incarcerated, renewed skepticism concerning the long-term rehabilitative effectiveness of incarceration, and high costs of maintaining large carceral populations (Carson and Golinelli 2013; Harding et al. 2014; Minton and Zeng 2015; Travis 2005; West et al. 2010). Not only have the economic costs of mass incarceration reached an historical high, but "this level of incarceration has devastated the children, the neighborhoods, the lifetime livelihoods, and even the very health, of the imprisoned themselves" (Thompson 2014, p. 1). In response to such devastation, the American Academy of Social Work and Social Welfare is calling for a movement "From Mass

A.L. Begun (✉) · A.I. Hodge, · T.J. Early
Ohio State University, Columbus, Ohio, USA

© The Author(s) 2017
S. Stojkovic (ed.), *Prisoner Reentry*,
DOI 10.1057/978-1-137-57929-4_3

Incarceration to Smart Decarceration" as one of 12 recently adopted Grand Challenges for Social Work (Pettus-Davis and Epperson 2015). While a "perfect storm" of factors has contributed to an apparent shift in our nation's unsustainable but prolonged era of mass incarceration (Carson and Golinelli 2013; Petersilia and Cullen 2015, p. 1), the reality remains that 95 % or more of incarcerated individuals eventually reenter the community (Hughes and Wilson 2002; Sabol et al. 2009; Travis 2005; Wool and Stemen 2004).

In 2009, the number of individuals released from state prisons exceeded the number admitted for the first time in over 31 years (Carson and Golinelli 2013). Over 637,000 individuals left U.S. state and federal prisons during 2012 (Carson and Golinelli 2013). Over 11.4 million individuals were admitted to jails between mid-year 2013 and mid-year 2014,—most of whom experience release to the community within 2 years (Minton 2013; Minton and Zeng 2015). At the end of 2014, many jurisdictions in the United States reported that the proportion of their adult correctional population being supervised in the community was larger than the proportion incarcerated in jails or prisons (Kaeble et al. 2015). Approximately 80 % of prisoners eventually return to living in the community under supervision (Hughes and Wilson 2002).

Prisoner reentry is not a new phenomenon nor is the science related to reentry issues. In addition to recidivism risk, the ability of individuals to establish conventional lifestyles and achieve reintegration after release is an important reentry outcome (Harding et al. 2014; Petersilia 2009). Evidence shows that meeting the physical, economic, housing, physical health, mental/behavioral health, and addiction treatment needs of previously incarcerated individuals is vitally important to their reentry success; failure to do so greatly increases the risks both for these individuals and for the communities to which they return (Begun et al. 2016; Freudenberg et al. 2008; Kerr and Lockshin 2010; Osher et al. 2002, 2003). Two parts to this reentry equation are (1) better preparing incarcerated individuals on how to get their needs met during reentry and (2) ensuring that effective and accessible systems are in place to integrate or reintegrate individuals back into community living (Begun et al. 2010, 2011; Draine and Munoz-Laboy 2014; Pettus-Davis and Epperson 2015; Travis 2004). As communities engage in intensified decarceration efforts and downsize their incarcerated populations, previously un- and under-recognized problems may arise. To date, existing literature on how to downsize effectively is limited (Petersilia and Cullen 2015).

Communities seeking tools to better anticipate likely issues and assess available options might turn to another historic, major dein-stitutionalization experience: moving the population of individuals experiencing mental illness or developmental disabilities out of long-term psychiatric institutions. During the 1960s and 1970s, deinsti-tutionalization of the mental health system was widely implemented in states, counties, and cities across the nation—assisted by passage of the Community Mental Health Centers Act. The era of deinsti-tutionalization in the mental health sector taught us an important lesson: Families frequently faced many overwhelming difficulties as they had to shoulder the primary responsibility of care for their relatives who were experiencing a serious mental illness (Benson 1994; Gallagher and Mechanic 1996; Goldman 1982; Gubman and Tessler 1987; Thompson and Doll 1982). An observation by Hairston, Rollin, and Jo (2004) reflects the relevance of this exam-ple: "Although most reentry policies and programs focus on the roles and functions of formal organizations, there is an underlying assumption that prisoners' families and friends, not the state, will be the major source of concrete aid and social and emotional support" (p. 1). These transitions are profound experiences for families, and family remains an important feature of the social and emotional landscape for individuals of any age.

In a similar vein, the purpose of this chapter is to critically analyze prisoner reentry from a family systems perspective: As families are profoundly affected by a member's incarceration, so too are they powerfully affected by the reentry process. An abundance of studies from multiple disciplines test assumptions concerning the ways in which family life and social bonds might affect the emergence of, or protection against, criminal offending that leads to incarceration. Far fewer address the ways in which a member's incarceration might affect the family (Western et al. 2004). Very few address the ways that families might experience a member's community reentry following release from incarceration.

This chapter examines theories about family systems; these theories are applicable to understanding the prisoner reentry process. Specifically, the chapter's focus is on adults being released from jails, prisons, and transitional incarceration facilities. One purpose of this work is to help inform practitioners, policy decision-makers, and researchers concerned with developing strategies that promote positive reentry outcomes. Another goal is to help inform audiences about how to understand and support families grappling with the challenges of (re)integrating a member released from incarceration. Literature and data specific to individuals in the criminal justice system are explored, along with lessons learned through the literature about families experiencing analogous reintegration circumstances.

The chapter begins with an overview of relevant family systems constructs, exploring the nature of families as dynamic systems and how a family member's incarceration and reentry might be experienced. The discussion next turns to an analysis of prisoner visitation evidence relevant to preserving a sense of family connectedness. Ideas for meeting the special needs of these families are then explored. Finally, conclusions are drawn concerning practice, policy, and future directions for research.

Families as Dynamic Systems

The concept of family systems was introduced in the early 1970s, at a time when mental health professionals and scholars were expanding their perspectives from an emphasis on individual behavior to an emphasis on understanding the ways in which individuals' behavior and development are influenced by their physical and social environments. This person-in-environment viewpoint quickly evolved to include consideration of the multi-directional ways in which individuals influence the environments in which they function, as well. Not only does family affect the development, behavior, and well-being of its individual members, so too does each individual member affect the family's development, behavior, and well-being. Over time, through this iterative process, the individual and the family to which he or she belongs help shape each other in patterned ways that Salvador Minuchin (1974) termed a *circularity of influence*.

A major contribution of family systems thinking was to supplement descriptions of family behavior with attempts to address complex *family processes*, as well. The roots of family systems thinking lie in general systems theory about living organisms (attributed largely to Ludwig von Bertalanffy's work of the 1950s). Systems theory examines the nature and significance of interdependence and interactions among components of an ever changing (dynamic) system that are viewed as a whole, rather than in terms of its individual parts. Living organisms, humans included, are dynamic systems comprised of interdependent, interacting component systems. Similarly, the "family" can be viewed as a dynamic, living organism comprised of interdependent, interacting elements. Not only are we concerned with how individual members develop and function as complex organisms, we are also concerned with the complex dynamics around which family members' interactions become organized into a "family system."

Clinicians and scholars during the 1960s and 1970s adopted systems theory to describe the relationships and interactions that take place within the emotional unit defining itself as "a family," and that result in the ways that individual members, and the family as a whole, function. Family systems theory offers a way of thinking about family behavior—the roots of functional and dysfunctional family patterns of behavior— as well as the iterative nature of influences between individuals and the family system (Bowen 1974). Family systems theory also explores how families operate within their immediate environmental contexts, which operate within larger social systems. For example, specific behaviors or expressions of family relationships can have very different meanings and functions in different cultural contexts (Rothbaum et al. 2002), such as the different value and meaning of promoting each individual members' autonomy and independence versus recognizing, accepting, and appreciating a certain degree of interdependence among family members.

Four critical features of family systems form the structure for presenting a number of concepts important to understanding family-related aspects of prisoner reentry. These are: (1) the family system is greater than the sum of its parts, (2) change in any part of the family system affects the entire family, (3) subsystems are embedded in the larger family system, and (4) family systems operate within a larger system context.

The Family System Is Greater than the Sum of Its Parts

In short, what this is saying is that we can never fully understand a family simply by knowing about its membership or composition. While knowing about the members is necessary, it is not sufficient to our understanding of the family as a whole. The concept of, and identity as, *a family* have profound meaning to its members; individuals often act in ways that will promote family interests and the integrity of the family, sometimes even at great individual cost or detriment. Families are constructed through the addition of members (e.g., marriage, birth, adoption) and are reshaped periodically by the loss of members (e.g., death, divorce, other forms of permanent separation). However, the nature and character of families are heavy influences on, as well as heavily influenced through, the functions by which they serve their members.

Family Functions

A family "is a task performing unit that meets both the requirements of external agencies in the society, and the internal needs and demands of its members" (Hill 1971, p. 12). In other words, families serve specific functions that benefit society, communities, and individuals. The specific tasks that families perform vary by culture, over time, and in response to family circumstances. However, several key family functions involve:

1. Feeding, clothing, sheltering, protecting, and otherwise addressing the basic needs of its individual members;
2. Adding and releasing members, for example through birth, adoption, or marriage, and through launching young adult members into independent living, or divorce;
3. Socialization of members into family and societal roles, as well as about social norms;
4. Maintaining order within the family, as well as maintaining relationships with the world outside the family boundaries;
5. Creating and maintaining a family identity, as well as motivation to preserve the family;

6. Producing and distributing goods and services necessary to maintain the family.

These sorts of tasks give direction and meaning to family behaviors and activities (Hill 1971). Family dysfunction can be assessed in terms of how these types of functions are met or fail to be met. It is worth noting that a parent's incarceration—particularly a mother's—may place minor children and adolescents at greater risk of inadequate care, a lack of family support, and exposure to traumatic experiences compared to age-mates whose mothers are not incarcerated (Johnston 1995).

Change in Any Part of the Family System Affects the Entire Family

Families are characterized by interdependent relationships among members. As a result of this interdependence, any change in the way that one member behaves will lead to change in the behavior of other family members (Hill 1971). Think of a pebble being dropped in a still pool of water: the ripples extend outward in all directions. In the same way, when changes occur within any individual member or in the relationships among them, the changes reverberate throughout the family system, affecting all of the other members and relationships. Systems are best able to engage in their routine functions when there is relatively little need to respond to change demands.

Families experience several phases in adjusting to change. The first phase often involves the experience of crisis and disorganization (McCubbin et al. 1980). Eventually, the family is able to establish a sense of reorganization and equilibrium, provided that they have the requisite internal and external resources to do so.

Homeostasis and Equilibrium

Family systems, by design, attempt to maintain internal stability, balance, and constancy; in systems terminology, homeostasis is the self-regulating principle of a system preserving its equilibrium. Family systems cannot afford to remain totally fixed and rigid because there are constantly changing conditions to which they must respond. For example, a family system may have worked out patterns of behavior that allow it to efficiently get everyone where they need to be on a school/work day. But, consider what happens when a weather emergency occurs or a member becomes ill: The system needs to adapt to the changed circumstances. However, adaptation demands effort and energy being redirected from regular functions. Thus, families represent "equilibrium-seeking and adaptive organizations" (Hill 1971 p. 12).

The processes of adaptation and adjustment are at the heart of the dynamic systems we call family. Because adaptation requires the expenditure of considerable energy and effort, events that push for a change response are experienced by the family system as stressful. This is true of any kind of change: happy events (marriage, birth of a baby, a job promotion, graduation) and unhappy events (divorce, serious illness, job loss). These change-provoking events produce tensions that the family must manage (McCubbin and Patterson 1983).

It is important to recognize several principles regarding the sources, nature, and complexity of family stressor events and a bit about family adaptability.

Internal and External Sources of Change

Stressor events can just as easily originate from within the family as they can be imposed from the outside. Families have to adjust to an individual member's developmental changes, such as a child learning to talk and becoming part of the conversational dynamic, or a child developing peer relationships outside of the family and introducing the family to new ideas or experiences, or even an aging family member losing the ability to live independently. Families also have to adjust to changes imposed from outside forces, such as the legal demand for children to attend school at specific ages, or social norms that dictate a family's responsibility to ensure the provision of care for an individual member whose life structure comes unraveled as a result of physical disability or mental illness.

With regard to the experience of incarceration, the criminal justice system places many change demands on individuals and their families over time. For example, a specific incarceration and reentry episode may be experienced within the context of a family's longitudinal "revolving door" experiences. Evidence for this comes from an ethnographic study of 50 male prisoners' families in which Braman and Wood (2003) found that the men's current family reintegration effort was just one in a series of incarceration cycles for a majority of the families interviewed. Families not only struggled to cope with the family member's incarceration but also with that family member's community reentry.

Normative and Paranormative Events

Stressor events may be normative or paranormative in nature. Many individual developmental changes, or the death of an elderly family member, might be relatively predictable, familiar, and normative in our society. Examples of events that are paranormative in our society include death or disability experienced by a young person, grandparents assuming primary responsibility for rearing grandchildren, and a family member's experience with addiction. An event may be paranormative for one of two reasons (or both together): It may be an "off-time" event, happening too early or too late in life to be normative, or it may be something not commonly experienced by the majority in a culture, community, or society. The forces of change associated with paranormative events are often difficult to anticipate, and families often lack physical and social resources and role models for helping them adapt. A family member's incarceration is a paranormative event, and as noted by Braman and Wood (2003), families struggle to adapt first to the incarceration and then to the community reentry events.

Concomitant Events

Certain stressor events may come with or lead to a host of concomitant hardships, contributing to a "pile-up" of stressors and associated strains demanding family adaptation (McCubbin and Patterson 1983). Again, incarceration of an adult provides an informative example: The family is emotionally and organizationally challenged by the member's absence, economically strained by legal costs and loss of income, and psychologically burdened with stigma, social isolation, shame, grief, and possibly anger regarding the situation. When beset with multiple concurrent or consecutive adaptive demands, a family system may exhaust its adaptive energies and resources (McCubbin and Patterson 1983).

Adaptability

A family's capacity to shift its behavior in response to change demands is referred to as adaptability. Adaptability is a resilience feature, and a family's ability to prevent a change-provoking event from causing irreversible harm to the system is referred to as its resistance capabilities (McCubbin and Patterson 1983). Social support is considered to be an important adaptive resource predicting family adjustment (Cobb 1976).

Subsystems Are Embedded in the Larger Family System

Family systems develop a large number of routines and familiar patterns of behavior as a means to increasing interactional efficiency. It would be tremendously time and energy consuming if the family members had to negotiate every task and function every time it needed to be executed. As a result, certain subsystem routines emerge over time. Several common subsystems are the marital/intimate partner subsystem (the interactions about their relationship), the parental subsystem (parent-child relations, as well as the relationship between parents about parenting), sibling subsystems (brothers, sisters, step- and half- siblings), and the extended family subsystem (grandparents, aunts/uncles, cousins, and others).

In this context, two topics warrant further attention. The first is a review of literature describing how certain family subsystems might be affected by a member's incarceration. The second concerns the specific roles related to family subsystems and how these might be affected by a member's incarceration and family reintegration efforts during community reentry.

Reentry Implications of Incarceration Effects on the Couple Subsystem

The experience of incarceration has a demonstrably destabilizing and disruptive effect on couples' relationships. Utilizing data from the Fragile Families study, controlling for a variety of factors, investigators observed that marriage or cohabitation of parents with young children is much less likely when the father has been incarcerated (Western et al. 2004). "The analysis provides strong evidence that the relative effects of [fathers'] incarceration on marriage and cohabitation are large, on the order of 20 to 40 percent" (Western et al. 2004, p. 40).

Schafer (1994) argued that spousal relationships are among the most precarious of a prisoner's family relations, at least for incarcerated men. He indicated that many men are divorced while incarcerated and that a felony conviction is grounds for divorce in most states (p. 28); divorce on the grounds of felony conviction requires a lengthy period of incarceration in some states, while in others a shorter sentence served in jail meets the criteria. Furthermore, incarceration significantly reduces the likelihood of unmarried parents remaining in a committed relationship or entering into marriage (Dyer et al. 2012). It seems that the impact of incarceration on couples' relationships has everything to do with the quality of the relationship prior to incarceration, and family contact during incarceration mediates the effects in terms of post-release family support and relationships (La Vigne et al. 2005): "in-prison contact can be a negative influence if intimate partner relationships are already poor" (p. 314). Thus, individuals whose relationships were tenuous prior to incarceration may not be expected to benefit greatly from engagement with these partners or spouses during the community reentry process; however, individuals in supportive relationships prior to incarceration may derive benefit in reintegration with these partners or spouses following release, as long as their relationships were appropriately tended to during incarceration.

Reentry Implications of Incarceration Effects on the Parent-Child Subsystem

Parent-child relationships are vulnerable to the disruptive effects of a parent's incarceration—an event that "places an indescribable burden on the relationships between these parents and their children" (Travis 2005, p. 119). As a result of incarceration, parents may have decreased influence on and knowledge of their children's activities, as well as how they are being cared for by others. This, in turn, "can lead to incarcerated parents losing custody of children" (Gordon 1999, p. 120). This is an important consideration based on sheer numbers alone. In 2007, 52 % of state and 63 % of federal prison inmates were parents to over 1.7 million children under the age of 18 years (Glaze and Maruschak 2008). Many of these individuals, particularly mothers (45 %), were the parents of multiple children (Mumola 2000). In one intervention study with women in jail, 80 % were mothers with an average of two to three children (Begun and Rose 2011). In the United States, on any particular day, an estimated 2.7 million children have at least one parent incarcerated in prison or jail according to the National Resource Center on Children and Families of the Incarcerated (Damron 2014).

A significant contribution to the understanding of families with an incarcerated parent is the dynamic perspective offered by Naudeau (2010): Parental incarceration is a process where the before, during, and after are all of great importance to the child and family.

Before Incarceration

In the majority of instances, incarcerated mothers lived with their children prior to being incarcerated in either jail or prison, as did a large percentage of fathers (64.3 % and 43.8 % respectively in the study reported by Mumola 2000). The data are a bit challenging to interpret because it is not uncommon for an incarcerated parent to have children with more than one partner, and to have been living with some but not all of their children (Johnston 2001). The important point is that these parents played an integral role in their children's lives prior to incarceration, thus incarceration has great potential for disruption of the parent-child relationship—especially when the parent is a mother (Laughlin et al. 2008).

On the other hand, a parent's incarceration may not represent the point at which a family's problems first began: "Rather, it often adds to the stress of a family already struggling with such life circumstances as poverty, discrimination, instability, violence, and limited access to sources of support" (Naudeau 2010, p. 51). An additional consideration is the ripple effect through the extended family system. The majority of children with an incarcerated parent are in kinship care, living with and under the care of other family members (Johnson and Waldfogel 2004).

During Incarceration

Naudeau (2010) described some of the emotional consequences of parental incarceration in terms of the disruption to attachment relationships. Emotionally, children may progress through a series of developmental phases in adjusting to the experience: (1) emotional numbness, (2) intense yearning, (3) psychological disorganization and depression, and, (4) reorganization, where the child establishes a new emotional equilibrium. Children vary widely in terms of the timing of these steps, and whether they make progress through the phases at all. Evidence indicates that stability in placement following a mother's incarceration is a critical factor in determining children's ability to form secure attachments. More than one placement disruption is associated with a much poorer (85 times less) ability to do so (Poehlmann 2005).

A parent's incarceration comes with a host of concomitant stressors for children, over and above the emotional and attachment factors associated with the forced separation. These quite possibly include change in economic stability (with concomitant changes in food, housing, and health care security), residence (with concomitant changes in school, neighborhood, and social network), and/or custody (extended family or placement with a foster family). While a majority of children remain with a family member (other parent, grandparent, or other relatives), a disconcerting percentage end up in the care of social service agencies or non-relative foster care arrangements—as many as 18 % in one study of mothers who were incarcerated (Casey-Acevedo et al. 2004). Permanency planning policies (such as the Adoptions and Safe Families Act) in the child welfare arena may contribute to the termination of parental rights, particularly when long-term sentences are being served, although this varies markedly by state (Begun and Rose 2011). Ideally, the changes resulting from placements where parental rights are terminated include greater stability compared to the period prior to a parent's incarceration, and perhaps involve removal of criminogenic factors for the developing child or adolescent. Removal of a parent whose behavior is dangerous may be beneficial for the child (Eddy and Reid 2003); prior to incarceration a child may be exposed to a host of disruptions, exploitation, and violence (Murray et al. 2014).

Unfortunately, and all too often, the opposite is true, especially when children's placement status remains in flux: The changes, relationship disruptions, and questionable quality of care experienced by children of incarcerated parents may become contributing factors in pervasive, enduring mental and physical illness, traumatic stress reactions, juvenile delinquency or adult criminal involvement, substance abuse, peer and intimate relationship problems, and/or school failure (Gabel and Johnston 1995; Johnson and Easterling 2012; Kampfner 1995; Murray et al. 2014; Myers et al. 1999; Naudeau 2010). Parental incarceration has been described as being a direct risk mechanism, in addition to being a risk correlate, for child development concerns (Murray and Farrington 2005).

A role-related concept that has received insufficient empirical attention, but holds great potential significance for this population of families, is that of *compensatory parenting*. Theoretically, who delivers what a child needs matters less in child development outcomes than whether or not what is needed was delivered by someone. In other words, others in the child's social environment may be able to pick up the missing functions when a primary parent becomes unable or unavailable to meet the child's care and development needs. The individuals providing this compensatory care may be the other parent, other members of the family or extended family, and/or other individuals in regular, close contact with the child and remaining family system.

Early research into the nature of resilient children identified that the child's ability to elicit this type of care from others in the social environment was of great benefit in terms of the child's ultimate resistance to developing problems later in life (e.g., Masten 2011; Rutter 1985; Shonkoff and Phillips 2000; Werner and Smith 1982).

Reentry Following Incarceration

Parke and Clarke-Stewart (2003) noted a somewhat surprising tendency for families to experience reunion following incarceration as being more stressful than the period of incarceration. This is evident in family stress and tension associated with the difficulties a parent might be experiencing in terms of reestablishing their bonds and regaining authority with their children (Naudeau 2010).

Returning fathers in one study reported many challenges that stemmed from difficulties in their relationships with the children's mother, her new partner, and her family; a primary factor determining the fathers' involvement with their children was how well they were "getting along" with the mothers of their children (Nurse 2004, p. 81). In short, weak inter-parental bonds translated into weak father-child bonds. Mothers tended to control access to the children; the issue was further complicated when the mothers had new partners with whom the children related as a father.

Preparation for Reentry

As part of the reentry planning process, it is important to consider how parents and children are prepared for family reintegration. For example, the investigators of the longitudinal *Returning Home* study noted that about 75 % of prisoners believed that it would be very or pretty easy to renew their family relationships following release, and that their family members would be supportive of them at reentry (Visher, La Vigne, and Travis 2004). In reality, family supportiveness was realized for 80–90 % of them, and participants believed that family support was critical for staying out of prison in the future. Clearly, family support matters and is often available; however, this does not mean that it is easy on any of the family members. Parenting in particular cannot be "put on hold" with the expectation that it can be easily picked up again at a later date (Scharff Smith 2014). And, we do not know what happened with participants who dropped out of the *Returning Home* study along the way; it is necessary to point out that their family support networks could look very different from those of participants who completed the longitudinal study.

Individuals reintegrating with the family system may not be adequately prepared to fulfill the family roles they are expected to assume or resume, such as caregiver, bread winner, and relationship partner (Braman and Wood 2003). Recognizing the reciprocal nature involved with being part of either an intimate couple partnership or parenting a child is a good starting point. Both sides of the equation need to be ready to (re)engage in their reciprocal roles in order for the relationship to work well.

Parenting is one reciprocal role of particular significance. Great opportunities lie in the arena of preparing incarcerated mothers and fathers to effectively assume/resume parenting roles with their children. While prison-based parenting education programs exist, there is relatively little systematically gathered evidence concerning best practices that can inform decision-makers about how to best prepare incarcerated mothers and fathers to succeed in fulfilling these important roles following release and how to best address their unique circumstances (Parke and Clarke-Stewart 2003).

The Childcare Opinions Questionnaire (COQ) Study[1]

The COQ study was a small-scale, cross-sectional survey conducted with incarcerated mothers to determine what they know and believe about appropriate behaviors in caring for young children. The survey was modified from one used to compare parents and child welfare workers'

[1] We would like to acknowledge the contributions of the students who assisted with the study and the mothers who participated, as well as funding provided by the Coca–Cola Critical Difference for Women program administered through The Ohio State University.

beliefs about children's care and well-being (Rose and Meezan 1996). The purpose of the COQ study was to help inform parenting education programs about what these mothers already know and what they need to know if the programs delivered in jails and prisons are to be as useful as possible. A total of 101 mothers in state prisons, aged 19–46 years (mean age 30.5), rated on a 5-point scale how serious they felt 67 caring behaviors were to a typical six-year old child. They were also asked to identify the one behavior that they deemed was most serious and the one that was least serious.

Table 1 specifies the mean ratings for nine categories of caregiving behavior, allowing for a comparison of those considered least to most serious. Shelter was the category that the mothers scored as being of least serious consequence to child well-being. This category included several items describing sub-standard housing conditions that would often be out of the control of a low-income family. For example, items included the living room serving as a bedroom, a leaky roof, house in poor condition, and no designated play area, as well as items about dirty dishes and food scraps left in rooms outside of the kitchen. This finding is noteworthy because child welfare workers

Table 1 Ratings by incarcerated mothers (N = 97) of seriousness for nine categories of caregiving behavior

Behavior category	Range for category means (1–5 scale)	Overall category mean (1–5 scale)	SD
Inadequate food	3.29–5.00	4.56	.40641
Inadequate clothing	2.17–5.00	4.08	.71447
Inadequate medical care	3.20–5.00	4.56	.47036
Inadequate shelter	2.13–5.00	3.86	.73834
Inadequate supervision	3.08–5.00	4.62	.33935
Exposure to unwhole-some social environment	3.00–5.00	4.27	.37170
Inadequate emotional care	2.88–5.00	4.57	.52043
Inadequate attention to education	2.50–5.00	4.27	.68096
Exploitation of the child	3.33–5.00	4.78	.38104

may hold these factors in high regard when determining housing adequacy for the return of child custody.

The most informative finding in the COQ study for parenting education is that the vast majority of the mothers demonstrated knowledge about the critical elements essential to adequate care for a child. Anecdotally, some of the mothers shared with the team that they found parenting education classes to be inadequate in other ways, calling them "rather lame." Specifically, they found that the content tended to lack relevance for the circumstances, conditions, and constraints they experienced living in the "real" world. For example, they felt that they did not need to be told what a healthy diet contained but rather how to secure a healthy diet for their children when they lived with their families in "food deserts" or faced other food insecurity conditions. Several of the mothers also expressed shame and guilt about some of their own parenting mistakes, especially those related to child neglect attributed to their involvement with drugs or alcohol. One mother turned in her survey, tearfully stating: "I have done so many of these things myself." In this light, parenting education programs delivered from a blaming and shaming perspective about past behaviors will not effectively help parents cope with their children's current and future developmental and relationship needs. Their inability in the past to fulfill their role responsibilities is not a sufficient indicator for how they will fare in the future. Thus, programs should seek to empower individuals for the roles they will be entering upon their release.

Role Theory Applied to Family Systems

Role theory offers an additional way to think about individual behavior within the family context. In general, role theory suggests that much of social behavior is determined by the nature of the social roles that individuals occupy. The nature of behaviors associated with social roles are learned through socialization, social learning, and social norms, and role behavior is heavily influenced by role expectations held by the individual and others in the social environment. While a specific role may be enacted by an individual, certain roles are occupied only in the context of reciprocal relationships: to be a caregiver requires someone to be a care receiver, for example.

Individuals occupy multiple roles simultaneously, which is one reason why we may behave differently in different social contexts. One way of thinking about an individual's multiple roles is to consider a related cluster of roles as being integrated into a position. For example, the position "mother" might include a cluster of roles related to interactions with her children, such as caregiver, resource manager, disciplinarian, educator, playmate, and others. Concurrently, this individual may also have roles related to other positions in her life: spouse, employee, and extended family member, for example.

A family system is comprised of a complex set of interacting and interdependent positions, each of which may be comprised of a complex set of roles. A final construct of relevance here is that of a role career. The career perspective takes into account the dimension of time, recognizing that expected roles and role behavior may change with time. For example, parenting a child during early adolescence requires role behaviors that differ markedly from those involved with parenting an infant; interactions may differ for couples after decades compared to when the relationship was new; siblings may interact differently as adults compared to when they were young children.

Role Problems

Role dysfunction and role failure come about in a variety of ways. This includes, but is not limited to:

1. Social norms associated with a specific role have not been acquired by the individual occupying that role. A very young man may not have adequately internalized the role expectations or learned the behaviors associated with becoming a father to his child, for example.
2. Role confusion occurs when the norms and expectations communicated by different socialization agents conflict. An individual might experience role confusion in the workplace when the employer, co-workers, and his/her own observations of parents or siblings in the employee role dictate different or conflicting expectations about what it means to be an employee.

3. With reciprocal roles, one of the partners might not behave as expected. For example, an older sibling may not be able to successfully function in a sibling caretaking role if the younger sibling fails to accept his or her authority. Similarly, when a previously incarcerated individual is reintegrating with the family, reciprocal roles in the couple subsystem may be difficult to reestablish.

4. Role void occurs when the system experiences a temporary or permanent vacancy for a much needed role. In the case of incarceration, the family system has to determine how to deal with the roles that the incarcerated member leaves vacant. The options include having other family members take over in each vacated role (which they may be ill-prepared to do), leaving the roles vacant (which may disadvantage the family over time), or bring in a new "replacement" member from outside the family system. Reintegration of the incarcerated family member during reentry demands that the family readjust their solution either by evicting the current occupant and having the returning individual take it over again, allowing the individual to resume a role left vacant, or permanently excluding the individual from the role.

5. Role strain occurs when an individual occupies different roles that may come into conflict with each other. For example, a woman returning to her family after release from jail may find that the demands of caring for her children (role: mother) conflict with the demands of conforming to an addiction treatment plan (role: patient), criminal justice system demands (role: person on probation), and demands of the child welfare system (role: client).

6. Role overload is experienced by an individual who attempts to fulfill too many different roles and becomes overwhelmed. We might expect to see this in the head of household left behind when an individual is incarcerated: The remaining partner is not only responsible for all of the roles he or she previously occupied, but perhaps for those left vacant by the incarcerated family member, as well. Fishman's (1990) ethnographic study described how the wives of incarcerated men, in absorbing the roles left vacant by their husbands, experienced high levels of stress as a result. This type of stress can result in health risks, as well as in poor parenting, which in turn contribute to children's emotional and

behavioral problems; together, these make functioning in the assumed roles even more challenging.

7. Role loss is experienced when an individual no longer occupies a role that was previously of great significance to him or her. A common example is the experience of individuals who retire from careers that gave meaning to them—great, gaping, grievous holes are left in their life structures. When a previously incarcerated individual attempts family reintegration and the family system does not allow reengagement in previously vacated roles, that individual may have to contend with the experience of significant role loss. The family system may allow the individual to occupy its least preferred roles (e.g., trash remover), but this token involvement does not compensate for the experience of losing previous, preferred roles (e.g., those involved with parenting). Nurse (2004) summarized this point regarding the high levels of stress experienced by men in relation with their wives and children following release from prison:

> A primary reason for this is that the children and women have undergone many changes in the men's absence. As a result, the men are no longer able to occupy their former roles in the family and find themselves unsure of how to act around their family members (p. 84).

Family Systems Operate Within a Larger System Context

Many social analyses apply an ecological systems model, first attributed to Urie Bronfenbrenner (Bronfenbrenner 1979, 1989). When applying the ecological systems model to individuals, the family is often considered part of the individual's immediate microsystem. Alternatively, when we think of the family as the unit of analysis, the family microsystem becomes those individuals with whom the family engages on a regular, frequent, highly impactful basis. This may include close relatives, immediate neighbors, friends, co-workers, and classmates. Extending the analogy from individual to family units, the family mesosystem includes individuals, organizations, institutions, and communities where interactions are less intimate and less regular, but still may have significant implications for family life. For example, the larger neighborhood context, children's schools, parents' workplaces, and places where social, behavioral health, and medical services are delivered on a regular basis might be part of the mesosystem for a family. The family's interactions become increasingly remote as we move out from the center of the model; however, even the largest of the systems (society, global community) continue to have an impact on how families function and experience their lives.

Being embedded in a larger system context is a two-way street. Not only are families affected by their contexts, they also exert certain amounts and types of influence on those contexts. Their mutual, circular patterns of influence are most evident as they interface with their microsystem over time. While the influence of more remote systems (meso- to macro-) on families is no less significant, the influence of any individual family becomes increasingly difficult to discern.

Later versions of Bronfenbrenner's social ecological model incorporate time as another critical dimension: the chronosystem. Time has a great deal of relevance to family systems. Family awareness of their past and future has great power to influence present behavior. This perspective is integrated into the family's awareness of its multigenerational nature, as well. Past and future generations have meaning to the family in its present experience. An individual family member "doing time" has added meaning in terms of the family system: The family continues to change, adapt, and develop over the time when the incarcerated individual does not move with them. As a result, during the process of community reentry, the individual and the family system may be very much out of sync. Maintaining contact between family members throughout the incarceration period has potential for helping to address some of the concerns raised so far.

Prisoner Visitation

Research indicates that successful outcomes during post-incarceration reentry are strongly influenced by prisoners' social support systems that may be disrupted during incarceration with limited or non-existent visitation. Since the 1950s and 1960s, scholars were demonstrating that family visitation and family support were associated with successful completion of parole (Schafer 1994). "Most current empirical findings support the view that visitation tends to reduce inmate recidivism" (Laughlin et al. 2008). Several studies specifically demonstrated a positive, significant relationship between family visits and post-release behavior, as well as a decreased risk of recidivism (Bales and Mears 2008; Cochran 2014; MN DOC 2011). Among the positive reentry outcomes associated with family involvement during the period of incarceration is a reduction in substance use disorders among those formerly incarcerated (Smith et al. 2004). Furthermore, visitation between parents and their children is a recognized correlate of successful reunification following release (Sharp 2003).

While the effects of family contact opportunities on family relationships is well-documented, relatively little is known about *how* visitation shapes the course of relationships among family members. The presumed mechanism of effect involves the maintenance of a social support continuum from prison to the community during reentry (MN DOC 2011). Social capital theories may have applicability here. In essence, social capital refers to an individual's (or family's) ability to "secure benefits by virtue of membership in social networks or other social structures" (Portes 1998, p. 6). Preserving connections with members of the community during a period of incarceration may contribute to leaving jail or prison with greater social capital to facilitate the reentry process (Hairston and Rollin 2006; Wolff and Draine 2004). Furthermore, a family's social capital has implications for an individual member's well-being (Wright et al. 2001)—individuals can benefit from their family's social networks even if their own are disrupted. One study, however, demonstrated that emotional support from families significantly predicted lower reoffending, whereas the provision of instrumental support did not (Taylor 2016).

There is, of course, a potential concern with what has been termed "negative social capital" (e.g., Liu 2004), whereby an individual retains connections to undesirable benefits, such as drugs or networks supporting illegal behavior. However, the evidence more heavily lies on the side of family connections during incarceration as an explanation for lessened recidivism following release. This may, in part, relate to the principle of an individual's "stake in conformity" and how it may serve as a deterrent to criminal behavior (Spohn 2007). Stake in conformity reflects the strength of a person's bonds to conventional society; presumably, greater stake in conformity motivates an individual to behave consistently with general (prosocial) societal norms, and lower stake in conformity contributes to more variability in behavior. Individuals lacking in social capital or having a low stake in conformity may be more likely to reoffend (Sherman et al. 1992; Spohn 2007).

Consistent with a social capital perspective, Gordon (1999) summarized several studies showing that family visits are associated with higher post-release employment rates, better parole outcomes, and lower post-release recidivism rates. Despite a relative lack of evidence to support the historical belief that exposure to a family subculture characterized by criminogenic values leads to criminal behavior (Liu 2004), this mindset continues to influence beliefs, policy, and practices related to family visitation—visits might be discouraged because it is believed that the individual may again fall under the influence of a criminogenic family system following release (negative social capital), or that engaging in contact with the incarcerated family member will "infect" the visitors with criminogenic values. Neither hypothesis has been demonstrated through systematic study. While some visits may be discouraged, many families are unable to visit because of distance.

Prison consolidation is increasingly being adopted as a strategy for containing or cutting costs: The National Conference of State Legislatures reported that at least 15 states closed correctional facilities during 2011 or 2012, and prison consolidation can significantly reduce cost to the state prison system, which accounts for almost 90 % of what is spent on corrections (Lawrence 2013). However, prison consolidation may have a significant potential impact on prisoner visitation patterns. As prisoners are moved to increasingly centralized locations, distances from inmates' home communities widen, and decreased visitation becomes a potential side effect with considerable secondary implications (Cochran et al. 2016). Furthermore, privatization of incarceration systems often necessitates inmate transfers to new geographical locations, which may further impede prisoner visitation

(Shichor, and Sechrest 2002) and intensify already-existing racial/ ethnic barriers to this means of preserving social ties during incarceration (Cochran et al. 2014; Cochran et al. 2016).

Even before the era of prison consolidation, because facilities for women were relatively scarce, the average distance between incarcerated mothers and their children was 160 miles (Hagan and Coleman 2001)—large distances become prohibitive for regular visitation due to time constraints, travel costs, and lack of transportation to remote locations (Bales and Mears 2008; Bedard, and Helland 2004; Christian 2005; Christian et al. 2006; Fuller 1993; Jackson et al. 1997; Schafer 1994). Because they are often so remotely located, more time may be spent traveling for a visit than the amount of time a visitor can spend with an incarcerated family member (Gordon 1999).

Fortunately, evidence also indicates that important and impactful family connections can be maintained outside of visitation through other forms of interaction, such as telephone calls, mail, and video visitation (Visher and Travis 2003). Unfortunately, these alternatives may not be sufficiently supported by institutions or may be too costly for inmates and their families to engage in them on a regular basis.

The Ohio Prisoner Visitation Study[2]

Utilizing 2011 data provided by Ohio's Department of Rehabilitation and Corrections (ODRC), a secondary analysis was conducted to investigate visitation patterns in the state's prison facilities. The original dataset included information on numerous variables about each of the state's 50,056 prisoners' visits during the previous five years. The data were drawn from prison records routinely maintained by prison staff. Prisoners with no approved visitors, having no chance of community

---

[2] We would like to acknowledge the contributions of Dr. Nate Doogan in conducting analyses related to the Ohio prisoner visitation study reported here, all of the students who assisted with the study, and the Ohio Department of Rehabilitation and Corrections

reentry, or who were residents of another state were excluded from analyses. The final data set included information about visits for 37,752 men (95%) and women (5%) in 31 state prison facilities prior to consolidation.

The probabilities of visits from each possible type of visitor for each possible week during the five years (or since the inmate was admitted) were estimated using generalized linear mixed models with several predictor variables entered into the tested models (cross-classified, random effects, discrete time event history model). First, each visitor was recoded as a family member or friend based on the prison visitation records. Family members included a wide range of types, including spouse/ significant other (husband, wife, common law spouse), parent (mother, father, step-parent, in-law parent), "child" (son, daughter, step- with no indication whether this was an adult or minor-aged child; son or daughter in-law), sibling (brother, sister, half-, step-), grandparent, aunt, uncle, or cousin. Others were included in the friend category; professional visits from lawyers, counselors, or others with a professional reason for visiting were excluded from the data.

The model predictors included: (1) static prisoner characteristics (gender, age, marital status at admission, and length of sentence); (2) visitor relationship (family member or friend/professional); and (3) time varying characteristics (distance between prisoner's home zip code and current institutional placement, and indicator of first or last six months of sentence being served). The tested models were adjusted for prisoners' level of security since visitation frequency is limited by policy based on security level. Minimum security (31% of inmates) allowed the greatest frequency of visits, medium security (45%) allowed fewer, and closed/ maximum security (24%) allowed no or very few visits.

The greatest number of visits during the five years for any inmate was 880, and a disproportionately large number of inmates had no visits at all during their incarceration: 37%. The median number of visits across all inmates was four, and across only those receiving any visits was 17. The inmates' sentences served so far ranged from days to more than five years served at the time of measurement. The median court-assigned sentence duration was 48 months. Furthermore, there was a slight decline in overall visitation rates from 2006 to 2011.

The men had significantly more institutional moves, greater numbers of ODRC approved visitors, and more visits than did the women. For both men and women, younger prisoners and prisoners in an intimate partner relationship were significantly more likely to receive visitors than their older and single counterparts; the mean prisoner age was 32 years and 84 % self-reported as being single. Prisoners were significantly more likely to receive visits from family members than from friends. Men were significantly less likely to receive a visit during the first and last six months of their sentences compared to the rest of their sentence; women were significantly less likely to receive a visit during their first six months but were no less likely to receive a visit six months before release than during the rest of their sentences. For the women, visits from children dropped to zero more quickly than did visits from other types of family relatives.

Finally, each additional mile of distance from an inmate's home zip code to his or her current institutional placement was associated with a significant reduction in the probability of any visits from family or friends: a 1.4 % reduction in likelihood per additional mile for women, and a 1.6 % reduction in likelihood per additional mile for men. In addition to distance, feasibility of visiting was also analyzed in a qualitative manner. Many institutions had policies in place that produced significant barriers to visitation. For example, in order to attend visiting hours at several prison facilities (beginning at 6 pm on a week day), visitors had to check in at the facility at 3 pm that same day. There were no available indoor waiting areas, food services, or restroom facilities for the 3 hours between check-in and visiting periods.

The study team utilized online mapping services, bus company schedules, fuel and toll cost calculators, and prison-specific visitation policies to estimate the feasibility of travel from one highly populated, centrally located community (Columbus, Ohio) to each of the state's 31 prison facilities. Depending on the type of vehicle, the projected cost of a round trip visit was $20–$30. Bus service was available to only 15 of the 31 facilities, for an average roundtrip fare of $45 (ranging from $22 to $73). However, the bus schedules were often inhospitable (requiring an overnight stay or arriving too late to meet the visitor check-in policy of the institution) and would often place a visitor only in the general vicinity, requiring additional resources to arrive at the facility itself. Video visits were available in only four facilities. Finally, prison visitation was closed on state holidays and subject to change without notice (most likely due to emergency "lock down" situations).

In combination, the results from the Ohio visitation study dovetail with what others have presented in the literature. First, most incarcerated individuals do not see their families on a regular basis, and many in prison never do (Hairston et al. 2004). Men generally receive more visits than women; women tend to be visited more by friends than by family (Casey-Acevedo and Bakken 2002), and the majority do not receive visits from their minor-aged children (Casey-Acevedo et al. 2004). Distance and travel costs/difficulties presented a tremendous potential barrier to family visitation, especially for children, and a critical distance from place of incarceration to home community seems to be 100 miles (Casey-Acevedo and Bakken 2002; Hairston et al. 2004; Schafer 1994). Families who rely on public transportation are additionally disadvantaged in their ability to visit facilities where public transportation systems do not provide a route (Clark 2001).

Visitation as a Family Experience

Assuming that reentry outcomes are influenced by supportive social networks (family and friends), increased centralization of incarceration locations due to downsizing of a prison system may impede visitation which, in turn, may negatively affect support network strength. Social work interventions to enhance supportive family and friend networks during the months prior to community reentry are important to explore, as are their potential impact on reentry outcomes. However, the visitation experience of family members is also an important factor to consider. Prison and jail visits can be emotionally, physically, and economically difficult activities in which to engage, especially when functioning as a single-parent family system under difficult circumstances becomes emotionally depleting (De Claire and Dixon 2015). Family members must be highly motivated to maintain contact and support the incarcerated individual in order to meet many of the challenges and demands associated with making a visit happen. For example, lack of privacy, restrictions on physical contact, difficult interactions with staff, negative experience in waiting areas, and concerns about exposure to the behavior of other inmates are not uncommonly experienced by visiting family members (Dyer et al. 2012).

Pierce (2015) examined the perceptions of incarcerated men concerning the impact of their visitation experiences on their family relationships, and what the men believed the facilities could do to help decrease the negative influences of their incarceration on their families. Some of these suggestions include making the environment more visitor-friendly, including by making them more child-friendly with activities and snacks being available in the visiting areas. Another category of suggestions related to staff attitudes and behaviors toward visitors: "Research has established that visitors are often treated poorly by staff when visiting a correctional facility" (Pierce 2015, p. 388). Additionally, greater use of alternatives to incarceration, particularly for non-violent offenses, might reduce the overall negative impact that incarceration can have on the family system as a whole by removing it from the equation (Pierce 2015).

Non-visitation

According to Travis (2005), in a small percentage of cases, continued parental involvement may not be in the child's best interest. This includes: where family violence was directed toward an intimate partner and/or child, a sex crime was perpetrated against a child, severe child maltreatment in the form of neglect occurred, or "yo-yo" parenting where the parent is only aware of the child when incarcerated and not when living in the community (Scharff Smith 2014; Travis 2005). Furthermore, in some instances incarcerated parents are so preoccupied with their own problems or so lacking in parenting abilities that they have little to offer to their children who might visit; in these instances, visitation might be ill-advised (Scharff Smith 2014).

Sometimes the incarcerated person decides to "opt out" of family visits for a variety of reasons such as not wanting to put the family members through the stress or costs of visiting and not wanting to be seen under their current circumstances (Scharff Smith 2014). In this case, helping children understand the reasons why their parent opted out of visitation is an important process that can reduce their tendency to conclude that the parent does not care about them—a conclusion that renders later relating exceedingly difficult (Scharff Smith 2014). A variety of other processes may need to be addressed in order to adequately support families through the reintegration process.

Meeting Families' Reintegration Needs

In many instances of family separation and reunion, the family system is required to adapt to changes in the presence/absence/reappearance of one of its members: Examples include military deployment, the transition period during employment relocation, physical or mental illness, addiction and recovery, adult children returning to live with the family of origin (the "not-so-empty nest"), and dissolution of a co-parenting couple's relationship. The family-level consequences of military deployment, for example, include a wide array of symptoms that increase in frequency or intensity (Saltzman et al. 2011). These symptoms may be long-lasting, as well: "... current research shows that reintegration issues, such as role stress, role confusion, individual/family adjustment can last months, even years after the ... [return] home" (Marek and D'Aniello 2015, p. 443). Families may not be expecting the stress and threat to system homeostasis imposed by the role changes necessitated by a family member's reintegration, and not recognize the reintegration process as the beginning of the family's future course, rather than the end of the past (MacDermid Wadsworth 2013).

Reintegration Stress

The family risk factors identified by Saltzman et al. (2011) under circumstances of military deployment have relevance to family systems experiencing a member's absence due to incarceration; Table 2 outlines family process risks, outcomes/family symptoms, and potential strategies

Table 2 Implications of risks and outcomes associated with a family member's deployment for understanding a family member's incarceration and reentry

Risk in incarceration situation[1]	Potential outcomes	Possible program responses
Incomplete understanding		
• Incomplete understanding of impact of incarceration and stress on family members • Inaccurate developmental expectations	• Misinterpretation of each other's behaviors and reactions • Anger, confusion, frustration • Inappropriate parent reactions and support • Guilt, blame • Excessive worry about children	• Psychoeducation • Developmental guidance • Proactive family planning for absence and reentry • Positive reframing of problem and goal statements • Train to manage the loss reminders • Highlight family strengths
Impaired family communication		
• Prolonged parent absence, disparate experiences, and inability to appreciate these differences • Lack of open emotional expression	• Isolation and estrangement • Reduced family cohesion, warmth, and appropriate support • Unclear, inconsistent, distorted information • Lack of collaborative process (planning, problem solving, decision making) • Increased irritability and conflict	• Share individual narratives, co-create shared family narratives • Perspective taking • Process the distortions and misattributions • Communication skills training • Family meetings
Impaired parenting		
• Problematic parent leadership and reactivity (related to parent distress, PTSD, depression, anxiety disorders) • Reduced parental availability, engagement, and monitoring	• Inconsistent care routines • Inconsistent discipline and parenting styles applied • Lack of coordinated co-parenting • Family relationship stress and conflict • Disruptive child behavior	• Processing parenting differences and misunderstandings • Parent leadership training • Developing shared goals and support of co-parenting • Skill training in collaborative decision-making, problem solving, goal setting, emotional regulation

(continued)

Table 2 (continued)

Risk in incarceration situation[1]	Potential outcomes	Possible program responses
Impaired family organization		
• Overly rigid or chaotic structure that is easily disrupted under stress	• Rigid or chaotic parenting styles • Poorly defined boundaries, roles, responsibilities • Erratic care routines • Disengagement of family member(s) • Decreased cohesion, confidence, optimism	• Shared parenting narratives to support effective co-parenting • Activities/assignments to enhance family structure and closeness • Training on collaborative family skills and maintaining care routines • Crisis contingency planning
Lack of guiding belief systems		
• Lack of framework to provide coherence and make meaning out of adversity • Lack of shared beliefs to support family identity, optimism, and mobilize coping efforts • Lack of access to supportive community, rituals, and transcendent values	• Feelings of isolation, hopelessness, pessimism • Loss of sense of coherence, life being comprehensible, manageable, meaningful • Lack of common family mission and "esprit de corps"	• Family narrative creation to increase coherence and make sense of experiences • Normalize and contextualize adverse experiences • Highlight strengths and past successes • Reframe negative • Support family's spiritual or religious inclinations

[1] Adapted from Saltzman et al. (2011)

for supporting resilience among families experiencing a member's incarceration and reintegration post-release.

Reintegration stress is an important concept relevant to family and community reentry following release from incarceration. The concept represents an identified challenge affecting military families experiencing a member's return following a period of deployment (Marek and D'Aniello 2015). Analogous under these two conditions are lengthy separations, possibly occurring in multiple cycles, as well as significant concerns for the absent family member's safety and well-being.

Furthermore, any assumptions about a family member returning home to the status quo following deployment or incarceration are erroneous. The family members and family system continue to adapt and change over time, despite the missing member's absence. The family's systems of operation and patterns of behavior have had to be adapted around the absence—the individual is reentering an environment that is perhaps so dramatically changed that it might be more appropriately referred to as entering for the first time.

Exceptional Needs, Exceptional Family Demands

A final consideration related to family reintegration during community reentry is the fact that many of these families were experiencing significant stressors affecting family functioning at the outset, prior to, and during the member's period of incarceration. This section explores some additional, compounding, complicating factors with which these families may be struggling to contend: housing, physical health, mental health, and substance use problems. Results from a study conducted in Ohio form a context for sharing this information.

Project RISE[3]

The following sections discuss background related to, and results emerging from, a longitudinal, primary data collection study called Project RISE (Reentry Inventory of Service Engagement). Project RISE was developed to determine the reentry needs of individuals from jails, prisons, and community-based correctional facilities (CBCFs), as well as what services were actually engaged and barriers encountered in meeting those needs. A total of 137 adult men and women (55 % vs 45 % respectively) were first interviewed during their final weeks of incarceration in jail (16 %), prison

---

[3] We would like to acknowledge the contributions of all the students who assisted in conducting this study, funding from the Ohio Association of County Behavioral Health Authorities and the Ohio State University College of Social Work, and each of the men and women who participated in the study.

(53 %), or a CBCF (31 %) and again during early reentry, two to three months following release. At the beginning of the study, 309 pre-release interviews were conducted; those who were lost to follow-up did not differ significantly from those retained on any demographic variables. Attrition rates were slightly higher, however, among those being released from jail compared to the other two types of facilities (67 % vs 50 % and 56 %).

Prior to release, the men and women were interviewed to gather data concerning: various demographic variables (including criminal justice system history); quality of life indices; past substance use (AUDIT-ID); past, present, and anticipated need for physical health, mental health, addiction treatment, and housing assistance services; past use of these four types of services; as well as past and anticipated barriers to receiving needed services. During reentry, participants engaged in similar inter-views asking about their need, use of, and barriers experienced for the same four types of services. Greater detail concerning methodology and portions of the study results are presented in a published manuscript (Begun et al. 2016), while other results are presented for the first time in the relevant sections below.

Housing and Economic Needs

Incarceration is responsible for "forcefully transforming the material and social lives of families," and for a host of concomitant problems that present extreme challenges to fragile families (Braman and Wood 2003, p. 159). For example, following release from incarceration, individuals frequently encounter significant barriers to being able to contribute to their family's economic security (Harding et al. 2014). In essence, a family member's return may actually become a family's economic liabi-lity if economic contributions do not compensate for the additional costs of the member being present.

Stable, secure, affordable housing may be difficult to access as land-lords may be disinclined to rent to individuals with a criminal record (Travis et al. 2001). However, achieving housing stability is required for successful family reunification (Arrigo and Takahashi 2007). Economic and housing stability are essential aspects of family functions related to providing for the basic needs of all family members described earlier in this chapter.

Men with a history of incarceration are far more likely than men without such histories to experience frequent moves and to face housing insecurity issues (Geller and Curtis 2011). Women, too, find it more difficult to secure stable housing through public assistance if they have criminal records (Richie 2001). Increased rates of recidivism, parole violations, re-arrest, and return to incarceration are associated with homelessness and shelter living by individuals during reentry, and finding a secure place to live is one of the greatest struggles upon community reentry (Baillargeon et al. 2010; Belenko 2006; Geller and Curtis 2011; Roman and Travis 2004; Seredycz 2010).

Housing stability is a critically important issue, connected to other important services these individuals may need. For example, in one study, women who secured stable living arrangements and steady work following release from incarceration had a significantly greater likelihood of completing post-release substance abuse treatment than did their unhoused, unemployed counterparts (Hohman et al. 2000). Unfortunately, many communities suffer from a shortage of affordable family housing, contributing to long waiting lists and housing insecurity (Hammett et al. 2001).

There exists an empirical knowledge gap concerning housing insecurity issues and supportive housing services for individuals engaged in community reentry following incarceration (Fontaine et al. 2012; Geller and Curtis 2011). Draine and Herman (2007) argue that the Critical Time Intervention model might be relevant for the population of individuals experiencing mental illness (with or without co-occurring substance use disorders) as they return to the community following a period of incarceration: A key emphasis in this type of intervention is housing security. Becoming homeless is a greater risk during reentry by inmates with mental illnesses than among other reentering inmates; these individuals are also more likely to co-habit with other ex-offenders or those abusing substances than are other reentering individuals (Baillargeon et al. 2010). While state and local policies on public housing exclusion vary (Geller and Curtis 2011; Lundgren et al. 2010), persons with sexual offenses or substance use histories may face additional challenges in securing placement in subsidized housing programs, and entire families may be evicted from public housing units should one co-habiting member engage in criminal behavior during their residency (GAO 2005; Geller and Curtis 2011; Heinle 2009; Lundgren et al. 2010; van Olphen et al. 2006).

Housing Results from Project RISE

Individuals had greater housing dependency on families and friends following release from incarceration compared to pre-incarceration. Between these two time periods, the ratio of individuals living in their own houses or apartments compared to those living in the homes of friends or relatives changed: 57 % (prior to incarceration) versus 38 % (post-release) lived in their own homes or apartments, and 37 % (prior to incarceration) versus 54 % (post-release) lived in the homes of friends or relatives. The rates at which they described themselves as being homeless (2 %) or living in some other arrangement (5 %), such as institutional, correctional, or residential programs, remained stable.

Participants' ratings of the stability and reliability of their living situations were relatively high: 78.6 % used ratings of very or mostly stable/reliable to describe their circumstances following release. This was actually an improvement compared to pre-incarceration when 69.4 % of participants awaiting release retrospectively used these higher ratings for housing stability and reliability. Participants also retrospectively rated their feelings about their pre-incarceration housing situations: The majority (60 %) being either mostly or very pleased, and 21.3 % felt terrible or mostly dissatisfied with what their housing situations were at that time. Following release, their feelings about their current housing situations were unchanged.

Housing stability did not differ by gender at either time period, nor was it different prior to incarceration for individuals in jail, prison, or a CBCF. However, housing stability during community reentry was significantly related to type of facility from which a person was released (chi-square analysis, $\chi^2(4) = 12.088$, $p < .05$) where the lowest degree of housing stability was reported by individuals released from jail. This may be due to the fact that jail stays are relatively short (up to one year) when compared to prison stays (usually one year or longer), rendering little time for engaging in reentry service preparation prior to release. Feelings about their living situations did not differ by gender or type of facility at either time point.

Just over half of participants did not need housing help during the reentry period from social service providers (55.9 %), 16.2 % needed a little or some help, and 28 % needed a lot of help with housing. The barrier rated as most serious was not being able to afford it (mean rating of 3, significant barrier, on a 4-point scale). Not knowing where to go for housing was the second most serious barrier (mean rating 1.95, somewhat of a barrier, on a 4-point scale). The average number of housing barriers that these individuals reported encountering was 4.0 out of 10 possible (median=3.0). This mean did not differ significantly on one-way analysis of variance by either gender or type of facility.

Physical Health

The types of infectious and chronic disease conditions often encountered in the population of individuals returning to the community following incarceration include HIV/AIDS, Hepatitis C, MRSA, tuberculosis (including treatment resistant forms), asthma, hypertension, sexually transmitted infections, and diabetes, as well as orthopedic, chronic pain, and seizure disorders (Cuellar and Cheema 2012; Freudenberg 2001; Goldstein et al. 2009; Hipp et al. 2009; Marquart et al. 1996; Seredycz 2010; Teitelbaum and Hoffman 2013; van Olphen et al. 2006; Woods et al. 2013; see also CDC at http://www.cdc.gov/correctionalhealth/health-data.html). "On average, prisoners are four to ten times more likely than the general population to suffer from infectious disease" (Teitelbaum and Hoffman 2013, p. 1334). Physical health problems among previously incarcerated women that are frequently unaddressed also include reproductive health issues and sexually transmitted infections (Richie 2001; Richie et al. 2001).

Failure to adequately address and treat these conditions during incarceration and community reentry has significant implications for the public health of the families and communities to which these individuals return

(Freudenberg et al. 2008; Hipp et al. 2009; Teitelbaum and Hoffman 2013; Woods et al. 2013), as well as to the quality of life experienced by these individuals. For individuals beginning a diagnosis and treatment plan during incarceration, continuity of care when back in the community is critical (Hammett et al. 2001). As a result of not engaging in routine preventive care or regular monitoring of chronic conditions, ex-offenders often resort to utilizing emergency departments rather than primary care when health care services are needed (Hawkins et al. 2010). Individuals may enter into a vicious cycle whereby health concerns impede their ability to engage in sustainable employment (many available jobs involve high physical demands), and a lack of employment impedes their ability to secure rehabilitative (non-emergency) medical care.

Unfortunately, this population experiences significant barriers to accessing health care services, including an inability to pay for health care, problems with navigating the system, a need for nonjudgmental health care providers, and poor collaboration between the criminal justice and community-based health care systems (Hawkins et al. 2010; Sung et al. 2011; Urban Institute 2002). Post-release employment difficulties contributed significantly to health care access problems (Belenko 2006; Hipp et al. 2009). Historically, problems with Medicaid or state health insurance interruption and insufficient documentation have contributed to long delays in securing medical coverage during community reentry (Baillargeon et al. 2010; Cuellar and Cheema 2012; Hammett et al. 2001). Recent policy changes included in Medicaid expansion and the Patient Protection and Affordable Care Act are expected to provide greater access to health care by ex-offenders but may also contribute to greater strain on the health care systems in many communities (ACA 2012); it is perhaps too soon to tell at this time.

Physical Health Care Results from Project RISE

While incarcerated, health and physical conditions interfered with day-to-day functioning at least sometimes for 36.5 % of participants in Project RISE. Medications were being prescribed for 41 % during incarceration and almost three-quarters of participants (72 %) expected that after release they would have concerns about being able to get their prescribed medications due to inability to pay, inability to find a prescribing doctor or someone to administer them, or medications going missing/being stolen. Half of the participants predicted that they would have at least some need for medical care following release.

During community reentry, 32 % of participants reported that their overall health and physical condition interfered with day-to-day functioning, and 15 % had received needed health care for a serious or chronic condition or injury during the reentry period. This included 7 % with prescriptions for serious or chronic health conditions, 7 % who received regular medical follow-up for serious or chronic health conditions, 5 % with at least one emergency room visit, 4 % who received diagnostic tests, and 3 % who received some other form of medical services for a serious or chronic medical condition. During the reentry period, 36 % of participants reported having received prescriptions for medication and, among them, 61 % had concerns about being able to get their medication at least some of the time; 37 % had these concerns often or always after release. In addition to these concerns, 25 % had other concerns about their medications; only 10 % of these individuals had their medication concerns addressed often or always.

Just over half of participants experienced a need for physical health care during the reentry period (57 %), with 27 % needing a little or some, and 30 % needing a lot of it. The barrier to receiving needed health care that was rated as most serious was not being able to pay for it (mean rating of 2.66, between somewhat and significantly a barrier, on a 4-point scale). Not having transportation to get health care was the second most serious barrier (mean rating 1.66, somewhat of a barrier, on a 4-point scale). The average number of barriers to engaging needed physical health care that these individuals reported encountering was 3.25 out of 10 possible (median=3.0). This mean did not differ significantly on one-way analysis of variance by either gender or type of facility.

It is worth noting that only 28 % of individuals were employed full-time by the second or third month of the reentry period, and whether or not they were eligible for health care plans through this employment is not known. Those employed part-time (15 %) most likely were not. Half of the participants were unemployed and some self-identified as being disabled (7 %). The impact of the Affordable Care Act on access to physical health care services, implemented after the study was completed, remains to be seen. Needless to say, an individual who cannot secure his or her own health care benefits may not be able to assist the rest of the family in getting their health care needs met either.

Mental Health and Addiction

The rates of mental health, post-traumatic stress, and substance use disorders are disproportionately high among incarcerated men and women compared to rates in the general population: from three to 21 times higher depending on the condition being considered, particularly among incarcerated women (Belenko 2006; Blitz et al. 2005; Mears and Cochran 2012; Seredycz 2010; Teitelbaum and Hoffman 2013), and the measurement methods utilized (Prins 2014). This translates to an estimated 61 % of individuals in state prisons and 44 % of those in jails meeting criteria for recent mental health diagnoses, and 74 %–76 % of individuals in prisons and jails meeting criteria for a recent substance use disorder (James and Glaze 2006).

Evidence indicates that, despite being very important in assuring reentry success, services to these populations too often are fragmented, difficult to access, lack adequate transition planning, and lack clinical meaningfulness (Baillargeon et al. 2010; Begun et al. 2016; Cuellar and Cheema 2012; Hatcher 2007; Kerr and mo Lockshin 2010; Lovell et al. 2002; Lurigio 2001; Mojtabi et al. 2011; Osher et al. 2002, 2003; Thompson et al. 2003; Wilson and Draine 2006). Post-release, continued problems with substance use interfere considerably with reentry success, recidivism deterrence, and an individual's ability to benefit from other services, such as tending to physical health care needs (Richie et al. 2001; van Olphen et al. 2006). The co-occurrence of psychiatric and substance use disorders are also over-represented in criminal justice settings, for a variety of reasons related to the likelihood of engaging in behaviors that lead to arrest and to violating conditions of community supervision (Peters et al. 2015). Outside of the criminal justice system, having serious, persistent mental health problems can interfere with retention in substance-related treatment programs and vice versa. Within the criminal justice system, for women experiencing both mental health and substance use problems, their substance use can be reduced by effective engagement in mental health services (Freudenberg et al. 2008).

Problems with mental health, substance use, or both affect not only the individuals reentering community living but also affect their families. According to Glaze and Maruschak (2008), a considerable majority of individuals incarcerated for substance-related offenses are parents, and a majority of the incarcerated parents met clinical criteria for a substance use disorder (67 % among those in state prisons and 56 % among those in federal prisons). Stigma and other issues related to a parent's long-term incarceration for substance-related offenses can lead to overwhelming negative effects on children (Mazza 2006).

Mental Health and Addiction Service Results from Project RISE

In the short-term, longitudinal reentry study described earlier and more extensively in a published article (Begun et al. 2016), the rates of mental health and substance use problems were similarly disproportionately high as those reported in the literature. When first interviewed, a majority of participants (56.5 %) anticipated they would need mental health services during reentry. More than half (54 %) had received mental health care prior to or during incarceration and even more (68.5 %) reported having been prescribed medication for mood, behavior, or emotional issues in the past. During reentry, compared to before release, a smaller percentage (48 %) of participants stated they needed mental health services; relatively few (15 %) reported having received mental health services since release.

The results for substance use problems, anticipated need, and actual service receipt are similar: Prior to release, a considerable majority (62.5 %) of participants anticipated a need for substance use services, a smaller percentage (44 %) reported experiencing this need during early reentry, and an even smaller percentage reported problematic use of substances during early reentry. A substance use screening test addressing the year immediately prior incarceration revealed serious problems being experienced by most participants: 82.5 % reported alcohol and/or other substance use to a degree that indicated they were at risk of or already had a substance use disorder, and 64 % were at very high risk. Further, nearly half (49 %) of participants reported binge or risky drinking (five or more drinks in a day at least monthly) and more than half (56 %) reported using other substances from two times per week to daily, during the year prior to incarceration. During early reentry, only 16 % of participants were at risk for a substance use disorder and only 7 % were at very high risk; 8 % reported engaging in risky drinking and 1 % reported using other substances twice per week to daily. Despite these reductions in use compared to pre-incarceration, 44 of participants still felt a need for substance use services during reentry. Participants from CBCFs had significantly higher (worse) scores on the alcohol and drug use screening tool than participants being released from prisons or jails.

Individuals reported encountering more barriers to receiving substance use services (average of 5.6 barriers) than mental health services (average of 4.54 barriers) during early reentry. The number of barriers to receiving substance use services was significantly higher for individuals released from jails (average of 9.55 barriers) compared to individuals released from prison (average of 2.94 barriers) or CBCFs (average of 3.65 barriers). Similarly, barriers to receiving mental health services differed significantly by type of facility, with individuals released from jails encountering the largest number of barriers on average: 8.81 for jails, 5.43 for prison, and 4.05 from CBCFs.

In summary, large percentages of individuals scheduled for release from prison, jails, and CBCFs expected to need substance use services, mental health services, or both. CBCFs were releasing individuals with the most serious substance use problems and concomitant need for extended services. Jails were releasing individuals who subsequently encountered considerably more barriers to receiving either type of treatment. This seems to indicate that prisons and CBCFs make linkages to treatment in the community or better prepare individuals to make linkages on their own, relative to jails. And, developing ways of circumventing or eliminating the multiple barriers to service engagement might make a considerable difference in outcomes for these individuals and their families.

Implications for Practice, Policy, and Future Research

"Every individual sent to prison leaves behind a network of family relationships" (Travis 2005, p. 119). Of great concern is how policy and systems of care might work together to ensure that the family relationships to which they return are as mutually supportive as possible. Not only do we hope to see families serve as natural support systems during reentry following incarceration (Travis and Waul 2003), we also hope to see families being well-supported during reintegration for their own sake.

Fostering positive family experiences during reentry begins during incarceration. The literature is mixed concerning the effects of family visits on inmates' disciplinary behavior during incarceration: Various studies have reported less, more, or no difference in inmate infractions as a function of visits from family members (Casey-Acevedo et al. 2004). There is little doubt that visitation during incarceration can have a positive impact on post-release outcomes for inmates and their families. A variety of contact-visitation models have been successfully pilot-tested in different types of institutional settings (Tebo 2006), but too few implementation studies have been conducted to conclude that translating these models "to scale" in widespread adoption can succeed and be sustained. Another visitation enhancement approach also warrants closer attention: visit coaching (Beyer et al. 2010). Through visit coaching, inmates can be helped to understand and prepare for the behavior of their family members during visits, cope with their own feelings, and adjust their own behaviors as a means of making the visits that do occur as productive as possible.

Significant dilemmas are encountered by jail and prison administrators in creating a positive climate for visitation, however. The first and foremost priority of jail and prison administrators is to ensure the safety and security of inmates, staff, and visitors. In some cases, the necessary restrictions that make visitation less hospitable are in place for this primary purpose, not with the direct intent of interfering with visitation.

In addition, budgetary constraints at the institutional, community, and state levels are very real barriers. While more flexible and visitor-friendly procedures that decrease barriers to visitation may be considered, facilities too often lack the resources for staffing or otherwise accommodating these options (Clark 2001). Decreases in visitation opportunities are a direct result of increasing budgetary pressure on jails and prisons (Pierce 2015). Casey-Acevedo and Bakken (2002) concluded that states need to dedicate resources to support prison visitation because families do not have the means to visit with any regularity. However, such a conclusion erroneously presumes that resources for this purpose are available at the state level. Meaningful differences exist in the funding of jails compared to prisons, with jails typically funded at the city or county level and prisons funded at the state or federal level. As a result, locales with greater funding may have greater opportunity to support innovative jail visitation programs compared to what might be available in state prisons, which might be under-resourced; and, vice versa, prisons may be better funded than local or regional jails, allowing them to implement visitation programs that the local institutions cannot afford.

Second, issues of family reintegration following release from incarceration are, often by necessity, entwined with child welfare family reunification issues, at least where the well-being of minor children is involved. Child welfare systems suffer from many of the same budgetary constraints impinging on the criminal justice system, often lacking the ability for case workers or foster families to accompany children to facilities for parent-child visitation to occur (Begun and Rose 2011). There are other ways in which reentry barriers might interface with the child welfare system: An inability to secure stable housing and employment, for example, may impede a parent's ability to regain custody of minor-aged children, thus potentially interfering with the children's ability to experience stable placement (Laughlin et al. 2008). These two interfacing systems, together with systems for addressing intimate partner violence, lack valid and reliable tools for definitively assessing when it is better to fight for disruption or for preservation of family bonds. Knowing this would help determine how to help families plan for and prepare for either reentry scenario: an individual's reintegration into the family system or becoming independent of the family system.

Third, multiple agencies, programs, and service delivery systems could be coordinated in efforts to support the reentry process with individuals and their families. For individuals, the integrative Assess, Plan, Identify, and Coordinate (APIC) model is one example of an approach detailing specific roles and responsibilities of the criminal justice and mental health/addiction treatment systems in assessing, planning for treatment, identifying community resources, and coordinating a transition plan for individuals with co-occurring mental health and substance use disorders as they return to the community (Osher et al. 2002). Several treatment models have been applied with success to treating these co-occurring disorders among individuals in the community; they have not been systematically applied during community reentry following incarceration, however (Peters et al. 2015). For families, interventions may be offered from the public, private, volunteer, and faith-based sectors; through children's, family, mental health, and criminal justice services; in schools, neighborhoods, religious centers; and, more (Toth and Kazura 2010). A model to consider serves families reintegrating a member after a period of military deployment (Saltzman et al. 2011).

In all of these scenarios, current funding models may pose certain barriers to integration. Expenditure of resources from one system of care may lead to significant savings overall, but the savings are often realized in another system. For example, a 1992 study in California demonstrated $1.5 billion in savings over an 18-month period attributed to substance abuse treatment, and estimated that for every treatment dollar spent, $7 were gained in terms of future savings (Harrison 2001). However, the treatment dollars spent came from one service delivery system, whereas the future savings were realized in the form of reduced crime and health care costs—not systems where the resources were initially expended.

Policy can both facilitate and impair the reentry reintegration process for individuals and families. Many policies serve to extend needed social, economic, housing, health care, and mental health services to individuals and families. For example, the 2008 Second Chance Act supported a variety of efforts to improve reentry outcomes at the state, local, tribal, and agency levels (Pogorzelski et al. 2005). On the other hand, policies may preclude individuals convicted of a drug-related felony offense from receiving assistance such as Temporary Aid to Needy Families (TANF), Supplemental Nutrition Assistance Program (SNAP/food stamps), federally subsidized housing, and higher education benefits (GAO 2005; McCarty et al. 2015). A double-bind is experienced by many individuals returning to the community following incarceration for a substance-related offense. They are often mandated to attend 12-step or other support-group sessions as a condition of community supervision or probation. These are not always accessible in every community, at times and locations that fit hourly work schedules, and all too often are accepted as a form of treatment in lieu of immediately available, evidence-based, addiction-specific, gender-appropriate, intensive treatment services of sufficient duration to adequately meet treatment needs (Freudenberg et al. 2008; Harrison 2001; Redko et al. 2006; Sung et al. 2011).

Two things currently lacking could help improve the reach and impact of family reintegration programs: (1) greater awareness and utilization of evidence-supported models and (2) greater coordination of the programs and services available to these families. In addition, locating programs within destigmatized contexts could increase willingness among families who might benefit from these programs to actually utilize them; integrating them into community-based family resource centers, for example (Toth and Kazura 2010).

Finally, there are important implications for future research and scholarship related to family systems and reentry processes for individual family members. First, little is known about how the experience might differ for families at different points in the family life cycle. Incarceration and community reentry may intersect with other significant family transitions. This concordance, while amplifying adaptive stress demands on the family system, also offers opportunities for intervening to shape the family development outcomes. Second, it is difficult to identify and locate the body of knowledge that has been produced concerning efficacy of various approaches to enhancing the family visitation experience, capitalizing on its potential and minimizing its risks. A systematic review of this literature would be helpful, as would ensuring that studies evaluating these approaches be conducted with strong methodologies. Third, criminal justice and mental/behavioral health practitioners would be greatly assisted by the development of psychometrically tested assessment tools with greater predictive reliability than currently exist. These assessment tools are needed to inform decisions regarding the development of appropriate visitation plans during the period of incarceration, as well as decisions concerning options for housing, physical health, mental health, and addiction services for reintegrating individuals and their families. Finally, implementation science has much to offer in terms of helping to move effective family reintegration strategies into the "best-practices" spotlight. This, in turn, can inform efforts to change policy and practices that might improve family reintegration experiences and individuals' reentry outcomes.

References

American Correctional Association (ACA). (2012). Key elements of the Affordable Care Act: Interface with correctional settings and inmate health care. Coalition of Correctional Health Authorities monograph, *1*(1), 1–12.

Arrigo, B. A., & Takahashi, Y. (2007). Theorizing community reentry for male incarcerates and confined mothers: Lessons learned from housing the homeless. *Journal of Offender Rehabilitation, 46*(1/2), 133–162.

Baillargeon, J., Hoge, S., Penn, J. V. (2010). Addressing the challenge of community reentry among released inmates with serious mental illness. *American Journal of Community Psychology, 46*(3/4), 361–375.

Bales, W. D., & Mears, D. P. (2008). Inmate social ties and the transition to society: Does visitation reduce recidivism? *Journal of Research in Crime and Delinquency, 45*(3), 287–321.

Bedard, K., & Helland, E. (2004). The location of women's prisons and the deterrence effect of "harder" time. *International Review of Law and Economics, 24*(2), 147–167. doi:10.1016/j.irle.2004.08.002

Begun, A. L., Early, T. J., Hodge, A. (2016). Mental health and substance abuse service engagement by men and women during community reentry following incarceration. *Administration and Policy in Mental Health and Mental Health Services Research, 43*(2), 207–218. doi:10.1007/s10488-015-0632-2

Begun, A. L., & Rose, S. J. (2011). Programs for children of parents incarcerated for substance-related problems. In S. L. A. Straussner & C. H. Fewell (Eds.), Children of substance-abusing parents: Dynamics and treatment (pp. 243–267). New York, NY: Springer.

Begun, A. L., Rose, S. J., LeBel, T. (2010). How jail partnerships can help women address substance abuse problems in preparing for community reentry. In S. Stojkovic (Ed.), *Managing special populations in jails and prisons, Vol. II* (pp. 1–23). Kingston, NJ: Civic Research Institute, Inc.

Begun, A. L., Rose, S. J., LeBel, T. (2011). Intervening with women in jail around alcohol and substance abuse during preparation for community reentry. *Alcohol Treatment Quarterly, 29*(4), 453–478.

Belenko, S. (2006). Assessing released inmates for substance-abuse-related service needs. *Crime & Delinquency, 52*(1), 94–113. doi:10.1177/0011128705281755

Benson, P. R. (1994). Deinstitutionalization and family caretaking of the seriously mentally ill: The policy context. *International Journal of Law and Psychiatry, 17*(2), 119–138.

Beyer, M., Blumenthal-Guigui, R., Krupat, T. (2010). Strengthening parent-child relationships: Visit coaching with children and their incarcerated parents. In Y. Harris, J. A. Graham, G. J. Oliver Carpenter (Eds.), *Children of incarcerated parents: Theoretical, developmental, and clinical issues* (pp. 187–214). New York, NY: Springer.

Blitz, C. L., Wolff, N., Ko-Yu, P., Pogorzelski, W. (2005). Gender-specific behavioral health and community release patterns among New Jersey prison inmates: Implications for treatment and community reentry. *American Journal of Public Health, 95*(10), 1741–1746. doi:10.2105/AJPH.2004.059733

Bowen, M. (1974). Alcoholism as viewed through family systems theory and family psychotherapy. *Annals of the New York Academy of Sciences, 233*(1), 115–122.

Braman, D., & Wood, J. (2003). From one generation to the next: How criminal sanctions are reshaping family life in urban America. In J. Travis & M. Waul (Eds.), *Prisoners once removed: The impact of incarceration and reentry on children, families, and communities* (pp. 157–188). Washington, DC: The Urban Institute Press.

Bronfenbrenner, U. (1979). *The ecology of human development.* Cambridge, MA: Harvard University Press.

Bronfenbrenner, U. (1989). Ecological systems theory. *Annals of child development, 6,* 187–249.

Carson, E. A., & Golinelli, D. (2013, revised 2014). *Prisoners in 2012: Trends in admissions and releases, 1991–2012.* Washington, DC: Department of Justice. http://www.bjs.gov/content/pub/pdf/p12tar9112.pdf

Casey-Acevedo, K., & Bakken, T. (2002). Visiting women in prison: Who visits and who cares? *Journal of Offender Rehabilitation, 34(3),* 67–83.

Casey-Acevedo, K., Bakken, T., Karle, A. (2004). Children visiting mothers in prison: The effects on mothers' behavior and disciplinary adjustment. *The Australian and New Zealand Journal of Criminology, 37*(1), 418–430.

Christian, J. (2005). Riding the bus. *Journal of Contemporary Criminal Justice, 21*(1), 31–48. doi:10.1177/1043986204271618

Christian, J., Mellow, J., Thomas, S. (2006). Social and economic implications of family connections to prisoners. *Journal of Criminal Justice, 34*(4), 443–452. doi:10.1016/j.jcrimjus.2006.05.010

Clark, T. A. (2001). The relationship between inmate visitation and behavior: Implications for African American families. *Journal of African American Men, 6*(1), 43–58.

Cobb, S. (1976). Social support as a moderator of life stress. *Psychosomatic Medicine, 38*(5), 300–314.

Cochran, J. C. (2014). Breaches in the wall: Imprisonment, social support, and recidivism. *Journal of Research in Crime and Delinquency, 51*(2), 200–229.

Cochran, J. C., Mears, D. P., Bales, W. D. (2014). Who gets visited in prison? Individual- and community-level disparities in inmate visitation experiences. *Crime & Delinquency,* 1–24. doi:10.1177/011128714542503

Cochran, J. C., Mears, D. P., Bales, W. D., & Stewart, E. A. (2016). Who gets visited in prison? Individual-and community-level disparities in inmate visitation experiences. *Journal of Research in Crime and Delinquency, 53*(2), 220–254.

Cuellar, A. E., & Cheema, J. (2012). As roughly 700,000 prisoners are released annually, about half will gain health coverage and care under federal laws. *Health Affairs, 31*(5), 931–938.

Damron, N. (2014). *Life beyond bars: Children with an incarcerated parent* (Fact sheet #7 from the University of Wisconsin Institute for Research on Poverty). http://nrccfi.camden.rutgers.edu/files/Factsheet7-Incarceration.pdf

De Claire, K., & Dixon, L. (2015). The effects of prison visits from family members on prisoners' well-being, prison rule breaking, and recidivism: A review of research since 1991. *Trauma, Violence, & Abuse*, 1–15. http://www.bjs.gov/content/pub/pdf/iptc.pdf

Draine, J., & Herman, D. B. (2007). Critical time intervention for reentry from prison for persons with mental illness. *Psychiatric Services, 58*(12), 1577–1581.

Draine, J., & Munoz-Laboy, M. (2014). Commentary. Not just variance in estimates: Deinstitutionalization of the justice system. *Psychiatric Services, 65*, 873.

Dyer, W. J., Pleck, J. H., McBride, B. A. (2012). Imprisoned fathers and their family relationships: A 40-year review from a multi-theory view. *Journal of Family Theory & Review, 4*(1), 20–47.

Eddy, J. M., & Reid, J. B. (2003). The adolescent children of incarcerated parents: A developmental perspective. In J. Travis & M. Waul (Eds.), *Prisoners once removed: The impact of incarceration and reentry on children, families and communities* (pp. 233–258). Washington, DC: The Urban Institute Press.

Fishman, L. T. (1990). *Women at the wall: A study of prisoners' wives doing time on the outside.* Albany, NY: State University of New York (SUNY) Press.

Freudenberg, N. (2001). Jails, prisons, and the health of urban populations: A review of the impact of the correctional system on community health. *Journal of Urban Health, 78*(2), 214–235. doi: 10.1093/jurban/78.2.214

Fontaine, J., Gilchrist-Scott, D., Roman, J., Taxy, S., Roman, C. (2012). Supportive housing for returning prisoners: Outcomes and impacts of the returning home—Ohio pilot project. Urban Institute Justice Policy Center. http://www.urban.org/UploadedPDF/412632-Supportive-Housing-for-Returning-Prisoners.pdf. Accessed 9 November 2013.

Freudenberg, N., Daniels, J., Crum, M., Perkins, T., Richie, B. E. (2008). Coming home from jail: The social and health consequences of community reentry for women, male adolescents, and their families and communities. *American Journal of Public Health, 98*, S191–S202. doi:10.2105/AJPH.2004.056325

Fuller, L. G. (1993). Visitors to women's prisons in California: An exploratory study. *Federal Probation, 57*(4), 41–47.

Gabel, K., & Johnston, D. (Eds.). (1995). *Children of incarcerated parents.* New York, NY: Lexington Books.

Gallagher, S. K., & Mechanic, D. (1996). Living with the mentally ill: Effects on the health and functioning of other household members. *Social Science & Medicine, 42*(12), 1691–1701.

Geller, A., & Curtis, M. A. (2011). A sort of homecoming: Incarceration and the housing security of urban men. *Social Science Research, 40*(4), 1196–1213. doi:10.1016/j.ssresearch.2011.03.008

Government Accountability Office, United States (GAO). (2005). Drug offenders: Various factors may limit the impacts of federal laws that provide for denial of selected benefits. http://www.gao.gov/new.items/d05238.pdf

Glaze, L. E., & Maruschak, L. M. (2008, revised 2010). Parents in prison and their minor children. Bureau of Justice Statistics Special Report. http://www.bjs.gov/content/pub/pdf/pptmc.pdf

Goldman, H. H. (1982). Mental illness and family burden: A public health perspective. *Hospital and Community Psychiatry, 33*(7), 557–560.

Goldstein, E. H., Warner-Robbins, C., McClean, C., Macatula, L., Conklin, R. (2009). A peer-driven mentoring case management community reentry model: An application for jails and prisons. *Family & Community Health, 32*(4), 309–313

Gordon, J. (1999). Are conjugal and familial visitations effective rehabilitative concepts? Yes. *The Prison Journal, 79*(1), 119–124.

Gubman, G. D., & Tessler, R. C. (1987). The impact of mental illness on families: Concepts and priorities. *Journal of Family Issues, 8,* 226–245.

Hagan, J., & Coleman, J. P. (2001). Returning captives of the American war on drugs: Issues of community and family reentry. *Crime & Delinquency, 47*(3), 352–367.

Hairston, C. F., & Rollin, J. (2006). Prisoner reentry: Social capital and family connections. In R. Immarigeon (Ed.), *Women and girls in the criminal justice system: Policy issues and practice strategies* (pp. 1–6). Kingston, NJ: Civic Research Institute.

Hairston, C. F., Rollin, J., Jo, H. (2004). *Family connections during imprisonment and prisoners' community reentry.* Jane Addams Center for Social Policy and Research, Jane Addams College of Social Work, University of Illinois at Chicago. https://jacsw.uic.edu/research_public_service/files/familyconnections.pdf

Hammett, T. M., Roberts, C., Kennedy, S. (2001). Health-related issues in prisoner reentry. *Crime & Delinquency, 47*(3), 390–409.

Harding, D. J., Wyse, J. J. B., Dobson, C., Morenoff, J. D. (2014). Making ends meet after prison. *Journal of Policy Analysis and Management, 33*(2), 440–470.

Harrison, L. D. (2001). The revolving prison door for drug-involved offenders: Challenges and opportunities. *Crime & Delinquency, 47*(3), 462–485.

Hatcher, S. (2007). Transitional care for offenders with mental illness in jail: Mapping indicators of successful community reentry. *Best Practices in Mental Health, 3*(2), 38–51.

Hawkins, A., O'Keefe, A., & James, X. (2010). Health care access and utilization among ex-offenders in Baltimore: Implications for policy. *Journal of Healthcare for the Poor and Undeserved, 21*, 649–665.

Heinle, T. E. (2009). Guilty by association: What the decision in Boston Housing Authority v. Garcia means for the innocent family members of criminals living in public housing in Massachusetts. *New England Journal on Criminal and Civil Confinement, 35*(1), 213–242.

Hill, R. (1971). Modern systems theory and the family: A confrontation. *Social Science Information, 10*(5), 7–26. doi:10.1177/053901847101000501

Hipp, J. R., Jannetta, J., Shah, R., Turner, S. (2009). Parolees' physical closeness to health service providers: A study of California parolees. *Health & Place, 15*(3), 649–658.

Hohman, M. M., McGaffigan, R. P., Segars, L. (2000). Predictors of successful completion of a postincarceration drug treatment program. *Journal of Addictions & Offender Counseling, 21*(1), 12–22.

Hughes, T., & Wilson, D. J. (2002). *Reentry trends in the United States.* Washington, DC: Department of Justice, Bureau of Justice Statistics. http://bjs.ojp.usdoj.gov/content/pub/pdf/reentry.pdf

Jackson, P., Templer, D. I., Reimer, W., LeBaron, D. (1997). Correlates of visitation in a men's prison. *International Journal of Offender Therapy and Comparative Criminology, 41*(1), 79–85. doi:10.1177/0306624x9704100108

James, D. J., & Glaze, L. E. (2006). *Mental health problems of prison and jail inmates.* Washington, DC: U.S. Department of Justice, Bureau of Justice Statistics. http://bjs.gov/content/pub/pdf/mhppji.pdf

Johnson, E. I., & Easterling, B. (2012). Understanding unique effects of parental incarceration on children: Challenges, progress, and recommendations. *Journal of Marriage and Family, 74*(2), 342–356. doi:10.1111/j.1741-3737.2012.00957.x

Johnson, E. I., & Waldfogel, J. (2004). Children of incarcerated parents: Multiple risks and children's living arrangements. In M. Patillo, D. F. Weiman,

B. Western (Eds.), *Imprisoning America: The social effects of mass incarceration* (pp. 97–131). New York, NY: Russell Sage Foundation.

Johnston, D. (1995). Intervention. In K. Gabel & D. Johnston (Eds.), *Children of incarcerated parents* (pp. 199–236). San Francisco, CA: Jossey-Bass, Inc.

Johnston, D. (2001). *Jailed mothers.* Pasadena, CA: Pacific Oaks Center for Children of Incarcerated Parents.

Kaeble, D., Glaze, L., Tsoutis, A., Minton, T. (2015, revised 2016). Correctional populations in the United States, 2014. Bureau of Justice Statistics. http://www.bjs.gov/content/pub/pdf/cpus14.pdf

Kampfner, C. J. (1995). Post-traumatic stress reactions in children of imprisoned mothers. In K. Gabel & D. Johnston (Eds.), *Children of incarcerated parents* (pp. 89–102). San Francisco, CA: Jossey-Bass, Inc.

Kerr, S., & Lockshin, A. (2010). Legal standards for securing reentry services. In H. A. Dlugacz (Ed.), *Reentry planning for offenders with mental disorders: Policy and practice* (pp. 2–1 to 2–25). Kingston, NJ: Civic Research Institute, Inc.

Laughlin, J. S., Arrigo, B. A., Blevins, K. R., Coston, C. T. M. (2008). Incarcerated mothers and child visitation: A law, social science, and policy perspective. *Criminal Justice Policy Review, 19*(2), 215–238.

La Vigne, N. G., Naser, R. L., Brooks, L. E., Castro, J. L. (2005). Examining the effect of incarceration and in-prison family contact on prisoners' family relationships. *Journal of Contemporary Criminal Justice, 21*(4), 314–335.

Lawrence, A. (2013, January). *Shrinking prisons.* State Legislatures Magazine. http://www.ncsl.org/research/civil-and-criminal-justice/shrinking-prisons.aspx

Liu, J. (2004). Subcultural values, crime, and negative social capital for Chinese offenders. *International Criminal Justice Review, 14*, 49–68.

Lovell, D., Gagliardi, G. J., Peterson, P. D. (2002). Recidivism and use of services among persons with mental illness after release from prison. *Psychiatric Services, 53*(10), 1290–1296.

Lundgren, L. M., Curtis, M. A., Oettinger, C. (2010). Postincarceration policies for those with criminal drug convictions: A national policy review. *Families in Society, 91*(1), 31–38.

Lurigio, A. (2001). Effective services for parolees with mental illnesses. *Crime & Delinquency, 47*(3), 446–461.

MacDermid Wadsworth, S. M. (2013). Understanding and supporting the resilience of a new generation of combat-exposed military families and their children. *Clinical Child and Family Psychology Review, 16*(4), 415–420.

Marek, L. I., & D'Aniello, C. (2015). Reintegration stress and family mental health: Implications for therapists working with reintegrating military families. *Contemporary Family Therapy*, *36*(4), 443–451.

Marquart, J. W., Merianos, D. E., Cuvelier, S. J., Carroll, L. (1996). Thinking about the relationship between health dynamics in the free community and the prison. *Crime & Delinquency*, *42*(3), 331–360. doi:10.1177/0011128796042003001

Masten, A. S. (2011). Resilience in children threatened by extreme adversity: Framework for research, practice, and translational synergy. *Development and Psychopathology*, *23*(2), 493–506.

Mazza, C. (2006). Children of incarcerated parents. In N. K. Phillips & S. L. A. Straussner (Eds.), *Children in the urban environment: Linking social policy and clinical practice* (pp. 191–215). Springfield, IL: Charles C. Thomas, Publisher, Ltd.

McCarty, M., Falk, G., Aussenberg, R. A., Carpenter, D. H. (2015). Drug testing and crime-related restrictions in TANF, SNAP, and housing assistance. Washington, DC: Congressional Research Service. https://www.fas.org/sgp/crs/misc/R42394.pdf

McCubbin, H. I., Boss, P. G., Wilson, L. R., Lester, G. R. (1980). Developing family invulnerability to stress: Coping patterns and strategies wives employ. In J. Trost (Ed.), *The family in change* (pp. 1–27). (International Sociological Association, Committee on Family Research.) Västeras, Sweden: International Library.

McCubbin, H. I., & Patterson, J. M. (1983). The family stress process: The double ABCX model of adjustment and adaptation. *Marriage & Family Review*, *6*(1/2), 7–37. doi:10.1300/J002v06n01_02

Mears, D. P., & Cochran, J. C. (2012). U.S. Prisoner reentry health care policy in international perspective: Service gaps and the moral and public health implications. *Prison Journal*, *92*(2), 175–202. doi:10.1177/0032885512438845

Minnesota Department of Corrections (MN DOC). (2011). *The effects of prison visitation on offender recidivism*. St. Paul, MN: Minnesota Department of Corrections.

Minton, T. D. (2013). *Jail inmates at midyear 2012—Statistical tables* (NCJ241264). Washington, DC: U.S. Department of Justice, Bureau of Justice Statistics.

Minton, T. D., & Zeng, Z. (2015). *Jail inmates at midyear 2014*. Washington, DC: U.S. Department of Justice, Bureau of Justice Statistics. http://www.bjs.gov/content/pub/pdf/jim14.pdf

Mojtabi, R., Olfson, M., Sampson, N. A., Jin, R., Druss, B., Wang, P. S., et al. (2011). Barriers to mental health treatment: Results from the national comorbidity survey replication. *Psychological Medicine*, *41*(8), 1751–1761.

Minuchin, S. (1974). *Families and family therapy*. Cambridge, MA: Harvard University Press.

Mumola, C. J. (2000). *Incarcerated parents and their children*. Washington, DC: U.S. Department of Justice, Bureau of Justice Statistics. http://www.bjs.gov/content/pub/pdf/iptc.pdf

Murray, J., Bijleveld, C. C. J. H., Farrington, D. P., Loeber, R. (2014). *Effects of parental incarceration on children: Cross-national comparative studies*. Washington, DC: American Psychological Association.

Murray, J., & Farrington, D. P. (2005). Parental imprisonment: Effects on boys' antisocial behavior and delinquency through the life-course. *Journal of Child Psychology and Psychiatry*, *46*(12), 1269–1278.

Myers, B. J., Smarsh, T. M., Amlund-Hagen, K., Kennon, S. (1999). Children of incarcerated mothers. *Journal of Child and Family Studies*, *8*(1), 11–25.

Naudeau, S. (2010). Children of incarcerated parents: Developmental trajectories among school-age children. In Y. R. Harris, J. A. Graham, G. J. Oliver Carpenter (Eds.), *Children of incarcerated parents: Theoretical, developmental, and clinical issues* (pp. 47–71). New York, NY: Springer Publishing Co.

Nurse, A. M. (2004). Returning to strangers: Newly paroled young fathers and their children. In M. Patillo, D. F. Weiman, B. Western (Eds.), *Imprisoning America: The social effects of mass incarceration* (pp. 76–96). New York, NY: Russell Sage Foundation.

Osher, F., Steadman, H. J., Barr, H. (2002). *A best practice approach to community re-entry from jails for inmates with co-occurring disorders: The APIC model*. Delmar, NY: The National GAINS Center.

Osher, F., Steadman, H. J., Barr, H. (2003). A best practice approach to community re-entry from jails for inmates with co-occurring disorders: The APIC model. *Crime & Delinquency*, *49*(1), 79–96.

Parke, R. D., & Clarke-Stewart, K. A. (2003). The effects of parental incarceration on children: Perspectives, promises, and policies. In J. Travis & M. Waul (Eds.), *Prisoners once removed: The impact of incarceration and reentry on children, families, and communities* (pp. 189–232). Washington, DC: The Urban Institute Press.

Peters, R. H., Wexler, H. K., Lurigio, A. J. (2015). Co-occurring substance use and mental disorders in the criminal justice system: A new frontier of clinical practice and research (Editorial). *Psychiatric Rehabilitation Journal, 38*(1), 1–6.

Petersilia, J. (2009). *When prisoners come home: Parole and prisoner reentry.* New York, NY: Oxford University Press.

Petersilia, J., & Cullen, F. (2015). Liberal but not stupid: Meeting the promise of downsizing prisons. *Stanford Journal of Criminal Law and Policy, 2*(1), 1–43.

Pettus-Davis, C., & Epperson, M. W. (2015). *From mass incarceration to smart decarceration* (Grand Challenges for Social Work Initiative Working Paper No. 4). Cleveland, OH: American Academy of Social Work and Social Welfare. http://aaswsw.org/wp-content/uploads/2015/12/WP4-with-cover.pdf

Pierce, M. B. (2015). Male inmate perceptions of the visitation experience: Suggestions on how prisons can promote inmate-family relationships. *The Prison Journal, 95*(3), 370–396.

Poehlmann, J. (2005). Representations of attachment relationships in children of incarcerated mothers. *Child Development, 76*(3), 679–696.

Pogorzelski, W., Wolff, N., Pan, K., Blitz, C. L. (2005). Behavioral health problems, ex-offended reentry policies, and the "Second Chance Act". *American Journal of Public Health, 95*(10), 1718–1724. doi:10.2105/AJPH.2005.065805

Portes, A. (1998). Social capital: Its origins and applications in modern sociology. *Annual Review of Sociology, 24*(1), 1–24.

Prins, S. J. (2014). Prevalence of mental illnesses in US state prisons: A systematic review. *Psychiatric Services, 65*(7), 862–872.

Redko, C., Rapp, R. C., Carlson, R. G. (2006). Waiting time as a barrier to treatment entry: Perceptions of substance users. *Journal of Drug Issues, 36*(4), 831–852.

Richie, B. E. (2001). Challenges incarcerated women face as they return to their communities: Findings from life history interviews. *Crime & Delinquency, 47*(3), 368–389.

Richie, B. E., Freudenberg, N., Page, J. (2001). Reintegrating women leaving jail into urban communities: A description of a model program. *Journal of Urban Health: Bulletin of the New York Academy of Medicine, 78*(2), 290–303.

Roman, C. G., & Travis, J. (2004). Taking stock: Housing, homelessness, and prisoner reentry. Urban Institute. Retrieved 3/1/2017 from http://webarc hive.urban.org/publications/411096.html

Rose, S. J., & Meezan, W. (1996). Variations in perceptions of child neglect. *Child Welfare, 75*(2), 139–160.

Rothbaum, F., Rosen, K., Ujiie, T., Uchida, N. (2002). Family systems theory, attachment theory, and culture. *Family Process*, *41*(3), 328–350.

Rutter, M. (1985). Resilience in the face of adversity: Protective factors and resistance to psychiatric disorders. *The British Journal of Psychiatry*, *147*, 598–611.

Sabol, W. J., West, H. C., Cooper, M. (2009). *Prisoners in 2008* (NCJ 228417). Washington, DC: US Department of Justice, Bureau of Justice Statistics. http://bjs.ojp.usdoj.gov/index.cfm?ty=pbdetail%26;iid=1763

Saltzman, W. R., Lester, P., Beardslee, W. R., Layne, C. M., Woodward, K., Nash, W. P. (2011). Mechanisms of risk and resilience in military families: Theoretical and empirical basis of a family-focused resilience enhancement program. *Clinical Child & Family Psychology Review*, *14*(3), 213–230.

Schafer, N. E. (1994). Exploring the link between visits and parole success: A survey of prison visitors. *International Journal of Offender Therapy and Comparative Criminology*, *38*(1), 17–32.

Scharff Smith, P. (2014). *When the innocent are punished: The children of imprisoned parents*. New York, NY: Palgrave Macmillan.

Seredycz, M. A. (2010). *Offender drug abuse and recidivism: An access to recovery program*. El Paso, TX: LFP Scholarly Publishing LLC.

Sharp, S. F. (2003). Mothers in prison: Issues in parent-child contact. In R. Muraskin (Series Ed.), & S. F. Sharp (Vol. Ed.), *Prentice Hall's women in criminal justice series. The incarcerated woman: Rehabilitative programming in women's prisons* (pp. 151–166). Upper Saddle River, NJ: Prentice Hall.

Sherman, L. W., Smith, D. A., Schmidt, J. D., Rogan, D. P. (1992). Crime, punishment, and stake in conformity: Legal and informal control of domestic violence. *American Sociological Review*, *57*(5), 680–690.

Shichor, D., & Sechrest, D. K. (2002). Privatization and flexibility: Legal and practical aspects of interjurisdictional transfer of prisoners. *The Prison Journal*, *82*(3), 386–407. doi:10.1177/003288550208200305

Shonkoff, J. P., & Phillips, D. A. (Eds.) (2000). *From neurons to neighborhoods: The science of early childhood development*. Washington, DC: National Academy Press.

Smith, A., Krisman, K., Strozier, A. L., Marley, M. A. (2004). Breaking through the bars: Exploring the experiences of addicted incarcerated parents whose children are cared for by relatives. *Families in Society—The Journal of Contemporary Human Services*, *85*(2), 187–195.

Spohn, C. (2007). The deterrent effect of imprisonment and offenders' stakes in conformity. *Criminal Justice Policy Review*, *18*(1), 31–50. doi:10.1177/0887403406294945

Sung, H.-E., Mahoney, A. M., Mellow, J. (2011). Substance abuse treatment gap among adult parolees: Prevalence, correlates, and barriers. *Criminal Justice Review*, *36*(1), 40–57. doi:10.1177/ 0734016810389808

Taylor, C. J. (2016). The family's role in the reintegration of formerly incarcerated individuals: The direct effects of emotional support. The Prison Journal, 96(3), 331–354.

Tebo, M. F. (2006). A parent in prison: states slowly beginning to help inmates' children, and advocates say it's overdue. *American Bar Association Journal*, *92*(2), 12–13.

Teitelbaum, J. B., & Hoffman, L. G. (2013). Health reform and correctional health care: How the affordable care act can improve the health of ex-offenders and their communities. *Fordham Urban Law Journal*, *40*(4), 1323–1356.

Thompson, H. A. (2014, July 9). Dodging decarceration: The shell game of "getting smart" on crime. Huffington Post. http://www.huffingtonpost. com/heather-ann-thompson/dodging-decarceration-the_b_5485361.html

Thompson, E. H., & Doll, W. (1982). The burden of families coping with the mentally ill: An invisible crisis. *Family Relations*, *31*(3), 379–388.

Thompson, M., Reuland, M., Souweine, D. (2003). Criminal justice/mental health consensus: Improving responses to people with mental illness. *Crime & Delinquency*, 49(1),30–51

Toth, K., & Kazura, K. (2010). Building partnerships to strengthen families: Intervention programs and recommendations. In Y. Harris, J. A. Graham, G. J. Oliver Carpenter (Eds.), *Children of incarcerated parents: Theoretical, developmental, and clinical issues* (pp. 161–186). New York, NY: Springer.

Travis, J. (2004). Reentry and reintegration: New perspectives on the challenges of mass incarceration. In M. Patillo, D. F. Weiman, B. Western (Eds.), *Imprisoning America: The social effects of mass incarceration* (pp. 247–268). New York, NY: Russell Sage Foundation.

Travis, J. (2005). *But they all come back: Facing the challenges of prisoner reentry*. Washington, DC: The Urban Institute Press.

Travis, J., Solomon, A. L., Waul, M. (2001). *From prison to home: The dimensions and consequences of prisoner reentry*. Washington, DC: The Urban Institute Press.

Travis, J., & Waul, M. (Eds.) (2003). *Prisoners once removed: The impact of incarceration and reentry on children, families, and communities*. Washington, DC: The Urban Institute Press.

The Urban Institute (2002). *Public health dimensions of prisoner reentry: Addressing the health needs and risks of returning prisoners and their families* (pp. 1–21). Los Angeles, CA. National Reentry Roundtable.

van Olphen, J., Freudenberg, N., Fortin, P., Galea, S. (2006). Community reentry: Perceptions of people with substance use problems returning home from New York City jails. *Journal of Urban Health, 83*(3), 372–381. doi:10.1007/s11524-006-9047-4

Visher, C. A., La Vigne, N., Travis, J. (2004). *Returning home: Understanding the challenges of prisoner reentry. Maryland pilot study: Findings from Baltimore.* Washington, DC: The Urban League.

Visher, C. A., & Travis, J. (2003). Transitions from prison to community: Understanding individual pathways. *Annual Review of Sociology, 29*(1), 89–113.

Werner, E. E., & Smith, R.S. (1982). *Vulnerable but not invincible: A longitudinal study of resilient children and youth.* New York, NY: McGraw Hill.

West, H.C., Sabol, W.J., & Greenman, S.J. (2010). Prisoners in 2009. Bureau of Justice Statistics Bulletin, NCJ 231675. Retrieved from https://www.bjs.gov/content/pub/pdf/p09.pdf

Western, B., Lopoo, L. M., McLanahan, S. (2004). Incarceration and the bonds between parents in Fragile Families. In M. Patillo, D. F. Weiman, B. Western (Eds.), *Imprisoning America: The social effects of mass incarceration* (pp. 21–45). New York, NY: Russell Sage Foundation.

Wilson, A. B., & Draine, J. (2006). Collaborations between criminal justice and mental health systems for prisoner reentry. *Psychiatric Services, 57*(6), 875–878.

Wolff, N., & Draine, J. (2004). Dynamics of social capital of prisoners and community reentry: Ties that bind? *Journal of Correctional Health Care, 10*(3), 457–490. doi:10.1177/107834580301000310

Woods, L. N., Lanza, A. S., Dyson, W., Gordon, D. M. (2013). The role of prevention in promoting continuity of health care in prisoner reentry initiatives. *American Journal of Public Health, 103*(5), 830–838.

Wool, J., & Stemen, D. (2004). Issues in brief: Changing fortunes or changing attitudes? Sentencing and corrections reforms in 2003. *Federal Sentencing Reporter, 16,* 294–306. http://www.vera.org/pubs/changing-fortunes-or-changing-attitudes-sentencing-and-corrections-reforms-2003

Wright, J. P., Cullen, F. T., Miller, J. T. (2001). Family social capital and delinquent involvement. *Journal of Criminal Justice, 29*(1), 1–9. doi: 10.1016/s0047-2352(00)00071-4

Audrey L. Begun joined Ohio State University's College of Social Work as an associate professor in 2009 after 22 years at the University of Wisconsin-Milwaukee, Helen Bader School of Social Welfare and the Center for Applied Behavioral Health. She received her BS (1976), MSW (1978), and PhD (1987) from the University of Michigan. Dr. Begun's scholarship primarily addresses issues in the area of substance abuse and addictions. In addition to publishing multiple articles and book chapters, as well as presenting at professional conferences, Dr. Begun edited the National Institute of Alcohol Abuse and Alcoholism social work curriculum and coauthored the book *Conducting Substance Use Research*. She teaches an online course, the content of which is also available from iTunes University, Theories and Biological Basis of Addiction, and is present in ResearchGate.

Ashleigh I. Hodge has a BA in Sociology from the University of Michigan—Dearborn, and MSW from the Ohio State University, and is currently working toward a PhD in social work. Her interests are broadly captured under the umbrellas of criminal and juvenile justice-related issues, though more specifically, she is concerned about the role of trauma in offending behavior and trauma-informed care among service providers for people with offending histories. She is a student alumna of the "Inside-Out Prison Exchange Program," which sparked her passion for wanting to make a difference in the lives of individuals who find themselves part of the justice system.

Theresa June Early is an affiliate of the Center for Latin American Studies at the Ohio State University, a member of the 2102 Council on Social Work Education Research Delegation to Cuba. In 2011–12, she was a Fulbright-Garcia Robles research fellow at the National Autonomous University of Mexico in Mexico City. She has published more than two dozen articles and book chapters in social work and mental health journals. Her article on the strength perspective in social work practice and families, appearing in the journal *Social Work*, was the 27th most highly cited article in social work journals in the decade from 2000–2009. She has served as a consulting editor for *Social Work Research, Children & Schools, Journal of the Society for Social Work and Research,* and *Journal of Social Work Research and Evaluation: An International Publication.*

Root & Rebound: An Innovative Program Paints the Reentry Landscape

Leah A. Jacobs, Katherine Katcher,
Pascal Krummenacher, and Sonja Tonnesen

Prisoner reentry programs in the United States are in crisis. These programs, which aim to facilitate the successful reentry of formerly incarcerated individuals into society, experience an ever-expanding volume of people in reentry, facing extraordinary and seemingly insurmountable challenges in reintegration, and receiving an inadequate degree of state support to address their needs. The governmental response to prisoner reentry has largely been insufficient with respect to both scope and funding; the laissez-faire approach, which devolves responsibility to municipalities and nonprofit agencies and allocates a small proportion of criminal justice funds to reentry efforts, has not built a reentry infrastructure strong enough to facilitate the successful reentry of formerly incarcerated people.

L.A. Jacobs (✉)
School of Social Work, University of Pittsburgh, Pennsylvania, USA

K. Katcher · P. Krummenacher · S. Tonnesen
Root & Rebound, Oakland, USA

© The Author(s) 2017   **145**
S. Stojkovic (ed.), *Prisoner Reentry*,
DOI 10.1057/978-1-137-57929-4_4

While reentry programs across the country work diligently to provide services, their ability to meet the demand and complex needs of those reintegrating is greatly diminished by the discontinuous and impoverished nature of the reentry landscape.

This chapter illustrates the current crisis in prisoner reentry from the perspective of a reentry legal resource center, Root & Rebound, which serves people in reentry and their advocates throughout the state of California. Primarily comprised of attorneys and legal staff, Root & Rebound works through a model of public education to reduce the impact of collateral consequences and barriers to reentry on the lives of people who are justice involved, thereby increasing access to justice and opportunity. To lay the foundation for and contextualize the experiences of Root & Rebound, this chapter first briefly reviews some of the scholarly literature on prisoner reentry and prisoner reentry programs. The chapter then discusses Root & Rebound's accomplishments and challenges to date, as well as the perceived facilitators and barriers to the program's operations and mission. Because Root & Rebound is based in California, we discuss reentry within the context of this State. However, given California's history as a leader in correctional reform nationally and the national need for decarceration, the circumstances we describe likely transcend state borders (Petersilia 2008). Based on the extant literature and Root & Rebound's experience, we conclude that successful reentry is dependent on the degree to which individuals reentering society have access to resources and services that will address both socioeconomic and legal needs, reentry programming that is continuous and collaborative, and welfare state and penal policies that both increase access to basic resources and opportunities and decrease legal barriers to reentry.

Background

The increasing enactment and utilization of punitive penal policies from the 1970s to the 1990s contributing to hyperincarceration (commonly referred to as "mass incarceration") occurred during a period of significant economic and social instability in the United States (Garland 2001; Weaver 2007). Simultaneous to the enactment of these punitive policies, the welfare state entered a period of retrenchment (Pierson 1995). Thus, the period of hyperincarceration can be characterized as one during which punitive approaches to dealing with economic and social instability replaced Johnson-era welfare state and community economic development approaches, having particularly harmful repercussions for poor, urban communities of color (Wacquant 2001; Wacquant 2009).

In contrast to the expanding correctional population of the past 40 years, the nation's rate of incarceration dropped in 2011. The subsequent downward trend, in part, represents bipartisan recognition that punitive policies of hyperincarceration fail to enhance safety or social stability. While gradual recognition of the enormous failure of hyperincarceration is now leading to penal reform, the state's social welfare response remains stagnant. Ultimately, charged with addressing the socioeconomic, as well as legal, needs of the reentry population, reentry programs do so in the context of the social welfare void of the current political era. In the following section, we discuss the importance of and challenges to successful community reentry faced by individuals reentering, highlighting how both individual barriers to reentry and structural inadequacies of state responses determine the nature of reentry programming.

Prisoner Reentry: A Key Component of and Challenge to Decarceration

Front-end penal reform strategies, such as diversion and sentencing reform efforts, are necessary to reduce the number of individuals who enter correctional systems. Reversing hyperincarceration, however, also requires the successful reintegration of individuals incarcerated or recently released from incarceration. The current reality of reentry efforts, however, is bleak; more than 75 % of those released from prison return to custody within 5 years due to either a revocation or a new conviction (Durose et al. 2014). In California, over half of all inmates released from state prison will return to custody within 2 years (California Department of Corrections and Rehabilitation 2015). This failure rate is a barometer of both the degree to which reentering individuals face barriers to successful reentry, as well as the capacity of reentry services to assist members of the reentry population in overcoming these barriers.

The challenges experienced by individuals reentering communities from jail and prison, both socioeconomic and legal, are significant [see Pogrebin, West-Smith, Walker and Unnithan chapter in this volume for a full discussion]. An extensive body of research has identified several common socioeconomic barriers to reentry, including those related to housing instability [e.g., lack of access to affordable housing and housing discrimination (Petersilia 2003; Makarios et al. 2010)], unemployment [e.g., lack of education and skills, lack of experience, stigma and discrimination (Makarios et al. 2010; Petersilia 2003; Raphael 2011)], strained familial relationships (Berg and Huebner 2011), and substance misuse (Makarios et al. 2010; Petersilia 2003). Many of these socioeconomic barriers are echoed in self-reported accounts of reentering individuals, especially unmet needs related to housing, education, and social support (Morani et al. 2011; O'Brien 2001; O'Brien and Leem 2007; Parsons and Warner-Robbins 2002). Firsthand accounts also highlight difficulty desisting from illegal activity, meeting parole conditions, addressing health and mental health needs, and meeting basic needs (e.g., transportation, food, and clothing) as barriers to reentry (Morani et al. 2011; O'Brien and Leem 2007).

While less frequently addressed in social science literature, formerly incarcerated people also face significant legal barriers to reentry. These "collateral consequences" or "invisible punishments" are civil punishments enacted against reentering individuals post release (Pinard 2010; Travis 2005). Collateral consequences take two forms, including sanctions automatically triggered because of a crime committed and discretionary disqualifications that may be enacted by civil courts (State Council of State Governments, n.d.). These sanctions and disqualifications can greatly constrain opportunities available by barring reentering individuals from public benefits and housing, student loans, and licensure for certain areas of employment. They can also lead to deportation, loss of retirement pensions, voting disenfranchisement, and sex-offender registration.

Expanded under the War on Drugs and other law and order policies of the 1980s and 1990s, these invisible punishments have never before been as extensive and entrenched (Pinard 2010). The American Bar Association has determined that today in the United States, people with criminal convictions face 44,000 federal, state, and local restrictions because of their records (American Bar Association 2015). Yet, most reentry programs tend to be built on existing social service systems staffed by social workers, case managers, and mental health practitioners (not attorneys), and to focus on individual rehabilitative interventions (e.g., vocational training, behavioral health treatment, etc.), not legal education and advocacy tools. Thus, they are not necessarily based on the needs of the reentry population or able to adequately address collateral consequences.

Reducing Recidivism and Aiding Decarceration: Policies and Programs for Successful Reentry

Over the course of the past 20 years, prisoner reentry has risen to public and political awareness as a legitimate social problem warranting policy and programmatic intervention (Jonson and Cullen 2015). Federally, two major pieces of legislation have contributed to the proliferation of reentry interventions. The first of these policies, the Serious and Violent Offender Reentry Initiative of 2003, allocated $110 million dollars to 89 reentry programs across the country. More recently, the Second Chance Act (SCA) of 2007 has allocated over $475 million dollars since its inception. Dispersed to state, local, and tribal governments, as well as community-based agencies, these funds are intended to support training and programs that facilitate a safe reentry into communities for those returning from jail and prison. According to the Bureau of Justice Assistance (BJA), "SCA programming provides support to eligible applicants for the development and implementation of comprehensive and collaborative reentry strategies specifically designed to increase public safety by reducing recidivism" (BJA n.d., para. 1).

These policies represent an explicit interest in supporting reentry efforts at the federal level; however, concern regarding their adequacy and effectiveness is justified. The millions of dollars invested in these efforts may certainly sound substantial, but they fail to reach a majority of individuals reentering communities each year. As sociologist Loic Wacquant (2010) notes, the SCA's annual allocation of $165 million dollars comprises less than 1 % of the total correctional budget; if disseminated across each individual released from custody, this sum amounts to the cost of about one sandwich per person per week. In actuality, from the SCA's initiation in 2009 through March of 2015, funded programs have only served 113,328 individuals (BJA n.d., no page). Thus, only a small fraction of the approximately 630,000 individuals released annually benefit directly from the SCA (Carson 2015). In addition to such inadequacy in investment, the claims that funds are being used to support "comprehensive" or "collaborative" reentry services are equivocal. The SCA is structured such that individual organizations and locales must compete for funding. In turn, the SCA promotes a reentry landscape characterized more by cottage nonprofit organizations than a cooperative or organized network of services and resources.

Passing additional legislation, state governments have attempted to supplement decarceration and reentry efforts at the federal level. With the second largest correctional system in the country, California in particular is in significant need of effective decarceration strategies. In 2011, the Supreme Court mandated a population release due to the California Department of Corrections and Rehabilitation's (CDCR) violation of the 8th Amendment; the State's prison facilities were overcrowded to the degree that their conditions constituted cruel and unusual punishment (Rappaport and Dansky 2010). In response, the State enacted Assembly Bill 109: The Public Safety and Realignment Act (2011).

Touted as the "cornerstone of California's solution to reduce overcrowding, costs, and recidivism," the Public Safety and Realignment Act essentially devolves state responsibilities to counties (e.g., county probation departments are now responsible for supervising low-level felony offenders formerly overseen by state parole agencies, and low-level felony offenses are now punished via incarceration in county jails instead of state prisons). Administrators, activists, and scholars have raised a number of concerns regarding the intention and operationalization of the Act (ACLU

2012; Krisberg and Taylor-Nicholson 2011; Rubin 2015). Among these concerns is the variability in operationalization between counties. Given that each county was required to submit their own plan for enacting realignment, some counties could initiate reforms focused on programs and services, while other counties could instead focus on surveillance and custody approaches (Turner et al. 2015). In an evaluation of a sample of 12 counties, Turner et al. (2015) find more than 90 % have increased their jail capacity as a result of Realignment. Of those counties investing in programs and services, there is significant variation in the services and programs supported through Realignment. While the State has attempted to promote some coordination within counties through the mandating of Community Corrections Partnerships, these bodies are largely impotent, lacking fiscal resources and legislative authority, and failing to create collaboration or continuity across California's counties. Thus, like the SCA, state funds have largely promoted the continuation of a disparate, fragmented, and equivocally adequate reentry approach for California.

Reentry Programs and Services

While federal and state policies have promoted the proliferation of reentry programs over the course of the past decade, this expansion has not resulted in the development of a cohesive reentry approach or a clear vision of best practice. No single definition of a "reentry program" exists and those that self-identify as such vary with respect to their location, population served, and services provided. Reentry programs can be prison-, parole-, or community-based. Alternatively, they can span these physical domains. Some programs focus on prerelease inmates, while others focus on individuals post release. They may also further narrow their focus to certain groups of reentering individuals based on need, risk, or demographics. The reentry terrain is also characterized by an array of practice scopes, including programs focused on reentry planning, education and employment, substance abuse and mental health treatment, surveillance (e.g., parole and probation), and wraparound comprehensive approaches (e.g., case management, reentry courts). For example, under California's Realignment policy, counties report utilizing programs that range in focus from education (often GED (General Educational Development) test prep), to employment (often skills training), substance abuse services and mental health treatment (often group counseling and cognitive behavioral), reentry units, and day reporting centers (Turner et al. 2015). Some of these approaches are utilized inside county jails or probation departments, while most are subcontracted to community-based providers.

The plurality of approaches to reentry services is accompanied by a lack of clarity surrounding effective practice (Wilson and Davis 2006). The variation in organization, target population, and services of reentry programs, coupled with the dearth of rigorous and comparative evaluations, makes it difficult to make overarching claims regarding the effectiveness of reentry models [see Ndrecka et al. 2016, as well as reviews by Seiter and Kadela (2003), Petersilia (2004), and Raphael (2011)]. In the case of California, while Realignment promotes the utilization of reentry programming, it fails to require any systematic evaluation of these services. Despite the challenges to and state disinterest in evaluating reentry programs, scholarly studies suggest several key components to successful reentry programs. Elements of successful reentry programs include their ability to intervene at the time of or shortly after release (Mellow and Christian 2008; Wilson and Davis 2006), the ease with which they can be navigated (Radice 2012), and the ability to meet participants' self-perceived needs (Morani et al. 2011; Mellow and Christian 2008; Zhang et al. 2006; Wilson and Davis 2006). In addition, who administers programming can impact effectiveness. For example, the goals of some services may conflict with parole and probation's surveillance and penal goals and potentially enhance the reluctance of individuals to seek or participate in such programs (Radice 2012).

From federal and state policies to local initiatives and programs, a stated commitment to addressing hyperincarceration and facilitating reentry exists. The way in which these policies are operationalized and programs function, however, often seems to undermine the very goals they seek to achieve. The contemporary crisis in community reentry is characterized by three deficits. First, the current level of investment in reentry programs cannot possibly meet the needs of the nearly 640,000 individuals reentering communities annually. As states, such as California, attempt to roll back the punitive approaches leading to hyperincarceration and larger numbers of individuals exit correctional facilities each year, this inadequacy will only deepen in the absence of increased investment. Second, federal and state policies alike promote piecemeal, fragmented approaches to reentry; utilizing competitive funding mechanisms and devolving responsibility from federal and state justice systems, collaboration is both disincentivized and hindered. Such fragmentation also impairs cross-county, state, or national evaluations, ultimately weakening our ability to develop shared knowledge of "what works" in facilitating successful reentry. Third, efforts to invest in reentry services have predominately expanded the provision of services through existing models and social service organizations. Utilizing the existing service infrastructure likely has several practical benefits. However, it does not necessarily indicate these services are most effective nor does it make space for less common, but not necessarily less essential, approaches. This is especially problematic given the lack of effort to address structural barriers, such as collateral consequences or lack of employment opportunities, to successful reentry. In sum, the existing lack of investment, poor continuity, and limited focus of existing approaches fail to comprise a reentry infrastructure that would adequately and systematically address socioeconomic and legal barriers to reentry.

In the following section, we describe a case example of a reentry program, Root & Rebound, which attempts to help formerly incarcerated individuals overcome these challenges, as well as to address the systemic barriers to developing a more comprehensive and effective reentry infrastructure. Following an introduction to the program's history, approach, successes, and challenges, we discuss the facilitators and barriers to successful reentry service delivery from the perspective of Root & Rebound's staff. Among these facilitators, we highlight the importance of collaboration, listening to and forefronting the perspectives of people in reentry, utilizing technology and media, and garnering public and political support. Among these barriers, we highlight the way in which gaps and redundancies in reentry infrastructure coupled with the continued divestment and fragmentation of social welfare systems impairs delivery of effective reentry services.

Root & Rebound: The Program

Root & Rebound is a reentry legal resource center, a prisoner reentry program that combines direct services, education, and policy advocacy to achieve its mission: to increase access to justice and opportunity for people in reentry from prison and jail, and to educate and empower those who support them, fundamentally advancing and strengthening the reentry infrastructure across the State of California. Founded by an attorney and working through the lens of legal advocacy and education, the organization looks systemically to understand key legal barriers to successful community reintegration, and works to provide people in reentry and those who interface with them (case managers, advocates, family members) with the information and tools to successfully advocate and navigate through these issues.

The program has its genesis in UC Berkeley's Boalt Hall Law School, where, from 2010 to 2013, student Katherine Katcher worked on criminal justice issues and prisoner rights issues, confronting the deplorable conditions men and women face throughout the criminal justice system. Speaking to clients who were anticipating the immense challenges of release, Katcher was shocked to learn of how few resources clients were given, how little reentry coordination was happening statewide, and how dire were the needs of the reentry population. She also saw a gap—no legal reentry resource organization working in states across the country providing education, information, and assistance on these issues.

After developing the idea for a legal organization dedicated to helping individuals in reentry in California and across the United States, Katcher enlisted the help of her colleague, Sonja Tonnesen, to help with the formation and development of the organization. In Fall of 2013, the nascent organization began a 4-month needs assessment and design phase. To better understand the gaps, needs, and existing best practices in reentry, the two-person team interviewed over 70 people in the field of reentry, including attorneys, social workers, formerly incarcerated advocates, educators, and academics (Katcher and Tonnesen 2014). Echoing and expanding the aforementioned literature on prisoner reentry needs, the assessment identified several limitations of the existing reentry infrastructure. Most notably, participants indicated difficulty in:

- connecting with service providers before release;
- having a sense of what to expect in the reentry process and how to prepare for success;
- having a consistent and stable support team throughout the continuum of reentry;
- advocating to be paroled to the appropriate county where they had access to programs, services, and social support;
- securing basic necessities like clothing, cell phones, transit, and livable income;
- finding safe and affordable housing;
- acquiring and maintaining gainful employment;
- accessing federal, state, and local public benefits (e.g., food stamps and social security income);
- family reunification support, including family law and dependency law services;
- finding affordable medical care, substance abuse treatment, and mental health facilities;
- understanding financial obligations and the impact they can have on civic life.

The needs assessment also illuminated several institutional barriers to reentry. These barriers largely centered on a lack of continuity and decentralization in services and resources. Findings indicated that current programs did not adequately bridge the divide between life in custody and life in reentry. Findings also indicated that an established reentry infrastructure existed, but it was highly decentralized; California's reentry landscape in 2013 was a quagmire of friends, family, social service agencies, housing facilities, legal advocacy groups, education programs, substance abuse facilities, corrections departments, and government agencies. All acted separately and with specialized knowledge, but without the resources or ability to connect their programs and services. Services were further fragmented because of California's Realignment policy, which siloed funding by distributing criminal justice money to individual counties and only for certain populations (e.g., low-level offenders who were now under county supervision) and not for others, like elderly prisoners who were coming out under state parole supervision.

After completing the needs assessment, Root & Rebound initiated a pilot phase and began working directly with people in reentry on their legal cases. Although they now better understood the gaps and needs faced by persons in reentry and the systemic issues that exacerbate those problems, staff had discovered there were very little data available on universal best practices in reentry, particularly when it came to understanding legal reentry service models and how and where attorneys could be most effective in this work. No model had been discovered that went beyond a direct service traditional legal aid approach, and questions still remained about how and whether a broader solution could be brought to fruition that would remain effective in meeting people's self-perceived needs and resolving legal issues. To dig more deeply into the issues and work to find a broad solution, Root & Rebound spent its first year of operation providing direct client services and taking on cases, seeing over 185 clients on a range of legal reentry issues, through full representation or brief advocacy. Client cases included issues of parole transfer and termination, family law issues, and employment questions.

Through the process of working directly with clients, it became readily apparent that people in reentry faced thousands of barriers across all areas of life; complex legal issues and questions would likely follow most of them for the remainder of their lives, as they navigated acquiring employment, housing, financial stability, education, and the like. Yet, information on the law, where to get relief, and how to navigate government agencies and systems was opaque and would be impossible to decipher without legal advocates conducting detailed research. Root & Rebound realized it would be impossible for clients and the agencies, family, friends, and advocates who worked to support them to navigate these issues. At the same time, Root & Rebound saw the 1:1 direct service model as extremely limiting. With approximately 100,000 people released from adult institutions in California each year (CDCR 2015) and hundreds of thousands more preparing for parole board hearings and release, the need to create a broad solution was pressing. An alternative model was necessary, one which would allow Root & Rebound to become a resource that could serve the needs of hundreds of thousands of people grappling with reentry issues across the state who would never be able to make it to a local office for support.

Upon the suggestion of an advisor, the team began documenting all of the issues and the legal research that came out of its cases, with the initial goal of capturing the information internally and possibly writing a guide on one or two areas of law that seemed most pressing. Instead, it became readily apparent that, if Root & Rebound chose to focus exclusively on housing law, readers would be unable to apply for housing if they did not know how to get a state ID or had unpaid traffic tickets that would prevent them from obtaining a state ID. If Root & Rebound focused on employment, people would also need information on when in the reentry process they could clear their criminal record. If Root & Rebound covered education law for people in reentry, this information might be moot if potential students did not know how to apply for benefits to sustain their studies or about the potential for occupational licensing bans in their field of choice. In sum, to fully solve the information gap, the guide would need to be holistic, comprehensive, and focus broadly across areas of need. A narrow focus would fail to meet the array of needs faced by reentering individuals and only contribute to an already fragmented reentry landscape. Yet, because such a broad and comprehensive resource had never been published for the reentry population, there was great doubt from many advisors: How would the guide stay updated? Would people in prison actually spend time reading such information? Didn't people need lawyers to walk them through these issues in person?

After 14 months of research and writing by a team of 4 staff, 10 interns, and countless volunteers, Root & Rebound published the *Roadmap to Reentry: A California Legal Guide* (2015). Available in print and online, the guide is an easy-to-use navigation tool covering the major barriers in reentry. The guide caters to a broad audience, including people preparing for reentry as well as their families, social workers and case managers, teachers, community supervision officers, and attorneys. It is comprehensive in scope, with the following nine chapters spanning law and civic life: housing, public benefits, parole and probation, education, understanding and cleaning up your criminal record; ID and voting, family and children, court-ordered debt, and employment. Each chapter is divided by topic and further subdivided in a question-and-answer format. The answers are written in an easily accessible and simple language, making use of charts and visual explanations. In order not to overwhelm readers, answers that involve complicated procedures or lengthy legal explanations are contained in chapter appendices. The challenge after creating such a comprehensive and holistic resource was outreach, making sure that the information and resources it contained actually reached people on the ground who need it most.

Root & Rebound's Model

Today, Root & Rebound's model is built around the *Roadmap to Reentry* and the idea that through the democratization of information and knowledge, legal advocates can empower people in reentry and those who support them to successfully navigate the challenges ahead. Root & Rebound's model includes (a) public education through dissemination of the guide, development of toolkits, and legal trainings; (b) hotline and letter writing assistance; and (c) system reform advocacy.

To bring the *Roadmap to Reentry* information to more communities, Root & Rebound provides community-based, prison- and jail-based, and web-based trainings on how to navigate and successfully overcome reentry barriers. Individual trainings are tailored to meet the specific needs of participating groups and individuals, including currently and formerly incarcerated people, their families, and the professional agencies that support them. The trainings familiarize participants with the guide and deepen participant knowledge of the content covered through exercises and discussion, with the goal of empowering participants to more successfully navigate these issues on their own. Trainings typically focus on two to three sections for half days or cover the entire guide during one full day.

Root & Rebound supplements its public education program with direct assistance through prison mail writing and a weekly legal reentry hotline. The mail writing and legal reentry hotline programs are free resources staffed by attorneys and law student volunteers, who provide case-specific support to the large number of individuals contacting the organization with specific legal issues. Dozens of individuals send letters to Root & Rebound every week with legal questions and referral requests, many of whom have previously attended trainings or received the *Roadmap to Reentry Legal Guide*. Root & Rebound's staff and volunteers individually answer each letter with detailed responses and refer individuals to other resources and service providers if requests fall outside of Root & Rebound's purview. The hotline, which runs all day once a week, allows callers to ask case-specific questions. Using the *Roadmap to Reentry* guide as the frontline tool, Root & Rebound's legal staff answer reentry-related questions; help solve issues; and provide critical resources, information, and referrals. Due to the vast and complicated nature of reentry-related issues, staff sometimes have to research more complex questions or those presenting new issues and write back to callers with further information post call.

While the majority of Root & Rebound's resources are devoted to its programmatic public education work, the organization also engages in systems reform work by documenting its experience on the ground and feeding this information to other stakeholders in the reentry field, including government, policy organizations, and litigation firms. It is Root & Rebound's belief that this feedback loop galvanizes policy-makers into pushing positive and necessary reform. The data collected through public education and hotline support services speak power-fully to stakeholders, ensuring that reforms are grounded in true needs. Additionally, Root & Rebound regularly develops and pub-lishes reports on major issues in an effort to educate reentry stake-holders (see, e.g., Katcher and Tonnesen 2014; Katcher and Tonnesen forthcoming).

As Root & Rebound becomes more established, other organizations regularly contact Root & Rebound to collaborate on projects. These collaborations have become a key component to Root & Rebound's model, and include relationships with governmental (e.g., Los Angeles Mayor's Office of Reentry), faith-based (e.g., Prison Fellowship, which provides trainings and Christian faith-based programming to people inside and outside of prison), and other nonprofit (e.g., Project Rebound, which assists formerly incarcerated individuals in pursuing higher education) organizations and coalitions. As discussed in the ensuing pages, such collaborations are critical to efficiently disseminating knowledge, building an infrastructure that holistically addresses the needs of reentering individuals, and reforming the criminal justice system.

Root & Rebound's Current Size and Scope

Since launching the *Roadmap to Reentry* guide in May 2015, Root & Rebound has refined the model described earlier. The team now has six full-time employees, and a large team of interns, fellows, and volunteers. Root & Rebound's budget has also grown, with a 40 % increase between 2014 and 2015. This financial growth has allowed Root & Rebound to significantly expand operations, while retaining strong leadership.

The education branch of the Root & Rebound model, the crux of its work, has grown most starkly. The guide has gained a wide readership. To date, over 6,000 people have read *Roadmap To Reentry* online (approximately 600 new online readers a month) and over 2,835 hard copies have been distributed to 56 of the 58 counties across California. The vast majority of these guides were sent to people currently incarcerated and preparing for release inside state prisons, jails, and federal prisons. Of the 2,835 people who received hard-copy guides in 2015, 90 % were directly impacted by the criminal justice system, including formerly incarcerated individuals, currently incarcerated individuals, and family members; 1 % worked in community supervision; and 9 % were advocates from the nonprofit/education sector, legal aid organizations, government social service providers, and clergy. Additionally, all 125 CDCR facilities now have copies of the guide in their law library. As of March of 2016, there were over 3,150 people currently on the wait list for the guide, scheduled to be republished in April of 2016.

Trainings on the guide have had a far reach. By the end of 2015, in over 22 trainings in 15 counties across California, 640 individuals representing 250 organizations were trained in *Roadmap to Reentry*. Of those trained in 2015, 21 % were directly impacted by the criminal justice system, including formerly incarcerated individuals, currently incarcerated individuals, and family members, 20 % worked in community supervision, 21 % worked in the nonprofit/education sector, 14 % were legal advocates, 17 % were government social service providers, 3 % were clergy, and 4 % identified as other. In all, these trainings had an estimated ripple effect of 20,000 people.

In 2015, Root & Rebound also built and strengthened relationships with local and regional partners, facilitating trainings across diverse audiences. Among the most notable trainings were a full-day training with 100 men inside Soledad State Prison, a general training for 75 community-based practitioners from across the reentry landscape in Los Angeles County, a family law training in our Oakland office for community-based practitioners and loved ones, and tailored trainings for supervision departments in the cities of Fresno and Sacramento, including parole offices within the Division of Adult Parole Operations and probations departments across the state in collaboration with the Chief Probation Officers of California.

As of March 2016, Root & Rebound has over 70 training requests from a wide range of organizations across California. The organization prioritizes outreach to remote and underserved areas. For example, Root & Rebound is currently working with Abby Abinanti, Chief Justice of the Yurok Tribe and Root & Rebound board member, and other tribal leaders to create and implement a plan to provide legal reentry support for tribal communities by adapting Root & Rebound's programs and resources. Based on reports from tribal representatives, there is a great need for reentry legal information and resources relevant to tribal communities and their laws, policies, and circumstances. Root & Rebound's work with the Yurok Tribe, the largest group of Native Americans in California, will serve as a pilot project for expanding reentry support to other tribes. Similarly, through their network of rural reentry partners, Root & Rebound will continue to reach other rural communities throughout the state and provide technical follow-up support in rural communities.

As education and trainings have expanded, Root & Rebound's direct service assistance has also grown steadily. Today, the legal hotline typically takes over 40 calls a month. These calls come from 26 California counties, and 6 additional counties across the United States.

To date, Root & Rebound's attorneys have served 270 callers on a wide range of issues; such issues include reunification with a child or child custody payments, support and guidance about employment options, sudden and significant changes to parole length or other conditions that greatly affect quality of life (where one may live, how far one can travel, the ability to work etc.), housing options for loved ones preparing for release, advocacy resources for challenging restrictive living conditions in transitional housing, and reentry resources and support in rural California. When reviewing the *Roadmap to Reentry* chapter topics covered in each call, callers ask about parole and probation (26 %), housing (17 %), employment (12 %), education (3 %), cleaning up a criminal record (12 %), court-ordered debt (4 %), family and children (7 %), identification and voting (4 %), public benefits (5 %), and community resources (21 %). All calls cover multiple issues. The individuals who call the legal hotline largely reflect the demographics, including racial inequalities, of the California penal system (see Table 1 for participant descriptors). Root & Rebound also receives and responds to nearly 150 letters per week. The majority of letters come from people in state prison and jails, as well as federal prisons, for whom letter writing is the primary communication method.

In its systems reform work, Root & Rebound employs what it learns on the ground in education and service provision to change things on a

Table 1 Legal hotline service recipients by race/ethnicity, gender, and status

Race/ethnicity		Gender		Status	
Hispanic	11 %	Men	60 %	Formerly Incarcerated Person	29 %
Native American/ Alaska Native	1 %	Woman	33 %	Currently Incarcerated Person	43 %
Asian	4 %	Other	7 %	Community Service Provider	3 %
African-American	26 %			Family or Friend	14 %
White	35 %			Educator	1 %
Hawaiian	1 %			Attorney	1 %
Multiracial	5 %			Community Supervision	1 %
Other	17 %			Other	8 %

systemic level. To this end, the organization has created partnerships with advocacy organizations, elected officials, and other stakeholders, providing feedback to these partners regarding on the ground needs. The organization also regularly composes letters of support and opposition for reentry-related measures. As Root & Rebound's experience (and thus reputation) has grown, it is increasingly afforded opportunities to engage in broader creative efforts to reform systemic barriers for people in reentry, but chooses to keep its work in this arena focused on areas where big policy organizations are not working. For example, in response to requests from partners in Los Angeles County, Root & Rebound is currently working with the Los Angeles Mayor's Office of Reentry, the L.A. Employer Advisory Council, and others to develop a fair hiring toolkit for private employers. This toolkit will be Los Angeles centered, but will be largely relevant to private employers in other California counties. Root & Rebound is also engaged in system change work in the area of decreasing legal barriers to reentry. In one such project, the organization is working with formerly incarcerated students and alumni of Project Rebound at San Francisco State University to improve the utilization of California's Certificate of Rehabilitation program, a heavily underused mechanism designed to reduce collateral consequences.

Root & Rebound's Accomplishments and Challenges to Date

Root & Rebound's staff identifies three areas of programmatic accomplishment, including increasing access to critical information, strengthening the reentry infrastructure statewide, and developing the organization to facilitate sustainable growth. The trifecta of Root & Rebound's programmatic offerings, the *Roadmap to Reentry Legal Guide*, legal trainings, and technical assistance provided in the reentry hotline, has proven an effective means of disseminating critical information. This chapter has already discussed Root & Rebound's reach in disseminating information. In addition, evaluations conducted to date reveal that Root & Rebound's public education programming is perceived positively among participants. First, data suggest complex legal information is conveyed in a manner that people can understand. Of those surveyed after reading the *Roadmap*, 100 % said the guide was either easy to understand or very easy to understand. The data also shows that the *Roadmap* guide and trainings have greatly increased the knowledge and confidence of communities reached. While 86 % of those surveyed reported knowing either "nothing," "some," or a "moderate" amount of information about reentry before reading the guide, 72 % reported either "high" or "very high" knowledge after reading it. For those participating in trainings, average confidence levels in navigating reentry also increased from moderate to high after participating. The perceived utility of the guide is also supported by survey results indicating 62 % of attendees would use the guide weekly, several times a week, or daily. Finally, 98 % of hotline callers report being completely satisfied with the service, making the hotline Root & Rebound's most positively received educational program to date.

Root & Rebound's second area of accomplishment is in strengthening the reentry infrastructure statewide. By bringing together reentry stakeholders across communities statewide through educational programming, Root & Rebound increases connection, coordination, and know-how among these groups. Beyond boosting what organizations, agencies, and families can do for their clients and members, and thus strengthening infrastructure, trainings are an opportunity for people to recognize and meet other members of their own communities who can serve as reentry supports. Trainings are attended by people currently and formerly incarcerated, their family members, supervision officers, nonprofit workers, lawyers, clergymen and women, and government social service providers. As mentioned earlier, of the 640 people directly trained in 2015, 21 % were directly impacted by the criminal justice system, including formerly incarcerated individuals, currently incarcerated individuals, and family members; 20 % worked in community supervision; 21 % worked in the nonprofit/education sector; 14 % were legal advocates; 17 % were government social service providers; 3 % were clergy; and 4 % identified as other. All attendees introduce themselves and their work before each session, work together on interactive exercises, and often develop relationships with other important stakeholders in their communities who were previously unknown to them—forging new connections for client referrals to strengthen wraparound services.

Root & Rebound's third arena of accomplishment is in building sustainability by creating a strong team and fostering leadership development. This development is characterized by attracting and retaining strong staff and volunteers. As previously discussed, Root & Rebound has six strong full-time staff members and a team of dedicated fellows, interns, and volunteers. Root & Rebound's philosophy in attracting and retaining staff is to build leaders. This requires identifying candidates who are excited about building an organization, managing large projects and volunteers, and desire to work in a creative and dynamic workplace. With regard to volunteers, Root & Rebound has had success in retaining volunteers by similarly finding individuals interested in taking on meaningful projects and by entrusting these volunteers with independent projects they can follow through to fruition. This also requires increasing staff capacity to supervise and manage effectively, including trainings and education for staff. Finally, Root & Rebound's growth is in part facilitated by successes in garnering financial support to expand its operations.

In addition to the three aforementioned areas of accomplishment, three areas remain a challenge for the organization, including evaluation, funding, and maintaining mission consistency. Tracking long-term outcomes, especially for the reentry population, is especially challenging. Although immediate surveys are easy to conduct after interventions such as trainings and hotline calls, it is challenging to track what difference this intervention makes over time. Because people's reentry circumstances change so quickly, including moving homes or jobs and changes in family life, it can be challenging to maintain contact with people served. To tackle the challenges of long-term tracking, Root & Rebound has enlisted the assistance of local academics to develop survey methodology that tracks the progress of guide readers, training attendees, and hotline callers. These data can then be compared to general California-wide statistics and against a control group of individuals who have contacted the organization, but are still waiting on their guides or trainings. These new data will prove invaluable in determining the organization's impact.

Second, with such immense breadth and depth of needs among reentering individuals and within reentry systems, acquiring sufficient funding to meet these needs is ever pressing and often challenging. Maintaining a sustainable funding stream is a particular challenge for Root & Rebound given the specific aims and structure of the organization. Public and private funding opportunities are often narrowly defined, with a specific focus only on certain geographic areas, issues, or modalities of service. Many foundations are exclusively focused on employment, housing, and mental health services, and fund many of the groups Root & Rebound trains, whose outcomes and impact are more easily quantified (e.g., number of job placements).

With regard to public funding, as previously mentioned, Realignment provides California counties with funds that may be used for reentry programs. However, these funds are usually administered by county probation departments, which typically allocate to nonprofits who work in their respective counties. For an organization like Root & Rebound, which holds trainings and events statewide, and takes calls from many different counties, the program is largely ineligible for County-specific funding. Because Root & Rebound's work is substantively and geographically broad in scope and because the organization does not provide a tangible service or resource (e.g., housing, vocational training, mental health services), funding opportunities are limited. For Root & Rebound to exist and thrive, however, they must convince funders of the importance of crosscutting and systemic interventions previously neglected in the reentry landscape.

Finally, Root & Rebound recognizes maintaining mission consistency as an area of ongoing challenge. Given the level of competition in applying for grants and because funding promotes individually focused (vs. systemic), geographically specific, and social-service-oriented programs, mission drift away from a broader public education and systemic intervention model is incentivized. Overcoming this challenge means often saying no to grant opportunities that would cause us to drift away from Root & Rebound's mission, expertise, and core values.

Practitioner Reflections: The Facilitators and Barriers to Successful Reentry Programming

This section conveys lessons learned from the perspective of a burgeoning reentry program. Later in this chapter, we summarize Root & Rebound staff's perceived facilitators and barriers to program operations (i.e., education, technical assistance, and systems reform) and achieving program goals (i.e., increase access to justice and opportunity for people in reentry from prison and jail, to educate and empower those who support them, and to advance and strengthen reentry infrastructure).

Among Root & Rebound's four perceived facilitators of successful reentry programming and achieving program goals are *collaboration, listening to and upholding firsthand experiences, utilizing technology and social media*, and *leveraging growing public support*. As described earlier, Root & Rebound collaborates with a diverse array of stakeholders in both its information dissemination and policy advocacy efforts. Collaboration enhances the efficiency with which Root & Rebound can disseminate knowledge; by strengthening what probation and parole officers, case managers, and family members can do for their clients and participants, Root & Rebound is able to reach far more people in reentry than it could on its own. For example, through "train the trainer" events, where Root & Rebound's staff educates service providers who then host their own trainings and build their own curriculum, the organization is able to create community educators who empower others in their locality. Through ongoing consultation with collaborating organizations, Root & Rebound also continues to support the transfer of information from organizations to clients.

Root & Rebound commonly hears stories exemplifying the effectiveness of such collaboration. One such story from our collaboration with Prison Fellowship is that of Jenny[1], who, after 15 years in prison, brought our *Roadmap to Reentry* guide to her parole hearing. Jenny referenced the great work she had done with Prison Fellowship's 4-week *Roadmap to Reentry* workshop, and informed the Commissioners that she was prepared for reentry because of participating in the workshop, and because she could always look up any of her questions in the guidebook. Having been previously denied, this time the BPH (The Board of Parole Hearings) granted Jenny's release to parole, and the final decision is now on the governor's desk for consideration. By training and educating professionals in the field, as well as family and loved ones, Root & Rebound is equipping the field at large to

---

[1] Pseudonym used to protect confidentiality.

be better prepared for the needs of people coming home in such high numbers. In addition to enhancing knowledge transfer via trainings and ongoing consultation, Root & Rebound brings collaborators together to promote the development of interagency relationships. By leveraging the existing reentry infrastructure through these forms of collaboration, Root & Rebound facilitates knowledge, skill, and resource sharing among stakeholders, and enhances political power in policy and system change efforts.

Second, a key facilitator of Root & Rebound's work is listening to and upholding firsthand experiences of reentry so that the model remains needs-based and informed by those with direct experience of reentry challenges. Root & Rebound is first and foremost based on the on-the-ground perspectives of individuals gleaned through the in-depth needs assessment previously discussed (Katcher and Tonnesen 2014). The voices of those most directly impacted continue to reach the Root & Rebound team through letters and hotline calls, surveys, and focus groups that the organization runs, particularly when taking on new project and initiatives. Information from these points of communication are then integrated into operational change efforts, as well as advocacy and system change efforts. For example, pre-training needs assessments and post-training satisfaction survey data have been critical to revising trainings to ensure content remains relevant and of sufficient depth, and that improvements and changes are made to the education curriculum to more adequately meet the needs of participants. The firsthand narratives of reentering individuals are also forefronted in all of Root & Rebound's public media campaign efforts, as discussed further, later in this chapter.

Third, Root & Rebound has found utilization of technology and social media to be fundamental to public education and outreach. In addition to providing access to informational materials online, Root & Rebound maintains an active social media presence. Staff use social media as a means of conveying individual narratives of people facing reentry challenges and sharing information that can contribute to changes in public perception and increase public will for policy and system change. In 2016, the organization is further leveraging technology to create an online training platform, so that people across the state can log on and access free basic and advanced trainings on topic areas where they have interest or need. The organization is also exploring how to create more digital trainings for currently incarcerated individuals, and how to work with institutions (where people incarcerated lack access to the Internet) to get the videos approved for viewing inside.

Finally, growing public support for criminal justice and reentry reform has become a central facilitator of Root & Rebound's work, as support from the Bay Area and California-wide community is key to expanding its work. It has always been Root & Rebound's belief that criminal justice reform in the United States is the central human rights issue of our time. This understanding of the problem seems to have gained traction in the past few years, and the public imagination has shifted immensely. The number of young people engaged in this issue and enthusiastic about volunteering is a testament to this shift. Foundations are much more open to funding criminal justice reform and reentry, and to recognize their ties to poverty, than they were just a few years ago. Such recognition and public support facilitates Root & Rebound's work by increasing resources, volunteers, and access to funds, as well as creating a window of opportunity for systemic policy change.

Among Root & Rebound's three barriers are *system fragmentation, insufficient provision of basic services and social goods to the reentry population,* and *lack of political and public will.* The first and perhaps most significant barrier to Root & Rebound's work is the degree of fragmentation that permeates the reentry landscape. In seeking to achieve their aim to increase collaboration and coordination across the reentry landscape, Root & Rebound has come to see fragmentation as more than just a descriptor; it is a logic with material and operational consequences. As a logic, system fragmentation promotes individual and competitive services, while devaluing overarching models of service delivery, collaboration, and continuity. Reentry services rarely bridge the divide between incarceration and release, but rather are typically administered to those formerly incarcerated, or currently incarcerated, with few programs that follow individuals through the entire process of reentry.

As a result many potential clients of Root & Rebound may be lost even before they receive information about the resources available through the program. No large state-wide body, which saves correctional bodies like parole or probation (whose impact is limited by their role within the penal system), exists to oversee and ensure stability and support throughout the process. Meanwhile, certain geographical areas become seriously underserved, and those programs that do exist receive little government oversight. Root & Rebound attempts to bridge the disconnect between life in custody and out of custody, resolve the gaps in geographic resources, and increase collaboration, but there are limits to what the organization can build; it cannot rebuild the reentry infrastructure, nor does it have the authority to oversee and ensure continuity and collaboration in the work of individual actors.

In addition to reentry infrastructure fragmentation, Root & Rebound faces the barrier of insufficient provision of basic services and social goods to the reentry population. In doing this work, it has become clear that where many Americans assume government assistance and support exist, it does not. The reentry population is disproportionately indigent. California offers a dearth of affordable housing options and people leaving prison or jail are not given access to food, housing, or other basic necessities with regularity. Rather, people leaving prison are given $200 and a bus ticket home, no matter how much time they have served. Many individuals leaving prison and jail can only find temporary housing in substance abuse treatment facilities. As a result, up to 50 % of parolees become homeless (State Council of Governments, n.d.) When the government fails to provide individuals with basic necessities like housing, food, and clothing, it undermines Root & Rebound's ability to provide legal education and advocacy. Rather, staff must provide clients with social service referrals and access to basic necessities before the legal needs of clients can be addressed. Root & Rebound has attempted to address these needs, in part by identifying and providing resources in all 58 California counties. While this must be done before Root & Rebound can effectively meet legal needs, these activities absorb staff time and impairs legal advocacy efforts.

Finally, while growing public and political support for the issue of reentry is a facilitator of our work, there remains a lack of political will by some legislators. Although the overall political climate in California and across the country has shifted on this issue, the shift has not been paralleled by adequate investment in the reentry landscape. For example, the Legal Services Corporation (LSC), the largest national funder of civil legal aid established by congress, restricts its funding from organizations doing criminal legal work. This means that organizations working on collateral consequence issues, for example, are ineligible for LSC funding. Within California, as discussed, while there is an enormous wave of people being released from custody, adequate funding has not followed this population; thus, in many ways, the population has been set up for failure and organizations like Root & Rebound, overwhelmed and understaffed, are left trying to holistically and comprehensively meet needs. Unlike federal social insurance programs that provide stable funding streams for services and benefits to other disadvantaged populations (e.g., Social Security Disability Insurance, Supplemental Security Income), those providing services to the reentry population are deeply vulnerable to the vicissitudes of political will. As for public support, while criminal justice reform is widely and passionately discussed now, it is unclear if it will remain so in 5 or 10 years. This is particularly concerning if reentry programs are unable to meet the needs of people in reentry, and as a result, recidivism levels remain high. If interest in this issue diminishes, it would harm the entire reentry population and the movement to support them.

Conclusion

While reentry policies providing critical funding have emerged and programs seeking to facilitate reentry exist, any hope that accompanies this attention and growth is tempered by the tremendously high demand of the ever-growing reentry population and the significant systemic barriers that impede effective reentry program implementation. The socioeconomic and legal challenges faced by the reentry population are great, and the challenges to developing effective reentry service programs that can help individuals overcome these barriers are similarly profound. Reflections from an innovative and ambitious young reentry program, such as Root & Rebound, suggest that the ability to adequately support the reentry population is hindered by the existing reentry and social welfare landscapes characterized by system fragmentation, insufficiency in the provision of basic material and social goods, and vulnerable to the shifting tides of political and public will. In such a landscape, however, there are also tools that can assist reentry programs in their work. From the perspective of Root & Rebound, these facilitators include collaborative relationships with other state and nonprofit actors, upholding the voices of those most impacted, harnessing the power of technology to bridge informational and social gaps, and garnering public interest and support for the work. By directly confronting some of the barriers to reentry programming, such as system fragmentation, Root & Rebound's leadership is optimistic that their model is scalable on a national level. The program intends to expand services into other states with large reentry populations in the coming years.

Given hyperincarceration and the resulting reentry crisis is largely the result of a series of policy decisions, the ability to truly assist the reentry population is likely dependent on our ability to make new policy decisions. It is evident from Root & Rebound's work on the ground in California that the reentry infrastructure is decentralized, inefficient, and inadequate. When policies incentivize private parties to enter the reentry landscape and force them to compete for limited resources, it creates both gaps in services and redundancies. It is also evident that the extensive needs of the reentry population necessitate enhancing access to social and economic resources, as well as legal advocacy. Thus, for reentry programs to really work, policies that strengthen the state's capacity to provide social and economic resources and penal policies that dismantle legal barriers to social advancement are dually necessary. In the meantime, Root & Rebound and partners will do their best, continuing to work through and despite these gaps in order to provide education and tools necessary for successful community reentry.

References

American Bar Association (2015). *Collateral consequences of criminal conviction.* http://www.abacollateralconsequences.org/

American Civil Liberties Union. (2012). Public safety realignment: California at a crossroads. www.aclunc.org/realignment

Berg, M. T., & Huebner, B. M. (2011). Reentry and the ties that bind: An examination of social ties, employment, and recidivism. *Justice Quarterly*, *28*(2), 382–410.

Bureau of Justice Assistance. (n.d.). The Second Chance Act. https://www.bja.gov/ProgramDetails.aspx?Program_ID=90

California Department of Corrections & Rehabilitation. (2015). *2014 outcome evaluation report*. Sacramento, CA: California Department of Corrections. www.cdcr.ca.gov/adult_research_branch

Carson, A. E. (2015). *Prisoners in 2014.* (No. NCJ 248955). Washington, DC: Bureau of Justice Statistics.

Durose, M. R., Cooper, A. D., Snyder, H. N. (2014). *Recidivism of prisoners released in 30 states in 2005: Patterns from 2005 to 2010.* Washington, DC: Bureau of Justice Statistics.

Garland, D. (2001). *The culture of control: Crime and culture in contemporary society.* Chicago, IL: University.

Jonson, C. L., & Cullen, F. T. (2015). Prisoner reentry programs. *Crime & Justice*, *44*, 517–557.

Katcher, K. L., Esq., & Tonnesen, S. C., Esq. (2014). Voice from the field: Major gaps and unmet needs in reentry & best practices for starting a reentry program (Rep.). http://static.squarespace.com/static/52f9700ee4b0eea0230aeb19/t/53892447e4b0cfc7f0c4bee1/1401496647881/Voices%20From%20the%20Field-FINAL.pdf

Katcher, K. L., Esq., & Tonnesen, S. C., Esq. (forthcoming). Root & Rebound Guide for California Employers: Hiring People with Criminal Records (Rep.).

Krisberg, B., & Taylor-Nicholson, E. (2011, August 30). Realignment: A bold new era in California corrections. The Chief Justice Earl Warren Institute on Law and Social Policy, University of California, Berkeley Law School.

Makarios, M., Steiner, B., Travis, L. F. (2010). Examining the predictors of recidivism among men and women released from prison in Ohio. *Criminal Justice and Behavior*, 0093854810382876.

Mellow, J., & Christian, J. (2008). Transitioning offenders to the community: A content analysis of reentry guides. *Journal of Offender Rehabilitation*, *47*, 339–355.

Morani, N. M., Wikoff, N., Linhorst, D. M., Bratton, S. (2011). A description of the self-identified needs, service expenditures, and social outcomes of participants of a prisoner-reentry program. *The Prison Journal, 91*(3), 347–365.

O'Brien, P. (2001). Making it in the "free world": Women in transition from prison. Albany, NY: State University of New York Press.

O'Brien, P., & Leem, N. (2007). Moving from needs to self-efficacy: A holistic system for women in transition from prison. *Women and Therapy, 29*, 261–284.

Parsons, M. L., & Warner-Robbins, C. (2002). Factors that support women's successful transition to the community following jail/prison. *Health Care for Women International, 23*, 6–18.

Petersilia, J. (2003). *When prisoners come home: Parole and prisoner reentry.* New York, NY: Oxford University Press.

Petersilia, J. (2004). What works in prisoner reentry? Reviewing and questioning the evidence. *Federal Probation, 68*, 4–8.

Petersilia, J. (2008). California's correctional paradox of excess and deprivation. *Crime and Justice, 37*(1), 207–278.

Pierson, P. (1995). *Dismantling the welfare state?: Reagan, Thatcher and the politics of retrenchment.* Chicago, IL: Cambridge University Press.

Pinard, M. (2010). Reflections and perspectives on reentry and collateral consequences. *Journal of Criminal Law and Criminology, 100*, 1213–1224.

Radice, J. (2012). Administering justice: Removing statutory barriers to reentry. *University of Colorado Law Review, 83*, 715.

Raphael, S. (2011). Incarceration and prisoner reentry in the United States. *The Annals of the American Academy of Political and Social Science, 635*(1), 192–215. doi:10.1177/0002716210393321

Rappaport, A., & Dansky, K. (2010). State of emergency: California's correctional crisis. *Federal Sentencing Reporter, 22*(3), 133–143.

Root & Rebound. (2015). *Roadmap to reentry: A California Legal Guide.* Oakland, CA: Root & Rebound. http://objects.dreamhost.com/roadmap guide/RoadmapGuide.pdf

Rubin, A. (2015, July). California's Jail-building Boom. *The Marshall Project.* https://www.themarshallproject.org/2015/07/02/california-s-jail-building-boom#.b8RWBnQHk

Seiter, R. P., & Kadela, K. R. (2003). Prisoner reentry: What works, what does not, and what is promising. *Crime & Delinquency, 49*(3), 360–388.

State Council of State Governments. (n.d.). *Homelessness and prisoner reentry.* Lexington, KY: Council of State Governments. http://www.endhomeless ness.org/page/-/files/1082_file_RPC_Homelessness_one_pager_v8.pdf

Travis, J. (2005). *But they all come back: Facing the challenges of prisoner reentry.* Washington, DC: The Urban Institute.

Turner, S., Fain, T., Hunt, S. (2015). *Public safety realignment in twelve California counties.* Santa Monica, CA: The RAND Corporation. www.rand.org

Wacquant, L. (2001). Deadly symbiosis when ghetto and prison meet and mesh. *Punishment & Society, 3*(1), 95–133.

Wacquant, L. (2009). *Punishing the poor: The neoliberal government of social insecurity.* Durham, NC: Duke University Press.

Wacquant, L. (2010). Prisoner reentry as myth and ceremony. *Dialectical Anthropology, 34*(4), 605–620.

Weaver, V. M. (2007). Frontlash: Race and the development of punitive crime policy. *Studies in American Political Development, 21*(2), 230–265.

Wilson, J. A., & Davis, R. C. (2006). Good intentions meet hard realities: An evaluation of the project Greenlight reentry program. *Criminology and Public Policy, 5,* 303–338.

Zhang, S. X., Roberts, E. R., Callanan, V. J. (2006). Preventing parolees from returning to prison through community-based reintegration. *Crime & Delinquency, 52,* 551–571.

Leah A. Jacobs is an Assistant Professor in the School of Social Work at the University of Pittsburgh, Pennsylvania. She holds a BS in psychology from Northeastern University, an M.A. in social policy/child development from Tufts University, and an MSW from the University of California, Berkeley. She is currently a fellow of the National Institute of Justice and will be an assistant professor in the University of Pittsburgh's School of Social Work by January, 2017.

Katherine Katcher is the Founder and Executive Director of Root & Rebound. She received her BA in anthropology from Columbia University and a JD from the University of California, Berkeley School of Law. Katherine has been working in the nonprofit sector for over 10 years.

Pascal Krummenacher is a Swiss law student at Queen Mary University of London in the United Kingdom. He joined Root & Rebound as a volunteer in October, 2015, after working in both homeless advocacy and eviction defense organizations in San Francisco.

Sonja Tonnesen is Deputy Director and founding staff member of Root & Rebound. She received her BA in urban studies from the University of Pennsylvania and her JD from the University of California, Berkeley School of Law.

What Works in Reentry and How to Improve Outcomes

Mirlinda Ndrecka, Shelley Johnson Listwan,
and Edward J. Latessa

Introduction

For the past decade or so there has been increased attention given to the process men and women go through when returning to their communities after being in a jail or prison. Offenders have been "re-entering" society ever since we began incarceration, so there is nothing new about the challenges that they face, so why the sudden interest? First, the number of ex-prisoners released each year is staggering, over 600,000 (which should come as

---

M. Ndrecka (✉)
Henry C. Lee College of Criminal Justice and Forensic Science,
University of New Haven, Connecticut, USA

S.J. Listwan
Department of Criminal Justice and Criminology,
University of North Carolina, Charlotte, USA

E.J. Latessa
School of Criminal Justice, University of Cincinnati, Cincinnati, USA

© The Author(s) 2017   **177**
S. Stojkovic (ed.), *Prisoner Reentry*,
DOI 10.1057/978-1-137-57929-4_5

no surprise to anyone that is familiar with the correctional system in the United States) (Bureau of Justice Statistics 2014). Second, there is concern about the high failure rates of ex-inmates and the effect it may have on public safety (Pew Center 2011). Given failure often leads to re-incarceration there are the high costs associated with failure. Moreover, the high failure rates lead to issues of prison and jail crowding which limits our ability to offer meaningful jail and prison programs, which in turn contributes to higher recidivism rates (Petersilia and Cullen 2015). In response, we have seen an increase in funding provided to states and jurisdictions across the country to improve programs and services offered in the reentry process.

In recent years, a great deal has been written about the challenges that ex-prisoners face. It almost seems that there are as many different types of programs and services offered as the number of offenders released. While many of the efforts are created with the best of intentions, sifting through those that are effective in reducing recidivism from those that are not is always challenging, particularly given that nearly all programs claim to be "evidence based." It is our intent with this chapter to examine what the empirical evidence tells us about prisoner reentry and how programs should be designed and implemented.

This chapter is divided into a number of topic areas. First we will review the emergence of the "reentry" phenomenon and some of the major initiatives that have been created over the past decade. Second, we will examine the diversity of reentry programs and the development of the reentry services model away from a strictly crime control approach. Third, will be a review of what it means to be evidence based and the guiding principles behind the research. The fourth section will dive into the research on reentry program including a look at some of the large studies as well as meta-analysis. Next, we will provide a strategy for designing and implementing evidence-based reentry programs including the importance of assessment, identifying and focusing on appropriate targets for change, effective treatment models and the use of core correctional practices with both probation and parole officers as well as what we call "influencers"—those individuals in an offenders life that can help guide and support them. We will also discuss the importance of making sure that fidelity and quality assurance is part of our efforts.

Finally, we will review what often gets in the way of designing and implementing effective reentry programs and some strategies for overcoming or removing the barriers.

The Emergence of the Reentry Phenomenon

The State of Corrections in 1999–2000

A decade and a half ago, Petersilia (2001) wrote about a topic, previously ignored, that was gaining momentous attention among policy makers and criminal justice practitioners. According to her, in light of increasing numbers of ex-prisoners returning to communities, the process of dealing with them once they exited prison had been termed "prisoner reentry." At the time, the American correctional system was starting to experience the full effects of the mass incarceration movement that started in the mid-1970s. Prison populations had reached 1.3 million in 1999, all state prison facilities were operating between 1 % and 17 % above their capacities (depending on the state), and federal prisons were operating at 32 % above their capacity (Beck 2000). More importantly, the number of ex-prisoners coming home became increasingly larger every day.

The growth in prison populations was driven by numerous changes in policies that took place starting in the mid-1970s and continued for more than two decades. First, the late 1970s and early 1980s saw an upsurge in prosecutors seeking tougher sentences for marginal felony cases. Prison sentences were being sought more often for crimes that were assigned community sentences or jail incarceration in the past. Blumstein and Beck (1999) found that the massive increase in incarceration during the 1990s was a direct effect of the increase in prison commitments per arrest. The criminal justice system simply started incarcerating more individuals (Travis 2005; Zimring et al. 2003).

Second, as part of the truth-in-sentencing movement and sentencing reform, the federal government passed the Sentencing Reform Act of 1984 and Sentencing Guidelines and abolished discretionary parole. Many states followed suit by establishing sentencing commissions and instituting state guidelines that determined how much time would be served by offenders, and by eliminating parole boards. The truth-in-sentencing-legislation radically curbed the discretionary powers of parole boards even in the states that maintained them. The amount of good time that offenders could obtain while in prison was also dramatically reduced because of these laws, and offenders convicted of certain violent crimes were required to serve 85 % of their sentences before they were eligible for parole. Not only were more people going to prison, but they were also spending longer periods in prison (Petersilia 2003; Simon 2012; Travis 2005).

Third, the "crack epidemic" panic that swept the nation was reflected in the dramatic increase of drug arrest and prosecutions, which in turn, affected the imprisonment rates. This trend started in the mid-1980s with the passage of the crack-cocaine laws by Congress and continued well into the 1990s with the "War on Drugs" policies. Under these new statues, individuals caught with 5 grams or more of crack cocaine would receive minimum mandatory sentences of 5 years. Thus, in 1980 there were about 300 arrests for drug crimes per 100,000 US adults. By 1996, the drug arrest rate had more than doubled to 700 arrests for 100,000 adults (Travis 2005). This rate increase was also accompanied by a boom in incarceration rates for nonviolent offenders; from 1978 to 1996 the number of incarcerated nonviolent offenders tripled, while the number of incarcerated drug offenders increased sevenfold. At the end of 1998, the Department of Justice reported that 52.7 % of state prison inmates and 87.6 % of federal inmates were imprisoned for offenses that involved neither harm nor the threat of harm to the victim (Irwin et al. 2000).

Last, the 1990s were characterized by an increase in popularity of very conservative and punishment-oriented measures that targeted repeat offenders. Despite a substantial reduction in crime (13 %), during the "tough-on-crime" era, the federal government and many states increased sentences for many offenders, eliminated many early release mechanisms, and sanctioned for sentence enhancements for felons that had prior convictions—the most famous example being California's three-strikes law that allowed for application of life sentences for felons who had two or more serious convictions. Other states and the federal government passed similar laws against repeat offenders, but the California legislation had the harshest provisions (Travis 2005; Zimring et al. 2003).

The results were not only more individuals in prison, but also more formerly incarcerated individuals being returned to prisons in higher numbers than ever before. Because more ex-prisoners were coming out on parole, more of them were eligible for parole violations—eligible to return to prison on technical violations. Furthermore, because of the punishment-oriented climate of the 1990s, and the increase in arrest rates in general, more parolees were being arrested and returned to prison. Between 1980 and 2000, the number of parole individuals being sent to prison for parole violations increased seven times (Travis 2005). Indeed by 2000, over 630,000 individuals were being released from prison, and many of them were returning to correctional facilities soon after their release (Beck and Mumola 1999; Petersilia 2001).

Coining the Term "Reentry"

The Bureau of Justice Statistics routinely surveys inmates in jails and prisons and collects statistics on admissions and releases from state prisons. Yet, until 2000 there were no national data delineating the characteristics of individuals leaving prisons, nor there were any descriptions of their lives in the months following release (Visher and Travis 2012). Correctional facilities considered their duties fulfilled once the offenders were released from their premises. While studies of ex-prisoners existed, few empirical studies had aimed to compile data on the profile of individuals leaving prisons. Little was known about the challenges and barriers that they faced once released, and on what would help them achieve successful reentry (Mears and Cochran 2015).

The launch of the multitude of efforts, initiatives, programs, and empirical studies to understand ex-prisoners and their challenges in returning to their communities, came as a result of a simple question that was asked after a routine meeting at the National Institute of Justice (NIJ). In the spring of 1999, Attorney General Janet Reno asked the director of the NIJ, Jeremy Travis and his colleague Laurie Robinson, Assistant Attorney General for Justice Programs: "What are we doing about all the people coming out of prison?" (Travis 2005, p. xi). Early in their investigative efforts, both Travis and Robinson realized that efforts to assist ex-prisoners were almost nonexistent (Travis 2005).

While working on the project, Travis suggested the term "reentry" to capture the totality of the phenomenon. Given that many ex-prisoners were being released without any supervision, his inquiry could not be restricted to parolees. The term "reentry" seemed appropriate when referring to all offenders being released from custody. Furthermore, Travis hoped that the term was broad enough to grip the attention and acceptance of both sides of the political spectrum, liberals, and conservatives, without inciting any discussions about sentencing policies and parole. While the term was coined by John Irwin in 1970, it was not until Travis' contribution that "reentry" as a term and as a movement appeared on the criminal justice national radar. The work of Travis and his colleagues spawned a series of initiatives that have made prisoner reentry the prevalent topic that it is today (Rhine and Thompson 2011; Jonson and Cullen 2015).

The Reentry Movement

Efforts to address the problem of prisoner reentry started soon after identifying the lack of support for the individuals leaving prison. In October of 1999, Attorney General Janet Reno held a press conference where she emphasized the urgency faced by the criminal justice agencies concerning the large numbers of ex-prisoners returning to society. During that press conference she announced a call for proposals from jurisdictions that were interested in developing reentry courts. Furthermore, during the same year, The NIJ, working in collaboration with the Corrections Program Office and the Office of Community Oriented Policing Services launched Reentry Partnerships in five locations. These partnerships aimed to improve reentry planning for ex-prisoners by bringing together correctional, police, and community agencies (Travis 2005).

On a national level, the Clinton administration was the first to dedicate funds to the reentry effort. In 2000, Clinton designated $60 million to "Project Reentry"—a federal program that provided job training, promoted responsible fatherhood among offenders, and established reentry courts (Petersilia 2001). That same year, the Urban Institute launched a multi-year Reentry Roundtable, a development that brought together academics, researchers, practitioners, service providers, formerly incarcerated individuals, and policy makers in getting a better understanding of the challenges faced by both reentrants and the agencies that attempted to handle the unprecedented numbers of individuals coming back to communities (Rhine and Thompson 2011).

The reentry efforts continued even after the change in political administrations at the federal level, signaling the fact that the reentry issue was seen as a crucial subject in criminal justice by both sides of the political spectrum. Thus in 2001, the federal government launched the Reentry Partnership Initiative (RPI), a project that encouraged courts, police, correction, and community agencies to work together in helping nonviolent formerly incarcerated offenders find employment and housing upon their return to their communities. The RPI model promoted collaboration between agencies in providing wraparound services for the reentrants (Rhine and Thompson 2011).

Another important venture was the creation of the Re-Entry Policy Council in 2001 by the Council of State Governments (CSG). The US Department of Justice, the US Department of Labor, and the US Department of Health and Human Services also partnered with CSG in establishing the plan and mission for the Re-Entry Policy Council. Its purpose was and remains the development and promotion of policies intended to assist the reintegration of the individuals leaving jails and prisons. In 2005, the Council also generated guidelines and recommendations for jurisdictions and agencies seeking to implement reentry initiatives by using experiences, guidance, and suggestions from 10 project partners and more than 100 administrators of correctional agencies (Rhine and Thompson 2011).

Furthermore, as part of the faith-based correctional initiatives that were popular during the presidency of George W. Bush, in 2003 the US Department of Labor in collaboration with the Department of Justice, Public/Private Ventures (a research company), and a consortium of private foundations launched Ready4Work (R4W). This was a faith-based, 3-year pilot program that offered employment training, job placement, corporate mentoring, case management, and other transitional services to individuals returning from prisons. The pilot was launched in 11 sites across the United States and ran until August 2006 (US Department of Justice 2003).

By expanding the Ready4Work platform, during the 2004 State of the Union, President Bush announced the Prisoner Reentry Initiative (PRI). In involving partnerships between federal and local agencies, the PRI sought to reduce recidivism by providing employment, housing, and holistic transitional services to nonviolent offenders returning to urban areas across the country. The Federal government dedicated $300 million over a period of 4 years. In November 2005, the PRI awarded the first grants of the initiative to 30 faith-based agencies located in 20 states (http://www.justice.gov/archive/fbci/progmenu_programs.html).

One of the largest efforts in assisting the needs of ex-prisoners by the Federal government was made through the development, implementation and evaluation of the Serious and Violent Offender Reentry Initiative (SVORI). Starting in 2003, the US Departments of Justice, Labor, Education, Housing and Urban Development and Health and Human Services started a multi-year collaboration that sought to reduce recidivism rates specifically for adult and juvenile serious offenders. Participants ranged from 14–35 years, and included both male and female offenders. The SVORI grants amounted to $100 million dollars and 69 grants were awarded to 89 state and local agencies throughout the 50 states and the District of Columbia. The initiative was designed to require collaboration between agencies and targeted a variety of reintegration barriers faced by offenders. Thus, services from the SVORI included employment, housing, family and community involvement, substance abuse, mental health issues, physical health, and case management. The SVORI sites had freedom in selecting their participants and in the types of services that they provided (Lattimore and Visher 2009).

During this same time, the National Institute of Corrections established the Transition From Prison to Community (TPC) initiative that aimed to encourage strategic systemic changes in states that were engaging in reentry efforts. As part of the TPC, the National Institute of Corrections in partnership with the Center for Effective Public Policy and the Urban Institute offered technical assistance to eight participating states. The states involved were assisted in building reentry programs or partnerships that were interdisciplinary, involved non-correctional stakeholders, implemented evidence-based practices backed by research and developed a capacity to change for future improvements. In 2009, TPC selected six additional states to receive technical assistance as part of the ongoing project (National Institute of Corrections Offender Reentry Transition; nicic.gov/tpcmodel).

Moving forward, in August 2008, President George W. Bush signed into law the Second Chance Act. The bill authorized $165 million in grants to state and local criminal justice agencies, as well as nonprofit organizations in developing and implementing programs that reduced recidivism rates by assisting ex-prisoners make a successful reintegration to their communities. The Act has supported both juvenile and adult initiatives and has funded a multitude of services for ex-offenders including substance abuse treatment, employment, housing, mentoring programs, victim services, and reentry courts. Additionally, the Act allocated funds for evaluation and research as well as training and technical assistance. Since 2009 over 300 government and nonprofit agencies from 48 states have received funds from the Second Chance Act. In 2015, Congress reauthorized the Act through the year 2020 (see also https://csgjusticecenter.org/nrrc/projects/second-chance-act/).

More recently, in 2011, the then-Attorney General Eric Holder founded the Federal Interagency Reentry Council. The council is a collaborative effort among 20 federal departments and agencies whose mission is to assist those returning from prison by removing federal barriers to a successful reentry, making communities safer through reductions in recidivism, lowering correctional costs, and identifying and supporting effective reentry programs. Currently, the Council is chaired by the Attorney General Loretta Lynch (Reentry Council 2016).

Diversity of Reentry Programs

The substantial involvement of federal and state governments in the reentry movement has resulted in the development of countless reentry programs and services across the United States. To address the multiple issues and barriers that are faced by reentrants when first leaving correctional institutions, reentry programs are very diverse in their focus, and by the nature of services that they provide (Ndrecka 2014; Seiter and Kadela 2003; Visher and Travis 2011). Some programs are multidimensional, offering several services and targeting multiple offender needs in a wraparound style of treatment (Lattimore and Visher 2009), while others specialize in the delivery of only one type of program such as substance abuse, or mental health (Kesten et al. 2012).

Furthermore, the structure of reentry programs differs widely. For example, some programs begin while the offenders are still incarcerated and continue their services after the offenders' release into the communities (Inciardi et al. 1997; Robbins et al. 2009), certain programs concentrate on providing prerelease services (Wilson and Davis 2006), and other reentry programs start providing services only after the offenders have reentered society (Zanis et al. 2003). Programs also differ with regard to the populations that they serve, with some reentry programs focusing only on juveniles (Josi and Sechrest 1999), some focusing on female offenders (Heilburn et al. 2008), and some focusing only male offenders (Lattimore and Visher 2009). A more detailed description of a variety of reentry programs is given in the ensuing pages.

Reentry Employment Programs

Employment is one of the criminogenic risks that are identified by the Risk, Need, and Responsivity (RNR) model (Andrews et al. 2006) and is considered an important way of reducing recidivism and facilitating offender reintegration after release (Valentine and Redcross 2015; Visher et al. 2005). Having quality employment after incarceration has also been shown to impact recidivism rates; however, many offenders tend to come into the system with spotty employment histories and few job-related skills. Additionally, many of them find it difficult to secure employment once released because of the social stigma associated with incarceration (Petersilia 2003; Travis 2005).

Employment, work-release, job-training, and job-placement programs are some of the most predominant existing reentry programs. Among these, work-release programs are the oldest and the most prevalent. Work-release programs were written into legislature in 1913 by then-Wisconsin State Senator Henry Huber. The bill, which proposed for prisoners to be employed during the day while incarcerated, came to be commonly known as the Huber Law and resulted in the launch of prison work-release programs (Grupp 1963). As of 2008, all but one of the 50 states reported having such a program in correctional facilities. Work-release programs are designed to teach inmates how to work productively when nearing their release so that the learned working habits persist once they are released into the community. In many states, offenders also participate in treatment programs while on work release and are subject to random drug screenings (Duwe 2015; Turner and Pertersilia 1996).

Job-training and placement programs entered the scene in the 1960s after the passing of the Manpower Training Act in 1962. Consequently, in the 1970s and 1980s, The US Department of Labor funded numerous federal projects that created work possibilities for ex-offenders including two experimental evaluations of community employment programs, the Living Insurance for Ex-Prisoners, and the Transitional Aid Research Project. While funding and support for these types of programs declined during the nineties, the reentry movement inspired their resurgence. Unlike work-release, job-placement, and job-training programs work with offenders once they are already into the community by training them in resume writing, job interview skills, and transitional job placement until permanent employment is obtained (Visher et al. 2005).

One of the most well-known transitional employment programs is the program by the Center for Employment Opportunities (CEO) in New York City. The CEO serves about 2,500 parolees that are returning to the city after incarceration. As part of the program, parolees are enrolled in a 5-day pre-employment class and placed into a transitional paid position that includes performing maintenance and repair work for city and state agencies. Their job performance and on-the-job behavior are monitored daily by site supervisors, while job coaches help them build their resumes and prepare them for job interviews. The clients are encouraged to apply for permanent positions if their job performance is satisfactory (Redcross et al. 2012).

Reentry Housing and Homelessness Programs

Housing is the most pressing issue for offenders when they are released. As Travis (2005, p. 4) puts it: "On the first day after prison…the released prisoner's immediate concern is 'Where will I sleep tonight?'" (p. 4). Most prisoners, will live with family in the months following their release, but these arrangements can be temporary in many cases. Visher et al. (2010) found that 7 months after their release 52 % of reentrants still had not found temporary housing, 35 % had lived at more than one address during that same time, while others had already entered a homeless shelter. Additionally, some prisoners enter prisons with a history of homelessness, which makes it more likely that they will be homeless once they are released (Metraux and Culhane 2004). In fact, a study of state and federal prisoners found that the rate of homelessness among ex-prisoners was four to six times higher than the rate of homelessness in the general population. Mental illness and substance abuse can also increase the chances of homelessness that are estimated to be as high as 20 % among mentally ill ex-prisoners (Greenberg and Rosenheck 2008). In turn, homeless ex-prisoners, or those who enter shelters after their release are more likely to abscond from supervision than reentrants who have secured stable housing (Metraux and Culhane 2004).

Traditionally, transitional housing for ex-prisoners has been provided by halfway houses. During the 1970s and 1980s, the providing basic necessities such as food, clothing, and a place of residence were the primary purposes of halfway houses (Latessa and Allen 1982). But while halfway house operations have changed to include an array of treatment programs for returning offenders (Latessa et al. 2010), their capacities cannot sustain the increasing numbers of offenders coming back from prison. As a result, halfway houses are mostly used to house ex-prisoners that have substance abuse needs and other types of transitional housing programs have been put in place to alleviate the problem (Roman and Travis 2006).

In recent years, housing programs for ex-offenders have been modeled after housing programs that were originally designed to accommodate non-correctional populations with disabilities or those who had chronic homelessness problems. Usually the ex-prisoners are referred to these programs through correctional reentry or parole services and they receive housing vouchers in low-income housing developments. For instance, the Frequent User Service Enhancement program is a collaboration between multiple agencies and has been implemented in several cities including New York and Chicago. The program is designed to help offenders with severe mental health problems and a history of chronic homelessness find stable housing in an attempt to reduce recidivism rates, decrease homeless shelter use, and reduce homelessness (Fontaine et al. 2012; Fontaine et al. 2011).

Reentry Substance Abuse Programs

Substance abuse problems are prevalent among correctional populations, with rates of lifetime disorders ranging from 70 % to 74 % (Feucht and Gfroerer 2011; Mumola and Karberg 2004, National Center on Addiction and Substance Abuse 2010). Rates among jail populations are also high with half of those convicted being under the influence of drugs or alcohol at the time of their arrest, and 68 % of jail inmates meeting the criteria for a drug dependency diagnosis (Karberg and James 2005). Furthermore, substance abuse can be linked to higher rates of recidivism (LeBel and Maruna 2012). Alcohol has been frequently linked violent behavior while drugs can influence involvement in property crime (Kunic and Grant 2006; Weekes et al. 1999; Weekes et al. 2013). Lastly, prisoners with a substance abuse history are more likely to have been sentenced multiple times when compared to prisoners who do not have the same problem (Mumola and Karberg 2004).

Reentry substance abuse programs are quite diverse. On one hand, substance abuse treatment is delivered by many halfway houses (Latessa et al. 2010; Lowenkamp and Latessa 2005). In other instances, substance abuse treatment can begin while the individual is still incarcerated. Once released, conditions of supervision require the offender to continue the substance abuse treatment and to reside in a community corrections agency (Heilburn et al. 2008). Additionally, courts often contract with nonprofit community-based organizations to deliver substance abuse treatment. Treatment is a required condition of supervision in these cases as well (Zanis et al. 2003).

Within prisons, therapeutic communities (TCs) have been a popular option for offering substance abuse treatment (Ndrecka 2014). TC programs usually involve a three-stage intervention. The first stage begins when the offenders are still incarcerated, usually 6–9 months prior to their release. During the second stage, the offenders are usually released under the supervision of a community agency. They continue to receive substance abuse treatment and can also be involved in other types of treatment based on their needs. The third stage consists of the after-care component of the treatment; the offenders receive treatment while the offenders are under the supervision of probation or parole agencies. While variations of the TC can include differences in supervision requirements and types of treatments available, most of them follow the treatment model closely (Hiller et al. 1999; Inciardi et al. 1997; Olson et al. 2009; Robbins et al. 2009; Wormith et al. 2007).

Reentry Mental Health Programs

The incidence of mental illness among correctional populations is higher than among the general population. One study estimated that rates of the mentally ill in prison were three to six times higher than the rates of mentally ill in the general population (Steadman et al. 2009). Another study compared rates of serious mental illness and found that in correctional institutions, the rate of serious mental illness is two to four times higher than at society at large (Hammett et al. 2001). Other data suggest that prisons are housing three to five times more mentally ill than psychiatric hospitals (Fellner 2006).

Offenders with mental illness tend to have a tougher time adjusting to prison life (Petersilia 2003). Additionally, while some data show that mental illness does not affect incarceration rates (Frank and Glied 2006), certain studies have found that mental illness can be related to recidivism. Thus, Cuellar et al. (2007) found that individuals with mental illnesses tend to have higher rates of arrests for minor crimes, and about half of mentally ill people have been arrested at some point in their life. A study of Utah prisoners examined compared time to recidivism among recently released offenders and found that those with mental illness returned to prison much quicker (median of 385 days) than prisoners without serious mental illness (median of 743 days) (Cloyes et al. 2010). Lastly, mental illness can contribute to what Travis (2005) calls the "churning" effect, with mentally ill offenders continuously moving in and out of correctional facilities (Baillargeon et al. 2009; Schlager 2013; see also Skeem et al. 2010; Slate et al. 2013).

Data on reentry programs that concentrate on mental health care are scarce but the reentry movement has inspired the creation of a few diverse options. One response has been the creation of mental health courts, the first one created in Broward County, Florida. Similar to drug courts in the way that they operate, mental health courts seek to meet the needs of offenders with mental disorders who have had frequent contact with criminal justice agencies. Court supervision is combined with a community-based treatment and a holistic case management approach (McGaha et al. 2002; Schalger 2013).

Other responses include the creation of specialized parole units for offenders with mental health issues. Officers that are assigned to these parole units have specific training in mental health issues and are equipped to provide continuity of treatment, including referral to appropriate treatment and crisis response (Schlagger 2013). Lastly, some jurisdictions have created programs for offenders with co-occurring mental health and substance abuse disorders. These programs provide treatment that is usually residential and includes aftercare components while the offenders remain under criminal justice supervision (Sacks et al. 2004).

Reentry Violent Offender Programs

The typical ex-prisoner returning to society is likely male, aged under 40 years, and has served time for committing a violent offense. He has little education, few if any employment skills, a spotty employment history, is likely to have a substance abuse and mental illness, and is from a disadvantaged background (Carson and Sabol 2012; Mears and Cochran 2015). The profile of reentrant individuals has not changed much since initial years of reentry efforts. And in order to address all of the problems of reentry populations the federal government developed the SVORI in 2003. At the time, reentry programs had a tendency to address only one domain of need for offenders. In contrast, the SVORI initiatives were designed to address multiple need areas for offenders and sought to improve outcomes across a range of domains (Lattimore and Visher 2009).

Through funding from the federal government, 69 agencies developed 89 SVORI programs. To qualify for funding the SVORI programs had to serve serious or violent offenders age 35 or younger (male, female, or juvenile), they had to employ a risk and needs assessment tool, and they had to encompass three stages of reentry—in prison, post-release supervision, and post-supervision. In addition, programs had to include partnerships between community organizations, correctional agencies, and faith-based organizations. The SVORI programs sought to improve outcomes in five areas: recidivism, housing, employment, health, and education. While, similar in goals, the SVORI programs varied greatly in the types of services that they provided and the type of offender population that they served (Lattimore and Visher 2009).

Another example of programs targeting violent offenders is the Boston Reentry Initiative (BRI), developed by funds from the Second Chance Act. The programs was started in 2001 as an interagency collaboration between the Boston Police Department, the Suffolk County Sherriff's Department, and a number of faith-based organizations and community service providers. It targeted high-risk offenders aged 18 to 32 years that had histories of violence and gang affiliation. The program was designed to provide a comprehensive support system for these offenders, in an attempt to prevent further involvement in crime while facilitating their transition (Braga et al. 2009).

Reentry Programs for Female Offenders

Women constitute only a small proportion of the total inmate population—the statistic was 7 % in 2012 (Carson and Sabol 2012). Even so, the rates of incarceration have increased more dramatically for women than for men during recent decades (Harrison and Beck 2005). Women offenders tend to be different from male offender across multiple dimensions. Thus, they are more likely to be incarcerated for drug offenses and less likely to be in prison for violent offenses (Carson and Sabol 2012). They are more likely to have been victimized and suffer from trauma, have a substance addiction, and report mental health issues (Mumola and Karberg 2004; Blackburn et al.

2008; Mears and Cochran 2015). Lastly, women are significantly more likely to have children and to be the primary caretaker for them than males (Holsinger 2014; Mears and Cochran 2015).

Historically, correctional programs were developed for males and then expanded to accept female offenders. Some programs, like the CREST work-release program in Delaware, serve both men and women. However, the program allows both males and females to live in the same quarters and has been criticized for having a sexually tense environment (Robbins et al. 2009).

Other programs have been designed specifically for women and seek to address women-specific issues and needs. For instance, the New Jersey Department of Corrections collaborated with the Community Education Centers, a private correctional organization partnered up to develop a community-based program for women prisoners who have substance abuse issues. The program also helps women with housing, employment, domestic violence, physical and mental health issues, and child reunification issues through a variety of treatment modalities (Heilburn et al. 2008). Nevertheless, many scholars have criticized reentry efforts available for women as lacking on their capacity to serve women's needs and in the range of needs that are addressed (Scroggins and Malley 2010; Schlager 2013).

Reentry Courts

Reentry courts are a relatively new addition to the criminal justice field. Modeled after drug courts, they were created by the US Department of Justice national initiative in 1999 (Travis 2005). The purpose of reentry courts is to monitor and assist offenders in the period immediately after release from incarceration, when risk of recidivism is very high. Just as in drug courts, a judge is actively involved in the planning and monitoring of services for each of the offenders. Offenders are required to obtain jobs or enroll in school to maintain successful status, the process involves graduated sanctions, and rewards are presented to celebrate milestones and achievements in the course of the program. Graduations are also held to mark successful completion of the program and they are usually attended by the offenders' families and friends. One of the first reentry court initiatives was started in East Harlem, New York. The program is over a decade old and has been subject to many evaluations. Today, there are at least 24 reentry courts operating throughout the United States (Hamilton 2011; Taylor 2013).

Halfway Houses

Halfway houses can be considered the oldest reentry efforts. They are residential transitional services that house either the offenders that are coming back to the community from prison, or the offenders that have violated their community sentence terms and are ordered to reside there. In this sense, they can serve as "halfway-into-prison" or "halfway-out-of-prison" facilities (Latessa and Allen 1982). Gaining popularity in the 1950s and up until the 1970s, halfway houses were frequently used as alternatives to incarceration or as places of residence for offenders who had trouble keeping compliance with terms of community sanctions. During this time, halfway houses also provided basic necessities such as food, clothing, and a place of residence for the offenders while they looked for permanent housing and employment (Latessa and Allen 1982; Petersilia 2003).

In recent decades, halfway houses have provided a range of treatment for offenders returning from prison that include employment readiness, educational services, and substance abuse services. Some halfway houses provide specialized treatment services like sex-offender treatment, mental health services, and even faith-based treatment services (Latessa et al. 2010; Willison et al. 2010). For instance, the Ridge House in Reno, Nevada, is a faith-based halfway house that provides reentry substance abuse and employment services to ex-prisoners. Eligible inmates arrive there shortly after their release and stay for about 90 days. Other services offered include parenting classes, financial classes, and health education. Additionally, offenders can obtain referrals to services offered from other agencies (Willison et al. 2010).

Reentry Programs and the Shift Toward the Service Model

More than a decade since its emergence, it seems evident that the reentry movement has established itself at the center of correctional policy and discourse. It also seems unlikely that it will fade away in the near future (Jonson and Cullen 2015). The support from federal and state governments has created countless reentry programs, employment opportunities, and community organizations. Furthermore, the attention to prisoner reentry has crossed criminal justice academic and practitioner circles and spilled into the public arena. Prisoner reentry has become a popular subject in politics, the mainstream media, and even television programming. There is a bipartisan collaboration in considering prisoner reentry issues in Congress and the federal government, President Barack Obama made front-page news in visiting a federal prison, and a simple search into the major national newspapers reveals that even presidential candidates are weighing in on the issue of prisoner reentry reform. Furthermore, Sesame Street, a longtime children's television show, introduced a Muppet character with an imprisoned father.[1] Lastly, the topic of reentry was thoroughly covered by an episode of Last Week Tonight, an award-winning news satire television program airing on HBO that tackles American current issues (Season 2, Episode 33).

In the context of correctional practices, reentry programs present an opportunity for change on both the individual and the social levels. By monitoring and assisting offenders, reentry programs cater to the issue of public safety. On the social level, reentry initiatives provide an opportunity to establish partnership among multiple governmental and community agencies. Reentry coordinators, units, and programs are now ubiquitous throughout practically all jurisdictions. And shrinking state budgets have made impossible for the "tough on crime" policies to be implemented even among those who still take them to heart (Crow and Smykla 2014).

---

[1] *Little Children, Big Challenges: Incarceration* is an educational resource video from *Sesame Street* released in 2013.

Yet some scholars caution that the reentry movement is likely to falter like many previous correctional initiatives have done before, if programs designed and implemented under the reentry umbrella do not show effectiveness in the long run. The success of reentry programs is contingent upon using evidence-based practices that produce visible reductions in recidivism. Otherwise, policy makers will turn their attention and budgets to the next, newest solution (Crow and Smykla 2014; Listwan et al. 2006).

When it comes to reentry this issue becomes especially complicated, since reentry programs come is so many diverse formats. Nevertheless, the "what works" literature, by providing a consistent theme of effective correctional rehabilitation programs, can become an impeccable road-map in outlining effective practices and interventions in the reentry realm. Whether reentry programs are effective or not depends on whether they follow this roadmap, namely the "principles of effective intervention" (Listwan et al. 2006).

Evidence-Based Practices and the RNR Model

As mentioned earlier, while parole has existed for a number of years, the current reentry phenomenon is unique in its character and purpose. The complexity facing the reentry movement rests with the dynamic nature of the population and services available given the large number of inmates that need to assimilate back into the community each year. Unfortunately, the services for re-entering inmates discussed in the previous section are not necessarily based on theoretical and empirically derived principles. It is shortsighted to believe that individuals can change their life-course trajectory by simply having a few weakly related risk factors such as housing and employment attended to; reentry is founded upon common sense strategies (e.g., gain employment) rather than empirically based policies (see Mears and Cochran 2015; Jonson and Cullen 2015). States and local jurisdictions must have a clear framework by which to build services for those with a higher risk of returning to prison.

Prominent criminological theories such as life-course, general strain, differential association, and social learning theories provide a rich understanding of offender behavior that have clear policy implications.

For example, with regard to life-course theory, a number of scholars have studied why and how some people desist from crime while others persist in their criminal careers (see Mulvey et al. 2014). Desistence from crime is seen as a process that can be influenced through a treatment strategies directed toward factors that promote desistence (Bushway and Paternoster 2014). With regard to general strain theory, researchers have begun exploring whether exposure to prison based strain (e.g., victimization) can impact the reentry process (Listwan et al. 2013). Understanding whether the prison environment is criminogenic could justify the need for changes to the prison culture and services for those leaving. Still others have examined the impact of social learning theory through peer group influences on offending (Warr and Stafford 1991), particularly in the context of reentry (see Visher and Travis 2003). All of these factors are key to understanding criminal decision-making and offender change. However, when it comes to policy development, the field of corrections has a long history of relying on approaches that are developed with little theoretical background (Gendreau 1996).

We argue that programs would benefit from following the principles set forth in the RNR approach. The RNR model is not a criminological theory but rather a treatment theory that is theoretically informed. As will be discussed in the next section, the research on the existing reentry programs is understandably mixed, however, a meta-analysis by Ndrecka (2014) found that promising reentry programs were those that adhered to a RNR model.

Risk, Need, and Responsivity Framework

The RNR framework provides a backdrop for effective programming because it is theoretically informed and empirically supported. The foundation of the RNR perspective is based on the theories discussed earlier in this chapter. For example, the criminogenic needs outlined by the RNR framework are similar to many of the desistence factors promoted by life-course theorists. Moreover, two of the most important criminogenic needs, attitudes and peers, are based on social learning theories of crime. In addition, the RNR perspective supports the use of cognitive behavioral treatment strategies to teach coping skills (among other techniques) that are directly related to all of theories noted above, particularly general strain theory which argues that criminal coping strategies are often the result of strain. The most beneficial aspect of using the RNR approach, however, is its practical application. The RNR framework provides a clear blueprint for practitioners working in the field. In particular, the model provides direction about who should be targeted (i.e., higher risk), what should be targeted (i.e., crimino-genic needs) and how it should be done (i.e., cognitive behavioral approaches). While there has been some discussion that the RNR approach should be augmented to achieve even greater reductions in recidivism (see Porporino 2010), the reality is that most current reentry programs have not yet fully implemented the RNR model. Once this foundation is established, then programs can begin fine-tuning their processes to achieve even greater reductions.

Risk Principle

The relevance of the RNR model to reentry programs is clear given that many of those re-entering the community are at high- to moderate-risk failure in the community. The risk principle suggests that intensive services should be dedicated to this moderate and high-risk offenders. But perhaps more importantly, low-risk clients should be diverted from intensive services lest we increase their chances of failure. Lowenkamp and Latessa (2005), for example, found that residential programs treating low-risk offenders increased recidivism by up to 29 %. Individuals iden-tified as low risk are likely engaged in a number of prosocial behaviors and placing them in intensive services and may increase their propensity for crime by removing them from the very prosocial activities we wish for them to engage (Andrews et al. 2006).

In contrast, higher risk individuals are less likely to have prosocial ties to the community and could be beneficial from intensive services as they may in limiting access to criminal opportunities. Research has been supportive of the risk principle, showing that client risk level predicts recidivism (Andrews and Bonta 1998; Andrews and Dowden 2006; Andrews et al. 2012; Bonta et al. 2000; Bourgon and Armstrong 2005;

Landenberger and Lipsey 2005, Lovins et al. 2007). A meta-analysis by Andrews and Dowden (2006) of over 300 studies revealed "solid support for the risk principle," with a modest treatment effect for the higher risk offenders and little to no effect for those who were low risk (p. 96). Finally, a study by Sperber et al. (2013) found that providing higher risk offenders a higher dosage of treatment of at least 200 hours led to substantial decrease in recidivism.

Need Principle

The second principle of the RNR model refers to targeting the criminogenic needs that are highly correlated with criminal behavior. These criminogenic needs are theoretically informed dynamic risk factors increase the likelihood that an individual will engage in criminal behavior (see Andrews et al. 1990; Gendreau 1996). Criminogenic needs include pro-criminal values, attitudes, and beliefs, associating with pro-criminal peers, personality factors such as impulsivity, lack of achievement in employment or school, family dysfunction, lack of pro-social leisure activities, and substance abuse.

Not surprisingly is the degree to which these criminogenic needs are found among the re-entering population. As we briefly discussed earlier, research finds that the vast majority of those re-entering the community have a history of substance abuse, are undereducated, lack employment skills, and reported family dysfunction (Petersilia 2003). With regard to employment, two-thirds of ex-prisoners report having employment before incarceration, however; most offenders have difficulty finding a job afterwards (Visher and Kachnowski 2007) with up to 75 % of ex-offenders remaining unemployed up to a year after release (Pager 2007). Ex-inmates are often limited to obtaining jobs on the "spot market" where they are only given temporary or seasonal work, instead of permanent employment (Petersilia 2003). One study also found that over 40 % of employers stated they would "probably not" or "definitely not" be willing to hire someone with a criminal record, and only 20 % indicated that they would definitely or probably hire a person with a criminal record (Holzer et al. 2004). Even with the recent "ban the box" legislation, those who are formerly incarcerated struggle to develop a stable lifestyle post release. Reentry programs should focus on the core criminogenic needs when developing services for clients. Unfortunately, reentry programs find it easier to work with some criminogenic needs over others as evidenced by the proliferation of employment-based programs rather than cognitive behavioral programs.

Responsivity Principle

The third principle of the RNR model is responsivity. Responsivity covers two broad areas of study. First, the specific responsivity principle refers to the importance of delivering an intervention that is appropriate and matches the abilities and styles of the client. Specific responsivity factors can range from individual level characteristics such as motivation and cognitive ability/intelligence to external factors such as transportation, childcare, and homelessness. For example, study of re-entering violent offenders in Nevada found that many clients were concerned how they would meet the obligations for parole or treatment if they did not have access to transportation and how they would manage to care for their dependents and simultaneously fulfill the requirements of treatment or how they would raise money for a down payment for housing (Listwan 2008). Later in this chapter, we will discuss the importance of using assessment results to identify and plan for barriers such as those discussed earlier.

Providing the most effective treatment approaches to reduce criminal behavior is the second area of focus under the responsivity principle. As noted earlier, one of the core criminogenic risk factors are pro-criminal attitudes, values, and beliefs. Those re-entering the community often have pro-criminal value systems that guide their interactions with the world around them. Put another way, people who believe it is acceptable to commit crime by justifying and minimizing their criminal behavior are more likely to engage that behavior (Cullen and Gendreau 2000). While a variety of treatment services are needed to attend to someone who is high risk and need, the empirical literature supports the use of strategies based on cognitive and social learning theories. These theories suggest that those who exhibit pro-criminal decision-making and have poor problem-solving and coping skills are more likely to be involved in criminal behavior.

Cognitive behavioral therapy focuses on how core beliefs influence emotions and behaviors. A core feature of this type of therapy is focus on how a dysfunctional cognitive processes influences emotions and behavior. Cognitive and social learning theories suggest that we learn these cognitions through interactions with intimate others. Programs can improve outcomes teaching clients to change or cope with these cognitions. Albert Ellis and Donald Meichenbaum's early work led to the widespread use of cognitive behavioral treatment to treat issues such as anger, trauma, stress, depression, and problematic relationships (Beck et al. 1985; Beck 1995; Beck and Fernandez 1998; Ellis 1973; Jaremko and Meichenbaum 2013; Meichenbaum 2014; Meichenbaum and Deffenbacher 1988). While certainly not to be oversold, cognitive behavioral treatment is one of the most effective approaches with offender populations with meta-analyses finding treatment effects in the range of 7–38% (Andrews et al. 1990; Carey 1992; Dowden and Andrews 1999; Drake et al. 2009; Nagayama Hall 1995; Landenberger and Lipsey 2005; Wilson et al. 2005).

Research on Reentry Programs

The significant growth in the numbers of reentry programs has increased the necessity for evaluating the effectiveness of these programs in assisting ex-prisoners reintegrate into their communities. Additionally, in the last two decades, practitioner and policy maker interest in the reentry movement has soared, and so has the funding of reentry programs and initiatives. Amidst the variety of programs that target an equally diverse range of needs for the offenders, the question that Petersilia (2004) asked more than a decade ago still begs for an answer: "which programs should government agencies, nonprofit organizations, and faith-based communities invest in?"(p. 4). The following section will explore the available research on the different types of reentry programs.

Research on Substance Abuse Programs

Reentry substance abuse programs fall mostly under two categories: TCs and aftercare programs. The research on aftercare programs has been mixed and a systematic review of aftercare programs concluded that the vague definition of what constitutes an aftercare program does not allow for proper examination of such programs. The same study maintained that previous research on aftercare programs was plagued by methodological problems, and more studies are needed to determine which characteristics of aftercare programs are most effective in reducing relapse to substance use (Pelissier et al. 2007).

On the other hand, there has been considerable research exploring the effects of prison TCs that have community components and recidivism. Pearson and Lipton (1999) conducted a meta-analysis of correctional treatment. They identified seven studies as evaluations of TCs. Analysis showed that TCs were effective in reducing recidivism by about 13 %. However, the authors pointed out that none of the studies were rated as methodologically rigorous, and to exert caution when interpreting the results (Belenko et al. 2012).

Similarly, in a meta-analytic review of prison drug treatments in North America and Western Europe, Mitchell and colleagues assessed 26 eligible studies resulting in 32 different effect sizes. Seventeen of the effect sizes were calculated from TC programs. While the overall effects on recidivism were modest, TC programs produced the strongest effects. However, the authors cautioned on the methodological weaknesses of the studies included in the meta-analysis (Mitchell et al. 2007). More recently, a meta-analysis of reentry programs identified 12 of its studies as TCs. The TC programs were statistically significant in reducing recidivism. The author concluded that the continuity of treatment from prison to community that is typical of the TC model that may account for treatment effectiveness (Ndrecka 2014).

Research on Mental Health Programs

Evaluations of reentry programs that target mentally ill offenders tend to be scarce, but even the studies that exist seem to reveal that improving symptoms of mental illness might not affect recidivistic behavior. Thus, in organizing the research on interventions for mentally ill offenders, Skeem and her colleagues maintain that mental health-centric models, such as Forensic Assertive Community Treatments (FACTs), have not been effective in reducing recidivism, but criminal justice-based models, such as specialized courts or supervision units, show some promise (Skeem and Peterson 2012; Skeem et al. 2010).

FACTs are based on Assertive Community Treatment (ACT) programs who were developed in the 1970s for non-correctional individuals that had comorbid health disorders and were at high risk for institutionalization. The programs combine treatment, rehabilitation, and support services from a team of professionals coming from a variety of disciplines including nurses, psychiatrists, and vocational counselors. The development of FACTS became necessary after the significant increase in mentally ill offenders returning to communities (Schlager 2013). Consequently, two experimental evaluations of ACT programs have not revealed an effect on recidivism rates. In one of the studies, a comparison between the ACT participants and those who received standard case management did not produce any significant differences in police contacts over a 3-year period (Clark et al. 1999). The second study, compared ACT, Integrated Dual Diagnosis Treatment, and treatment and usual and found no differences in arrests and incarceration (Calsyn et al. 2005; Skeem and Peterson 2012).

Evaluations of mental health courts have been more promising. Thus, Redlich (2005) found that participants of mental health courts recidivate less that those who do not. Specifically, in examining the case processing in seven mental health courts, Steadman et al. (2005) found that 1 year after enrollment in the court, participants were four times less likely to be arrested than in the year prior to their enrollment in the program. However, most mental health courts have been used as means to divert individuals into community programs rather than a prison sentence, or have been used with probation and jail populations (McGaha et al. 2002; Sarteschi et al. 2011); therefore, their effectiveness in addressing the needs of reentry populations is still questionable. Lastly, evaluations of specialized criminal justice programs for mentally ill offenders or offenders with co-occurring mental illness and substance dependency have exhibited significant reductions in recidivism (Kesten et al. 2012; Sacks et al. 2012; Sacks et al. 2004).

Research on Employment Programs

Considering the number of employment programs that exist for ex-prisoners, few studies have examined the effects of such programs on employment and recidivism outcomes. Additionally, the research that exists has produced mixed results. Thus, only nine studies have examined the effect of work-release programs and most of the results have not been favorable to this type of programs. Most of the studies have found that work release does not reduce recidivism (Drake 2007; Duwe 2015; Jeffery and Wolpert 1974; Lamb and Goertzel 1974; LeClair and Guarino-Ghezzi 1991; Rudoff and Esselstyn 1973; Turner and Petersilia 1996; Waldo and Chiricos 1977; Witte 1977).

The majority of the evaluations of work-release programs in the 1970s produced contradicting results. Thus, Rudoff and Esselstyn (1973) found that work release significantly reduced recidivism, while Lamb and Goertzel's (1974) evaluation of a jail work release in California revealed no significant differences in re-incarceration rates between program participants and the control group. On the other hand, an evaluation of a similar program (jail work release) in the same state by Jeffery and Wolpert (1974) found the program effective only among offenders with longer criminal histories, while ineffective among those who were only first- or second-time offenders. A few years later, Witte's (1977) North Carolina work-release evaluation found that work-release participants were arrested for lesser offenses than the comparison group counterparts, while Waldo and Chiricos (1977) found no significant effects in their assessment of a Florida program.

Two decades later the mixed theme of the results stayed consistent, as one study (LeClair and Guarino-Ghezzi 1991) reported that work release significantly reduced recidivism rates among participants, while the other (Turner and Petersilia 1996) cautioned that a quarter of the work-release participants returned to prison, while also reporting that the program did not reduce correctional costs. More recently, in reevaluating Washington's state work-release program, Drake (2007) found that it significantly reduced recidivism while being cost-effective. On the other hand, Duwe (2015) found that even though cost-effective, the Minnesota work-release program produced only modest reductions in reoffending.

The transitional job-placement and job-training program evaluations have also yielded miscellaneous results. Thus, two studies that have evaluated the Transitional Jobs Reentry Demonstration (TJRD), a program that provides vocational training and transitional employment for newly released offenders, have found that the program is ineffective on both employment and recidivism outcomes. Accordingly, while being part of the TJRD increased employment initially, the effects disappeared after the participants left the transitional job positions. In relation to recidivism, the TJRD did not significantly reduce arrests, reconvictions, or returns to prison (Jacobs 2012; Valentine and Redcross 2015).

However, other similar programs seem to fare better. The CEO program has been evaluated multiple times, and evaluations have revealed that while the effects of the program on employment tend to fade after participants leave the transitional job positions, the program significantly reduces recidivism both at a 3-month follow-up period (Redcross et al. 2012) and at a 2-year follow-up period (Valentine and Redcross 2015). Similarly, Duwe (2012) found significant results in recidivism reduction and increasing employment in his evaluation of Minnesota's EMPLOY program, a job-training and job-readiness program that commences in the institution and follows offenders up to a year after their release. Finally, Visher et al. (2005) conducted a meta-analysis of eight random-assignment employment programs and found that employment programs did not significantly reduce recidivism.

In attempting to make sense of the results of research on reentry employment programs Latessa (2012) reaffirms the importance of employment as an important step to community reintegration. However, he argues that the reason why so many employment programs fail in reducing recidivism is because they tend to address acute dynamic risk factors rather than targeting the dynamic factors that take time to change. Most employment programs help offenders develop a resume and find a job position, but they fail to address offenders' attitudes toward work, their poor problem-solving skills, or poor coping skills. It is by targeting the way that offenders think and feel about work, and by teaching them prosocial coping skills that change truly happens. Only by addressing these factors can employment programs become effective.

Evaluations of Reentry Courts

Research on reentry courts has begun to examine their effects on recidivism rates. However, with few exceptions, the available research on reentry courts is beleaguered by methodological limitations (Close et al. 2008; Spelman 2003; Hiller et al. 2002), or is in the preliminary stages of evaluation, focusing on the implementation process of courts procedures (Lindquist et al. 2014; Administrative Office of the Courts 2012). It should be noted that while all reentry courts have the same core concepts, they differ on their daily operations. For instance, participation in the Harlem reentry court is mandatory (Hamilton 2011), while the Student Transition and Recovery (STAR) program in Pennsylvania is voluntary (Taylor 2013). This might be one of the reasons why results from evaluation studies of reentry courts have produced miscellaneous results.

In one study, Farole (2003) conducted a process and an outcome evaluation of the Harlem reentry court using a quasi-experimental study. He found that reentry court participants were less likely to be reconvicted within a year of release than regular parolees, but they were more likely to return to prison than the comparison group. While neither of these findings were statistically significant, Farole (2003) concluded that the reentry court did not have an impact on recidivism. However, a reevaluation of Harlem court looking at participants after adjustments had taken places in daily operations found slightly more promising results. Thus, at a 2-year follow-up, Hamilton (2011) found that reentry court participants were being rearrested and reconvicted at significantly lower rates than traditional parolees. Nevertheless, participants had significantly higher technical violations than traditional parole pointing to the fact that closer supervision was resulting in possible iatrogenic effects for program participants.

Other reentry court evaluations have compared the outcomes from completers of the program to outcomes from non-completers. In examining the reentry court in Richland et al. (2006) examined the characteristics of participants and found that program completers were significantly different from non-completers. Completers were older, were more likely to be employed and were more likely to be more educated than non-completers suggesting that the success of the drug court depended more on participant characteristics rather than treatment available. Furthermore, at a 3-year follow-up period, 67 % of participants had not recidivated. The evaluation of the Delaware reentry court found similar positive results, with significant differences in recidivism between program completers and non-completers (9.14 % vs. 29.12 %) (Gebelein 2003).

More recent evaluations have found favorable results, although the evaluations have had methodological limitations. First, Close et al. (2008) compared program participants to a sample of matched traditional parolees and found that traditional parolees had participated in less services and had fewer sanctions and urinalyses; however, no data were provided for recidivism rates. Second, the evaluation of the Indiana reentry court found significantly lower rates of recidivism among court completers (41 %) and non-completers (52.7 %) than the expected national rate (67.5 %) (Pearson-Nelson 2009). Third, the California Administrative Office of the Courts (AOC) released a preliminary study of reentry courts in six counties in 2012. Comparing returns to prison rates after 1 year, they found that only 31 % of court participant's recidivated as compared to 46 % of all offenders released from California state prisons. (AOC 2012). Lastly, Taylor (2013) used a matched comparison group design in examining the STAR program in Pennsylvania, and found that participation in the program was associated with a significant reduction in revocations, but no differences in rearrests.

Finally, in attempting to identify effective characteristics of reentry courts, the federal government has funded a few multi-site evaluation of drug courts. The first multisite evaluation attempt was launched by the Office of Justice Programs in 2000 and resulted in a process evaluation for the first nine reentry court sites that were developed as part of the

Reentry Court Initiative, however funds were not appropriated for further studies (Lindquist et al. 2003). A decade later, with the passing of the Second Chance Act initiatives, the NIJ funded the Evaluation of Second Chance Adult Reentry Courts (NESCAARC). The funding has produced two process evaluations involving eight reentry court sites, while future funding is planned for a matched comparison group impact evaluation of all the participating sites examining outcomes that include recidivism, employment, substance abuse, and housing (Lindquist et al. 2013; Lindquist et al. 2014).

Evaluations of Halfway Houses

While evaluations of specific halfway houses exist (Dowell et al. 1985; Willison et al. 2010), few studies have assessed their effectiveness as a category of programs. Since many offenders who leave prisons are required to reside in halfway houses before being released into the community, assessing the effectiveness of halfway houses in how they impact the reentry process becomes an important issue for reentry scholars. There have been a few extensive halfway house evaluations in recent years. In the first one, Lowenkamp and Latessa (2005) assessed the effectiveness of 53 community-based residential programs that served parolees—38 halfway houses and 15 community-based correctional facilities (CCFs) across Ohio. Offenders who successfully completed treatment in these facilities were compared to a group of offenders who were not placed in residential programming for a follow-up period of 2 years. The evaluators calculated differences in recidivism rates for each of the program and by risk category of offenders.

The study found vast differences in the effectiveness of programs in reducing recidivism. Specifically, some programs reduced recidivism by over 30 %, while others had iatrogenic effects, some increasing recidivism rates by more than 35 %. When examining the risk categories, results showed that most programs were effective in reducing recidivism when high-risk offenders were targeted—about 70 % of them. But the effects were disastrous when low-risk offenders were included in treatment—about 67 % of the programs increased the recidivism rates of their participants. The results indicated that halfway houses can be effective when operated along the RNR model. They can be useful treatment venues for offenders that are not quite ready to return to the work force, have a substance abuse problem, and/or do not have prosocial families and networks when they leave prison (Lowenkamp and Latessa 2005).

In a similar study, Latessa et al. (2009) examined the effectiveness of halfway houses and community correction centers throughout the state of Pennsylvania. They evaluated 54 facilities with a total of 7,846 offenders. Data consistently showed that offenders placed in programs recidivated at higher rates than the offenders in the comparison group across all measures of recidivism (technical violation, rearrest, and re-incarceration). Similar to the Ohio study, the evaluation found that facilities were including low-risk offenders in treatment, and mixing the risk of offenders placed in treatment. This accounted for adverse effects on offender recidivism and poor performance of correctional programs.

Additionally, Latessa et al. (2010) conducted a follow-up study of the Ohio halfway houses. The new study improved on several methodological areas including an increased sample size, individual matching of the program participants, an examination of the characteristics for program participants and non-participants. The results were remarkably consistent with the findings from the original study. Halfway houses were successful in reducing recidivism, more so when only successful program completers were considered (5 %). However, the success of programs was still guided by the risk principle—higher reductions in recidivism were seen when program targeted high-risk offenders, while programs that targeted lower risk offenders had negative effects. Unfortunately, programmatic consistency had also persisted, as many programs that underperformed in the original study continued to perform poorly in the follow-up examination.

Lastly, Ostermann (2009) evaluated the New Jersey Parole Board Halfway Back Program, which uses halfway houses and day reporting programs to serve parolees. In his examination of halfway houses, Ostermann (2009) found that parolees who participated in halfway house programming were less likely to be arrested and reconvicted, and had a longer average time to recidivate than the comparison group. The halfway houses were also found to be cost-effective (White et al., 2011). In examining the work-release component of these same halfway houses, Routh and Hamilton (2015) found increased time to a technical violation and in the mean number of days until return to prison. However, no significant differences in recidivism were found between the halfway house participants and the comparison groups, raising questions about adherence to the RNR model in implementing these programs.

The SVORI Evaluation

The largest scale evaluation effort of reentry programs was the evaluation of the SVORI, conducted by the Urban Institute and RTI International. As mentioned previously, the SVORI agencies were awarded $100 million and created 89 programs for both adult and juvenile offenders. The evaluation of the SVORI included 16 programs (12 adult and 4 juvenile) throughout 14 states. Because the SVORI programs delivered different types of services and treatments, the evaluation did not concentrate on one type of reentry program, but instead it focused on the impact of services that the SVORI participants received. The evaluation examined differences on recidivism data, substance abuse, employment, and housing. Furthermore, interviews with offenders were conducted at 3, 9, and 15 months post release (Lattimore and Visher 2009).

Overall, the SVORI impact evaluation did not show significant differences between SVORI participants and non-SVORI participants in any of the measures including recidivism, housing, and substance abuse. Specifically, at the 15-month follow-up, the SVORI had no significant effects on securing housing for adult or juvenile offenders. Furthermore, drug use tended to increase over time for adult males, adult females, and juvenile offenders. While the SVORI participants reported less drug use, differences between the SVORI participants and non-participants were insignificant at the 15-month follow-up. The SVORI had a modest effect on employment for all offenders, with more SVORI participants reporting having worked significantly more days in the 15 months than the non-SVORI participants. However, when comparing re-incarceration rates, there were no significant differences between the SVORI participants and non-participants (Lattimore and Visher 2009).

Another evaluation was conducted at a 56-month follow-up for adult offenders and a 24-month follow-up for juveniles, and found that the SVORI participants had fewer arrests and longer times to arrest for all the three groups. The SVORI adult males were also less likely to get incarcerated and had a longer time to incarceration, but the results were not statistically significant. For adult women and juveniles, differences in incarceration were not significant (Lattimore et al. 2012).

Comprehensive Reviews of Reentry Research

To date, only two studies have attempted to systematically review and organize the research on reentry programs. The first review was conducted by Seiter and Kadela (2003). The authors examined 32 reentry studies that were published between 1975 and 2001. Using the Maryland Scale of Scientific Methods (MSSM) the reentry programs were ranked on methodological rigor (Sherman et al. 1998). Studies assigned a score of one were marked as methodologically weak (no control group, correlation measured between program and recidivism), while studies assigned a score of five were considered the strongest in internal validity (random assignment of program participants in experimental and control group).

In determining what programs were effective in reducing recidivism the authors took a two-step approach. First, the 32 studies were divided into different categories: drug rehabilitation programs, vocational and work programs, educational programs, sex offender and violent offenders, halfway house programs, and prison-prerelease programs. Second, a category of programs were classified as "working" when two or more evaluations with a score of at least three on the MSSM, and a statistical significant finding existed for that particular category (Seiter and Kadela 2003).

Based on these criteria, four different categories of reentry programs were determined to be effective in reducing offender recidivism: drug rehabilitation programs, vocational and work programs, halfway houses, and prison-prerelease programs. Sex offender and violent programs were deemed to be promising, but authors cautioned for additional research in the area, while educational programs were found unsuccessful in reducing recidivism. More importantly, Seiter and Kadela (2003) were the first to elaborate a definition for reentry programs: (a) programs that focused on the transition of the offenders from prisons to the community, (b) programs that provided a continuity of care from correctional programs into community. This was quite an important development considering the variety of reentry programs.

More than a decade later, Ndrecka (2014) conducted a meta-analysis of 53 studies published between 1980 and 2013, resulting in 58 effect sizes. Using Seiter and Kadela's (2003) definition of reentry programs, the meta-analysis found that overall, reentry programs reduced recidivism by 6 %. However, significant heterogeneity effects were found among the reentry programs examined, with some of them reducing recidivism as much as 39 % while others increasing recidivism by 17 %. These findings are consistent with prior research examining correctional program effectiveness. Thus, the overall effectiveness of correctional programs hovers around 10 % (Andrews et al. 1990; Losel 1995), but similarly to this meta-analysis, prior research has shown considerable variability in program effectiveness.

Next, in attempting to determine which program characteristics were associated with larger reductions in recidivism, Ndrecka (2014) examined a number of program characteristics. Generally, her findings were consistent with the "what works" literature. Specifically, it was found that programs were more effective when they exemplified a "true" reentry program model and offered treatment in three phases: an institutional phase, a transitional phase, and a community phase. Programs that assisted offenders in making the transition from the institution to the community had higher reductions in recidivism. Thus, two-phase (es=.12; CI =.08 to.17) and three-phase programs (es=.11; CI=.04 to.18) were significantly more effective in reducing recidivism than one phase programs (es=.06; CI=.04 to.08). Prior research suggests that structuring programs in this manner ensures that changes in the offender's life are addressed as they take place (Listwan et al. 2006; Seiter and Kadela 2003; Taxman et al. 2003).

Ndrecka also examined treatment effectiveness by location of treatment. Consistent with previous research (Gendreau 1996) programs that are delivered in the community were more effective in reducing recidivism than residential programs. In the case of reentry programs, programs that were delivered in the community (es = .04; CI = .02 to .07) and programs delivered in phases involving both the institution and the community produced significant reductions in recidivism (es = .11; CI = .08 to .15) further reinforcing the idea that the transition period is the most important in effective reintegration (Listwan et al. 2006; Taxman et al. 2003).

The effects of reentry programs were also scrutinized by the risk category of offenders. While many studies that were included in the meta-analysis failed to report the risk of program participants, analysis of the effect sizes in the studies that did report risk were in line with previous research (Latessa et al. 2009; Latessa et al. 2010; Lowenkamp and Latessa 2005c). Only programs that targeted high-risk offenders resulted in significant recidivism reductions (es = .07; CI = .01 to .13), while programs that targeted low-risk offenders did not result in significant results, or produced iatrogenic effects on recidivism (Ndrecka 2014).

Lastly, significant differences in effectiveness were also found when considering program length (Ndrecka 2014). Programs that continued for 13 weeks or longer has significant effects on reducing recidivism (es = .12; CI = .08 to .15), while programs lasting 12 weeks or less had no effect. These findings are in line with previous research that suggests that programs shorter than 3 months are insufficient in the length of time needed to produce changes in behavior (Gendreau 1996).

Each of these practices and policies attempt to provide avenues for agencies to follow when implementing best practices into their agencies. However, as was seen with the SVORI programs, implementing these programs is not without difficulties. These programs need multiple levels of support at the state and local levels, and they must be designed with best practices in mind. Designing and implementing evidence-based reentry programs based on these research findings requires careful attention and monitoring. The next section will out-line the various issues programs should consider when developing their programs.

Designing and Implementing Evidence-Based Reentry Programs

As noted in the review above, much of the literature on reentry services and programs is mixed. We argue that in order for reentry programs to be more effective, the focus should shift from only attending to acute needs (e.g., housing and unemployment) to focusing on those needs which have been found to be directly related to criminal behavior (e.g., problem-solving skills and pro-criminal attitudes). Further, one of the barriers impeding the development of effective reentry programming is the lack of coordinated and thoughtful cross system approach. Part of the problem in this regard is that the term reentry is still fairly broad as it can refer to any process involving the release of an inmate and can include "almost any experience that offenders have had during and after their incarceration" (Jonson and Cullen 2015, p. 522). Reentry programs, however, are not a typical "program" but rather represent a system of service delivery. While Taxman et al. (2003) are widely cited for their discussion of a three or more phased approach that begins with offering inmates services in the institution and extends for a period of service delivery and supervision in the community (and Ndrecka 2014 found support for this approach), the basic structure does not provide a clear path for how to design and implement reentry programs across multiple systems (e.g., prison, parole, halfway houses, community providers, work release, etc.).

In this section we will focus our attention on five core areas that will assist programs with design and implementation of reentry services. First, we will discuss the importance of planning for implementation prior to the development of a reentry program. Second, we will review the importance of using quality RNR assessments to guide the type, duration and dosage of treatment services for the client. Third, we will discuss targets for change that include important considerations like housing and jobs but also sustained efforts toward reducing recidivism.

In that context, we will discuss the importance of using core correctional practices. Fourth, we will discuss the importance of ensuring the community supervision officers are trained to assist the client with their treatment needs and also utilizing evidence-based approaches. Finally, we will consider the importance of fidelity that includes monitoring the degree to which the reentry program is operating as designed.

Program Development

Given that reentry programs are designed to begin in the institution and continue into the community, a high degree of collaboration among agencies is essential. Developing relationships among stakeholders in across multiple systems is challenging. For some states, this process is even more difficult given the structure inherent in states with separate departments of corrections and parole. Even in states without separate agencies, the degree of collaboration between supervising agencies varies. One such solution, as found in the SVORI model, is to require grantees to appoint a reentry coordinator who would be responsible for orchestrating the services and practices among the agencies both in the institution and community.

The reentry coordinator must be in a leadership position with responsibility for coordinating agencies and monitoring fidelity. Studies suggest that having leadership within programs is key for the implementation and sustainability of reentry programs. For example, Byrne et al. (2002) suggest that leaders can build consensus, support, and collaboration among agencies involved in the client's reentry process. Having a program director that is not only well versed in the literature but is also able to translate that knowledge to staff is key. This role may include bimonthly meetings, program visits, and data collection. Ultimately it is the reentry coordinator's responsibility to create a therapeutic alliance among stakeholders.

The reentry coordinator should be the "face" of the program and create a clear model to keep policy makers informed and build stakeholder support. The coordinator should be involved in all major decision steps from selecting appropriate clients into the program to making program termination decisions. The continuity provided by the coordinator has the potential to increase the quality of implementation. In fact, in a meta-analysis, Lipsey et al. (2010) found that three factors predicted program effectiveness: the type of intervention, the type of offender (high risk) and the quality of the implementation.

In order to design appropriate services, reentry programs should create selection criteria for program admittance. Written selection criteria allow organizations to screen out individuals who do not need intensive services and design appropriate services based on client's risks and needs. At a minimum, reentry programs should follow the risk principle and target those who are moderate to high risk of failure in the community. As discussed in previous sections, relying on one factor such as a violent charge will produce an eclectic group of clients to treat thereby making service delivery difficult to design and implement. The selection criteria should be based in part on empirically driven assessment results.

Assessment

As discussed in "Evidence-Based Practices and the RNR Model", the RNR model begins with the assessment process. The assessment process should begin while the client is institutionalized and should be flexible and responsive to changes in the clients' risks and needs. The selection of an empirically supported assessment tool(s) is important for reentry programs. There are several common tools currently in use throughout the country. For example, two of the most commonly used are the Level of Service-Case Management Inventory (LS-CMI) for adults (Andrews et al. 2004) and the Youth Level of Service-CMI for juveniles (Andrews and Hoge 2004). The tools include all of the core criminogenic needs (e.g., education/employment, family/marital, peers, etc.) and an assessment of responsivity considerations and case planning tools. The Ohio Revised Assessment System (ORAS) is another empirically supported assessment tool for adults (Latessa et al. (2010) and the Ohio Youth Assessment System (OYAS) for juveniles (Lovins and Latessa 2013) that were developed at the University of Cincinnati. The assessment contains five separate tools that can be used as stand-alone tools or as a set depending on the case plan of the client. The instrument covers all of the major risk factors including history, family and living arrangements, peers, education and employment, pro-social skills, substance abuse, mental health and personality, and values, beliefs and attitudes (Latessa et al. 2009). All of these assessment tools provide an indication of the client's overall risk and need profile. For example, the assessment tools indicate the client's risk for recidivism and whether the client is high risk within a specific domain (e.g., peers, family, pro-criminal cognitions). Depending on the clients selected for the program, the staff would also be advised to provide additional assessments of core criminogenic domains (e.g., addiction) or offense specific indicators (e.g., sex offending).

Planning for the eventual release of the client will involve assessing for both risk/need and responsivity factors that could impact the likelihood of failure. For example, it may be important to screening out low functioning offenders from services that require a high range of cognitive functioning or develop pre-treatment modules for those who score low on assessments of motivation. Depending on the tools chosen by the program, the reassessment process may occur prior to and immediately following the client's released into the community. The ORAS tool has several modules that can be utilized depending on whether the person is in prison (prison intake) or has entered the community (reentry).

Reassessing client's risks and needs is important for identify needs that may change once the client re-enters the community. Reassessments should continually occur throughout the duration of the reentry program. Reassessment can inform key stakeholders as to whether the program or services had an impact on the offender's overall risk, which can positively impact support for the program. For example, a study by Hollin et al. (2003) found that changes in risk level (as measured by the LSI-R) were significantly associated with reductions in recidivism among clients.

Changing Offender Behavior

Once the program adopts meaningful selection criteria and assessment tool (s), the staff can plan for the reentry program itself. The first few months post release are the highest risk time period for the client and the services should be intensive from the outset and last until the client's core crim-inogenic needs are addressed. However, many correctional programs are forced to devote resources to crisis management such as housing, medical, and transportation issues rather than core treatment needs such as antisocial peers, dysfunctional family patterns, or cognitions. This is an area where the leadership of the reentry coordinator is important. The coordinator should educate stakeholders to understand that the dosage of treatment should be sufficient in length to impact behavioral change. For higher risk individuals that dosage will likely need to reach a threshold of 200 hours of more of services to see significant reductions in recidivism (Sperber et al. 2013). This level of treatment will take time and requires a commitment on part of the reentry program stakeholders.

However, programs should be mindful that providing a certain dosage or amount of treatment is not the same as providing appropriately matched services. A client's time can easily be filled with activities that may not lead to sustained behavioral change. For example, employment programs likely fail because they focus on filling a client's time with simple activities (e.g., resume building and job seeking) rather than core issues such as the client's attitudes toward work, their poor problem-solving skills, or poor coping skills. Providing empirically supported strategies is more important than providing a certain number of service hours.

As we discussed in the Risk, Need, and Responsivity Framework section, cognitive behavioral treatment models are the most effective approach when dealing with pro-criminal attitudes, values and beliefs. As suggested by Haney (2002), many inmates return home from prison with entrenched antisocial attitudes and values due to their long histories with the criminal justice system. Cognitive behavioral programs target these risk factors and can teach clients skills that help them manage their behaviors across multiple settings (not just while they are in the program). Studies suggest that inmates who possess rational coping skills are more likely to experience better mental health and physical health outcomes in addition to reentry outcomes (Cochran 2012; Grennan and Woodhams 2007; Ireland et al. 2005; Liebling 1995).

In addition to skill building, programs based on a cognitive behavioral approach have several important features. These features are referred to as the core correctional practices (Andrews and Kiessling 1980; Andrews and Carvell 1998; Dowden and Andrews 2004; Gendreau 1996; Latessa et al. 2013). The core correctional practices include five broad components: effective use of authority, anti-criminal modeling and reinforcement, problem solving, use of community resources, and quality of relationships between clients and staff. Given reentry programs are not simply programs but incorporate the entire reentry process, these core correctional practices are relevant to all of the partners (e.g., program staff, parole officers). For example, effective use of authority not only means what it implies (i.e., that staff use authority in a successful way) but also incorporates the importance of developing rules and expectations that are clear and fair to the client throughout the reentry process. In a reentry program, the expectations for the client should be set forth from the beginning with the client kept informed of their progress throughout treatment. Having all stakeholders involved in the process and versed in these principles is key to this approach.

Second, staff acting as anti-criminal models and providing reinforcement for good behavior is another crucial aspect of cognitive behavioral approaches. According to Dowden and Andrews (2004), "the underlying goal of this approach is that offenders will learn prosocial and anti-criminal attitudinal, cognitive, and behavioral patterns from their regular interactions with front line staff" (p. 205). Cognitive and social learning theories suggest that we learn both vicariously and directly through our experiences with others. If staff model antisocial behavior the clients are likely to justify their antisocial behavior. The behavioral literature clearly finds that reinforced behavior is more likely to be repeated. Individuals who are reinforced for prosocial behavior are more likely to repeat that behavior and eventually that reinforcement motivates an individual to produce long term behavioral change (Bandura 1977). Third, the core correctional practices include skill-based approaches that teach clients a wide array of problem-solving skills to cope with strain in multiples areas of their lives (e.g., employment, peer pressure, relationships).

The fourth area, utilizing community resources, is particularly relevant to reentry coordinators. Reentry coordinators should be mindful of this during the implementation phase, however, it is also likely that the level of community involvement and support will fluctuate over time. For example, some programs enjoy a tremendous amount of community support during the implementation phase only to find that some partners lose interest post implementation. In other circumstances, stakeholders may be added or dropped due to the changing needs of the clients involved in the program. Having a qualified reentry coordinator is key in this area as he or she can socialize new stakeholders regarding the philosophy and goals of the program.

Finally, the quality of staff/client relationship is important. As we have discussed, "staff" in the context of reentry can include the prison staff, treatment staff, probation/parole officers, community stakeholders, mentors, and in some cases may include the client's family and supports. Quality relationships include factors such as warmth, respect, and trust can influence the therapeutic alliance between staff and client. In fact, Dowden and Andrews (2004) found that quality of interpersonal relations among staff and client were important features of effective programs. Within the context of staff, the role of probation and parole staff in the therapeutic alliance has recently gained quite a bit of attention.

Effective Community Supervision Practices

Recently the RNR model has been applied to community supervision officers to encourage their role in the offender change process. An analysis of audiotaped interactions among 62 Canadian probation officers and their clients "found relatively poor adherence to the RNR principles. For example, other than substance abuse and family/marital problems, most criminogenic needs were infrequently addressed. Pro-criminal attitudes were discussed in only 3 of cases. Furthermore, cognitive-behavioral techniques such as prosocial modeling and role playing along with practice were demonstrated in less than one-quarter of the sessions" (Bonta et al. 2010, p. 2). In response, Bonta et al. (2010) created a training program for community supervision officers called the Strategic Training Initiative in Community Supervision (STICS). The training program was designed to provide officers with a background in the RNR model and core correctional practices and teach them skills they could use in their one-on-one sessions with clients. Their research supports the use of this approach with offenders. Using a randomized control design they found that clients who were supervised by officers utilizing the STICS approach (particularly the cognitive techniques) were significantly less likely to recidivate compared to controls (Bonta et al. 2010). Other studies support training community supervision officers. For example, a study by Chadwick et al. (2015) that also found offenders supervised by officers trained in core correctional practices were less likely to recidivate.

Researchers at the University of Cincinnati developed a similar approach for both juvenile and adult probation/parole agencies referred to as the Effective Practices in Community Supervision (EPICS) model (Smith et al. 2012). As with the STICS protocol, officers are trained in core correctional practices and encouraged to provide brief skill-based interventions to probationers during their client meetings. The EPICS model has been implemented across the United States in both juvenile and adult agencies. Preliminary research finding are similar to those mentioned above with trained supervision officers performing better than untrained officers (Labrecque et al. 2013).

The University of Cincinnati is expanding the EPICS model to target what they refer to as "influencers." The goal of EPICS-I is to identify prosocial support in an offender's life and teach those influencers core correctional practices used within the EPICS model. An influencer can be any pro-social support in the client's life. For example, family, significant others, peers, mentors, coaches, religious figures, law enforcement, or social service agencies could be involved. By teaching these individuals these skills they could support the treatment process, encourage pro-social problem-solving skills and provide modeling and reinforcement for pro-social behavior.

Each of these models has one thing in common—creating an environment that supports offender change through utilizing theoretically informed and empirically supported treatment strategies. As noted in the above discussion, the more supports that can be brought into an individual's life, the higher the likelihood that we will see long-term offender change and desistence from crime. All of this discussion, however, is for naught if the reentry program is not implemented with fidelity. Next, we will discuss the importance of fidelity when implementing reentry programs and services.

Fidelity

Whether due to staff or leadership changes or simply program drift, all programs go through a process of change over time. Attending to this change and creating a culture that supports change while maintaining program fidelity is key. Earlier in this section, we noted the importance of leadership in program development and sustainability. In order to achieve this, the reentry coordinator should assume some role in training/educating staff in the various agencies serving clients. Socializing staff members on the philosophy of the intended program is important for sustaining the culture and ensuring that the program is implemented as designed. In effect, the coordinator must help establish a therapeutic alliance among multiple agencies and staff. Studies suggest that positive attitudes toward evidence-based practices among staff are partly due to the level of support and encouragement given (Aarons and Sawitzky 2006).

Up to this point we have placed quite a bit of responsibility on the reentry coordinator. It is naïve to assume that one person can design, implement and monitor the fidelity of any program. Developing a reentry leadership team is critical to assist with the responsibility of the program and building support for the program. Developing and sustaining interest and support among stakeholders is important. For example, studies find that those who report high levels of job satisfaction, which included high ratings of director leadership, were less likely to leave the organization (Garner et al. 2012).

In addition to leadership teams, coaching and continual training for staff members should be required to ensure the program is operating with fidelity (Landenberger and Lipsey 2005). Clinical supervision may be more likely to occur among social service agencies, but is it equally important for it to be provided for all of those providing services (e.g., community supervision officers). Research by Miller et al. (2004) found that training alone is typically insufficient to ensure staff becomes proficient in a particular skill such as motivational interviewing. In fact, they found that the officers who received training with feedback and coaching were the only ones who were able to maintain the skill during the 4-month follow-up period. Similarly, in both the STICS and EPICS training programs, probation officers receive coaching and are encouraged to meet monthly as a group to discuss benefits and problems with the approach. In addition, officers are required to submit audiotapes for review by highly trained staff that provides feedback on their performance. It is important to build this clinical supervision piece into the process early and create a culture where staff feels supported through the coaching process rather than made to believe they will be punished if found to be struggling with a concept.

Fidelity should also be monitored through performance data. Stakeholders should plan for evaluation and data collection from program outset. In addition to long-term outcome measures, such as reductions in recidivism, programs should also be interested in tracking intermediate outcomes. For example, measuring progress among program participants as they matriculate from the prison to the community can determine whether the services are working as designed. Other program traces include collecting data on client's education status, antisocial attitudes, motivation, employment, and substance use. Collecting these data at multiple points in time allows the program to assess for improvements in these areas. Documenting the performance or progress of program participants will help determine treatment effects. By focusing on performance rather than activities a reentry program can measure intermediate outcomes that should serve as a prelude to reductions in recidivism.

Shortcomings and Barriers to Change

So, what gets in the way of designing and implementing effective reentry programs and what are some of the shortcomings? Based on hundreds of program assessments[2], many involving reentry programs as well as several large studies (Latessa et al. 2010: Lowenkamp and Latessa

---

[2] Staff at the University of Cincinnati have conducted assessments of over 600 correctional programs throughout the United States using the Correctional Program Assessment Inventory or the Correctional Program Checklist.

2003, Lowenkamp 2003; Lowenkamp and Latessa 2005a; Lowenkamp and Latessa 2005b) a number of number of deficiencies, obstacles and barriers have been identified that often impede the development and implementation of effective reentry programs (Latessa et al. 2016).

Lack of Leadership

Reentry programs come in many forms. Some are self-contained programs, such as halfway houses, while others are coalitions of various agencies and service providers that come together in an attempt to assist offenders that are returning to the community. Regardless of the form, effective programs have strong leadership that is characterized by well qualified leaders that are involved in the design and overall management of the program. Unfortunately, many program suffer from a lack of leadership. Below are some of the issues we often see related to ineffective leadership:

- Give change lip service to using evidence-based practices, but do not really want to change approach
- No identified overseer of changes or unstable leadership
- Want to pick and choose elements from a model rather than implement the model as designed
- Reluctant to challenge staff and hold people accountable
- Too busy to get involved in the actual "program"
- Don't understand the model
- Fail to develop detailed program description and program manuals
- Failure to develop quality assurance processes (or to follow-through when given information)

Lack of Support from Supervisors

While strong leadership is necessary, it is not sufficient, and over the years we have learned that without the support and involvement of the supervisors, most change efforts fall flat. Since staff often take their cues from their immediate supervisors, without their commitment it is unlikely that change will occur. Some of the common barriers are as follows:

- Supervisors feel threatened (fear staff will know more than they do)
- Don't have the skills or competencies
- Fail to ensure staff are implementing the program as designed
- Are not part of the decision-making
- Afraid to challenge staff or hold them accountable
- Develop an "us against them mentality" (form alliance with staff to resist change)

Staff

In recent years there have been several studies that have demonstrated the importance of staff to effective interventions (Lowenkamp et al. 2010; Schaffer et al. 2012; Lowenkamp et al. 2006). In a study of halfway houses and CCFs, Makarios et al. (2016) found that the characteristic of staff, staff training, and staff supervision were all significantly related to positive outcomes. While staff often play a criterial role in reentry programs, unfortunately, there are also a great deal of shortcomings in this area. There are a number of issues related to staff and the challenges of implementing evidence-based programming:

- Natural resistance to change
- Are often "true" believers in existing model (sometimes because "it worked for them")
- Don't have the skills or competencies
- Requires work (I wasn't hired for this)
- Are not challenged or held accountable by supervisors
- High turnover
- Lack of training and coaching
- Poor supervision or no clinical support
- Staff are not selected based on values and skills

Assessment

Given the importance of the risk and need principles, it follows that offender assessment is an essential aspect of effective reentry programs.

While use of validate assessment tools are commonplace in probation and parole agencies (Jones et al. 1999). Jones), many reentry programs have yet to fully implement sound assessment practices. As a result, some of the common deficiencies are as follows:

- Rely on "clinical" assessments (often done by non-clinicians) rather than actuarial assessments
- Assess offenders then don't use it—everyone gets the same treatment
- Do not develop and/or update treatment plans
- Do not reassess
- Make errors and don't correct
- Do not adequately train staff in use or interpretation
- Assessment instruments are not validated or normed
- Do not budget for assessment cost
- Do not assess responsivity factors

Programming

As discussed earlier, the services and programs that are actually provided in the reentry process can vary tremendous and are often provided in a wide range of settings including institutions, residential placements such as halfway houses, and the community. We know that the type and quality of the programming and services can have a profound effect on outcomes such as recidivism. There are numerous deficiencies and obstacles in this area and the end results are reentry programs that are not effective in reducing recidivism.

- Failure to develop programming around an evidence-based model
- Failure to provide programming and services that target criminogenic areas, or density of targeting criminogenic needs is not sufficient
- One size fits all—everyone gets the same programming
- Unwillingness to adjust the program schedule (particularly when the dosage needs to be increased)
- Limited or no training of family
- Programs are not multimodality but rather focus on one of two areas

- Little if any actual skill development for participants
- Quick to conclude that changes to treatment aren't working (if a participant fails or treatment component requires modification)
- Lack of consistency in high fidelity program delivery

Program Quality

Perhaps the greatest challenge is one of continuous quality assurance, making sure the program is being implemented as designed. Of course being truly evidence based ultimately requires a program to gather information and data to see if it actually producing the desired effects. While conducing outcome studies is often beyond the expertise and scope of a program, ensuring that the program and its components are being consistently done well is not. Some of the shortcomings in this area include:

- Failing to identify or correct drifting from the program model
- Introduction of "new" program elements that are not always consistent with the program's model
- Failure to have develop or implement quality assurance processes, such as ongoing observation of service delivery with feedback
- Failure to develop performance measures
- Failure to examine outcomes
- Failure to develop meaningful completion criteria based on participant performance
- Failure to respond to findings from QA processes

Ten Suggestions for Overcoming Obstacles

Of course many of these barriers apply to almost all correctional programs, not just those focusing on reentry efforts and we would be remiss if we did not offer suggestions for developing more effective reentry programs and dealing with some of the obstacles.

1. There is a strong need for reentry programs to find leaders to serve as champions for the program and the more levels the better.

2. Supervisors are the key to successful implementation and they need to be involved in the process from an early stage. They also need to be given additional training and should serve as coaches for line-staff.

3. All staff need to be trained, but training alone isn't enough, they need ongoing coaching and support as well as booster sessions.

4. One way to make sure the program is focused on criminogenic needs is to distinguish between activities that can help someone adjust back to the community and those core correctional programs that will help reduce recidivism. By doing so, it will help reentry programs keep focus on criminogenic targets and reduce program drift, and it also allows for components that address more general needs that many offenders have as well.

5. The formal programming needs to be manualized. This provides structure and is easier to replicate and train staff, improves quality assurance, and improves consistency.

6. Develop quality assurance processes. These can include case file audits, regular observation of groups and other activities, provide staff coaching and peer review, conduct participant satisfaction surveys and or exit interviews, clinical supervision, and program audits by outside groups.

7. Data and evaluation makes a difference and all programs need to collect data and use the information to make changes as needed. Partnering with local colleges and universities to assist with research efforts is one approach that can be mutually beneficial.

8. Invest in staff. Provide training, both initial and ongoing, allow some input into the program, make sure they have enough time to learn and pilot new approaches and interventions, and provide support and supervision.

9. If the program employs licensed professional staff then they need to be involved in monitor groups and staff, provide training, and serve as coaches.

10. Remember, change is difficult. Don't try and do everything at once. Pilot new interventions and tools and develop realistic timeframes for implementation.

Conclusions

Reentry programs provide an important safety net for those leaving prisons and jails as well as the community. In an ideal setting, reentry programs would provide men and women the needed support they need to get back on their feet, as well as the programs and services needs to reduce recidivism. Unfortunately, as discussed throughout this chapter, most reentry efforts still have a long way to go to achieve this goal. The good news is that there is a large body of knowledge based on many years of research that has demonstrated that we know a great deal about what works in reducing recidivism. In addition, many of the characteristics of effective programs are that are well known and can be easily summarized are involved leadership, qualified and committed staff, good assessment practices, programming that is evidence based and delivered in a responsive manner, and using data and information to make sure the program is operating as designed.

As this chapter has attempted to illustrate, the challenge is not knowing what to do but rather making sure there is program integrity in what we do and it is done reasonably well. This is critical because in order for reentry efforts to maintain political and financial support they need to demonstrate effectiveness. Finally, while there are a great many obstacles and barriers to overcome we have also tried to provide a roadmap that can help lead the way to design and implement more effective reentry programs.

References

Administrative Office of the Courts (2012). *AOC briefing: A preliminary look at California parolee reentry court*. Judicial Council of California.

Aarons, G. A., & Sawitzky, A. C. (2006). Organizational culture and climate and mental health provider attitudes toward evidence-based practice. *Psychological Services, 3*, 61–72.

Andrews, D. A., & Bonta, J. (1998). The psychology of criminal conduct (2nd ed.). Cincinnati, OH: Anderson Publishing.

Andrews, D. A., & Carvell, C. (1998). Core correctional training–core correctional supervision and counseling: Theory, research, assessment and practice. Unpublished training manual, Carleton University, Ottawa, Canada.

Andrews, D. A., & Dowden, C. (2006). Risk principle of case classification in correctional treatment a meta-analytic investigation. *International Journal of Offender Therapy and Comparative Criminology, 50,* 88–100.

Andrews, D. A., & Hoge, R. D. (2004). *Youthful level of service/case management inventory (YLS/CMI).* Toronto, Canada: Multi-Health Systems.

Andrews, D. A., & Kiessling, J. J. (1980). Program structure and effective correctional practices: A summary of the CaVIC research. In R. R. Ross & P. Gendreau (Eds.), *Effective Correctional Treatment* (pp. 439–463). Cincinnati, OH: Anderson Publishing.

Andrews, D. A., Bonta, J., Wormith, J. S. (2006). The recent past and near future of risk and/or need assessment. *Crime and delinquency, 52,* 7.

Andrews, D. A., Bonta, J., Wormith, S. J. (2004). *The level of service/case management inventory (LS/CMI).* Toronto, Canada: Multi-Health Systems.

Andrews, D. A., Guzzo, L., Raynor, P., Rowe, R. C., Rettinger, L. J., Brews, A., et al. (2012). Are the major risk/need factors predictive of both female and male reoffending? A test with the eight domains of the level of service/case management inventory. *International Journal of Offender Therapy and Comparative Criminology, 56,* 113–133.

Andrews, D. A., Zinger, I., Hoge, R. D., Bonta, J., Gendreau, P., Cullen, F. T. (1990). Does correctional treatment work? A clinically relevant and psychologically informed meta-analysis. *Criminology, 28,* 369–404.

Baillargeon, J., Binswanger, I. A., Penn, J. V. Williams, B. A., Murray, O. J. (2009). Psychiatric disorders and repeat incarcerations: The revolving prison door. *The American Journal of Psychiatry, 166,* 103–109.

Bandura, A. (1977). Self-efficacy: Toward a unifying theory of behavioral change. *Psychological Review, 84,* 135–155.

Beck, A. J. (2000). *Prisoners in 1999.* Washington, DC: Bureau of Justice Statistics, U.S. Department of Justice.

Beck, A. J., & Mumola, C. (1999). *Prisoners in 1998.* Washington, DC: Bureau of Justice Statistics, U.S. Department of Justice.

Beck, A. T. (1995). *Cognitive therapy: Basics and beyond.* New York: Guilford Press.

Beck, A. T., Emery, G., Greenberg, R. L. (1985). *Anxiety disorders and phobias: A cognitive approach.* New York: Basic Books.

Beck, R., & Fernandez, E. (1998). Cognitive-behavioral therapy in the treatment of anger: A meta-analysis. *Cognitive Therapy and Research, 22,* 63–74.

Belenko, S., House, K. A., Welsh, W. (2012). Understanding the impact of drug treatment in correctional settings. In J. Petersilia & K.R. Reitz (Eds.),

The Oxford handbook of sentencing and corrections (pp. 463–491). New York: Oxford University Press.

Blackburn, A. G., Mullings, J. L., Marquart, J. W. (2008). Sexual assault in prison and beyond: Toward an understanding of lifetime sexual assault among incarcerated women. *The Prison Journal, 88*, 351–377.

Blumstein, A., & Beck, A. J. (1999). Population growth in the U.S. Prisons, 1980–1996. *Crime and Justice, 26*, 17–61.

Bonta, J., Bourgon, G., Rugge, T., Scott, T. L., Yessine, A. K., Gutierrez, L., Li, J., (2010). *The strategic training initiative in community supervision: Risk-need-responsivity in the real world 2010–01.* Ottawa: Public Safety Canada.

Bonta, J., Wallace-Capretta, S., Rooney, J. (2000). A quasi-experimental evaluation of an intensive rehabilitation supervision program. *Criminal Justice and Behavior, 27*, 312–329.

Bourgon, G., & Armstrong, B. (2005). Transferring the principles of effective treatment into a "real world" prison setting. *Criminal Justice and Behavior, 32*, 3–25.

Braga, A. A., Piehl, A. M., Hureau, D. (2009). Controlling violent offenders released to the community: An evaluation of the Boston Reentry Initiative. *Journal of Research in Crime and Delinquency, 46*(4), 411–436.

Bureau of Justice Statistics. (2014). *Prisoners, year end, 2012.* Washington, DC: Department of Justice.

Bushway, S. D., & Paternoster, R. (2014). Identity and desistance from crime. In J. A. Humprey and P. Cordella (Eds.), *Effective interventions in the lives of criminal offenders* (pp. 63–77). New York: Springer.

Byrne, J., Taxman, F., Young, D. (2002). *Emerging roles and responsibilities in the reentry partnership initiative: New ways of doing business.* Washington, DC: National Institute of Justice.

Calsyn, R., Yonker, R., Lemming, M., Morse, G., Klinkenberg, D. (2005). Impact of assertive community treatment and client characteristics on criminal justice outcomes in dual disorder homeless individuals. *Criminal Behavior and Mental Health, 15*, 236–248.

Carey, G. (1992). Twin imitation for antisocial behavior: Implications for genetic and family environment research. *Journal of Abnormal Psychology, 101*, 18–25.

Carson, E. A., & Sabol, W. J. (2012). *Prisoners in 2011.* Washington, D.C.: Bureau of Justice Statistics.

Center for Faith Based and Community Initiatives. (2010). *Ready4Reentry: Prisoner reentry toolkit for faith-based and community organization*. U.S. Department of Labor.

Chadwick, N., Dewolf, A., Serin, R. (2015). Effectively training community supervision officers: A meta-analytic review of the impact on offender outcome. *Criminal Justice and Behavior, 42*(10), 977–989.

Clark, S., Ricketts, S., McHugo, G. (1999). Legal system involvement and costs for persons in treatment for severe mental illness and substance use disorders. *Psychiatric Services, 50*, 641–647.

Close, D. W., Aubin, M., Alltucker, K. (2008). *The District of Oregon reentry court: Evaluation, policy recommendations, and replication strategies*. Research Report. Eugene: U.S. District Court of Oregon.

Cloyes, K. G., Wong, B., Latimer, S., Abarca, J. (2010). Time to prison return for offenders with serious mental illness released from prison: A survival analysis. *Criminal Justice and Behavior, 37*, 175–187.

Cochran, J. C. (2012). The ties that bind or the ties that break: Examining the relationship between visitation and prisoner misconduct. *Journal of Criminal Justice, 40*(5), 433–440.

Crow, M. S., & Smykla, J. O. (Eds.) (2014). *Offender reentry: Rethinking criminology and criminal justice*. Burlington, MA: Jones and Bartlett Learning.

Cuellar, A., Snowden, L. M., Ewing, T. (2007). Criminal records of persons served in the public mental health system. *Psychiatric Services, 58*, 114–120.

Cullen, F. T., & Gendreau, P. (2000). Assessing correctional rehabilitation: Policy, practice, and prospects. *Criminal Justice, 3*, 299–370.

Dowden, C., & Andrews, D. A. (1999). What works for female offenders: A meta-analytic review. *Crime & Delinquency, 45*, 438–452.

Dowden, C., & Andrews, D. A. (2004). The importance of staff practice in delivering effective corrections treatment: A meta-analytic review of core correctional practice. *International Journal of Offender Therapy and Comparative Criminology, 48*, 203–214.

Dowell, D. A., Klein, C., Krichmar, C. (1985). Evaluation of a halfway house for women. *Journal of Criminal Justice, 13*, 217–226.

Drake, E. (2007). *Does participation in Washington's work release facilities reduce recidivism?* Olympia: Washington State Institute for Public Policy.

Drake, E. K., Aos, S., Miller, M. G. (2009). Evidence-based public policy options to reduce crime and criminal justice costs: Implications in Washington State. *Victims and Offenders, 4*, 170–196.

Duwe, G. (2012). The benefits of keeping idle hands busy: An outcome evaluation of a prisoner reentry employment program. *Crime & Delinquency, 61*(4), 559–586.

Duwe, G. (2015). An outcome evaluation of a prison work release program: Estimating its effects on recidivism, employment, and cost avoidance. *Criminal Justice Policy Review, 26*, 531–554.

Ellis, A. (1973). *Humanistic psychotherapy: The rational-emotive approach.* Three Rivers Press.

Farole, D. J. (2003). *The Harlem parole reentry court evaluation: Implementation and preliminary impacts.* New York, NY: Center for Court Innovation.

Fellner, J. (2006). A corrections quandry: Mental illness and prison rules. *Harvard Civil Rights-Civil Liberties Law Review, 41*, 391–412.

Feucht, T. E., & Gfroerer, J. (2011). *Mental and substance use disorders among adult men on probation or parole: Some success against a persistent challenge.* Washington, DC: Substance Abuse and Mental Health Services Administration. National Institute of Justice.

Fontaine, J., Gilchrist-Scott, D., Horvath, A. (2011). *Supportive housing for the disabled reentry population: The district of Columbia frequent users service enhancement pilot program.* Washington, DC: Justice Policy Center. Urban Institute.

Fontaine, J., Gilchrist-Scott, D., Roman, J., Taxy, S., Roman, C. (2012). *Supportive housing for returning prisoners: Outcomes and impacts of the returning home-Ohio pilot project.* Washington, DC: Justice Policy Center. Urban Institute.

Frank, R. G., & Glied, S. A (2006). *Mental health policy in the United States since 1950: Better but not well.* Baltimore, MD: The John Hopkins University Press.

Garner, B. R., Hunter, B. D., Modisette, K. C., Ihnes, P. C., Godley, S. H. (2012). Treatment staff turnover in organizations implementing evidence-based practices: Turnover rates and their association with client outcomes. *Journal of Substance Abuse Treatment, 42*(2), 134–142.

Gebelein, R. S. (2003). *Delaware's reentry drug court: A practical approach to substance abusing offenders.* Paper prepared for Conference "European Perspectives on Drug Courts" Strasbourg, NCJ 207482.

Gendreau, P. (1996). Offender rehabilitation what we know and what needs to be done. *Criminal Justice and Behavior, 23*, 144–161

Greenberg, G. A., & Rosenberg, R. (2008). Homelessness in the state and federal population. *Criminal Behavior and Mental Health, 18*, 88–103.

Grennan, S., & Woodhams, J. (2007). The impact of bullying and coping strategies on the psychological distress of young offenders. *Psychology, Crime & Law, 13*(5), 487–504.

Grupp, H. (1963). Wisconsin's Huber law. *Wisconsin Counties Magazine, 10*(1), 110–130.

Hall, G. C. N. (1995). Sexual offender recidivism revisited: A meta-analysis of recent treatment studies. *Journal of Consulting and Clinical Psychology, 63*, 802–809.

Hamilton, Z. K. (2011). Adapting to bad news: Lessons from the Harlem parole reentry court. *Journal of Offender Rehabilitation, 50*, 385–410.

Hammett, T., Roberts, C., Kennedy, S. (2001). Health-related issues in prisoner reentry. *Crime & Delinquency, 47*, 390–409.

Haney, C. (2002). The psychological impact of incarceration: Implications for post prison adjustment. Paper prepared for the Urban Institute's Re-Entry Roundtable. Washington, DC.

Harrison, P. M., & Beck, A. J. (2005). *Prison and jail inmates at midyear 2004.* Washington, DC: Bureau of Justice Statistics.

Heilburn, K., DeMatteo, D., Fretz, R., Erickson, J., Gerardi, D., Halper, C. (2008). Criminal recidivism of female offenders: The importance of structured, community-based aftercare. *Corrections Compendium, 33*(2), 1–2.

Henwood, B. F., Cabassa, L. J., Craig, C. M., Padgett, D. K. (2013). Permanent supportive housing: Addressing homelessness and health disparities? *American Journal of Public Health, 103*(S2), S188–S192.

Hiller, M. L., Knight, K., Simpson, D. D. (1999). Prison-based substance abuse treatment, residential aftercare and recidivism. *Addiction, 94*, 833–842.

Hiller, M. L., Narevic, E., Leukefeld, C., Webster, J. M, (2002) *Kentucky reentry courts: Evaluation of the pilot programs.* http://courts.ky. gov/NR/rdonlyres/D5F5A4FD-DA42-4E38-B204B15593E2EA99/)/Kent uckyReentryCourtEvaluationofthePilotProgramsJuly2002.pdf

Hollin, C. R., Palmer, E. J., Clark, D. (2003). The level of service inventory-revised profile of English prisoners a needs analysis. *Criminal Justice and Behavior, 30*(4), 422–440.

Holsinger, K. (2014). The feminist prison. In F. T. Cullen, C. L. Jonson, M. Stohr (Eds.), *The American prison: Imagining a different future* (pp. 87–110). Thousand Oaks, CA: Sage.

Holzer, H. J., Raphael, S., & Stoll, M. A. (2004). *The effect of a criminal history on employer hiring decisions and screening practices: Evidence from Los Angeles.* National Poverty Center Working Paper Series, #04-15.

Inciardi, J. A., Martin, S. S., Butzin, C. A., Hooper, R. M., Harrison, L. D. (1997). An effective model of prison-based treatment for drug-involved offenders. *Journal of Drug Issues, 27,* 261–278.

Ireland, J. L., Boustead, R., Ireland, C. A. (2005). Coping style and psychological health among adolescent prisoners: A study of young and juvenile offenders. *Journal of Adolescence, 28*(3), 411–423.

Irwin, J. (1970). *The felon.* Pretince-Hall, Inc., NJ: Edgewood Cliffs.

Irwin, J., Schiraldi, V., Ziedenberg, J. (2000). America's one million nonviolent prisoners. *Social Justice, 27,* 135–145.

Jacobs, E. (2012). *Returning to work after prison: Final results from the transitional jobs reentry demonstration.* Research report. MDRC. New York, NY.

Jaremko, M., & Meichenbaum, D. (Eds.). (2013). *Stress reduction and prevention.* Springer Science & Business Media.

Jeffery, R., & Woolpert, S. (1974). Work furlough as an alternative to incarceration: An assessment of its effects on recidivism and social cost. *The Journal of Criminal Law & Criminology, 65,* 405–415.

Jones, D. A., Johnson, S., Latessa, E. J., Travis, T. F. (1999). Case classification in community corrections: Preliminary findings from a national survey. *Topics in Community Corrections,* National Institute of Corrections, U.S. Department of Justice, Washington, D.C.

Jonson, C. L., & Cullen, F. T. (2015). Prisoner reentry programs. *Crime and Justice, 44,* 517–575.

Josi, D. A., & Sechrest, D. K. (1999). A pragmatic approach to parole aftercare: Evaluation of a community reintegration program for high-risk youthful offenders. *Justice Quarterly, 16,* 51–80.

Kaeble, D., Glaze, L., Tsoutis, A., Minton, T. (2016). *Correctional populations in the United States, 2014.* Washington, DC: Bureau of Justice Statistics, U.S. Department of Justice.

Karberg, J., & James, D. J. (2005). *Substance dependence, abuse, and treatment of jail inmates, 2002.* Bureau of Justice Statistic Special Report. Washington, DC: U.S. Department of Justice.

Kesten, K. L., Leavitt-Smith, E., Rau, D. R., Shelton, D., Zhang, W., Wagner, J., et al. (2012). Recidivism rates among mentally ill inmates: Impact of the Connecticut Offender Reentry Program. *Journal of Correctional Health Care, 18,* 20–28.

Kunic, D., & Grant, B. A. (2006). *The Computerized Assessment of Substance Abuse (CASA): Results from the demonstration project (R-173).* Correctional Service of Canada, Ottawa.

Labrecque, R. M., Smith, P., Schweitzer, M., Thompson, C. (2013). Targeting antisocial attitudes in community supervision using the EPICS model: An examination of change scores on the Criminal Sentiment Scale. *Federal Probation, 77*, 15.

Lamb, H. R., & Goertzel, V. (1974). Ellsworth house: A community alternative to jail. *American Journal of Psychiatry, 131*, 64–68.

Landenberger, N. A., & Lipsey, M. W. (2005). The positive effects of cognitive–behavioral programs for offenders: A meta-analysis of factors associated with effective treatment. *Journal of Experimental Criminology, 1*, 451–476.

Latessa, E. (2012). Why work is important, and how to improve the effectiveness of correctional reentry programs that target employment. *Criminology & Public Policy, 11*, 87–91.

Latessa, E., & Allen, H. E. (1982). Halfway houses and parole: A national assessment. *Journal of Criminal Justice, 10*, 153–163.

Latessa, E., Listwan, S.J., Koetzle, D. (2013). *What works (and doesn't) in reducing recidivism*. Cincinnati, OH: Anderson Publishers.

Latessa, E., Lovins, B., Ostrowski, K. (2009). *The Ohio youth assessment system: Final report*. University of Cincinnati: Center for Criminal Justice Research.

Latessa, E., Lovins, L., Smith, P. (2010). *Follow-up evaluation of Ohio's community based correctional facility and halfway house programs – Outcome study*. Technical Report. Cincinnati, OH: Corrections Institute. University of Cincinnati.

Latessa, E., Lowenkamp, C., Bechtel, K. (2009). *Community corrections centers, parolees, and recidivism: An investigation into the characteristics of effective reentry programs in Pennsylvania*. Technical Report. Cincinnati, OH: Center for Criminal Justice Research. University of Cincinnati.

Latessa, E., Smith, P., Lemke, R., Makarios, M., & Lowenkamp, C. (2010). The creation and validation of the Ohio risk assessment system (ORAS). *Federal Probation, 74*(1), 16–22.

Latessa, E.J., Sleyo, J., Schweitzer, M. (2016). Researchers in the real world: Evidence-based practices, implementation barriers, and lessons learned. *Offender Programs Report, 19*, 65.

Lattimore, P. K., Barrick, K., Cowell, A., Dawes, D., Steffey, D., Tueller, S., et al. (2012). *Prisoner reentry service: What worked for SVORI evaluation participants?* Final Report. Research Triangle Park, NC: RTI International.

Lattimore, P.K., & Visher, C. A. (2009). *The multi-site evaluation of SVORI: Summary and synthesis*. Research Triangle Park, NC: RTI International.

LeBel, T., & Maruna, S. (2012). Life on the outside: Transitioning from prison to the community. In J. Petersilia & K. R. Reitz (Eds.), *The Oxford handbook of sentencing and corrections* (pp. 657–683). New York: Oxford University Press.

LeClair, D. P., & Guarino-Ghezzi, S. (1991). Does incapacitation guarantee public safety? Lessons from the Massachusetts furlough and prerelease programs. *Justice Quarterly, 8,* 9–36.

Liebling, A. (1995). Vulnerability and prison suicide. *British Journal of Criminology, 35*(2), 173–187.

Lindquist, C., Ayoub, L., Dawes, D., Harrison, P.M., Malsch, A. M., Hardison Walters, J., et al. (2014). *The national institute of justice's evaluation of second chance act adult reentry courts: Staff and client perspectives on reentry courts from year 2.* RTI International, NPC Research, Center for Court Innovation.

Lipsey, M. W., Howell, J. C., Kelly, M. R., Chapman G., & Garver, D. (2010). *Improving the effectiveness of juvenile justice programs: A new perspective on evidence based programs.* Washington, DC: Center for Juvenile Justice Reform, Georgetown University.

Lindquist, C., Hardison Walters, J. Rempel, M., Carey, S.M. (2013). *The national institute of justice's evaluation of second chance act adult reentry courts: Program characteristics and preliminary themes from year 1.* RTI International, NPC Research, Center for Court Innovation.

Lindquist, C., Hardison, J., Lattimore, P. (2003). *Reentry courts process evaluation (Phase 1), final report.* Research Triangle Park, NC: RTI International.

Listwan, S. J. (2008). Reentry for serious and violent offenders: An analysis of program attrition. *Criminal Justice Policy Review, 48,* 212–228.

Listwan, S. J., Cullen, F., Latessa, E. J. (2006). How to prevent prisoner re-entry programs from failing: Insights from evidence based corrections. *Federal Probation, 70,* 19–25.

Listwan, S. J., Sullivan, C. J., Agnew, R., Cullen, F. T., Colvin, M. (2013). The pains of imprisonment revisited: The impact of strain on inmate recidivism. *Justice Quarterly, 30,* 144–168.

Losel, F. (1995). Increasing consensus in the evaluation of offender rehabilitation: Lessons from research synthesis. *Psychology, Crime and Law, 2,* 19–39.

Lovins, B., & Latessa, E. J. (2013). Creation and validation of the Ohio youth assessment system (OYAS) and strategies for successful implementation. *Justice Research and Policy, 15,* 67–93.

Lovins, L. B., Lowenkamp, C. T., Latessa, E. J., Smith, P. (2007). Application of the risk principle to female offenders. *Journal of Contemporary Criminal Justice, 23,* 383–398.

Lowenkamp, C. T. (2003). *A program level analysis of the relationship between correctional program integrity and treatment effectiveness.* Doctoral Dissertation, University of Cincinnati.

Lowenkamp, C. T., & Latessa, E. J. (2005). Increasing the effectiveness of correctional programming through the risk principle: Identifying offenders for residential placement. *Criminology & Public Policy, 4,* 263–290.

Lowenkamp, C. T., & Latessa, E. J. (2003). *Evaluation of Ohio's halfway houses and community based correctional facilities.* Cincinnati, OH: Center for Criminal Justice Research, University of Cincinnati.

Lowenkamp, C. T., & Latessa, E. J. (2005a). *Evaluation of Ohio's CCA programs.* Cincinnati, OH: Center for Criminal Justice Research, University of Cincinnati.

Lowenkamp, C. T., & Latessa, E. J. (2005b). *Evaluation of Ohio's Reclaim funded programs, community correctional facilities, and DYS facilities.* Cincinnati, OH: Center for Criminal Justice Research, University of Cincinnati.

Lowenkamp, C., Makarios, M. D., Latessa, E. J., Lemke, R., Smith, P. (2010). Community corrections facilities for juvenile offenders in Ohio: An examination of treatment integrity and recidivism. *Criminal Justice and Behavior, 37,* 695–708.

Lowenkamp, C., T., Latessa, E., Smith. P. (2006). Does correctional program quality really matter? The impact of adhering to the principles of effective intervention. *Criminology and Public Policy, 5,* 575–594.

Makarios, M., Lovins, L., Latessa, E. J., Smith, P. (2016). Staff quality and treatment effectiveness: An examination of the relationship between staff factors and the effectiveness of correctional programs. *Justice Quarterly, 33,* 348–367.

Mallik-Kane, K., & Visher, C. A. (2008). *Health and prisoner reentry: How physical, mental, and substance abuse conditions shape the process of reintegration.* Washington, DC: Urban Institute Justice Policy Center.

McGaha, A., Boothroyd, R. A., Poythress, N. G., Petrila, J., Ort, R. G. (2002). Lessons from the Broward County mental health court evaluation. *Evaluation and Program Planning, 25,* 125–135.

Mears, D. P., & Cochran, J. P. (2015). *Prisoner reentry in the era of mass incarceration.* Thousand Oaks, CA: Sage.

Meichenbaum, D. (2014). Ways to bolster resilience in traumatized clients: Implications for psychotherapists. *Journal of Constructivist Psychology, 27,* 329–336.

Meichenbaum, D. H., & Deffenbacher, J. L. (1988). Stress inoculation training. *The Counseling Psychologist, 16,* 69–90.

Metraux, S., & Culhane, D. P. (2004). Homeless shelter use and reincarceration following prison release: Assessing the risk. *Criminology & Public Policy*, *3*, 201–222.

Miller, W. R., Yahne, C. E., Moyers, T. B., Martinez, J., & Pirritano, M. (2004). A randomized trial of methods to help clinicians learn motivational interviewing. *Journal of Consulting and Clinical Psychology*, *72*(6), 1050.

Mitchell, O., Wilson, D. B., MacKenzie, D. L. (2007). Does incarceration-based drug treatment reduce recidivism? A meta-analytic synthesis of the research. *Journal of Experimental Criminology*, *3*, 353–375.

Mulvey, E. P., Schubert, C. A., & Piquero, A. (2014). *Pathways to desistance*. Summary Technical Report. Washington, DC: U.S. Department of Justice.

Mumola, C. J., & Karberg, J. C. (2004). *Drug use and dependence, state and federal prisoners*. Washington, DC: Bureau of Justice Statistics.

National Center on Addiction and Substance Abuse. (2010). *Behind bars II: Substance abuse and America's prison population*. http://www.center onaddiction.org

Ndrecka, M. (2014). *The impact of reentry programs on recidivism: A meta-analysis*. Doctoral Dissertation, University of Cincinnati, ProQuest Dissertations Publishing.

Oliver, J. (Host), Avery, K., Carvell, T., Gondelman, J., Gurewitch, D., Haggerty, G., et al. (2015, November 8). Prisoner re-entry [Television series episode]. In D. Fitzgerald (Producer), J. Oliver, T. Carvell, J. Thoday, J. Taylor (Executive Producers), L. Stanton (Co-Executive Producer). *Last week tonight with John Oliver*. New York, NY: Home Box Office, Inc.

Olson, D. E., Rozhon, J., Powers, M. (2009). Enhancing prisoner reentry through access to prison-based and post-incarceration aftercare treatment: Experiences from the Illinois Sheridan Correctional Center therapeutic community. *Journal of Experimental Criminology*, *5*, 299–321.

Ostermann, M. (2009). An analysis of New Jersey's day reporting center and halfway back programs: Embracing the rehabilitative ideal through evidence based practices. *Journal of Offender Rehabilitation*, *48*, 139–153.

Pager, D. (2007). Two strikes and you're out: The intensification of racial and criminal stigma. In S. Bushway, M. Stoll, & D. Weiman (Eds.), Barriers to reentry? The labor market for released prisoners in post-industrial America (pp. 151–173). New York: Russell Sage Foundation.

Pearson, F., & Lipton, D. (1999). A meta-analytic review of the effectiveness of corrections-based treatments for drug abuse. *The Prison Journal*, *79*, 384–410.

Pearson-Nelson, B. (2009). *Allen County community corrections: Reentry court program impact evaluation.* School of Public and Environmental Affairs. Indiana University Purdue University. Fort Wayne, IN.

Pelissier, B., Jones, N., Cadican, T. (2007). Drug treatment aftercare in the criminal justice system: A systematic review. *Journal of Substance Abuse Treatment, 32,* 311–320.

Petersilia, J., & Cullen, F. (2015). Liberal but not stupid: Meeting the promise of downsizing prisons. *Stanford Journal of Criminal Law and Policy, 2*(1), 1–43.

Petersilia, J. (2001). When prisoners return to communities: Political, economic, an social consequences. *Federal Probation, 65,* 3–8.

Petersilia, J. (2003). *When prisoners come home: Parole and prisoner reentry.* New York: Oxford University Press.

Petersilia, J. (2004). What works in prisoner reentry? Reviewing and questioning the evidence. *Federal Probation, 68,* 4–10.

Pew Center on the States. (2011). *State of recidivism: The revolving door of America's prisons.* Washington, DC: Pew Charitable Trusts.

Porporino, F. J. (2010). Bringing sense and sensitivity to corrections: From programmes to "fix" offenders to services to support desistance. In J. Brayford, F. Cowe, J. Deering (Eds.), *What else works? Creative work with offenders* (pp. 61–85). Abingdon: Taylor & Francis Publishers.

Redcross, C., Millenky, M., Rudd, T., & Levshin, V. (2012). *More than a job: Final results from the evaluation of the center for employment opportunities (CEO) transitional jobs program.* Office of Planning, Research and Evaluation the Administration of Children and Families. U.S. Department of Health and Human Services.

Redlich, A. D. (2005). Voluntary, but knowing and intelligent? Comprehension in mental health courts. *Psychology, Public Policy and Law, 11,* 605–619.

Reentry Council (2016). Federal Interagency Reentry Council. Washington, DC: Department of Justice.

Richland, L. E., Morrison, R. G., & Holyoak, K. J. (2006). Children's development of analogical reasoning: Insights from scene analogy problems. *Journal of Experimental Child Psychology, 94,* 249–273.

Rhine, E. E., & Thompson, A. C. (2011). The reeentry movement in corrections: Resiliency, fragility, and prospects. *Criminal Law Bulletin, 47,* 177–209.

Robbins, C. A., Martin, S. S., Surrat, H. L. (2009). Substance abuse treatment, anticipated maternal roles, and reentry success of drug-involved women prisoners. *Crime & Delinquency, 55*(3), 388–411.

Roman, C. G., & Travis, J. (2006). Where will I sleep tomorrow? Housing, homelessness, and the returning prisoner. *Housing Policy Debate, 17*, 389–418.

Routh, D., & Hamilton, Z. (2015). Work release as a transition: Positioning success via the halfway house. *Journal of Offender Rehabilitation, 54*, 239–255.

Rudoff, A., & Esselstyn, T. C. (1973). Evaluating work furlough: A follow-up. *Federal Probation, 38*, 48–53.

Sacks, S., Chaple, M., Sacks, J. Y., McKendrick, K., Cleland, C. M. (2012). Randomized trial of a reentry modified therapeutic community for offenders with co-occurring disorders: Crime outcomes. *Journal of Substance Abuse Treatment, 42*, 247–259.

Sacks, S., Sacks, J. Y., McKendrick, K., Banks, S., Stommel, J. (2004). Modified TC for MICA offenders: Crime outcomes. *Behavioral Sciences and the Law, 22*, 477–501.

Sarteschi, C. M., Vaughn, M.G., Kim, K. (2011). Assessing the effectiveness of mental health courts: A quantitative review. *Journal of Criminal Justice, 39*, 12–20.

Schlager, M. (2013). *Rethinking the reentry paradigm: A blueprint for action.* Durham, NC: Carolina Academic Press.

Schaffer, M. A., Sandau, K. E., & Diedrick, L. (2012). Evidence practice models for organizational change: Overview and practical applications. *Journal of Advanced Nursing, 69*(5), 1197–1209.

Scroggins, J., & Malley, S. (2010). Reentry and the (unmet) needs of women. *Journal of Offender Rehabilitation, 49*, 146–163.

Seiter, R. P., & Kadela, K. R. (2003). Prisoner reentry: What works, what does not, and what is promising. *Crime & Delinquency, 49*, 360–388.

Sherman, L. W., Gottfredson, D. C., MacKenzie, D. L., Eck, J., Reuter, P., Bushway, S. D. (1998). *Preventing crime: What works, what doesn't, what's promising.* Washington, DC: U.S. Department of Justice, National Institute of Justice.

Simon, J. (2012). Mass incarceration: From social policy to social problem. In J. Petersilia & K. R. Reitz (Eds.), *The Oxford handbook of sentencing and corrections* (pp. 138–174). New York: Oxford University Press.

Skeem, J. L., & Peterson, J. K. (2012). Identifying, treating, and reducing risk for offenders with mental illness. In J. Petersilia & K. R. Reitz (Eds.), *The Oxford handbook of sentencing and corrections* (pp. 521–543). New York: Oxford University Press.

Skeem, J. L., Manchak, S., Peterson, J. P. (2010). Correctional policy for offenders with mental illness: Creating a new paradigm for recidivism reduction. *Law and Human Behavior, 35*, 110–126.

Slate, R. N., Buffington-Vollum, J. K., Johnson, W. W. (2013). *The criminalization of mental illness: Crisis and opportunity for the justice system.* Carolina Academic Press.

Smith, P., Schweitzer, M., Labrecque, R. M., Latessa, E. J. (2012). Improving probation officers' supervision skills: An evaluation of the EPICS model. *Journal of Crime and Justice, 35*(2), 189–199.

Spelman, J. (2003). An initial comparison of graduates and terminated clients in America's largest re-entry court. *Corrections Today, 65*, 74–77, 83.

Sperber, K. G., Latessa, E. J., Makarios, M. D. (2013). Examining the interaction between level of risk and dosage of treatment. *Criminal Justice and Behavior, 40*, 338–348.

Steadman, H. J., Osher, F., Robbins, P. C., Case, B., Samuels, S. (2009). Prevalence of serious mental illness among jail inmates. *Psychiatric Services, 60*, 761–765.

Steadman, H. J., Redlich, A. D., Griffin, P., Petrila, J., Monahan, J. (2005). From referral to disposition: Case processing in seven mental health courts. *Behavioral Sciences & the Law, 23*, 1–12.

Taxman, F., Young, D., Byrne, J. (2003). *From prison safety to public safety: Best practices in offender reentry.* Washington, DC: National Institute of Justice.

Taylor, C. J. (2013). Tolerance of minor setbacks in a challenging reentry experience: An evaluation of a federal reentry court. *Criminal Justice Policy Review, 24*, 49–70.

Travis, J. (2005). *But they all come back. Facing the challenges if prisoner reentry.* Washington, DC: The Urban Institute.

Turner, S., & Petersilia, J. (1996). Work release in Washington: Effects on recidivism and Corrections costs. *Prison Journal, 76*, 138–164.

U.S. Department of Justice, Bureau of Justice Statistics. (2003). *Education and correctional populations* (NCJ 195670). http://www.bjs.gov/index.cfm?typbdetail&iid814

Valentine, E. J., & Redcross, C. (2015). Transitional jobs after release from prison: Effects on employment and recidivism. *IZA Journal of Labor Policy, 4.* doi:10.1186/s40173-015-0043-8

Visher, C. A, & Travis, J. (2012). The characteristics of prisoners returning home and effective reentry programs and policies. In J. Petersilia & K. R. Reitz (Eds.), *The Oxford handbook of sentencing and corrections* (pp. 89–118). New York: Oxford University Press.

Visher, C. A., & Kachnowski, V. (2007). Finding work on the outside: Results from the "returning home" project in Chicago. *Barriers to Reentry*, 74, 80–114.

Visher, C. A., & Travis, J. (2003). Transitions from prison to community: Understanding individual pathways. *Annual Review of Sociology*, 29, 89–113.

Visher, C., & Travis, J. (2011). Life on the outside: Returning home after incarceration. *The Prison Journal*, 91, 102S–119S.

Visher, C., Winterfield, L., & Goggeshall, M. B. (2005). Ex-offender employment programs and recidivism: A meta-analysis. *Journal of Experimental Criminology*, 1, 295–315.

Visher, C., Yahner, J., La Vigne, N. G. (2010). *Life after prison: Tracking the experiences of male prisoners returning to Chicago, Cleveland, and Houston*. Washington, DC: Urban Institute.

Warr, M., & Stafford, M. (1991). The influence of delinquent peers: What they think or what they do. *Criminology*, 29(4), 856–866.

Waldo, G. P., & Chiricos, T. G. (1977). Work release and recidivism: An empirical evaluation of a social policy. *Evaluation Review*, 1, 87–108.

Weekes, J. R., Moser, A. E., Langevin, C. M. (1999). Assessing substance-abusing offenders for treatment. In E. J. Latessa (Ed.), *Strategic solution: The international community correctional association examines substance abuse* (pp. 363–371). Lanham: American Correctional Association Press.

Weekes, J. R., Moser, A. E., Wheatley, M., Matheson, F. I. (2013). What works in reducing substance-related offending? In L. A. Craig, L. Dixon, L., T. A. Gannon (Eds.), *What works in offender rehabilitation: An evidence-based approach to assessment and treatment* (pp. 237–254). Chichester, West Sussex: Wiley-Blackwell.

White, M.D., Mellow, J., Englander, K., Ruffinengo, M. (2011). Halfway back: An alternative to revocation for technical parole violators. *Criminal Justice Policy Review*, 22, 140–166.

Willison, J. B., Roman, C. G., Wolff, A., Correa, V., Knight, C. R. (2010). *Evaluation of the ridge house residential program: Final report*. Research Report. Washington, DC: Urban Institute.

Wilson J. A., & Davis, R. (2006). Good intentions meet hard realities: An evaluation of the Project Greenlight reentry program. *Criminology & Public Policy*, 5, 303–338.

Wilson, D. B., Bouffard, L. A., & Mackenzie, D. L. (2005). A quantitative review of structured, group oriented cognitive-behavioral program for offenders. *Criminal Justice and Behavior*, 32(2), 72–204.

Witte, A. D. (1977). Work release in North Carolina: A program that works! *Law and Contemporary Problems, 41*, 230–251.

Wormith, J. S., Althouse, R., Simpson, M., Reitzel, L. R., Fagan, T. J., Morgan, R. D. (2007). The rehabilitation and reintegration of offenders: The current landscape and some future directions for correctional psychology. *Criminal Justice and Behavior, 34*, 879–892.

Zanis, D. A., Mulvaney, F., Coviello, D., Alterman, A. I., Savitz, B., Thompson, W. (2003). The effectiveness of early parole to substance abuse treatment facilities on 24 month criminal recidivism. *Journal of Drug Issues, 33*, 223–235.

Zimring, F., Hawkins, G., Kamin, S. (2003). *Democracy and punishment: Three-strikes and you're out in California*. New York: Oxford University Press.

Mirlinda Ndrecka, PhD is an assistant professor at the Department of Criminal Justice in the Henry C. Lee College of Criminal Justice and Forensic Sciences at the University of New Haven. Dr. Ndrecka's research and teaching interests include criminological theory, offender risk assessment, effective correctional programming, and offender reentry. As part of her training, she had the opportunity to work on and manage numerous state grants and research projects that required working closely with correctional agencies.

Shelley Johnson Listwan is an associate professor at the Department of Criminal Justice and Criminology at the University of North Carolina, Charlotte. Prior to this, she held positions as an assistant professor at the University of Nevada, Las Vegas, and an associate professor at Kent State University. She received her PhD in criminal justice from the University of Cincinnati in 2001. Her areas of interest include corrections, criminological theory, psychology of crime, and victimization. She has authored 30 academic publications, including three books. Dr. Listwan also provides training to agencies throughout the country on the topics of classification and assessment, treatment planning, evidence-based services, problem-solving courts, and prisoner reentry.

Edward J. Latessa received his PhD from the Ohio State University in 1979 and has published over 150 works in the area of criminal justice, corrections, and juvenile justice. He is coauthor of eight books including *What Works (and Doesn't) in Reducing Recidivism, Corrections in the Community*, and *Corrections in America*. He has also received numerous awards and in 2013 he was identified as one of the most innovative people in criminal justice by a national survey conducted by the Center for Court Innovation in partnership with the Bureau of Justice Assistance and the US Department of Justice.

Can Released Prisoners "Make It"? Examining Formerly Incarcerated Persons' Belief in Upward Mobility and the "American Dream"

Thomas P. LeBel, Matt Richie, and Shadd Maruna

Introduction

Although it is often assumed that released prisoners can "make it if they so desire" (Petersilia 2003, p. 8) or "if [they] don't give up" (Irwin 2005, p. 178), we know little about the perceptions of formerly incarcerated persons themselves in regard to this "pull yourself up by the bootstraps" philosophy of individual responsibility (MacDonald 2003). To address this gap, this chapter examines the extent to which formerly incarcerated persons' "buy into" and believe in the possibility of upward mobility and the American Dream. Then, the characteristics of formerly incarcerated persons related to believing in the American Dream are examined. Finally, the chapter will discuss how

T.P. LeBel (✉) · M. Richie
University of Wisconsin-Milwaukee, Wisconsin, USA

S. Maruna
Rutgers University, New Jersey, USA

© The Author(s) 2017
S. Stojkovic (ed.), *Prisoner Reentry*,
DOI 10.1057/978-1-137-57929-4_6

believing in the American Dream is related to psychological well-being and successful prisoner reintegration more generally.

Literature Review

The American Dream and Upward Mobility

The source of the phrase "American Dream" is most often attributed to historian James Truslow Adams (1931) in his book titled, *The Epic of America*. Since that time, there have been many explanations of the criteria that constitute believing in the American Dream as well as the idea that America is a meritocracy (see, e.g., Barlett and Steele 2012; Bush and Bush 2015; Cullen 2003; Hacker 2008; Hanson and Zogby 2010; Hochschild 1995; McClelland and Tobin 2010; Messner and Rosenfeld 2013; Rank et al. 2014; White and Hanson 2011; Wysong et al. 2014; Zogby 2008, 2011). For example, Rank and colleagues (2014) argue that there are three key components to the American Dream, "first, having the freedom to engage and pursue one's interests and passions; second, the bargain that hard work should lead to economic security and success; and third, the importance of hope, optimism, progress, and successfully confronting the challenges of life" (p. 152).

In a similar vein, Longoria (2009) notes that "a meritocratic society is one that promotes smart, hard-working individuals regardless of which social strata they happen to be born in. . . . It is a society where equality of opportunity is a reality and where the restraints on individual success (except for innate capability) are eliminated as far as is possible" (p. 6). In general, Horatio Alger's "rags to riches" stories epitomize the American Dream in that anyone, regardless of their background or economic circumstances, has an equal opportunity to succeed through work and skill (see, e.g., McClelland and Tobin 2010; McNamee and Miller 2014; Messner and Rosenfeld 2013; Rank et al. 2014). In the United States, the view that the social structure is open, and that individual mobility is possible for all people, is perhaps so entrenched as to be considered the "dominant ideology" (Kluegel and Smith 1986; see also Major and Schmader 2001; Sidanius and Pratto 1993; Tajfel and Turner 1979). It is thought that cultural values such as the belief in the "American Dream" (see Messner and Rosenfeld 2013) and the "Protestant Work Ethic" (e.g., Ellemers 1993) influence Americans to believe in the opportunity for personal advancement as well as in personal responsibility for one's social status position in society (Major and Schmader 2001, p. 182).

McClelland and Tobin (2010; see also Rank et al. 2014) assert that "the hopes embedded in the Dream . . . invariably include three economic aspirations: a rising standard of living, financial security, and upward mobility" (p. 4). Moreover, they argue that "[e]conomic and social mobility . . . is one of the core concepts—arguably *the* core concept—of the American Dream" (McClelland and Tobin 2010, p. 41). Within the criminal justice literature, Messner and Rosenfeld (2013; see also Reiman and Leighton 2013) similarly assert that the American Dream refers to "a broad cultural ethos that entails a commitment to the goal of material success" (p. 6). Messner and Rosenfeld's (2013) work builds on that of Merton's (1938, 1968) "social structure and anomie" argument stressing the disjuncture between the cultural emphasis on the importance of monetary success as a major goal of American society and the appropriate (and possible) means of achieving this goal. Merton (1938, 1968) created a typology of adaptations to this lack of fit between goals and means which became the basis of "strain theory." The five modes of adaptation to anomie are conformity, innovation (give up on the means and engage in crime), ritualism (give up on the goals), retreatism (give up on both goals and means and live on the margins of society), and rebellion (rejection of goals and means and substitution of new ones). Importantly, Merton (1968, p. 225) posits that even for the "lowest strata" or most socio-economically disadvantaged persons, "deviant behavior is still the subsidiary pattern and conformity the modal pattern." In other words, the most common adaptation to anomie is thought to be conformity and striving for material success (i.e., the American Dream) through hard work, education, obtaining the necessary skills, etc.

Beliefs/Attitudes About Achieving the American Dream

Although there is certainly variability in the extent to which individuals buy into legitimizing myths that justify their group's position in society, evidence suggests that even the most disadvantaged endorse the view that the social structure is for the most part open (Crocker et al. 1998; Jost and Banaji 1994; Kluegel and Smith 1986). Zogby International Polling has been collecting survey data on the American Dream since 1998 (see, e.g., Hanson and Zogby 2010; White and Hanson 2011; Zogby 2008, 2011). Over its history, the Zogby polls have shown consistent support in the belief in the American Dream. For example, in the 2001 poll, three-fourths (76 %) of Americans believed it was possible for themselves and their families to achieve the American Dream. Support in the possibility of the Dream has declined somewhat since this time (to 67 % in 2008 and 57 % in 2010), but the majority of people still believe it is possible (Zogby 2011, p. 114).

Another poll conducted yearly by *CBS News/New York Times* (2012) over 15 years has asked the question, "Do you think it is still possible to start out poor in this country, work hard, and become rich?" The percentage of individuals answering "yes" has averaged between 70 and 85 %, indicating that the vast majority of the general public has continuously believed that it is possible to rise from "rags to riches" in America (*CBS News/New York Times Poll* 2012; Rank et al. 2014). Similarly, in a poll conducted by the National League of Cities (2004), about two-thirds of respondents indicated that the American Dream could be realized by "all or most people in this country." Moreover, an opinion poll on economic mobility and the American Dream conducted by Pew Charitable Trusts (2009) found that 68 % of those polled thought they either have achieved or would achieve the American Dream. In the criminal justice literature, Rose and Clear (2004) reported that 62 % of people who live in disadvantaged communities in Tallahassee, Florida, believe that the "American Dream" is possible for everyone.

Bush and Bush (2015, p. 123) report that when asked "To what extent do you expect to ever achieve the American Dream?" those with incomes less than $50,000 do not differ in their views from those making $101,000–$200,000, with about one-third agreeing a lot with this statement and slightly more than half agreeing somewhat. Importantly, only about one in seven (13.7 %) responded "not at all" about their expectations of achieving the American Dream. The top reasons for believing in the American Dream include affirmative responses to "I'm intelligent and work hard, so I should succeed" (59 %), and "America is the land of opportunity" (52 %) (Zogby 2011). Having a secure job or business and one's religious faith are also reasons for believing in the American Dream. In fact, nearly half (49 %) of frequent churchgoers attributed their optimism about the American Dream to their religious faith.

Despite the overwhelming support from the general public, White and Hanson (2011; see also Hanson and Zogby 2010) reviewed several recent polls about the American Dream and concluded that while the Dream is not in doubt, more people, since the economic crisis of 2008 (i.e., the great recession), believe that it is becoming harder to achieve. In particular, White and Hanson (2011, p. 11; see also McNamee and Miller 2014; Wysong et al. 2014) found that people believe the American Dream will be harder to achieve, with 75 % claiming it is not as attainable as it was in 2000, and more than half (59 %) believing that achieving the Dream will be harder for the next generation.

Hanson and Zogby (2010) also argue that the American Dream may no longer be focused on material wealth, but instead more on spiritual fulfillment. Zogby (2008, 2011) reports that when choosing the statement that "best represents your goals in life," there has been a shift from Traditional Materialists to Secular Spiritualists since polling began in 1998. The Secular Spiritualists respond "yes" to the statement "I believe you can achieve the American dream through spiritual fulfillment rather than material success." The two answers that receive the fewest affirmative responses are categorized by Zogby (2008, 2011) as the Deferred Dreamers and the Dreamless Dead. Deferred Dreamers believe that the American Dream is "more likely to be attained by my children and not me," while the Dreamless Dead respond affirmatively to the statement "I believe I cannot achieve the American dream, whether material or spiritual, nor can most middle-class Americans." Zogby (2008) reports that these two categories have accounted for between 15 % and 20 % of American adults between 1998 and 2008. Zogby (2011) notes that the number of Dreamless Dead alone jumped from 12 % to 20 % in November 2010, and that the recent jump in these views was greater among those with the lowest incomes, women, and those without college degrees.

The Myth of Meritocracy and the American Dream

A great number of books have appeared recently with titles suggesting that the possibility of achieving the American Dream are overblown: *American Dream Dying: The changing economic lot of the least advantaged* (McClelland and Tobin 2010); *The betrayal of the American Dream* (Barlett and Steele 2012); *The way we'll be: The Zogby report on the transformation of the American Dream* (Zobgy 2008); *Tensions in the American Dream: Rhetoric, reverie, or reality* (Bush and Bush 2015); *The great risk shift: The new economic insecurity and the decline of the American Dream* (Hacker 2008); *Chasing the American Dream: Understanding what shapes our fortunes* (Rank et al. 2014); and *The meritocracy myth* (McNamee and Miller 2014).

Rank and associates (2014, p. 64) refer to the "American paradox" as "the gap between the ideals of America, as found in the American Dream, versus the realities of everyday life." In a similar vein, Longoria (2009) states that a "substantial proportion believes that race, gender, social background, and personal connections make a difference in one's outcomes in life. The *vox populi* tells us that America is and is not a meritocracy" (p. 132). This negative view concerning the reality of the American Dream certainly has strong roots in conflict theory. For example, Reiman and Leighton (2013, p. 196) argue that " . . . the have-nots and have-littles must believe that they are not being exploited or being treated unfairly by the have-plenties." In a similar vein, McNamee and Miller (2014) write that "[f]or a system of inequality to be stable over the long run, those who have more must convince those who have less that the distribution of who gets what is fair, just, proper, or the natural order of things" (McNamee and Miller 2014, p. 3; see also Reiman and Leighton 2013; Sims 1997).

Rank and colleagues (2014) report that during any 10-year period, approximately half of Americans will experience at least 1 year of economic insecurity (p. 38), and that experiencing low income and poverty has become more common since the late 1960s. In fact, research indicates that the United States has less upward mobility than in many other western democracies, and that movement up the economic ladder is especially difficult for those at the bottom rung (Rank et al. 2014; Robinson 2007; Pew Charitable Trusts 2007). McNamee and Miller (214) assert that "... the *myth* of meritocracy is harmful: it provides an incomplete explanation for success and failure, mistakenly exalting the rich and unjustly condemning the poor" (p. 240; see also Reiman and Leighton 2013).

Similarly, Rank and colleagues refer to "cumulative disadvantage" and note that "initial...disadvantages can then result in further...disadvantages, producing a cumulative process in which inequalities are maintained or widened throughout the life course" (2014, p. 108; see also Sampson and Laub 1997). Thus, the American Dream appears to reward those with the most talent and effort, without taking into consideration the structural forces and factors that allowed them to start the race a few mile markers ahead of the most disadvantaged in society (Edin and Shaefer 2015; McNamee and Miller 2014; Reiman and Leighton 2013). Many researchers have reported trends antithetical to living the American Dream such as an increase in low-wage (often part-time) jobs with little opportunity for advancement (Edin and Shaefer 2015; Hacker 2008; Kalleberg 2011; Massey 2007; Wysong et al. 2014).

Peter Finn (1998, p. 105), in a comprehensive review of model ex-prisoner employment programs, found that the explicit goal of many of these programs is to change the mind-set of former prisoners so that they *buy into* status quo ideals such as holding an honest job and providing for one's family. Reiman and Leighton (2013) take this argument one step further and assert that "[t]he ultimate sanctions of criminal justice dramatically sanctify the present social and economic order, and *the poverty of criminals makes poverty itself an individual moral crime!"* (Reiman and Leighton 2013, p. 192). In a similar vein, Wakefield and Uggen (2010; see also Pew Charitable Trusts 2010) posit that mass incarceration not only creates inequality but also sustains it through the educational system and the job market.

Behavioral Responses for the Belief in the American Dream

Disadvantaged group members' "shared beliefs about the nature of the social structure" (Turner and Reynolds 2001, p. 134), particularly the belief in the possibility for a low-status group member to move to a higher-status group, is thought to have an important influence on the behavioral responses of members of disadvantaged groups (e.g., Ellemers 1993, 2001; Tajfel 1982; Wright 2001). Although conceptualized as a continuum, boundary permeability has most often been studied as a dichotomy—with the social structure considered either open or closed. An open context represents the meritocratic ideal in which anyone can get ahead in life based on individual effort and abilities, whereas in a closed context "one's social position is entirely dependent upon group memberships, and individual abilities are irrelevant" (Wright 2001, p. 224). A middle ground position, called "tokenism," has been postulated by Wright and colleagues (Wright 1997, 2001; Wright et al. 1990; see also Lalonde and Silverman 1994), in which boundaries are restricted and only a small number of qualified members of disadvantaged groups are able to improve their social status.

Major and Schmader (2001) define legitimacy appraisals as "subjective perceptions of the fairness or justice of socially distributed outcomes, including status, power, or any other differential, among individuals and groups" (p. 180). Jost and Banaji (1994) define system justification as "the psychological process by which existing social arrangements are legitimized, even at the expense of personal and group interests" (p. 2). System justification is similar to Lerner's (1980) "just world" theory in which it is hypothesized that human beings have a psychological need to believe that people basically get what they "deserve." Consequently, it is thought that members of disadvantaged groups who endorse legitimizing ideologies show a marked tendency to maintain the status quo even in objectively unjust (e.g., token or closed systems) circumstances (Major and Schmader 2001, p. 182).

The belief in legitimizing myths, of course, will also result in the reduction of disadvantaged group's motivation for social change (Major et al. 2002, p. 281; Tyler 2001, p. 355). Wright and Tropp (2002) argue that when an individual considers the social structure to be permeable, s/he will use a mobility strategy of individual normative action (i.e., Merton's idea of conformity). However, when the social structure is perceived as closed or highly restricted (i.e., tokenism), the strategy used is thought to depend on the interaction between perceived legitimacy and perceived stability. In fact, the questioning of legitimizing myths that sustain inequalities among groups is believed to be a necessary condition for all protest and liberation movements (Crocker et al. 1998, p. 510; see also Wright and Tropp 2002, p. 220). Consequently, it is likely that formerly incarcerated persons who perceive the criminal justice system as unjust will be more likely to support and become involved in advocacy-related activities to change the system (see LeBel 2009).

Formerly Incarcerated Persons' Beliefs about the Ability to "Go Straight" and Achieve the American Dream

Irwin (2005, p. 202) asserts that in his 50 years of contact with prisoners and former prisoners he has been "consistently reassured that *most* persons passing through the prison make up their mind to attempt to live a noncriminal life and stay out of prison." Despite this desire to live a noncriminal life, it is a well-known fact that about two-thirds (67.8 %) of prisoners will be rearrested within 3 years of their release, and about half returned to prison on a parole violation or a new conviction (Durose et al. 2014). The reality of reentry is much different from the "land of milk and honey" often imagined from behind bars. In fact, released prisoners must overcome many obstacles in order to succeed after prison including problems with employment, housing, returning to the same or similarly disadvantaged neighborhoods, and substance use and mental health issues (see LeBel and Maruna 2012 for a review of the obstacles in transitioning from prison to the community).

The view that former prisoners can "make it" or "go legit" after prison is shared by academics (Petersilia 2003; Bushway and Reuter 2002) and practitioners (Lynch 2001, pp. 53–54). Ironically, the optimism of being able to make it is perhaps most strongly held by former prisoners themselves, and has been consistently supported in research at the point of release, when most offenders express a strong desire and willingness to "go straight" (Burnett 1992; Lin 2000; Visher and Courtney 2007; Visher et al. 2004). Research from the Urban Institute's *Returning home* study consistently finds that prior to release, about three-fourths of respondents expected it to be "pretty easy" or "very easy" to stay out of prison following release (see, e.g., Visher and Courtney 2007; Visher et al. 2004). Prisoners often report that to be successful they must have will power, but also need to ask for help and support (Coalition for Women Prisoners 2008; Howerton et al. 2009). LeBel et al. (2008; see also Visher and Courtney 2007) found that soon-to-be-released prisoners' positive mind-set was a significant predictor of post-imprisonment outcomes. In particular, belief in one's ability to "go straight" or self-efficacy (hope) contributed positively to the reintegration process. Maruna (2001) found that persisters (i.e., former prisoners still engaging in criminal activity) believe that they are "doomed to deviance" and have little hope of making it in conventional society. Maruna (2004) posits that the understanding that one's outcomes are due to external, stable, and uncontrollable factors may be partly responsible for former prisoners continued involvement in crime.

Research also indicates that most prisoners and former prisoners have essentially the same goals and aspirations as the law-abiding public (Austin and Irwin 2012; Burnett 1992; Erickson et al. 1973, p. 97; Helfgott 1997; Irwin 1970, pp. 134–135; Petersilia 2003, p. 80; Visher and O'Connell 2012). Helfgott (1997), for example, noted that former prisoners' most common long-term goals were to own a home, to establish a career, to be self-employed and to own a business, to obtain an educational degree, to be able to help their children financially through college, and to have a "normal life". Moreover, Erickson and colleagues (1973) report that "the parolees' ideas and plans for success on parole stress struggle, hard work and self-restraint" (p. 78). Consequently, they conclude that "[t]he popular myth that the criminal has rejected society's values, that he is a 'public enemy' in the sense of not sharing the orientation towards the world of the law-abiding general public" is not supported (Erickson et al. 1973, pp. 78–79; see also Visher and O'Connell 2012).

However, research also suggests that for many returning prisoners, these expectations for "conventional" material success are unrealistic (Bucklen and Zajac 2009; Erickson et al. 1973; Glaser 1969; Irwin 1970) and perhaps need to be scaled back (Lin 2000). According to Irwin (2005, 174), "Most prisoners step into the outside world with a small bundle of stuff under their arm, a little bit of money, perhaps their $200 'gate' money, and that's all." In fact, in some states, the situation could be even worse. Indeed, a recent study of prisoners released in Houston, Texas found that many were released with $50 in gate money, about three-fourths had only one set of street clothing, and fewer than two in five (37 %) had non-prison issue photo identification (La Vigne et al. 2009b). Thus, returning prisoners might believe the social structure is more open than it actually is. Anderson (1999) asserts that the social structure is at best one of tokenism, and suggests that the "conventional culture is viewed by many blacks in the inner cities as profoundly unreceptive" (p. 287). He argues forcefully that:

> ... success brings class mobility to a fortunate few. Yet their very success serves to reproduce or legitimate the racialized class and status structures that continue to oppress those who either do not encounter the same opportunities or choose not to "sell out" in order to achieve the dominant society's version of success. (Anderson 2001, pp. 151–152)

A major consequence of being labeled as a criminal involves the exclusion of the labeled individuals from conventional opportunities (see especially Sampson and Laub 1997, for a discussion of "cumulative disadvantage"). Research indicates that former prisoners face considerable discrimination in competing for jobs, leading to reduced prospects for obtaining even low-wage employment (see Decker et al. 2015; Holzer et al. 2006; Pager 2007; Pettit and Lyons 2007). Laws frequently bar employers from hiring released prisoners (i.e., convicted felons) in many sectors of the economy including jobs involving childcare, elder care, health care, and financial services (Love 2006). Of course, many returning prisoners have poor employment skills and limited work experience to begin with (Petersilia 2003), leaving them doubly disadvantaged (Festen and Fischer 2002). Soon to be released prisoners and formerly incarcerated persons appear to recognize these employment-related roadblocks to reentry. After release from prison, men consistently report struggling most with finding a job (70 % at 1 month, 65 % at 1 year) and making enough money to support themselves (66 %, 56 %) (Visher and Courtney 2007; Visher et al. 2004).

In a comprehensive report of employment outcomes for released prisoners in three states, Visher and colleagues (2008) report that only 45 % were currently employed at 8 months. The majority (71 %) of male formerly incarcerated persons felt that their criminal record had negatively affected their job search (Visher et al. 2008). Women are even less likely than men to find full- or part-time employment in the first year after release from prison (La Vigne et al. 2009a). This may be due to women having a higher unemployment rate prior to admission to prison (Greenfeld and Snell 1999), having fewer job skills (Messina, Burdon and Prendergast 2001), having more extensive histories of substance use, and/or being much less likely to have received job training while in prison (La Vigne et al. 2009a).

A decent job can be a source of noncriminal contacts and also reinforce "legitimate" goals and values that promote the adoption of a law-abiding lifestyle. Sampson and Laub (1993), however, argue that employment "by itself" does not support desistance, rather, "employment coupled with job stability, commitment to work, and mutual ties binding workers and employers' reduces criminality" (p. 146). Moreover, Irwin (2009) argues that "doing good involves having a job with a 'living wage,' security, and job satisfaction" (p. 132; see also Uggen 1999). Unfortunately, many returning prisoners also appear to be frustrated and unhappy because they have few options besides "McJobs" (i.e., low-paying and "dead end" jobs) (see, e.g., Visher et al. 2008). Visher and colleagues (2008), for example, report that about half of released prisoners who do find work are unhappy with their pay. In addition, one's attitude toward work appears to play a role in whether a parolee is successful. Bucklen and Zajac (2009) report that parole violators had negative attitudes toward employment and unrealistic job expectations, and did not want to accept lower end jobs.

In a recent study, Harding and colleagues (2014) examined the "trajectories of well-being" for 22 released prisoners over a 2–3-year period. They report that nearly two-thirds of these individuals (14/22, 63.6 %) suffered from either continual hardship indicating "transitioning between extreme *desperation* and *survival* when they were not in custody" (p. 450), or "a vacillation between periods of *stability* and *survival*" (p. 450). Similarly, Austin and Irwin (2000, 156) estimate that more than 25 % of released prisoners "eventually end up on the streets, where they live out a short life of dereliction, alcoholism, and drug abuse." These findings with released prisoners are similar to those from Edin and Shaefer (2015) for those living in extreme poverty in which for one subject it was noted that she " . . . basically has no shot at achieving this dream . . . housing is too expensive, the jobs she might get pay far too little, and there's too little help" (Edin and Shaefer 2015, p. 91). Only 4 of the 22 (18.2 %) subjects in Harding and colleague's reentry study were classified as having trajectories of upward mobility showing "improvement in material conditions and economic security even after achieving stability, eventually resulting in *independence*" (p. 451). An additional four subjects obtained long-term economic stability—attained economic stability, but had no "opportunities for economic or material advancement" (Harding et al. 2014, p. 451). The few returning prisoners able to experience upward mobility received extensive material support from family and romantic partners, as well as assistance from their "rich social networks that they could provide leads to jobs with career ladders" (Harding et al. 2014, p. 461).

Factors Potentially Related to Believing in the American Dream

Race/Ethnicity

For the prisoner reintegration discussion, Petersilia (2003, p. 30) asserts that race is the "elephant sitting in the living room." A persons' race/ethnicity has a significant negative effect on finding employment, equal to or greater than the impact of having a criminal record (Decker et al. 2015;

Pager 2007; Pager et al. 2009). Pager (2007, p. 101), for example, noted that "while being black or having a criminal record each represent a strike against the [job] applicant, with two strikes, you're out." Likewise, racial differences in the quality of neighborhood attainment after incarceration have also been seen (Massoglia et al. 2012).

Rank and colleagues (2014) found that about three-fourths (74 %) of people of color "will encounter poverty in their lives without ever achieving affluence" (p. 126). African Americans are nearly three times as likely as whites to be living in poverty (26 % compared with 10 % in 2014), and about four in ten report that their race has made it harder for them to succeed in life (Pew Charitable Trusts 2016). In particular, about two-thirds or more African Americans report that it is harder to get ahead due to racial discrimination, failing schools, and a lack of jobs (Pew Charitable Trusts 2016). Additionally, Longoria (2009) reports that African Americans are much more likely than whites to believe that a lack of equal opportunity is a major cause of poverty. In *A theory of African American offending: Race, racism, and crime,* Unnever and Gabbidon (2011), argue that racial discrimination has cumulative effects that can lead to psychological, physical, and social complications; and the potential to lead an African American to a greater likelihood of offending. In a similar way, Cernkovich et al. (2000; see also Hochschild 1995) suggest that due to structural factors, in America, race matters even if those who are most affected by it do not realize it.

Despite these findings, polling about the American Dream has consistently found "[n]o racial difference on whether the American Dream is attainable" (Zogby 2011, p. 111). Moreover, others have reported similar findings showing no racial differences in the belief in upward mobility or that the American Dream is possible (Hochschild 1995; Rose and Clear 2004). Interestingly, Hochschild (1995) found that the worst off third of blacks remain committed to the American Dream despite the severity of their economic circumstances. Consequently, based on these contradictory findings, it is of interest to examine if black, non-Hispanic participants in this study of former prisoners have similar or different beliefs in the American Dream than their peers.

Sex

The Zogby Polls concerning the American Dream have documented some differences between women and men. Hanson (2011) reports that "[o]verall, the most consistent gender differences in the 2001 survey involve the *definition* of the Dream more than whether it is *achievable* or what *factors affect it.*" Women were less likely to say the American Dream is mainly about achieving material success, and more likely to report that it is about achieving spiritual goals (Hanson 2011). The Zogby polls also show that women (as compared to men) began to diverge in 2004 in their confidence that the American Dream is possible (Hanson 2011). For example, in 2004, Hanson (2011) reports that 65 % of women agreed with the statement "Do you feel that it is possible for you and your family to achieve the American Dream, or would you say it does not exist?" as compared to 80 % of men. The gap between women and men has remained significant in more recent surveys, with women being less optimistic about the Dream (Hanson 2011).

The reentry experiences of women are important to examine (see Leverentz 2014). It is generally believed that women returning home from prison must deal with more issues than their male counterparts (see, e.g., Bloom et al. 2003; O'Brien 2001; Richie 2001), especially concerning stigma and discrimination (LeBel 2012b; van Olphen et al. 2009). For example, LeBel (2012b) found that for formerly incarcerated persons, a higher percentage of women than men reported feeling discriminated against for nine of ten reasons, with three of the differences statistically significant: gender, diagnosed mental disorder, and sexual orientation. Therefore, in regard to the belief in upward mobility and the American Dream, it is important to assess if there are differences between formerly incarcerated women and men.

Social Bonds

Strong social bonds to conventional society are thought to be important for successful prisoner reintegration (see, e.g., Petersilia 2003; Western et al. 2015; Wolff and Draine 2004) and desistance from crime (e.g., Laub et al. 1998; Sampson and Laub 1993), and the strength of one's family relationships are typically seen as being of central importance (Braman 2004). Reentry studies have found that married men are less likely to self-report committing a new crime (Visher et al. 2009); women who were married were less likely to be reincarcerated (La Vigne et al. 2009a); and being married or living as married and higher-quality relationships with partners reduces self-reported drug use (Visher et al. 2009). Harding and colleagues (2014) also found that former prisoners with more social support from family and romantic partners were more likely to experience upward economic mobility. Based on these findings, it is hypothesized that formerly incarcerated persons with stronger social bonds, that is, who are married, will be more likely to believe in the American Dream.

The lack of formal education, especially being a high school dropout, has consistently been found to be related to becoming incarcerated at some point in a person's lifetime (see, e.g., Western 2006). In general, when talking about upward mobility and the American Dream, many people believe that education, especially graduating from college, is one of the keys to success (McClelland and Tobin 2010). Moreover, education has a powerful impact on the likelihood of experiencing affluence instead of poverty during one's lifetime (Rank et al. 2014, p. 124). However, about twice as many blacks (31 %) compared to whites (14 %) with a college degree describe themselves as lower class (Pew Charitable Trusts 2016). Also, blacks with some college education are more likely than those without it to report having been discriminated against because of their race (Pew Charitable Trusts 2016, p. 8). It is hypothesized that formerly incarcerated persons with lower levels of formal education will be less likely to believe that the American Dream is possible.

As noted from the Zogby polls, many people now see the American Dream "as a blend of material and spiritual goods, beliefs, and values" (D'Antonio 2011, p. 128). Moreover, one's religious faith is reported to be one of the top reasons why people believe in the American Dream (Zogby 2011). Some evaluation research suggests that engagement in faith-based programs may be beneficial for prisoner reintegration (e.g., Johnson 2004), and that religious conversion and spiritual transformation are key factors that aid former prisoners in overcoming reentry obstacles (e.g., Solomon et al. 2001; Johnson and Larson 2003). In this study of formerly incarcerated persons, it is hypothesized that those with stronger religious/spiritual beliefs will think that upward mobility is possible.

It is generally accepted that the more time one serves in prison, the more disconnected one becomes from the outside world (see, e.g., Irwin 2005). Similarly, Maruna (2001; see also Anderson 1999) argues that conviction and imprisonment often serve to reinforce a person's negative worldview and detachment from society. Consequently, it is hypothesized that the more extensive and serious a former prisoner's criminal history is the more likely he is not going to accept the American Dream as possible.

Stigma and Discrimination

McNamee and Miller (2014) posit that "[d]iscrimination is not just a nonmerit factor; it is the antithesis of merit" (p. 216). In regard to formerly incarcerated persons, Johnson (2002) argues,

> Released prisoners find themselves "in" but not "of" the larger society. Like lepers, we keep ex-prisoners at a distance and avoid them entirely when we can. Even under the best of conditions, ex-offenders face formidable obstacles to reassimilation in the community. (p. 319)

It is well documented that former prisoners suffer from many "civil disabilities" such as statutory restrictions placed on, public and private employment, voting, eligibility for public assistance and public housing, financial aid to attend college, firearm ownership, criminal registration, and the like (e.g., Legal Action Center 2004; Mauer and Chesney-Lind 2002; Travis 2002). Travis (2002) refers to these restrictions as "invisible punishments." Moreover, there is increasing acknowledgment that not only being labeled "ex-con" but also the perception that one is stigmatized by society may make prisoner reintegration difficult (Anderson 1999, 2001; LeBel et al. 2008; LeBel 2012a; Owens 2009; Winnick and Bodkin 2009).

Owens (2009), for example, suggests that perceptions of stigma likely have a negative impact on the belief in economic mobility and boundary permeability. It is important to continue to gain a better understanding of the impact that perceptions of stigma may have on the lives of formerly incarcerated persons. Based on the extant literature, it is hypothesized that stronger perceptions of stigma will negatively impact formerly incarcerated persons' belief that the American Dream is possible.

Normalization of Incarceration Experience in Neighborhood

Research consistently points to the fact that neighborhoods and residential context matter for a wide variety of social, health, behavioral, and economic reasons (Rank et al. 2014; Sampson 2012; Sharkey and Faber 2014). Sharkey (2008; see also Quillian 2003 for adults being stuck in high-poverty census tracts), for example, found that 72 % of black children growing up in the poorest quarter of American neighborhoods remained in similarly disadvantaged neighborhoods as adults. Thus, persistent poverty often affects consecutive generations of African American families (Sharkey and Faber 2014).

The geographic concentration of returning prisoners in inner-city minority neighborhoods has become an important topic of interest for prisoner reentry researchers (Sampson and Loeffler 2010; Travis et al. 2014). The reality of reentry is that at least half of released prisoners return to their old neighborhood (La Vigne et al. 2009b; Yahner and Visher 2008), or to a similarly disadvantaged community with high rates of crime and relatively few services and support systems to promote successful reintegration (see, e.g., Clear 2007; Harding et al. 2013; Travis et al. 2014). Released prisoners themselves certainly appear to recognize that their chances of success are diminished by returning to the same old neighborhood as many report that drug dealing is a major problem, that it is difficult to avoid crime, and that their neighborhood is not a good place to find a job (see, e.g., Brooks et al. 2008; La Vigne et al. 2009b; Visher and Courtney 2007). Additionally, prisoners who return to more disadvantaged and disorganized neighborhoods recidivate at a greater rate (Kubrin and Stewart 2006; Yahner and Visher 2008; see also Kirk 2009). Kubrin and Stewart (2006, p. 189) argue that "by ignoring community context, we are likely setting up ex-inmates for failure."

Several researchers suggest that incarceration may have lost much of its stigmatizing capacity due to the normalization of the experience for large segments of the population in inner-city communities (see, e.g., Anderson 1999; Clear 2007; Hirschfield 2008; Petersilia 2003; Western et al. 2015). Yet, in spite of the normalization of the prison experience for many young men in inner-city communities, Schnittker and Bacak (2013, p. 251; see also Braman 2004; Clear et al. 2001) report that incarceration is "more likely to be a mark of disgrace" rather than a "badge of honor" for African Americans living in communities where the going to jail or prison has become a normative experience.

Although the literature supports the view that former prisoners living in inner-city communities where incarceration rates are high are cognizant of their lower position in society, it is less clear what impact the normalization of this experience will have on former prisoners' perceptions of the American Dream and upward economic mobility. With such large numbers of former prisoners concentrated in inner-city communities, an examination of the impact that the normalization of the prison experience may have on the outlook of formerly incarcerated persons is warranted. Similarly, as the vast majority of prisoner reentry research has focused on the largest metropolitan areas in a state, it is important to assess (and compare) the perceptions and experiences of prisoners that return to smaller metropolitan areas as well.

Perceived Unjustness and Unfairness of the Criminal Justice System

The criminal justice literature is replete with examples of how unjust America's criminal justice system is, especially in regard to people of color (see, e.g., Alexander 2010; Reiman and Leighton 2013; Tonry 2011; Unnever and Gabbidon 2011). Former prisoners themselves often articulate that the system is unfair and unjust (e.g., Ross and Richards 2003). In a similar vein, Laub and Sampson (2003) conclude that "most persistent offenders (as well as ex-offenders) see society as a whole as corrupt" (p. 186). Moreover, Maruna (2001) reported that "in the desisting self-story, the 'System' may need more reform than the recovering individual himself or herself. . . . In fact, rather than overcoming a "criminal value system," the interviewees saw themselves as recovering from *society's* value system in some sense" (p. 107). Believing that the criminal justice system is illegitimate appears to imply that society as a whole is unfair and unjust. Moreover, other research involving social identity theory suggests that perceptions of illegitimacy will be inversely related to the belief that upward mobility is possible (Mummendey et al. 1999; Wright 1997). Consequently, it is hypothesized that stronger feelings that the criminal justice system is illegitimate will be related to formerly incarcerated persons' increased skepticism that the American Dream is possible.

Group Identification

The "us versus them" mentality of prisoners is a well-accepted facet of the prison environment (e.g., Irwin 1970). McAnany et al. (1974, p. 26) report that most former prisoners perceive the prison experience as unjust and postulate that this view "creates a positive identification—that of victim—for those who undergo it." They also found that the self-identity of many former prisoners was based on their common prison experience. In addition, once released, former prisoners who want to make it in a law-abiding way must struggle to overcome a similar set of obstacles.

Research from the social psychology perspective posits that people who ascribe to legitimizing ideologies are unlikely to identify with the devalued group (Ellemers 1993, 2001); especially if they believe that they can move upward into a higher-status group through their own efforts. In fact, the belief in individual (or upward) mobility may be inversely related to levels of group identification (Jost et al. 2001, p. 382). Branscombe and Ellemers (1998) posit that "individual mobility can be conceptualized as a strategy that is aimed at maintaining a positive *personal* identity, and it is likely to be preferred by people who self-categorize at the individual level in a given social context" (p. 244). Considerable research evidence indicates that stigmatized persons who do not identify with the group (low-group identifiers) prefer individualistic strategies such as attempting to leave the group, whereas persons who strongly identify with the disadvantaged group (high group identifiers) are more likely to endorse and engage in group-level strategies such as advocacy and collective action (Branscombe and Ellemers 1998; Ellemers 1993; Major 1994; Simon et al. 1998; Wright and Tropp 2002). A stronger belief that the American Dream is possible will likely decrease group identification with other former prisoners (see, e.g., Dion and Earn 1975; Ellemers 1993; Mummendey et al. 1999; Tyler et al. 1997). Therefore, it is hypothesized that the more formerly incarcerated persons identify with similarly stigmatized others, the less likely they will endorse the conformity inherent in the American Dream.

Psychological Well-Being and Behavioral Outcomes

Laub and Sampson emphasize that "personal agency looms large" in persistence and desistance trajectories (2003, p. 280). Many researchers note that the belief in one's ability to "go straight," or one's sense of self-efficacy, self-confidence, optimism, or hope may be necessary, if not sufficient condition for an individual to be able to succeed after prison and desist from crime more generally (see, e.g., LeBel et al. 2008; Maruna 2001; Nelson et al. 1999; O'Brien 2001; Visher and O'Connell 2012). For example, socio-cognitive research with former prisoners suggests that long-term, persistent offenders tend to lack feelings of agency, experiencing their lives as being largely determined for them in a fatalistic mind-set which Maruna (2001) refers to as being "doomed to deviance." The negative impact of this belief system also gains credibility from Maruna's finding that,

> The active offenders... seemed fairly accurate in their assessments of their situation (dire), their chances of achieving success in the "straight" world (minimal), and their place in mainstream society ("need not apply"). (2001, p. 9)

Based on this research, and other literature discussed above about desistance from crime and prisoner reentry, it is hypothesized that those who believe more strongly that the American Dream is possible will feel better about themselves (i.e., have higher self-esteem), express more satisfaction with their life right now, and show more optimism for the future (i.e., indicate a lower likelihood of rearrest). Additionally, it is hypothesized that those believing that the American Dream and upward economic mobility will be less likely to feel the need to conceal their criminal past on applications of various sorts.

Study Objectives

Little is known about the relationship (or impact) that formerly incarcerated persons' demographics, criminal history, and attitudes, may have on the belief that the American Dream is possible for all people in society, and particularly for those reentering society from prison. This examination of the factors that are related to formerly incarcerated person's belief in the American Dream is for the most part exploratory. The main objectives of this study are to examine the strength of the belief in the American Dream, the factors related to these beliefs, and to assess the relationship between these beliefs and psychological well-being (self-esteem and life satisfaction) and potential behavioral outcomes.

Four research questions are addressed: (1) To what degree do formerly incarcerated persons' think that any person can succeed in mainstream society in America? (2) To what degree do formerly incarcerated persons' agree or disagree that "A former prisoner that wants to can 'make it' in a law abiding way in society? (3) What factors account for any differences in these beliefs that the American Dream is possible? and (4) How is the belief that the American Dream is possible related to psychological well-being and potential behavioral outcomes such as the forecast of rearrest in the next 3 years and concealment of a felony conviction on applications?

Methods

Sample and Data Collection

In this study, a formerly incarcerated person is defined as: *someone who has served a prison sentence for a felony conviction.* A purposive and targeted sampling technique was used to recruit male and female formerly incarcerated persons from New York City and Upstate New York. Sampling was aimed at recruiting adults, aged 18 and older, who were currently receiving prisoner reintegration services of some kind, or working as a staff member (i.e., as a counselor, employment specialist, halfway house manager, etc.) for the organization. A total of 258 formerly incarcerated persons are included in this study; 229 clients and 29 staff members. Participants were recruited from six organizations providing a variety of services (e.g., counseling, drug/alcohol treatment, education, and employment services) to former prisoners. Female former prisoners were oversampled for this project. Whereas women make up only 6.4 % of the adults released from prison in New York State in 2003 (NYDOCS 2004), they make up 17.8 % of this sample.

This is a cross-sectional study and the method of data collection is a self-completed questionnaire that was delivered to groups of former prisoner clients at each of the organizations, and to staff members individually. Data collection was completed between April and September 2004. The questionnaire asked about a variety of topics concerning life as a formerly incarcerated person including: perceptions of stigma, social identity as a former prisoner, coping strategies, psychological well-being, demographics, and criminal history. The questionnaire primarily utilized a fixed-choice "closed" format with response sets ranging from five to eight items. The majority of participants completed the questionnaire in 30 min or less. Approval for the study was obtained from the University's Institutional Review Board and senior level personnel (e.g., executive director) at each of the organizations.

Analytical Strategy

OLS regression analysis (using SPSS version 22) is used to determine how well a set of variables explain the American Dream scale and the perception that any former prisoner can "make it" in a law-abiding way in society. These OLS regression analyses provide information on the characteristics. Attitudes and beliefs of formerly incarcerated persons are most strongly related to perceiving that the American Dream is possible. The mean substitution method is used to account for missing data, and following the suggestion of Cohen, Cohen, West, and Aiken (2003), a missing-data dummy variable is included in the OLS regression equation. Then, correlation analysis is used to examine the relationship between belief in the American Dream and psychological well-being (self-esteem and satisfaction with life), the forecast of rearrest in the next 3 years, and concealment of information about their criminal past when completing applications of various sorts.

The independent variables and four variables measuring psychological well-being and potential behavioral outcomes are discussed in the Measures section. Descriptive statistics are displayed in the Results section. As the key construct in these analyses, special attention is given to the indicators in the American Dream scale and the measure used to assess the view that any former prisoner can succeed after release from prison.

Measures

The American Dream

The belief in the possibility for a low-status group member to move to a higher-status group is known as boundary permeability or individual mobility. Former prisoners were asked to indicate their beliefs about boundary permeability with a 3-item scale using a 7-point Likert-type response set ranging from strongly disagree to strongly agree. The questions to address individual mobility have been modified from items used to measure meritocratic beliefs (e.g. Jost et al. 2003; Major et al. 2002). The sample of former prisoners was asked how much they disagree or agree that:

- Advancement in mainstream society is possible for all people.
- America is an open society where all people with skills can achieve higher status.
- Anyone who is willing to work hard has a good chance of succeeding in America.

These three items indicate the belief that "anyone" in society can "make it" or succeed in America if they work hard and have the necessary skills. A separate item asks the respondent to indicate his or her belief that "A former prisoner that wants to can 'make it' in a law-abiding way in society." Higher scores on these measures indicate the belief that the boundary is open and individual mobility and the ability to achieve the American Dream is a realistic possibility.

Demographic and Background Characteristics

Demographic information including age, sex, and racial/ethnic identity was collected. Age is a continuous variable in years, and for sex, males are coded as 1 with females coded as 0. An effort was made to over sample female former prisoners in relation to their percentage of the population released each year in New York State. Racial/ethnic identity is operationalized with black, non-Hispanic coded as 1 and all others coded as 0. Marital status was measured with the question, "What is your current marital status?" Response categories included: married; not married but living with someone as if married; have an intimate partner, but not married or living together; and single. This response set was used because it provides mutually exclusive categories that provide a clear indication of each respondent's *current* intimate relationship status. Marital status is dichotomized with those reporting currently being married coded as 1 and all others coded as 0. The location where the participant completed the interview is coded with 1 = New York City and 0 representing all others from Upstate New York (i.e., Albany, Buffalo, Syracuse). This study includes formerly incarcerated persons who are both clients receiving reentry-related services as well as staff members in these agencies. Staff members are coded as 1, with clients coded as 0.

Normalization of the Prison Experience

The geographic concentration of returning prisoners in the most socially and economically disadvantaged inner-city communities has become a topic of interest for prisoner reentry researchers (see, e.g., Travis et al. 2014).

Three items (e.g., "A kid growing up today in the neighborhood where I grew up will probably end up in prison someday") were combined to form a normalization scale where higher scores indicate that serving time in prison is seen as a likely occurrence and is not considered shameful in the neighborhood where the respondent grew up.

Education and Employment

The lack of formal education has consistently been found to be related to becoming incarcerated at some point in a person's lifetime (see, e.g., Western 2006) and may be related to believing in the American Dream. Education level is operationalized by the highest level of formal education completed and is a 7-item scale with those reporting 8th grade or less coded as 0 and those who have engaged in postgraduate study coded as 6. Respondents' employment status has been dichotomized with 1 indicating currently employed and 0 representing not employed.

Criminal History

The criminal history of participants was measured in three ways: number of felony convictions in lifetime, time served in lifetime, and number of times returned to prison for parole violations. Each of these measures involves self-report. The variables for number of felony convictions and parole violations resulting in a return to prison are coded from 0 to 4 or more. The variable for amount of time served represents the months spent incarcerated in respondents' lifetime. For the analyses to follow, the time served variable has been log transformed in order to account for positive skew.

Religious/Spiritual Beliefs and Remorse

In this study, participants were recruited from (at least) two organizations that may be considered to have elements of "faith-based" practice. In addition, many of the participants in these programs have been exposed to and/or currently attend Alcoholics Anonymous (AA) or Narcotics Anonymous (NA) programs. Both AA and NA have a spiritual or religious dimension. Therefore, participants were asked, "In living day to day, how important is practicing your religious beliefs or spiritual beliefs?" A 5-point Likert-type scale with a range from "not at all important" to "very important" is used for this question.[1] Higher scores indicate that practicing one's religious or spiritual beliefs is important.

A largely unexplored facet of the perspective of former prisoners is whether or not they feel sorry for their crime(s). However, feeling remorse is increasingly being linked to the desistance and recidivism process (see, e.g., Braithwaite 1989; LeBel et al. 2008). To measure remorse, participants were asked to respond to the statement, "I am sorry for the harm caused to others by my past criminal activities," using a 7-point Likert-type response set ranging from strongly disagree to strongly agree.

Group Identification

Group identification represents the extent to which respondents identify or feel close ties with other formerly incarcerated persons. The three indicators in this scale are similar to items used by many researchers to measure group identification (see, e.g., Ellemers et al. 1997). The specific items include: "I have a number of things in common with other former prisoners"; "I identify with other former prisoners"; and "Former prisoners need to stick together."

Illegitimacy of the Criminal Justice System

Legitimacy (or illegitimacy) is primarily concerned with the fairness and justifiability of the social structure in regard to the intergroup situation facing the disadvantaged group (e.g. Major 1994; Tajfel 1982; Tyler 2001).

---

[1] Respondents who checked the box indicating that "I'm not religious or spiritual" were recoded as 1 for practicing their religious or spiritual beliefs is "not at all important."

In this study, former prisoners' attitudes and beliefs about how fair, just, and legitimate they perceive the criminal justice system and laws to be is assessed. Three items were modified from previous studies (see Lipkus 1991; Major 1994; Schmitt et al. 2003; Tyler 1990; Wahl 1999; Wright and Tropp 2002) in order to address the issues relevant to a population of former prisoners. The specific items include "Unjust laws have put many people in prison"; "All in all, I think the criminal justice system treats people fairly"; and "All people receive the equal protection of the laws." A 7-point Likert-type scale with a range from strongly disagree to strongly agree is used for the three items in this scale. The last two items are reverse scored so that higher scores on this scale indicate stronger agreement that the criminal justice system and laws are unfair and unjust. Therefore, this is a scale of the perceived *illegitimacy* of the criminal justice system.

Personal Stigma

In this study, respondents were asked for their perceptions of what "people" think about them personally because of their status as a former prisoner. Items were modified from Link's (1987) devaluation–discrimination scale for persons with mental illness and Harvey's (2001) scale concerning stigma and race. In addition, several new items were developed (see LeBel 2012a). The 9-item scale includes many of the stereotypes of formerly incarcerated persons (e.g., dangerous, dishonest, untrustworthy), as well as indicators for being feared, discriminated against, and looked down on. A 7-point Likert-type scale from 1 (strongly disagree) to 7 (strongly agree) was used for the personal stigma scale.

Psychological Well-Being and Behavioral Outcomes

The psychological well-being of respondents is measured with the Rosenberg Self-Esteem Scale (Rosenberg 1965). This 10-item scale has five positively worded items (e.g., "I feel that I have a number of good qualities") and five negatively worded items (e.g., "I feel I do not have much to be proud of"). Negatively worded items were reverse scored so that higher scores on the scale reflect feelings of positive self-worth. A single question from Andrews and Withey (1976) was used to measure former prisoners' "global" well-being or life satisfaction, "How do you feel about your life as a whole?" This variable is scored using Andrews and Withey's (1976) D-T scale from 1 (terrible) to 7 (delighted).

The formerly incarcerated persons in this study were asked to predict or forecast the probability that they will recidivate (see, e.g., Dhami et al. 2006). Respondents were asked "Realistically, how likely or unlikely is it that you will be arrested for a new crime in the next three years?" A 5-point Likert-type scale from 1 (very unlikely to be rearrested) to 5 (very likely to be rearrested) was used to assess respondent's forecast of rearrest. A questionnaire used by Wahl (1999) included an item about the extent to which respondents avoid indicating their status as persons with a mental disorder on applications of all sorts. To assess the endorsement of concealing on applications, the formerly incarcerated persons in this study were asked: "Have you avoided indicating on written applications (for jobs, licenses, housing, school, etc.) that you have a felony conviction for fear that information will be used against you?" This variable is scored using a 5-point Likert-type scale from 1 (never) to 5 (very often). Importantly, this measure of concealment is broader than employment as it also includes applications for licenses, housing, school, or other reasons.

Results

Descriptive Statistics

Descriptive statistics are presented in Table 1. The sample of formerly incarcerated persons has a mean age of 36.88 years, is 82.2 % male, and is 57.2 % black, non-Latino. The mean score on the education measure is 2.58 (standard deviation [SD] = 1.50), with the median and mode = 2.00 for having a General Educational Develpoment (GED)/ High School Educational Development (HSED). About one-third (33.1 %) of respondents reported an education level involving the

Table 1 Descriptive statistics

Characteristic	Description	Mean	SD
Age	Years	36.88	9.59
Sex	0 = female; 1 = male	0.822	0.38
Black, non-Latino	0 = all others; 1 = black, non-Latino	0.572	0.50
Education level	Formal education completed. 0 = eighth grade or less; 6 = postgraduate study	2.58	1.50
Marital status	"What is your current marital status?" 0 = not married; 1 = married	0.224	0.42
Employment status	Current employment status. 0 = not employed; 1 = employed full-time or part-time	0.369	0.48
Location (New York City)	Location in which questionnaire was completed. 0 = Upstate New York; 1 = New York City	0.721	0.45
Staff member	Status of respondent at reentry program. 0 = client; 1 = staff member	0.112	0.32
Stigma (personal)	Perceptions of personally being stigmatized due to status as a former prisoner. 1 = strongly disagree; 7 = strongly agree. 9-item scale. α =.874	3.70	1.30
Group identification	The extent to which respondents' identify with other former prisoners. 1 = strongly disagree; 7 = strongly agree. 3-item scale. α =.543	5.14	1.05
Normalization	Normalization of prison experience in the neighborhood where the respondent grew up. 1 = strongly disagree; 7 = strongly agree. 3-item scale. α =.703	4.24	1.52
Remorse	Sorry for harm caused to others by past criminal activities. 1 = strongly disagree; 7 = strongly agree	5.79	1.67
Religious beliefs	"In living day to day, how important is practicing your religious beliefs or spiritual beliefs?" 1 = "not at all important" or "I'm not religious or spiritual" to 5 = "very important"	3.60	1.49
Illegitimacy	The belief that the criminal justice system and the laws are unfair and unjust. 1 = strongly disagree; 7 = strongly agree. 4-item scale. α =.542	5.52	1.03
Felony convictions	Number of felony convictions (lifetime) from 0 to 4 or more	2.16	1.02

(*continued*)

Table 1 (continued)

Characteristic	Description	Mean	SD
Time served	Time served in months (lifetime)	90.83	74.68
Parole violations	Number of parole violations resulting in a return to prison from 0 to 4 or more	0.78	1.13
Self-esteem	Rosenberg's Self-esteem Scale. 1 = strongly disagree; 7 = strongly agree. 10-item scale. $\alpha =.792$	5.48	0.95
Life satisfaction	"How do you feel about your life as a whole?" 1 = terrible; 4 = mixed feelings; 7 = delighted	4.50	1.24
Forecast of rearrest	"Realistically, how likely or unlikely is it that you will be arrested for a new crime in the next three years?" 1 = very unlikely to be rearrested; 5 = very likely to be rearrested	2.02	1.10
Concealment on applications	"Have you avoided indicating on written applications (for jobs, licenses, housing, school, etc.) that you have a felony conviction for fear that information will be used against you?" 1 = never; 5 = very often	2.76	1.49
American Dream is possible scale	The belief that all people can succeed in mainstream society. 1 = strongly disagree; 7 = strongly agree. 3-item scale. $\alpha =.634$	4.75	1.31
Any former prisoner can "make it"	"A former prisoner that wants to can 'make it' in a law-abiding way in society" 1 = strongly disagree; 7 = strongly agree	6.10	1.07

Note: SD = standard deviation.

completion of a GED/HSED, and nearly one-fourth (22.4 %) were currently married. Twenty-nine (11.2 %) of the formerly incarcerated persons were staff members of the agencies, and about three-fourths (72.1 %) of the total sample completed the questionnaire in New York City. Slightly more than one-third (36.9 %) of the respondents were currently employed. On average, participants served 90.8 months in prison during their lifetime with a median of 60 months. The mean for number of felony convictions in their lifetime is 2.16, while the mean for parole violations resulting in a return to prison is 0.78.

The mean of the personal stigma scale (3.70) was significantly below the midpoint of 4.00 (neither agree nor disagree), and the Cronbach's alpha coefficient for the scale is .874. About three-fourths of respondents (74.8 %) agreed or strongly agreed with the statement about feeling sorry for their past crimes.[2] In fact, the mean using a 7-point Likert-type scale from 1 for strongly disagree to 7 for strongly agree was 5.79 with a SD of 1.67. The mean for practicing religious/spiritual beliefs was 3.60 (SD = 1.49). Close to four in ten (39.8 %) respondents reported that practicing their religious/spiritual beliefs is very important to them as compared to 17.3 % who indicated that it is not at all important or that they are not religious or spiritual. The mean of the normalization scale (4.24) is slightly above the midpoint (neither agree nor disagree) of the scale and has a substantial amount of variation suggesting that some participants grew up in neighborhoods where a person going to prison was a common occurrence, while others did not. Many participants identified strongly ($M = 5.14$) with other former prisoners, and the Cronbach's alpha coefficient for this scale is .543. Similarly, the mean of the illegitimacy scale (5.52) was significantly above the midpoint of 4.00 (neither agree nor disagree), indicating that the former prisoners in this study generally think that the criminal justice system and laws are unfair and unjust.

For the psychological well-being measures, the mean of 5.48 on the self-esteem scale was quite high, and the mean of 4.50 for life satisfaction (i.e., "how you feel about your life as a whole") was halfway between the responses of "mixed feelings" and "pleased." The mean for concealment on applications was 2.76 (SD = 1.49) with a median of 3 (for sometimes). For the forecast of rearrest, the mean was 2.02 (SD = 1.10), where 2 indicates "unlikely to be rearrested" in the next 3 years.

---

[2] Braman (2004) likewise reported that "...no inmate whom I spoke with claimed to feel pride in being incarcerated. While there are undoubtedly some inmates who do feel this way, even the youngest and least abashed drug dealer I interviewed expressed shame and regret" (p. 108).

The American Dream

Table 2 displays means, SDs, factor loadings, and Cronbach's alpha for the American Dream scale. Higher scores indicate the extent to which formerly incarcerated persons think that anyone in society can "make it" or succeed in America if they work hard or have the necessary skills. A principal component factor analysis shows that all three indicators load on a single factor that explains 58.04 % of the total variance, and the scale has an alpha of .634.[3] The mean of the American Dream scale is 4.75 (SD = 1.31), significantly ($t_{1,\ 257} = 9.21$, $p < .001$) above the neutral score (4.0). Moreover, all three indicators have scores significantly above the midpoint (at $p < .05$). Table 1 shows that the mean for the measure that any former prisoner that wants to can "make it" is 6.10 (SD = 1.07), significantly ($t_{1,\ 256} = 31.34$, $p < .001$) above the neutral score (4.0). Therefore,

Table 2 The American Dream is possible scale

Indicator	Mean (SD)	Factor loading
"Anyone who is willing to work hard has a good chance of succeeding in America."	5.66 (1.33)	0.698
"Advancement in mainstream society is possible for all people."	4.29 (1.83)	0.734
"America is an open society where all people with skills can achieve higher status."	4.29 (1.93)	0.846
Scale	4.75 (1.31)	
Eigenvalue		1.741
Total variance explained		58.04 %
Cronbach's alpha		0.634

Note: N = 258. Principal component factor analysis is used. SD = standard deviation. 1 = strongly disagree, 7 = strongly agree.

---

[3] An alpha coefficient higher than 0.70 is generally considered an acceptable level of internal consistency (Nunnally 1978). Although this scale has an alpha slightly below this threshold, Schmitt (1996) argues that "there is no sacred level of acceptable or unacceptable level of alpha" (p. 353), and that scales with lower levels of reliability may be quite useful. However, interpretation of constructs with lower reliability has "the potential for underestimating any relationships between the measured variable and other variables of interest" (Schmitt 1996, p. 352).

overall, the majority of formerly incarcerated persons in this sample strongly believe that anyone (including former prisoners) who is willing to work hard can succeed in America, advancement in mainstream society is possible for all, and any person with skills can achieve higher status.

Explaining the Belief in the American Dream

Table 3 displays results for the OLS regression equation explaining the American Dream scale.[4] The table reports the unstandardized coefficients, standard errors, and the standardized coefficients (β) and statistical significance for each of the independent variables. The multiple regression analysis revealed that the independent variables contributed significantly to the model, $F (18, 254) = 3.37$, $p < .001$ and accounted for a respectable 20.4 % of the variation in the American Dream scale. Six of the independent variables uniquely predict the belief that the American Dream is possible. Formerly incarcerated persons who more strongly agree that the American Dream is possible for all people have lower perceptions of personally being stigmatized due to their status as a former prisoner, have lower scores on the scale for illegitimacy of the criminal justice system, have served less time in prison in their lifetime, completed less formal education, identify more strongly with other former prisoners, and feel more remorse for their past crimes.

Table 4 displays the results for the multiple regression model predicting the belief that any former prisoner that wants to can make it in a law-abiding way in society. This analysis shows that the independent variables contributed significantly to the regression model, $F (18, 248) = 7.071$, $p < .001$ and accounted for a substantial 35.6 % of the variation in the

---

[4] The OLS regression equations were checked for outliers (using regression diagnostic statistics) and for problems of multicollinearity among the IVs (using variation inflation factor [VIF] statistics). The regression diagnostics used to flag potentially problematic cases included centered leverage values of two times the mean to check for non-outlying influential cases; studentized residuals ±3 to check for extreme outliers; and Cook's D > .05 to check for influential cases (see Belsley et al. 1980; Cohen et al. 2003; Cook 1977). The regression results presented here are for OLS regression equations with outliers removed.

Table 3 Regression analysis results for the American Dream scale

Variable	B	SE B	β
Age	−.002	.009	−.015
Sex	.122	.240	.036
Black, non-Latino	−.227	.158	−.087
Education level	−.134*	.055	−.152
Marital status	−.077	.193	−.025
Employment status	.189	.185	.070
Location (New York City)	−.141	.184	−.049
Staff member	.043	.293	.010
Stigma (personal)	−.264***	.066	−.263
Group identification	.178*	.084	.144
Normalization	.016	.055	.019
Remorse	.094*	.048	.122
Religious beliefs	−.038	.056	−.043
Illegitimacy	−.214**	.082	−.168
Felony convictions	.010	.088	.007
Time served	−.235*	.112	−.156
Parole violations	−.022	.079	−.018
Missing data dummy	.221	.263	.053
Constant	6.975***	.721	
R^2	.204		

Note: Results for the regression equation with outliers removed ($n = 255$). SE = standard error. Mean substitution is used for missing data. *** $p \leq .001$ ** $p \leq .01$, * $p \leq .05$.

measure that any former prisoner can make it. The eight variables with significant relationships with stronger agreement that former prisoners can make it include identifying more strongly with other former prisoners, perceptions of less personal stigma, having more parole violations, feeling more remorse for past crimes, currently having a job, living in Upstate New York (not New York City), stronger perceptions that the criminal justice system is unfair and unjust, and currently being married.

Relationship Between Believing in the American Dream and Psychological and Behavioral Outcomes

In the next step, an assessment is made of the relationship (correlations) between believing in the American Dream and respondents' self-esteem, life satisfaction, forecast of rearrest in the next 3 years, and concealment

Table 4 Regression analysis results for any former prisoner can "Make It"

Variable	B	SE B	β
Age	−.005	.006	−.051
Sex	−.026	.146	−.012
Black, non-Latino	.040	.097	.023
Education level	.002	.033	.004
Marital status	.215#	.117	.103
Employment status	.316**	.114	.175
Location (New York City)	−.326**	.112	−.170
Staff member	−.239	.180	−.088
Stigma (personal)	−.228***	.039	−.342
Group identification	.301***	.050	.364
Normalization	−.005	.033	−.009
Remorse	.099***	.029	.192
Religious beliefs	.012	.034	.019
Illegitimacy	.116*	.049	.136
Felony convictions	.029	.053	.034
Time served	−.086	.068	−.086
Parole violations	.167***	.048	.214
Missing data dummy	−.031	.161	−.011
Constant	4.708***	.439	
R^2	.356		

Note: Results for the regression equation with outliers removed ($n = 249$). SE = standard error. Mean substitution is used for missing data. *** $p \le .001$ ** $p \le .01$, * $p \le .05$, # $p \le .10$.

of a felony conviction on applications. Table 5 displays the correlations (Pearson's r, two tailed) and statistical significance level of each of these relationships. Not surprisingly, the results show that the American Dream measures are positively related to self-esteem. Higher scores on the item for any former prisoner can make it is significantly related ($r = .195$, $p \le .01$) to self-esteem, while stronger agreement that the American Dream is possible for all people is related at a marginally significant level to self-esteem ($r = .118$, $p = .057$). The greater one's satisfaction with life, the more she/he agrees that the American Dream is possible ($r = .124$, $p \le .05$). The more a formerly incarcerated person forecasts the likelihood of getting rearrested in the next 3 years, the less she/he agrees that any former prisoner can make it in a law-abiding way in society ($r = −.162$, $p \le .01$). The higher a respondent's score on the

Table 5 Relationship between American Dream measures and psychological and behavioral outcomes

Characteristic	American dream is possible scale	Any former prisoner can "Make It"
Self-esteem	.118#	.195**
Life satisfaction	.124*	.101
Forecast of rearrest	.029	−.162**
Concealment on applications	−.148*	−.050

Note: Correlations are shown (two tailed). Pairwise deletion is used for missing data.
** $p \leq .01$, * $p \leq .05$, # $p \leq .10$.

American Dream scale, the lower will be the concealment of their criminal history (i.e., felony conviction) on applications ($r = -.148$, $p \leq .05$).

Discussion

The main objectives of this study were to examine formerly incarcerated persons' belief in the American Dream for all people in society as well as former prisoners. More specifically, this study examines the strengths of these beliefs, the factors related to these beliefs, and assesses the relationship between the strength of these beliefs and psychological well-being (self-esteem and life satisfaction) and potential behavioral outcomes such as the forecast of rearrest in the next 3 years and concealment of a felony conviction on applications. Essentially, this study examines if and why formerly incarcerated persons believe in the American Dream, and how these beliefs matter both psychologically and behaviorally for returning prisoners.

A scale with three indicators was developed to measure the belief that the American Dream is possible for all people. The mean for the scale ($M = 4.75$) was significantly above the midpoint (of 4.00 for neither agree or disagree), a principal component analysis indicated that all three indicators loaded on a single factor, and the internal consistency of the scale was good ($\alpha = .634$). Overall, the formerly incarcerated persons in this sample expressed the belief that advancement to a higher status in America is possible for all people who work hard and have skills. This finding was expected based on the extant literature showing that even the most disadvantaged individuals endorse the view that the social structure is for the most part open (Crocker et al. 1998; Jost and Banaji 1994; Kluegel and Smith 1986), and that people consistently support the belief that the American Dream is possible, especially around the year 2004 when this study was conducted (Zogby 2011). Essentially, despite the structural challenges formerly incarcerated persons face, they still subscribe to Horatio Alger's "rags to riches" story, in that with hard work and skills, anyone can achieve the American Dream (McNamee and Miller 2014).

The mean (6.10) for the question asking for agreement that "A former prisoner that wants to can 'make it' in a law-abiding way in society" was significantly above the midpoint (4.00). A staggering 42.8 % of respondents strongly agreed, while an additional 37.0 % agreed with this statement. In fact, only 2.4 % of the respondents disagreed in any way that a former prisoner can make it if he or she wants to do so. Additionally, about three-fourths of the formerly incarcerated persons in this study responded to the following statement: "Please indicate which of the three statements below most clearly represents your view of the chance for former prisoners to succeed in a law-abiding way in mainstream society." The three responses and results for this forced-choice question were as follows: "It is nearly impossible for a former prisoner to succeed in society" (2.9 %); "Only a select few former prisoners are truly given an opportunity to succeed in society" (22.8 %); and "Any former prisoner that is willing to work hard can succeed in society" (74.3 %). Thus, overall, formerly incarcerated persons in this sample strongly believe that any former prisoner can "make it" in mainstream society. These results for formerly incarcerated persons' belief in individual upward mobility for former prisoners lends support to the existing literature suggesting that most believe that the social and economic structure in America is more open than closed (e.g., Erickson et al. 1973; Irwin 1970; Lin 2000).

Although the two measures for the American Dream are related to one another ($r = .292$, $p < .001$), the findings described above suggest that formerly incarcerated persons express a stronger belief that any former prisoner can make it in a law-abiding way in society than in the belief that upward mobility is possible for all people in America. Despite the plethora of pitfalls that a returning prisoner must overcome to succeed, it is implausible to think that someone released from prison will engage in and be able to maintain a commitment to law-abiding behavior (e.g., the conformist for Merton 1938, 1968) and going straight without the belief that the pursuit of the American Dream is possible. These findings support the notion that one's sense of self-efficacy, self-confidence, optimism, or hope may be a necessary, if not sufficient condition for an individual to be able to succeed after prison and desist from crime more generally (see, e.g., LeBel et al. 2008; Maruna 2001; Visher and O'Connell 2012). LeBel and colleagues (2008) also assert that with an adequate sense of hope about the future, a formerly incarcerated person may both select into and take advantage of positive social opportunities, such as education, employment, or marital attachment.

Multiple regression models were used to provide empirical evidence regarding explanations for formerly incarcerated persons' belief that the American Dream is possible for all people in society and for former prisoners in particular. Four of the characteristics/attitudes/beliefs of formerly incarcerated persons were predictive of both measures of believing in the American Dream. In particular, believers in the American Dream perceive less personal stigma, identify more strongly with other former prisoners, and are more remorseful. The perception that the criminal justice system and laws are more illegitimate (i.e., unjust and unfair) was positively related to the belief that any former prisoner can make it in a law-abiding way, but negatively related to the belief that all people who work hard and have skills can succeed.

More specifically, in predicting the American Dream scale (Table 3), a comparison of the standardized coefficients indicates that higher perceptions of personal stigma ($\beta = -.263$) has the largest (negative) impact, while for the dependent variable for agreeing that any former prisoner can make it, feeling stigmatized ($\beta = -.342$) has the second largest impact. The set of indicators in the 9-item personal stigma scale include many of the stereotypes of formerly incarcerated persons (i.e., dangerous, dishonest, untrustworthy) as well as indicators for being feared, discriminated against, being looked down on, etc. For example, respondents were asked for their level of agreement with the following statement: "I personally am discriminated against because I'm a former prisoner." Consequently, it was not a surprise to find that formerly incarcerated persons perceiving higher levels of stigma fit most closely with Zogby's (2008, 2011) Dreamless Dead, who do not think that they personally, nor most middle-class Americans, can achieve the American Dream.

It was hypothesized that stronger feelings that the criminal justice system is illegitimate will be related to formerly incarcerated persons' increased skepticism that the American Dream is possible. Indeed, thinking that the criminal justice system is illegitimate (unjust and unfair) had the second largest impact ($\beta = -.168$) of the variables included in the model predicting the American Dream scale. The negative relationship between illegitimacy and upward mobility indicates that the more respondents regard the criminal justice system and criminal law as unfair and unjust, the less they view the American Dream as possible (for the link between illegitimacy and mobility more generally see Mummendey et al. 1999; Wright 1997). However, for the model explaining the level of agreement that any former prisoner can make it, stronger agreement that the criminal justice system is unfair was found to be *positively* related to the belief that any former prisoner can succeed in a law-abiding way. This finding may suggest that those who think the system is especially unfair may have lost hope that going straight is a realistic possibility for those returning home from prison. Based on the inconsistency of the findings involving perceptions of illegitimacy and the measures for the American Dream, more research is warranted to examine this relationship.

The measure for group identification represents the extent to which respondents identify, have a number of things in common with, and think that former prisoners need to stick together. When predicting the view that any former prisoner can make it (Table 4), the standardized coefficients show that higher scores for group identification with other former prisoners ($\beta = .364$) has the largest impact. In fact, group identification had a significant, and positive, relationship with the American Dream scale as well. These findings were not expected as prior research suggested that stronger beliefs that social mobility is possible will decrease group identification with other devalued group members (see, e.g., Dion and Earn 1975; Ellemers 1993, 1997; Mummendey et al. 1999; Tyler et al. 1997). However, perhaps the "need to stick together" with other former prisoners is a key factor in the belief that any former prisoner can make it. That is, it is harder for a former prisoner to believe that he or she can make it if they do not first believe that getting ahead in a law-abiding way is possible for their peers.

Feeling remorse, and more generally changing one's criminal identity to a more prosocial identity, is increasingly being linked to desistance from crime and the (successful) reentry process (see, e.g., Braithwaite 1989; LeBel et al. 2008; Maruna 2001). In this study, the prosocial view of feeling "sorry for the harm caused to others by my past criminal activities" was positively related to both measures of the American Dream. Feeling remorse for misdeeds, in a sense, may be an indication of conforming to the norms of society more generally (Merton 1938, 1968), and buying into the goal of material success and the means by which to achieve it.

In this study, currently employed respondents expressed stronger agreement that it is possible for any former prisoner to make it in a law-abiding way in society if they set their mind to it. The literature review emphasized that a core component of the American Dream is economic and social upward mobility (McClelland and Tobin 2010; Rank et al. 2014). For those returning from prison, obtaining and maintaining a job is likely the first, and most important, step required to move up the economic and social ladder (see Harding et al. 2014). When prisoners and parolees are asked to express their needs, employment and job training are typically at, or near, the top of the list (Erickson et al. 1973; La Vigne et al. 2007; Nelson et al. 1999; Visher and Lattimore 2007). The related needs of lack of money and lack of education are also perceived as major obstacles that must be addressed in order to succeed (Erickson et al. 1973; Visher and Lattmore 2007). Finding and maintaining employment after release has been shown to reduce recidivism (La Vigne et al. 2004; La Vigne et al. 2007; Rossman and Roman 2003; Visher and Courtney 2007; Visher et al. 2008; Yahner and Visher 2008). For example, Visher and colleagues (2008) note that the likelihood of reincarceration during the first year out is lower for individuals employed at 2 months compared to those who were unemployed.

Expanding transitional employment opportunities for recently released prisoners could have positive effects on employment outcomes and recidivism after incarceration (Finn 1998; Redcross et al. 2009; Rossman and Roman 2003). Redcross and colleagues (2009), in a rigorous evaluation of the Center for Employment Opportunities (CEO) in New York City, found that returning prisoners who received transitional jobs and post-employment support services were significantly less likely than a control group to be convicted of a crime over a 2-year follow-up period. Overall, for the current study, the relationship between having a job and believing that any former prisoner can make it in a law-abiding way in society suggests the belief that "if I can do it, so can you!" (see Chapter "Employment Isn't Enough: Financial Obstacles Experienced by Ex-prisoners During the Reentry Process" in this volume by Pogrebin, West-Smith, Walker, and Unnithan that questions the importance of employment to released offenders when facing mountains of debt upon release).

The hypothesis concerning a positive relationship between the seriousness of a respondent's criminal history and the belief in the American Dream is not well-supported in these analyses. The results in Tables 3 and 4 indicate that with the exception of parole violations for the view that any former prisoner can make it, and time served for the American Dream scale, the extent and seriousness of respondents' criminal history is, at most, only weakly related to believing in the American Dream. Moreover, having been returned to prison more times due to parole violations was positively related to believing that any former prisoner can make it if he or she wants to do so. It is possible that parole violators blame their lack of willpower for failing to succeed or do not plan to be law abiding, but think that other released prisoners that want to can succeed. Meanwhile, having served more time in prison in one's lifetime was negatively related to thinking that upward mobility is possible for all people in America. Perhaps long-term prisoners are less optimistic about the future, more generally, than their counterparts who have served a shorter sentence.

Formerly incarcerated persons who have completed more formal education reported less agreement that all people in society can achieve higher status (i.e., the American Dream scale). It is unclear why education is so strongly related to the belief that the American Dream is possible for all people, but is unrelated to the measure for any former prisoner can make it. Education may in some way radicalize former prisoners, or perhaps there is self-selection in the decision to go to college by persons with the most critical views of society and the "System." Former prisoners who have completed more schooling may be more cynical (or realistic) because they have higher aspirations which are not being realized (see, e.g., Sullivan 2004). Based on these findings, future research should continue to investigate the impact of formerly incarcerated persons' level of education on the belief that the American Dream is possible.

Currently, being married was a marginally significant predictor (at $p < .10$) of believing that any former prisoner can make it. This finding was expected as the quality of one's social bonds is important for successful prisoner reintegration more generally (Harding et al. 2014; Petersilia 2003; Western et al. 2015; Wolff and Draine 2004). Harding and colleagues found that released prisoners with more social support from romantic partners were more likely to obtain upward economic mobility. LeBel et al. (2008; see also Bucklen and Zajac 2009) found that self-characterization as a "family man" (i.e., a "good partner," a "good father," and/or a "good provider") contributes positively to the desistance process of formerly incarcerated persons. This finding suggests that stronger social bonds might act as a protective factor that supports reintegration and conformity with the norms (goals and means) of how to succeed in mainstream society.

Respondents completing the questionnaire at program locations in New York City are less likely to think that it is possible for any former prisoner to make it in a law-abiding way after release from prison. This finding of a "City effect" needs to be examined further as it could be an artifact caused by the nature of the programs where participants were recruited, or a remnant of the tragedy of the terrorist attack on the Twin Towers a couple of years before. Moreover, as much of the reentry literature has been focused on the largest metropolitan areas, it is important to continue to examine the reasons why city dwellers (as compared to their suburban and rural peers) may be more pessimistic about the possibility of upward mobility for returning prisoners that work hard.

It is also important to briefly mention the characteristics of formerly incarcerated persons in this sample that were not significant predictors of either measure of the American Dream. In particular, the variables unrelated to believing in the American Dream include the following: age, sex, race/ethnicity (black, non-Latino as compared to all others), religious/ spiritual beliefs, being a staff member (and not a client), normalization of the prison experience in the neighborhood where they grew up, and the number of felony convictions. Based on the extant literature, it is somewhat surprising that demographics and the background of formerly incarcerated persons are unrelated to their optimism about the ability to achieve upward mobility. Interestingly, despite the finding that employment status is related to thinking that any former prisoner can make it, the views of staff members at the agencies did not differ from the clients.

The relationship between believing in the American Dream and four potential psychological and behavioral consequences were examined. The literature on the American Dream and prisoner reentry more generally suggested that those believing more strongly in the American Dream would report more psychological well-being and be less likely to forecast rearrest for themselves or to conceal their criminal history on applications. Each of these hypotheses was partially supported in this study (see Table 5). Those who believe more strongly that any former prisoner can make it have significantly higher self-esteem and are significantly less likely to forecast that they personally will be arrested within the next 3 years. Importantly, research studies have typically found that prisoners who think it will be easier to stay out of prison are in fact less likely to be reincarcerated after release (LeBel et al. 2008; Visher and Courtney 2007). For the American Dream scale, those indicating a stronger belief that all people can succeed are more satisfied with their life as a whole right now, less likely to conceal their (felony) criminal history on applications, and expressed marginally higher self-esteem than their peers. These findings lend some support to the idea that feeling better about oneself, as well as hope for the future and self-efficacy, may be necessary conditions for someone to attempt to, and possibly, desist from crime and succeed in a material way after returning home from prison (see, e.g., LeBel et al. 2008; Maruna 2001; Visher and O'Connell 2012).

Implications of Formerly Incarcerated Persons' Modes of Adaptation to the American Dream

Using Merton's (1938, 1968) typology, it would appear that the correctional system in general would clearly like to have released prisoners use the adaptation of conformity. If not able to accept both the goals and means leading to monetary success in American society, the second and third choices for adaptation appear to be ritualism (being satisfied with your lot in life and an existence near the margins and the poverty line) and retreatism (living on the margins of society, such as homelessness, but not raising your head up enough to return to the prison system). In contrast, the correctional system does not want to produce innovators (committing more crime to survive) after release, and certainly does not want to see formerly incarcerated persons adapting through rebellion (e.g., involvement in advocacy work to drastically change the criminal justice system such as through the Black Lives Matter (BLM) movement [Taylor 2016; Pew Charitable Trusts 2016]).

Formerly incarcerated persons are increasingly speaking out and becoming more politically active. LeBel (2009), for example, found that many formerly incarcerated persons are interested in, or actively involved with, advocacy-related initiatives to change the criminal justice system. The results from this study (LeBel 2009) also indicated a basic incompatibility between an advocacy/activism orientation and criminal attitudes and behavior. These findings suggest that involvement in advocacy-related activities might have potential in facilitating the successful reintegration of some formerly incarcerated persons. These findings also suggest the potential for political organizing among recently released prisoners to support initiatives such as the BLM movement (Harris 2015) and the Fight for $15 campaign (Chen 2016; NELP 2015) to increase the minimum wage. About two-thirds (65 %) of African Americans support the BLM movement, with 41 % strongly supporting it. Most (59 %) African Americans also think that the BLM will be effective, in the long run in helping blacks to achieve racial equality, but only 20 % think it will be very effective.

In contrast, about 40 % of whites support the movement with only 14 % strongly supporting it (Pew Charitable Trusts 2016). Seventy percent of African Americans support a $15 minimum wage and two-thirds (67 %) feel that an increase in the minimum wage will help workers, rather than hurting them. Around half of whites oppose a minimum wage of $15 and 42 % feel that an increase in the minimum wage will hurt workers because businesses will hire fewer people (Moore 2015). Formerly incarcerated persons that have been released from prison more recently and are likely without college degrees, subsisting on low incomes, and with especially negative views of the system as unfair and unjust (i.e., the Dreamless Dead for Zogby 2011), may be increasingly willing to join activist movements such as the BLM and the fight for $15.

Limitations

Some limitations should be considered when interpreting the results of this study. The use of a purposive and targeted sampling technique (i.e., a nonrandom convenience sample) of formerly incarcerated persons in New York State who are attending or working at prisoner reentry programs poses a threat to the external validity of the study. In addition, the analysis is limited to a single state, and the questionnaires were completed less than 3 years after the devastating impact that the 9/11 terrorist attack had on New York City. That is, these results cannot be generalized to those in other states or to formerly incarcerated persons who are not currently attending reentry programs, or who are working in other fields and not currently under community supervision. This study employed a cross-sectional design, and as a result, it is not possible to establish causal direction for the relationships between believing in the American Dream and other variables of interest. Research on the American Dream suggests that beliefs vary over time based on larger economic and national or international events. Therefore, longitudinal research designs are needed to better examine and document the process of how and why formerly incarcerated persons' views about upward mobility may vary due to the challenges associated with reentry and changing economic circumstances. The measures for believing in the American Dream used in this study were fairly limited. Future research about formerly incarcerated persons' belief in the American Dream should consider using the same or similar measures to those used in the extant literature (e.g., the Zogby Poll). Finally, the data in this study were collected in late 2004.

However, after the recession of 2008, research consistently finds that people are more pessimistic about their own and their children's economic chances (Pew Charitable Trusts 2010, 2011). Consequently, if interviewed today, it is likely that released prisoners would reflect a similar more pessimistic view of the possibility for upward economic mobility. Moreover, an overwhelming majority of Americans are more concerned today with financial stability, rather than climbing the income ladder (Pew Charitable Trusts 2011). However, a recent Pew Charitable Trusts (2012) poll found that the majority of Americans believe their financial situation will be better in 10 years. These somewhat contradictory findings yield more support for a more up-to-date examination of formerly incarcerated persons' belief in, and responses to, the possibility of living the American Dream is warranted.

Conclusion

This study examined formerly incarcerated persons' belief in the American Dream, the factors related to believing that upward mobility is possible, and the relationship between believing in the Dream and psychological well-being and potential behavioral outcomes. The findings suggest that stronger beliefs in the American Dream, coupled with the provision of services to assist in climbing the economic ladder, might have a potentially positive impact on facilitating the successful reintegration of a substantial number of formerly incarcerated persons. Petersilia (2003, p. 14) argues that "if we fail to take advantage of this mindset, we miss one of the few potential turning points to successfully intervene in offender's lives."

References

Adams, J. T. (1931). *The epic of America*. Bethesda, MD: Simon.

Alexander, M. (2010). *The new Jim Crow: Mass incarceration in the age of colorblindness*. New York: The New Press.

Anderson, E. (1999). *Code of the street: Decency, violence, and the moral life of the inner city*. New York: W. W. Norton & Company.

Anderson, E. (2001). Going straight: The story of a young inner-city ex-convict. *Punishment & Society, 3*(1), 135–152.

Andrews, F. M., & Withey, S. B. (1976). *Social indicators of well-being*. New York: Plenum.

Austin, J., & Irwin, J. (2000). *It's about time: America's imprisonment binge*. 3rd edition. Belmont, CA: Wadsworth.

Austin, J., & Irwin, J. (2012). *It's about time: America's imprisonment binge*. 4th edition. Belmont, CA: Wadsworth.

Barlett, D. L., & Steele, J. B. (2012). *The betrayal of the American Dream*. New York: Public Affairs.

Belsley, D. A., Kuh, E., Welsch, R. E. (1980). *Regression diagnostics: Identifying influential data and sources of collinearity*. New York: Wiley.

Bloom, B., Owen, B., Covington, S. (2003). *Gender-responsive strategies: Research, practice, and guiding principles for women offenders*. Washington, DC: National Institute of Corrections.

Braithwaite, J. (1989). *Crime, shame, and reintegration*. Cambridge, UK: Cambridge University Press.

Braman, D. (2004). *Doing time on the outside: Incarceration and family life in urban America*. Ann Arbor, MI: University of Michigan Press.

Branscombe, N. R., & Ellemers, N. (1998). Coping with group-based discrimination: Individualistic versus group-level strategies. In J. K. Swim & C. Stangor (Eds.), *Prejudice: The target's perspective* (pp. 244–266). San Diego, CA: Academic.

Brooks, L. E., Solomon, A. L., Kohl, R., Osborne, J. W. L., Reid, J., McDonald, S. M., et al. (2008). *Reincarcerated: The experiences of men returning to Massachusetts prisons*. Washington, DC: The Urban Institute.

Bucklen, K. B., & Zajac, G. (2009). But some of them don't come back (to prison!): Resource deprivation and thinking errors as determinants of parole success and failure. *The Prison Journal, 89*(3), 239–264.

Burnett, R. (1992). *The dynamics of recidivism: Summary report*. Oxford, UK: University of Oxford, Centre for Criminological Research.

Bush, M. E. L., & Bush, R. D. (2015). Tensions in the American Dream: Rhetoric, reverie, or reality. Philadelphia, PA: Temple University Press.

Bushway, S. D., & Reuter, P. (2002). Labor markets and crime. In J. Q. Wilson & J. Petersilia (Eds.), *Crime: Public policies for crime control* (pp. 34–58). Oakland, CA: ICS Press.

CBS News/New York Times (2012). IPOLL Databank, The Roper Center for Public Opinion Research, University of Connecticut.

Cernkovich, S. A., Giordano, P. C., Rudolph, J. L. (2000). Race, crime, and the American Dream. *Journal of Research in Crime and Delinquency, 37*(2), 131–170.

Chen, M. (2016). Vote for $15. *Dissent, 63*(3), 42–46.

Clear, T. R. (2007). *Imprisoning communities: How mass incarceration makes disadvantaged neighborhoods worse.* New York: Oxford University Press.

Clear, T. R., Rose, D. R., Ryder, J. A. (2001). Incarceration and the community: The problem of removing and returning offenders. *Crime & Delinquency, 47*(3), 335–351.

Coalition for Women Prisoners. (2008). *My sister's keeper: A book for women returning home from prison or jail.* New York: Correctional Association of New York.

Cohen, J., Cohen, P., West, S. G., Aiken, L. S. (2003). *Applied multiple regression/correlation analysis for the behavioral sciences.* 3rd edition. Mahwah, NJ: Lawrence Erlbaum Associates.

Cook, R. D. (1977). Detection of influential observations in linear regression. *Technometrics, 19*, 15–18.

Crocker, J., Major, B., Steele, C. (1998). Social stigma. In D. T. Gilbert, S. T. Fiske, G. Lindzey (Eds.), *The handbook of social psychology*, Vol. 2, 4th edition (pp. 504–553). New York: McGraw-Hill.

Cullen, J. (2003). *The American Dream: A short history of an idea that shaped a nation.* New York: Oxford University Press.

D'Antonio, W. V. (2011). Religion and the American Dream: A Catholic reflection in a generational context. In S. L. Hanson & J. K. White (Eds.), *The American Dream in the 21st Century* (pp. 117–140). Philadelphia, PA: Temple University Press.

Decker, S. H., Ortiz, N., Spohn, C., Hedberg, E. (2015). Criminal stigma, race, and ethnicity: The consequences of imprisonment for employment. *Journal of Criminal Justice, 43*(2), 108–121.

Dhami, M. K., Mandel, D. R., Loewenstein, G., Ayton, P. (2006). Prisoners' positive illusions of their post-release success. *Law and Human Behavior, 30*, 631–647.

Dion, K. L., & Earn, B. M. (1975). The phenomenology of being a target of prejudice. *Journal of Personality and Social Psychology*, 32, 944–950.

Durose, M. R., Cooper, A. D., Snyder, H. N. (2014). *Recidivism of prisoners released in 30 States in 2005: Patterns from 2005 to 2010 (Special Report, NCJ 244205)*. Washington, DC: U.S. Department of Justice, Bureau of Justice Statistics.

Edin, K. J., & Shaefer, H. L. (2015). *$2.00 a day: Living on almost nothing in America*. New York: Houghton, Mifflin, & Harcourt.

Ellemers, N. (1993). The influence of socio-structural variables on identity enhancement strategies. In W. Stroebe & M. Hewstone (Eds.), *European review of social psychology*, Vol. 4 (pp. 27–57). Chichester, UK: Wiley.

Ellemers, N. (2001). Individual upward mobility and the perceived legitimacy of intergroup relations. In J. T. Jost & B. Major (Eds.), *The psychology of legitimacy: Emerging perspectives on ideology, justice, and intergroup relations* (pp. 205–222). Cambridge: Cambridge University Press.

Ellemers, N., Spears, R., Doosje, B. (1997). Sticking together or falling apart: In-group identification as a psychological determinant of group commitment versus individual mobility. *Journal of Personality and Social Psychology*, 72(3), 617–626.

Erickson, R. J., Crow, W. J., Zurcher, L. A., Connett, A. V. (1973). *Paroled but not free*. New York: Behavioral.

Festen, Marcia K., & Fischer, Sunny (2002). *Navigating reentry: The experiences and perceptions of ex-offenders seeking employment*. Prepared on behalf of The Chicago Urban League.

Finn, P. (1998). Job placement for offenders in relation to recidivism. *Journal of Offender Rehabilitation*, 28(1/2), 89–106.

Glaser, D. (1969). *The effectiveness of a prison and parole system*. Indianapolis: Bobbs-Merrill.

Greenfeld, L. A., & Snell, T. L. (1999). *Women offenders* (NCJ 175688). Washington, DC: U.S. Department of Justice, Bureau of Justice Statistics.

Hacker, J. S. (2008). *The great risk shift: The new economic insecurity and the decline of the American Dream*. New York: Oxford University Press.

Hanson, S. L. & Zogby, J. (2010). The polls—Trends: Attitudes about the American Dream. *Public Opinion Quarterly*, 74(3), 570–584.

White, J. K., & Hanson, S. L. (2011). The making and persistence of the American Dream. In S. L. Hanson & J. K. White (Eds.), *The American Dream in the 21st Century* (pp. 1–16). Philadelphia, PA: Temple University Press.

Harding, D. J., Morenoff, J. D., Herbert, C. (2013). Home is hard to find: Neighborhoods, institutions, and the residential trajectories of returning prisoners. *Annals of the American Academy of Political and Social Science*, *647*, 214–36.

Harding, D. J., Wyse, J. J. B., Dobson, C., Morenoff, J. D. (2014). Making ends meet after prison. *Journal of Policy Analysis and Management, 33*(2), 440–470.

Harris, F. C. (2015). The next civil rights movement? *Dissent, 62*(3), 34–40.

Harvey, R. D. (2001). Individual differences in the phenomenological impact of social stigma. *The Journal of Social Psychology, 141*(2), 174–189.

Helfgott, J. (1997). Ex-offender needs versus community opportunity in Seattle, Washington. *Federal Probation, 61*, 12–24.

Hirschfield, P. J. (2008). The declining significance of delinquent labels in disadvantaged urban communities. *Sociological Forum, 23*(3), 575–601.

Hochschild, J. (1995). *Facing up to the American Dream: Race, class, and the soul of the nation*. Princeton, NJ: Princeton University Press.

Holzer, H. J., Raphael, S., Stoll, M. (2006). Perceived criminality, criminal background checks, and the racial hiring practices of employers. *Journal of Law and Economics, 49*, 451–80.

Howerton, A., Burnett, R., Byng, R., Campbell, J. (2009). The consolations of going back to prison: What "revolving door" prisoners think of their prospects. *Journal of Offender Rehabilitation, 48*, 439–461.

Irwin, J. (1970). *The felon*. Englewood Cliffs, NJ: Prentice Hall.

Irwin, J. (2005). *The warehouse prison: Disposal of the new dangerous class*. Los Angeles, CA: Roxbury Publishing Company.

Irwin, J. (2009). *Lifers: Seeking redemption in prison*. New York: Routledge.

Johnson, B. R. (2004). Religious programs and recidivism among former inmates in prison fellowship programs: A long-term follow-up study. *Justice Quarterly, 21*(2), 329–354.

Johnson, B. R., & Larson, D. B. (2003). *The inner change freedom initiative: Evaluating a faith-based prison program, CRRUCS Report*. Philadelphia, PA: University of Pennsylvania, and New York: Center for Court Innovation, The Manhattan Institute.

Johnson, R. (2002). *Hard time*. 3rd edition. Belmont, CA: Wadsworth.

Jost, J. T., & Banaji, M. R. (1994). The role of stereotyping in system-justification and the production of false consciousness. *British Journal of Social Psychology, 33*, 1–27.

Jost, J. T., Burgess, D., Mosso, C. O. (2001). Conflicts of legitimation among self, group, and system: The integrative potential of system justification theory. In J. T. Jost & B. Major (Eds.), *The psychology of legitimacy: Emerging perspectives on ideology, justice, and intergroup relations* (pp. 363–388). New York: Cambridge University Press.

Jost, J. T., Pelham, B. W., Sheldon, O., Sullivan, B. N. (2003). Social inequality and the reduction of ideological dissonance on behalf of the system: Evidence of enhanced system justification among the disadvantaged. *European Journal of Social Psychology*, 13, 86–98.

Kalleberg, A. L. (2011). *Good jobs, bad jobs: The rise of polarized and precarious employment systems in the United States, 1970s to 2000s*. New York: Russell Sage Foundation.

Kirk, D. S. (2009). A natural experiment on residential change and recidivism: Lessons from Hurricane Katrina. *American Sociological Review*, 74, 484–505.

Kluegel, J. R., & Smith, E. R. (1986). *Beliefs about inequality: American's view of what is and what ought to be*. New York: Aldine de Gruyter.

Kubrin, C. E., & Stewart, E. A. (2006). Predicting who reoffends: The neglected role of neighborhood context in recidivism studies. *Criminology*, 44(1), 165–195.

La Vigne, N. G., Brooks, L. E., Shollenberger, T. L. (2007). *Returning home: Exploring the challenges and successes of recently released Texas prisoners*. Washington, DC: The Urban Institute.

La Vigne, N. G., Brooks, L. E., Shollenberger, T. L. (2009a). *Women on the outside: Understanding the experiences of female prisoners returning to Houston, Texas*. Washington, DC: The Urban Institute.

La Vigne, N. G., Shollenberger, T. L., Debus, S. A. (2009b). *One year out: Tracking the experiences of male prisoners returning to Houston, Texas*. Washington, DC: The Urban Institute.

La Vigne, N. G., Visher, C., Castro, J. (2004). *Chicago prisoners' experiences returning home*. Washington, DC: The Urban Institute.

Lalonde, R. N., & Silverman, R. A. (1994). Behavioral preferences in response to social injustice: The effects of group permeability and social identity salience. *Journal of Personality and Social Psychology*, 66, 78–85.

Laub, J. H., & Sampson, R. J. (2003). *Shared beginnings, divergent lives: Delinquent boys to age 70*. Cambridge, MA: Harvard University Press.

Laub, J. H., Nagin, D. S., Sampson, R. J. (1998). Trajectories of change in criminal offending: Good marriages and the desistance process. *American Sociological Review*, 63, 225–238.

LeBel, T. P. (2009). Formerly incarcerated persons' use of advocacy/activism as a coping orientation in the reintegration process. In B. Veysey, J. Christian,

D. J. Martinez (Eds.), *How offenders transform their lives* (pp. 165–187). Cullompton, UK: Willan.

LeBel, T. P. (2012a). Invisible stripes? Formerly incarcerated persons' perceptions of stigma. *Deviant Behavior, 33*, 89–107.

LeBel, T. P. (2012b). "If one doesn't get you another one will": Formerly incarcerated persons' perceptions of discrimination. *The Prison Journal, 92*(1), 63–87.

LeBel, T. P., & Maruna, S. (2012). Life on the outside: Transitioning from prison to the community. In J. Petersilia & K. Reitz (Eds.), *The Oxford handbook of sentencing and corrections* (pp. 657–683). New York: Oxford University Press.

LeBel, T. P., Burnett, R., Maruna, S., Bushway, S. (2008). The "chicken and egg" of subjective and social factors in desistance from crime. *European Journal of Criminology, 5*(2), 130–158.

Legal Action Center (2004). *After prison: Roadblocks to reentry: A report on state legal barriers facing people with criminal records.* New York: Legal Action Center.

Lerner, M. J. (1980). *The belief in a just world: A fundamental delusion.* New York: Plenum.

Leverentz, A. (2014). The ex-prisoner's dilemma: How women negotiate competing narratives of reentry and desistance. New Brunswick, NJ: Rutgers University Press.

Lin, A. C. (2000). *Reform in the making: The implementation of social policy in prison.* Princeton, NJ: Princeton University Press.

Link, B. G. (1987). Understanding labeling effects in the area of mental disorders: An assessment of the effects of expectations of rejection. *American Sociological Review, 52*, 96–112.

Lipkus, I. (1991). The construction and preliminary validation of a global belief in a just world scale and the exploratory analysis of the multidimensional belief in a just world scale. *Personality and Individual Differences, 12*(11), 1171–1181.

Longoria, R. T. (2009). *Meritocracy and Americans' views on distributive justice.* Lanham, MD: Lexington Books.

Love, M. C. (2006). *Relief from the collateral consequences of conviction: A state by state resources guide.* Buffalo, NY: William S. Hein, Inc.

Lynch, M. (2001). Rehabilitation as rhetoric: The ideal of reformation in contemporary parole discourse and practices. *Punishment & Society, 2*(1), 40–65.

MacDonald, H. (2003). How to straighten out ex-cons. *City Journal, 13*(2), 24–37.

Major, B. (1994). From social inequality to personal entitlement: The role of social comparisons, legitimacy appraisals, and group membership. In M. P. Zanna (Ed.), *Advances in experimental social psychology*, Vol. 26 (pp. 293–355). San Diego, CA: Academic Press.

Major, B., & Schmader, T. (2001). Legitimacy and the construal of social disadvantage. In J. T. Jost & B. Major (Eds.), *The psychology of legitimacy: Emerging perspectives on ideology, justice, and intergroup relations* (pp. 176–204). Cambridge: Cambridge University Press.

Major, B., Gramzow, R. H., McCoy, S. K., Levin, S., Schmader, T., Sidanius, J. (2002). Perceiving personal discrimination: The role of group status and legitimizing ideology. *Journal of Personality and Social Psychology, 82*(3), 269–282.

Maruna, S. (2001). *Making good: How ex-convicts reform and reclaim their lives.* Washington, DC: American Psychological Association Books.

Maruna, S. (2004). Desistance from crime and explanatory style: A new direction in the psychology of reform. *Journal of Contemporary Criminal Justice, 20*(2), 184–200.

Massey, D. S. (2007). *Categorically unequal: The American stratification system.* New York: Sage.

Massoglia, M., Firebaugh, G., Warner, C. (2012). Racial variation in the effect of incarceration on neighborhood attainment. *American Sociological Review, 78*(1), 142–65.

Mauer, M., & Chesney-Lind, M. (Eds.) (2002). *Invisible punishment: The collateral consequences of mass imprisonment.* New York: The New Press.

McAnany, P. D., Tromanhauser, E., Sullivan, D. (1974). *The identification and description of ex-offender groups in the Chicago area.* Chicago, IL: University of Illinois.

McClelland, P. D., & Tobin, P. H. (2010). *American Dream dying: The changing economic lot of the least advantaged.* Lanham, MD: Rowman & Littlefield.

McNamee, S. J., & Miller, R. K. (2014). *The meritocracy myth.* 3rd edition. Lanham, MD: Rowman and Littlefield.

Merton, R. K. (1938). Social structure and anomie. *American Sociological Review, 3*(5), 672–682.

Merton, R. K. (1968). *Social theory and social structure.* Enlarged edition. New York: The Free Press.

Messina, N., Burdon, W., Prendergast, M. (2001). *A profile of women in prison-based therapeutic communities.* Draft. Los Angeles, CA: UCLA Integrated Substance Abuse Program, Drug Abuse Research Center.

Messner, S. F., & Rosenfeld, R. (2013). *Crime and the American Dream.* 5th edition. Belmont, CA: Wadsworth.

Moore, P. (2015). *$15 minimum wage more divisive than smaller increases.* https://today.yougov.com/news/2015/07/30/15-minimum-wage-more-divisive/. Accessed 11 July 2006.

Mummendey, A., Kessler, T., Klink, A., Mielke, R. (1999). Strategies to cope with negative social identity: Predictions by social identity theory and relative deprivation theory. *Journal of Personality and Social Psychology, 76*(2), 229–245.

National Employment Law Project. (2015). *The Growing Movement for $15.* New York: NELP.

National League of Cities (2004). *The American Dream in 2004: A survey of American people.* Research Report, September.

Nelson, M., Deess, P., Allen, C. (1999). *The first month out: Post- incarceration experiences in New York City.* New York: Vera Institute of Justice.

Nunnally, J. C. (1978). *Psychometric theory.* 2nd edition. New York: McGraw-Hill.

O'Brien, P. (2001). *Making it in the "free world."* Albany, NY: SUNY Press.

Owens Jr., C. D. (2009). Social symbols, stigma, and the labor market experiences of former prisoners. *The Journal of Correctional Education, 60*(4), 316–342.

Pager, D. (2007). *Marked: Race, crime, and finding work in an era of mass incarceration.* Chicago: The University of Chicago Press.

Pager, D., Western, B., Sugie, N. (2009). Sequencing disadvantage: Barriers to employment facing young Black and White men with criminal records. *Annals of the American Academy of Political and Social Science, 623,* 195–213.

Petersilia, J. (2003). *When prisoners come home: Parole and prisoner reentry.* New York: Oxford University Press.

Pettit, B., & Lyons, C. (2007). Status and the stigma of incarceration: The labor market effects of incarceration by race, class, and criminal involvement. In D. Weiman, S. Bushway, M. Stoll (Eds.), *Barriers to re-entry: The Impact of incarceration on labor market outcomes* (pp. 202–226). New York: Russell Sage.

Pew Charitable Trusts. (2007). *Economic mobility: Is the American Dream alive and well?* Washington, DC: Pew Charitable Trusts, Economic Mobility Project.

Pew Charitable Trusts. (2009). *Findings from a national survey and focus groups on economic mobility.* Washington, DC: Pew Charitable Trusts, Economic Mobility Project.

Pew Charitable Trusts. (2010). *Collateral costs: Incarceration's effect on economic mobility*. Washington, DC: Pew Charitable Trusts.

Pew Charitable Trusts. (2011). *Economic mobility and the American Dream—Where do we stand in the wake of the great recession?* Washington, DC: Pew Charitable Trusts, Economic Mobility Project.

Pew Charitable Trusts. (2012). *Economic mobility and the American Dream: Examining racial and ethnic differences*. Washington, DC: Pew Charitable Trusts, Economic Mobility Project.

Pew Charitable Trusts. (2010). *A balance sheet at 30 months: How the great recession has changed life in America*. http://www.pewsocialtrends.org/files/2010/11/759-recession.pdf. Accessed 11 July 2016.

Pew Charitable Trusts (2016). *On views of race and inequality, Blacks and Whites are worlds apart*. http://www.pewsocialtrends.org/2016/06/27/on-views-of-race-and-inequality-blacks-and-whites-are-worlds-apart/. Accessed 5 July 2016.

Quillian, L. (2003). How long are exposures to poor neighborhoods? The long-term dynamics of entry and exit from poor neighborhoods. *Population Research and Policy Review, 22*, 221–249.

Rank, M. R., Hirschl, T. A., Foster, K. A. (2014). *Chasing the American Dream: Understanding what shapes our fortunes*. New York: Oxford University Press.

Redcross, C., Bloom, D., Azurdia, G., Zweig, J., Pindus, N. (2009). *Transitional jobs for ex-prisoners: Implementation, two-year impacts, and costs of the center for employment opportunities (CEO) prisoner reentry program*. A Report from MDRC-Building Knowledge to Improve Social Policy.

Reiman, J., & Leighton, P. (2013). *The rich get richer and the poor get prison: Ideology, class, and criminal justice*. 10th edition. Boston, MA: Pearson.

Richie, B. (2001). Challenges incarcerated women face as they return to their communities: Findings from life history interviews. *Crime & Delinquency, 47*, 368–389.

Robinson, E. (2007). Tattered dream: Who'll tackle the issue of upward mobility? *Washington Post*, 23November.

Rose, D. R., & Clear, T. R. (2004). Who doesn't know someone in jail? The impact of exposure to prison on attitudes toward formal and informal controls. *The Prison Journal, 84*(2), 228–247.

Rosenberg, M. (1965). *Society and the adolescent self-image*. Princeton, NJ: Princeton University Press.

Ross, J. I., & Richards, S. C. (2003). *Convict criminology*. Belmont, CA: Wadsworth.

Rossman, S. B., & Roman, C. G. (2003). Case managed reentry and employment: Lessons from the opportunity to succeed program." *Justice Research and Policy, 5*(2), 75–100.

Sampson, R. J. (2012). *Great American City: Chicago and the enduring neighborhood effect.* Chicago: University of Chicago Press.

Sampson, R. J., & Laub, J. H. (1993). *Crime in the making.* Cambridge, MA: Harvard University Press.

Sampson, R. J., & Laub, J. H. (1997). A life-course theory of cumulative disadvantage and the stability of delinquency. In T. P. Thornberry (Ed.), *Developmental theories of crime and delinquency* (pp. 133–163). New Brunswick, NJ: Transaction Publishers.

Sampson, R. J., & Loeffler, C. (2010). Punishment's place: The local concentration of mass incarceration. *Daedalus, 139,* 20–31.

Schmitt, M. T., Branscombe, N. R., Postmes, T. (2003). Women's emotional responses to the pervasiveness of gender discrimination. *European Journal of Social Psychology, 33,* 297–312.

Schmitt, N. (1996). Uses and abuses of coefficient alpha. *Psychological Assessment, 8*(4), 350–353.

Schnittker, J., & Bacak, V. (2013). A mark of disgrace or a badge of honor? Subjective status among former inmates. *Social Problems, 60*(2), 234–254.

Sharkey, P. (2008). The intergenerational transmission of context. *American Journal of Sociology, 113,* 931–969.

Sharkey, P., & Faber, J. W. (2014). Where, when, why, and for whom do residential contexts matter? Moving away from the dichotomous understanding of neighborhood effects. *Annual Review of Sociology, 40*(1), 559–579.

Sidanius, J., & Pratto, F. (1993). The inevitability of oppression and the dynamics of social dominance. In P. M. Sniderman & P. E. Tetlock (Eds.), *Prejudice, politics, and the American dilemma* (pp. 172–211). Stanford, CA: Stanford University Press.

Simon, B., Loewy, M., Sturmer, S., Weber, U., Freytag, P., Habig, C., et al. (1998). Collective identification and social movement participation. *Journal of Personality and Social Psychology, 74*(3), 646–658.

Sims, B. A. (1997). Crime, punishment, and the American Dream: Toward a Marxist integration. *Journal of Research in Crime and Delinquency, 34*(1), 5–24.

Solomon, A. L., Roman, C. G., Waul, M. (2001). *Summary of focus group with ex-prisoners in the district: Ingredients for successful reintegration.* Washington, DC: Urban Institute.

State of New York Department of Correctional Services (NYDOCS). (2004). *Characteristics of inmates discharged 2003*. Albany, NY: State of New York Department of Correctional Services.

Sullivan, M. L. (2004). Youth perspectives on the experience of reentry. *Youth Violence and Juvenile Justice, 2*(1), 56–71.

Tajfel, H. (1982). Social psychology of intergroup relations. *Annual Review of Psychology, 33*, 1–39.

Tajfel, H., & Turner, J. C. (1979). An integrative theory of intergroup conflict. In W. G. Austin & S. Worchel (Eds.), *The social psychology of intergroup relations* (pp. 33–47). Monterey, CA: Brooks/Cole Publishing Company.

Taylor, K. Y. (2016). *From #Blacklivesmatter to Black liberation*. Chicago: Haymarket Books.

Tonry, M. (2011). *Punishing race: A continuing American dilemma*. New York: Oxford University Press.

Travis, J. (2002). Invisible punishment: An instrument of social exclusion. In M. Mauer & M. Chesney-Lind (Eds.), *Invisible punishment: The collateral consequences of mass imprisonment* (pp. 15–36). New York: The New Press.

Travis, J., Western, B., Redburn, S., Eds. (2014). *The growth of incarceration in the United States: Exploring causes and consequences*. Washington, DC: National Academies Press.

Turner, J. C., & Reynolds, K. J. (2001). The social identity perspective in intergroup relations: Theories, themes, and controversies. In R. Brown & S. L. Gaertner (Eds.), *Blackwell handbook of social psychology: Intergroup processes* (pp. 133–152). Malden, MA: Blackwell.

Tyler, T. R. (1990). *Why people obey the law*. New Haven, CT: Yale University Press.

Tyler, T. R. (2001). Social justice. In R. Brown & S.L. Gaertner (Eds.), *Blackwell handbook of social psychology: Intergroup processes* (pp. 344–364). Malden, MA: Blackwell.

Tyler, T. R., Boeckman, R. J., Smith, H. J., Huo, Y. J. (1997). *Social justice in a diverse society*. Denver, CO: Westview Press.

Uggen, C. (1999). Ex-offenders and the conformist alternative: A job quality model of work and crime. *Social Problems, 46*(1), 127–151.

Unnever, J. D., & Gabbidon, S. L. (2011). *A theory of African American offending: Race, racism, and crime*. New York: Routledge.

van Olphen, J., Eliason, M. J., Freudenberg, N., Barnes, M. (2009). Nowhere to go: How stigma limits the options of female drug users after release from jail. *Substance Abuse Treatment, Prevention, & Policy, 4*, 1–10.

Visher, C., Debus, S., Yahner, J. (2008). *Employment after prison: A longitudinal study of releases in three states*. Washington, DC: The Urban Institute.

Visher, C., Kachnowski, V., La Vigne, N., Travis, J. (2004). *Baltimore prisoners' experiences returning home*. Washington, DC: The Urban Institute.

Visher, C. A., & Courtney, S. M. E. (2007). *One year out: Experiences of prisoners returning to Cleveland*. Washington, DC: The Urban Institute.

Visher, C. A., & Lattimore, P. K. (2007). Major study examines prisoners and their reentry needs (NCJ 219609). *NIJ Journal, 258*, 30–33.

Visher, C. A., & O'Connell, D. J. (2012). Incarceration and inmates' self perceptions about returning home. *Journal of Criminal Justice, 40*, 386–393.

Visher, C. A., Knight, C. R., Chalfin, A., Roman, J. K. (2009). *The impact of marital and relationship status on social outcomes for returning prisoners*. Washington, DC: The Urban Institute.

Wahl, O. F. (1999). *Telling is risky business: Mental health consumers confront stigma*. New Brunswick, NJ: Rutgers University Press.

Wakefield, S. & Uggen, C. (2010). Incarceration and stratification. *Annual Review of Sociology, 36*, 387–406.

Western, B. (2006). *Punishment and inequality in America*. New York: Russell Sage.

Western, B., Braga, A. A., Davis, J., Sirois, C. (2015). Stress and hardship after prison. *American Journal of Sociology*, 120(5), 1512–1547.

Winnick, T. A., & Bodkin, M. (2009). Stigma, secrecy, and race: An empirical examination of black and white incarcerated men. *American Journal of Criminal Justice*, 34(1/2), 131–150.

Wolff, N., & Draine, J. (2004). The dynamics of social capital of prisoners and community reentry: Ties that bind? *Journal of Correctional Health Care*, 10(3), 457–490.

Wright, S. C. (1997). Ambiguity, social influence and collective action: Generating collective protest in response to tokenism. *Personality and Social Psychology Bulletin, 23*, 1277–1290.

Wright, S. C. (2001). Restricted intergroup boundaries: Tokenism, ambiguity, and the tolerance of injustice. In J. T. Jost & B. Major (Eds.), *The psychology of legitimacy: Emerging perspectives on ideology, justice, and intergroup relations* (pp. 223–254). Cambridge, UK: Cambridge University Press.

Wright, S. C., & Tropp, L. R. (2002). Collective action in response to disadvantage: Intergroup perceptions, social identification, and social change. In I. Walker & H. J. Smith (Eds.), *Relative deprivation: Specification, development, and integration* (pp. 200–236). Cambridge, UK: Cambridge University Press.

Wright, S. C., Taylor, D. M., Moghaddam, F. M. (1990). Responding to membership in a disadvantaged group: From acceptance to collective protest. *Journal of Personality and Social Psychology*, 58(6), 994–1003.

Wysong, E., Perrucci, R., Wright, D. (2014). *The new class society: Goodbye American Dream?* 4th edition). Lanham, MD: Rowman & Littlefield.

Yahner, J., & Visher, C. (2008). *Illinois prisoners' reentry success three years after release*. Washington, DC: The Urban Institute.

Zogby, J. (2008). *The way we'll be: The Zogby report on the transformation of the American Dream*. New York: Random House.

Zogby, J. (2011). Want meets necessity in the new American Dream. In S. L. Hanson & J. K. White (Eds.), *The American Dream in the 21st Century* (pp. 105–116). Philadelphia, PA: Temple University Press.

Further Reading

Hanson, S. L. (2011). Whose dream? Gender and the American Dream. In S. L. Hanson & J. K. White (Eds.), *The American Dream in the 21st Century* (pp. 77–103). Philadelphia, PA: Temple University Press.

Harding, D. J. (2003). Jean Valjean's dilemma: The management of ex-convict identity in the search for employment. *Deviant Behavior*, 24, 571–595.

Isenberg, N. (2016). *White trash: The 400-year untold history of class in America*. New York: Viking.

McCain, J. (2008). *Concession speech*. Phoenix, Arizona, 5 November.

Obama, Barack (2008). Victory speech. Chicago, IL, 5 November.

Rose, D. R., & Clear, T. R. (2003). Incarceration, reentry, and social capital: Social networks in the balance. In J. Travis & M. Waul (Eds.), *Prisoners once removed: The impact of incarceration and reentry on children, families, and communities* (pp. 313–341). Washington, DC: The Urban Institute Press.

Society for Human Resource Management (SRHM) (2012). Background checking—The use of criminal backgrounds checks in hiring decisions. https://www.shrm.org/research/surveyfindings/articles/pages/criminalbackgroundcheck.aspx. Accessed 31 March 2016.

Western, B., Kling, J. R., Weiman, D. F. (2001). The labor market consequences of incarceration. *Crime & Delinquency*, 47(3), 410–427.

Thomas P. LeBel is an associate professor in the Department of Criminal Justice at the University of Wisconsin-Milwaukee. He is the author or coauthor of many publications about prisoner reintegration, desistance from crime, the stigma of incarceration, and interventions for criminal justice involving women with drug and alcohol problems. He has served as a scientific review board member, panelist, or discussant for prisoner reentry-related initiatives sponsored by the National Institute of Justice, the National Academy of Sciences—Committee on Law and Justice, the Urban Institute, and the National Institute of Corrections.

Matt Richie is currently a doctoral student in the Helen Bader School of Social Welfare at the University of Wisconsin-Milwaukee and former research assistant for the Milwaukee County Drug Treatment Court (MCDTC). He assisted in evaluating various aspects of the court, including the cognitive-behavioral treatment and trauma-informed care programs, as well as recidivism among drug court participants. His research interests include desistance from crime, the situational aspects of officer-involved shootings, police officer use of force, and risk assessment validation.

Shadd Maruna Prior to becoming Dean at Rutgers University Newark, Shadd Maruna has worked at Queen's University, Belfast, the University of Cambridge, and the University at Albany, SUNY. His book *Making Good: How Ex-Convicts Reform and Rebuild Their Lives* was named the "Outstanding Contribution to Criminology" by the American Society of Criminology (ASC) in 2001. More recently, he has received the Hans Mattick Award for Distinguished Contribution to Criminology in 2014 and the inaugural Research Medal from the Howard League for Penal Reform in 2012. He has been a Soros Justice Fellow, a Fulbright Scholar, and H. F. Guggenheim Fellow. He is the editor of the book series "Psychology, Crime and Justice" for American Psychological Association Books and coedited the book *Fifty Key Thinkers in Criminology* with Keith Hayward and Jayne Mooney (2010).

Employment Isn't Enough: Financial Obstacles Experienced by Ex-prisoners During the Reentry Process

Mark Pogrebin, Mary West-Smith, Alexandra Walker, and N. Prabha Unnithan

In the past three decades, the prison population in the United States has more than quadrupled, expanding from approximately 369,000 to more than 1.5 million inmates (U.S. Department of Justice 1982, 2012a). The tremendous growth in the inmate population has resulted in a subsequent increase in offenders returning to their communities, with as many as 730,000 offenders being released from federal and state correctional facilities per year (U.S. Department of Justice 2011). By 2011, 853,900 persons were being supervised in the community as parolees, while 80 %

M. Pogrebin
University of Colorado, Public Affairs, Denver, CO, USA

M. West-Smith (✉)
University of Northern Colorado-Criminal Justice, Greeley, CO, USA
e-mail: mary.westsmith@unco.edu

A. Walker · N.P. Unnithan
Colorado State University-Sociology, Fort Collins, CO, USA

© The Author(s) 2017
S. Stojkovic (ed.), *Prisoner Reentry*,
DOI 10.1057/978-1-137-57929-4_7

of persons who left prison that year did so under some form of parole supervision (U.S. Department of Justice 2012b, 2012c).

The parole population is in a state of constant flux. Within 1 year, the membership of the parolee population changes dramatically, with almost two thirds of the individuals on parole exiting parole through various ways, including completion of the terms of parole, return to incarceration, abscondence, deportation, and death (U.S. Department of Justice 2012c). However, only about one third of persons who exited parole in 2011 did so through successful reentry to their communities (U.S. Department of Justice 2012c). More than a decade ago, two thirds of released persons were rearrested within 3 years of release (U.S. Department of Justice 2002). While there has been a great deal of variability in the return-to-prison rates in individual states over the last decade, the frequency of parole failure remains stubbornly high (Pew Center on the States 2011).

It has been long recognized that there are several circumstances linked to successful reentry, including employment that pays wages that cover basic living expenses (Travis and Petersilia 2001). However, the use of criminal justice fees associated with parole conditions, such as payments for drug testing, treatment, and monitoring, are increasingly being assessed and may reduce available funds to pay for basic expenses (Bannon et al. 2010). Restitution, child support, and additional mandated expenses may also be contributing to financial barriers to successful reentry that available employment cannot overcome.

Literature Review

Individuals returning to their communities do not experience equally the multiple dilemmas of reentry, but the vast majority encounter difficulties in various areas of adjustment. Employment opportunities, access to governmental benefits, stable housing, treatment programs, family support, access to health care, and a positive parole experience are needed for successful reentry (Naser and LaVigne 2006, Travis and Petersilia 2001). Becker (1968) recognized decades ago that loss of human capital creates additional challenges for reentering prisoners. The depreciation of human capital resulting from incarceration diminishes prospects for success in many areas, but it is especially problematic when ex-offenders are trying to find employment. If employment is found, it is commonly unskilled work that pays low wages (Becker 1968; Kling 2006). Western et al. (2001) note that the experience of discrimination in employment and lowered chances for economic success for reentering prisoners has been well established.

Ex-inmates have lower earning capacities and rates of employment when measured against comparable groups (Freeman 1992; Grogger 1995; Lyons and Pettit 2011; Western et al. 2001). Compared to 18 % of the general population that does not have high school diplomas, 68 % of inmates reported having not completed high school while approximately one quarter received their GED (General Educational Determination) certificates, which serve as high school equivalency assessments, while serving time in an institution (U.S. Department of Justice 2003). People who lack the education and training employers value have difficulty finding employment, but, as Pager (2003, p. 956) notes "criminal records close doors in employment situations." Pager also found that employers stated they were twice as likely to hire nonoffenders as they were to give jobs to equally qualified offenders. According to Holzer et al.'s (2007) study involving employer surveys, two thirds of the respondents reported that they would not hire people with criminal backgrounds. Additionally, only 6 % of those surveyed reported that they would be willing to employ people who not only have criminal backgrounds but who also have spent time in prison, leaving 94 % of these surveyed employers as apparently viewing persons with prison stays ineligible for employment in their organizations.

Job applicants may try to hide their past criminal records by not informing prospective employers of their prior incarceration (Harding 2003). In a study of formerly incarcerated persons' perception of stigma, more than one third of the study participants reported they had avoided disclosure of their criminal histories on job applications in an attempt to avoid rejection based on their ex-inmate status (LeBel 2012). This risky strategy is effective primarily in situations where the job is short term or where background checks are not required (Harding 2003). More desirable jobs, especially those that have mandatory background checks, are likely out of their reach, since ex-inmates are unable to conceal their former inmate status.

Having a family support system also has been shown to be important for successful reentry (Kushel et al. 2005; LaVigne et al. 2004). Providing a home when a person leaves prison greatly relieves many financial pressures, but family members also can improve job opportunities for returning ex-prisoners through their network of friends, employers, and religious institutions (Visher et al. 2008). Parolees who find employment shortly after release often do so by making use of connections through friends and family members with whom they maintained contact during their incarceration (Cobbina 2009; Mallik-Kane and Visher 2008; Nelson et al. 1999; Visher and Kachnowski 2007). Without the help of family and friends, returning ex-inmates are likely to face much longer periods of time before finding employment, if they find it at all (Nelson et al. 1999).

Parolees who were employed prior to incarceration may be able to reestablish contact with former employers prior to release, which improves their chances of quickly finding employment (Visher et al. 2008). However, since many former inmates do not have decent legitimate employment records, few can likely take advantage of such former relationships. Although one of the best ways for ex-prisoners to find work is through family, community, and former employment contacts; many persons leaving prison lack connections that can lead to employment since many of their contacts in the community may be criminally active and are not in the position to offer leads for legitimate employment (Hagan 1993). Their stigmatized backgrounds, their deficiencies in education and appropriate skills, and their lack of prosocial contacts can affect many ex-inmates' ability to find work, which can inhibit both their current and future economic statuses (Pager 2003; Western 2006; Western et al. 2001).

The stakes for quickly finding employment are high for persons returning from prison. Parolees generally must have jobs to meet their parole conditions and the inability to find and keep work can result not only in a marginalized existence but also in a return to prison for violation of parole requirements. However, employment alone may not be sufficient for many persons leaving prison, since employment that may barely cover basic living expenses likely will not pay enough to meet the additional financial obligations that many parolees confront as they leave prison. Debts incurred prior to incarceration may continue to mount while a person is in prison. Griswold and Pearson (2005), in a study of child support obligations of incarcerated parents, found that parents often enter prison with thousands of dollars in unpaid child support and by the time they leave prison, the arrears they owe include not only the original debt but also interest and child support accumulated while in prison. In addition to child support obligations, ex-inmates are often released from prison with significant financial liabilities, such as court costs and fees, tax deficiencies, and other domestic bills (Richards and Jones 2004).

In the 15 states with the largest prison populations, expenses frequently assessed through the criminal justice system include restitution and fees associated with parole supervision, alcohol and drug testing, and mandatory treatment (Bannon et al. 2010). Additional noncriminal justice obligations such as child support and "poverty penalties," including late fees, interest fees, payment plan fees, and collection fees associated with the inability to pay debts, may further reduce funds available to cover basic living expenses and may contribute to a return to prison (Bannon et al. 2010, p. 19). Such fees may discourage ex-inmates from seeking legitimate employment if wages are garnished and income tax refunds are intercepted to pay debts incurred through criminal justice and other legal obligations.

Finding and maintaining employment, having a residence at which a parolee can be contacted, submitting to and paying for medical and DMG (Dimethylglycine) testing, and paying fees and restitution are now common standard conditions of parole (Travis and Stacey 2010). An increasing dependence on surveillance and ongoing treatment and testing in the community has shifted the costs from the supervising authorities to persons leaving prison. In the past, employment that ex-inmates may have had access to and that may have provided wages sufficient to pay for minimal living expenses might not be sufficient to cover the now-mandated additional expenses associated with parole.

While some states allow prisoners to voluntarily "max out" their sentences, thereby forgoing parole supervision (Ostermann 2011, p. 596), Colorado is not one of these states. In 1993, the Colorado Legislation passed H.B. 93-1302, which requires felony offenders to serve mandatory parole periods of 1–5 years after their first release from prison. From 1995 to 2011, the average daily parole population in Colorado increased from

1185 to 8422 (Colorado Department of Corrections 1999, 2013), a much larger increase than would be expected, based only on the increase in the prison population. With the dramatic increase in the parole population, the number of individuals returned to prison for parole violations also increased. From 1997 to 2013, the percentage of Colorado parolees who exited parole by returning to prison for technical violations of parole rose from 16.5 % to 40 % (Colorado Department of Corrections 1999, 2013), despite many intermediate sanctions steps taken by Colorado to minimize the number of parole violators returned to prison. In stark contrast, the national percentage of exits from state parole by return to prison for technical violations dropped from 25 % to 21 % between 2008 and 2011, and in 2012, this number dramatically decreased to 14 %, largely driven by California's efforts to curtail the use of prison as a response to technical parole violations (U.S. Department of Justice 2013). Nonetheless, Colorado's percentage of parolees who exit parole by returning to prison for technical violations is significantly higher than the national average.

Maintaining employment, if one is not physically or mentally disabled, is a typical parole condition requirement. Without the ability to find and maintain employment, parolees may have little chance of avoiding reincarceration. However, merely finding employment may not be sufficient to overcome other financial barriers that may prevent parolees from gaining any type of financial stability and, thus, a foothold in conventional society.

The purposes of the current study are multiple. First, we explore the employment and financial challenges that parolees confront as they leave prison in Colorado. Second, we seek to improve our understanding of how additional financial burdens may prevent parolees from achieving financial security. Finally, we focus on how such burdens and financial insecurity may create conditions where parolees believe they cannot successfully reenter society.

Method

The current study was approved by both the Colorado State University Institutional Review Board (IRB) and the Colorado Department of Corrections, the parent agency of the Division of Adult Parole. Data were collected from 70 parolees, 48 males and 22 females. The ethnic/racial composition of our study population was 45.6 % Anglo, 31.5 % Hispanic, and 18.4 % African American, which closely mirrors the ethnic and racial composition of the inmate population in Colorado. We recruited study participants from four district parole offices, two in urban locations and two in suburban areas, all within the greater Denver metropolitan area. The age range of respondents was from 23 to 57 (median = 29 years old) and the incarceration lengths ranged from 1 to 20 years (median = 5.8 years). Median time on parole at the time of the interview was 18 months.

We used a purposive sampling technique to contact potential research participants. We had approval to contact parolees at the time they had appointments to see their parole officers, to describe our research, and to ask if they were interested in participating in the research. Each person was told the purpose of the study and if they agreed to participate, they signed a consent form approved by the Colorado State University IRB. With the exception of one male parolee who declined to participate, all of the parolees we contacted agreed to be study participants. Study participants were told that their responses would be confidential and that they could choose not to tape the interview or stop the interview at any time. All of our 70 paroled ex-prisoners were cooperative, agreed to be recorded, and seemed willing to discuss the problems they were facing on parole. The men and women who were interviewed appeared to be open and frank in relating their personal experiences; although at times, relating difficult experiences was an emotionally painful process. While there is always concern regarding potential harm to research participants, as Linn (1997) noted, relating their stories may allow respondents to better comprehend their feelings about what they have experienced.

Interviews took place over an 18-month period and were conducted in private rooms at the four parole offices. Each interview lasted approximately 60 minutes and was digitally recorded with the participant's consent. A semistructured interview format was used, which relied on sequential probes to pursue leads provided by participants. This approach allowed the parolees to identify and elaborate on domains that characterized their parole experiences that they perceived as important rather than relying on the researchers to elicit responses to structured questions.

The interviews were transcribed for qualitative data analysis, which involved a search for general relationships among categories of observations, grounded theory techniques similar to those suggested by Glaser and Strauss (1967). The data were categorized into conceptual domains of parolees' experiences on parole as identified by the participants. These parole experiences may not be reflective of all reentered ex-prisoners who are on parole, but their narratives raised similar concerns and added voice and depth to the issues that parolees face when leaving prison and returning to the community (Ragin, 1994; Seidman, 1998).

While not part of formal data collection, between interviews we often had informal conversations with parole officers who were interested in discussing their perceptions of parolees' difficulties in finding employment and meeting their financial obligations. Their insights helped to better inform us about challenges specific to parolees in Colorado. In addition, information provided by parole officers did not conflict with parolees' accounts and gave us an increased confidence in the validity of our interview data.

Findings

Reentering offenders are in desperate need of employment to financially survive and to successfully complete the mandates of parole, but they may be in the position of facing a vast majority of employers unwilling to consider hiring them. This leaves very few employers and jobs available for the hundreds of parolees leaving Colorado prisons each month, most of whom appear to be competing with each other for the same low-wage positions. The accounts of our study participants revealed the difficulty and frustrations involved in trying to find work, which rarely resulted in employment shortly after leaving prison.

Seeking Employment

Felony convictions and incarceration hampering a search for employment were common themes among our research participants, as related by one male parolee.

I request an application, I'll go in there and fill it out and I'll return it, give it back to them. About a week or two later I'll give them a call back just to check on the status of my application, and they just say "They don't hire felons." That's the way it is. Or they tell me, "We will call you back," or something like that. But I never hear back.

This particular parolee's rejection in his job search was typical of the vast majority of our study participants.

At times, temporal circumstances prevented some of our study participants from obtaining employment; they claimed that they were not yet out of prison when a job they could have had opened up. One married, 37-year-old male parolee expressed his frustration in trying to get a public transportation position.

They were like "Sorry, we could have hired you back then" [when I was still in prison]. I could have had a job with RTD (Regional Transportation District) Access. Those small buses where they pick up elderly and mentally challenged people. I now have to wait four and a half months. I applied seven or eight months ago, me and my wife . . . she went ahead and filled out the application with me for the hell of it and she ended up getting a job.

In this parolee's account, his wife was laid off from a credit union where she had worked for 9 years. She had no criminal history and had excellent job references and was selected to be a Regional Transportation District (RTD) driver, the job her husband was seeking. The paroled applicant continued to try to get a job with RTD and was quite persistent in his attempts to gain employment with the public bus line.

I've been keeping contact with the district manager there. He knew me after I got my ankle bracelet off. I called him and he says, "There's another issue. They (RTD) want to make sure that you have been driving for a year. If you're still unemployed after a year, I'll hire you."

Returning ex-offenders often find themselves in "Catch-22" positions due to restrictions and requirements of parole that can inhibit a successful job search. Many people on parole are prevented from attaining certain types of employment due to state laws or parole rules. For example, they often cannot have a driver's license until a certain period of time has elapsed without a violation of parole. Such restrictions place many positions that pay decent wages out of reach. While this study participant had been led to believe that he could have had the job if only he had been out of prison, the requirement that he have held a valid license for 1 year prior to being hired would have prevented him from obtaining this desirable job shortly after leaving prison.

Job applicants may try to hide past criminal records from prospective employers, a risky strategy since not reporting one's past criminal history may be considered a technical violation of the conditions of parole and can result in a return to prison. However, parole officers may use their discretion to overlook this type of violation if the parolee is employed and complying with the other conditions of parole. For most jobs, employers conduct criminal background checks, but these checks are often not completed before the applicant is hired. Lying about a criminal history that is later discovered through a background check is grounds for termination. One participant described how he was willing to take this risk and was able to obtain and keep a job, despite failing to disclose his criminal history.

> I kind of told a white lie at my interview. It was the only way I could get my foot in the door. They (Subway) were interviewing hundreds of people. The lady that I was interviewing with, I told her that I was married and that my wife got in a car accident and passed away that's what I told her, to get in the door ... I'm 49 years old and I've been welding for some years. So, working in a sandwich shop, well, I had to do something to start paying the rent at the halfway house. I needed money coming in. I had to have a job to keep on parole, so I kind of told a white lie to get that job. Once I got in the door and showed them how hard I could work and everything, I 'fessed up and told them the truth.

This parolee, the only person out of all who were interviewed for this study who admitted to being deceitful on his job application, was very fortunate to not be fired when his criminal history came to light. His employer did not terminate him and he had been working for 7 months at the time he was interviewed for this study. Many employers are likely to not be so willing to retain an employee who not only lied on a job application but who also had a criminal record that included time spent in prison.

Family Networks and Employment

About 40 % of our study participants resided with their families upon release from prison. These respondents found employment more readily than those who did not parole to their families' homes. Numerous examples clearly demonstrated the role that family support and family members' knowledge of available jobs or contacts played in helping parolees find work. In the following examples, employers knew the respondents had been in prison and these parolees were able to find work without having to conceal their former inmate status or to face background checks. One male parolee described finding work through his mother's contacts.

> Luckily, my Mom knows the owner and is good friends with her. They go to the same church. She talked to her before I came home. So that's how I got the job. But, I put in many, many applications, several a day for weeks, and to this day, since I got out (8 months ago), I haven't got a call back once.

Another parolee offered an explanation of how he found work through friends of his father.

> My dad's got a lot of friends that have small firms, so I've been helping them all summer, tossing hay bales and doing all kinds of different stuff. My dad and me always do side work, like we built a cow shed. Stuff like that's been basically keeping me afloat. For a couple of months I had a job. That was nice.

While one study participant described that he was fortunate his mother owned a construction company that hired him immediately upon release, ex-inmates typically come from families with low-socioeconomic backgrounds and do not have family members who own profitable and legitimate businesses that can provide the type of employment required to meet parole conditions. Some of our study participants had family members and relatives who played major roles in utilizing community networks to help them find employment, but many returning parolees do not have family members who are willing or able to help them with their job searches. These parolees often depend on friends or acquaintances they knew prior to their imprisonment to help them find work.

Friend Networks and Employment

One female study participant described being fortunate to be rehired as a waitress where she had worked prior to incarceration. At the time of the interview, she had been promoted to night manager. However, her experience was uncommon among our research participants. Many men and women in our study had poor employment histories prior to incarceration and could not contact former employers and realistically hope to be rehired as they left prison.

A more common theme was that of using connections parolees had in their communities prior to their imprisonment, as described by one male participant.

> I have a friend that has got his own remodeling business. I have known him for 10 years, from the streets. He used to be my neighbor. I told him "Hey, I'm back out. I need work." [He said] "Okay, come on over." I remodel houses, drywall, and install floors.

Another ex-offender described making use of friendship connections.

> The best way to find jobs is through a friend or somebody you know. You ask around. You go there first. 'Cause that's how 90 % of people get jobs, through somebody they know. Then, from there, you crack down on other jobs, try to make them better. If it's crappy, you deal with it and then try to make it better. You try to get a better job.

At the time of the interview, this respondent held two jobs, both found by using his network of friends and acquaintances.

One important condition of parole is to not have contact with persons who have criminal records or those who are involved in criminal behavior. These restrictions are designed to prevent parolees from reconnecting with criminally oriented friends and falling back into criminal lifestyles. While they may reduce the chances of connecting with former criminal associates, they also can significantly narrow many offenders' networks of friends and acquaintances who could potentially offer job information tips.

Finding employment in recent years has been made even more difficult for persons leaving prison. Employment for citizens who have no criminal history has been difficult in our nation's depressed labor market and many unemployed law-abiding persons compete for similar low-wage positions that, in the past, ex-offenders often were able to obtain. Thus, the burden of finding any employment for those with a criminal record has been made even more challenging.

Employment Isn't Enough: Additional Financial Obligations

Parolees are expected to find work that pays wages adequate for self-sufficiency. Paying for room and board, if one is not living with family members, is just the beginning of many parolees' financial obligations. Some obligations are internal to parole, such as payment for drug testing, mandatory treatment, court costs and fines, and restitution. Other legal obligations outside of the conditions imposed by parole may include child support, tax liabilities, and family debt incurred prior to or during incarceration.

Financial obligations related to parole. Ex-prisoners who are not able to live with family members after release and who reside in halfway houses as per their parole plans face additional pressures to find work. Halfway houses in Colorado are operated by private for-profit or nonprofit vendors and have rules regarding rent payment. One halfway house resident spoke of the challenges he encountered in finding work.

We went out Monday through Friday about 7:30 AM in the morning until 4 PM in the afternoon looking for jobs. There were quite a few guys there in the halfway house, and I think about 60 to 80 of us were looking for work every day. There were some guys that had been there for months and hadn't found work.

Halfway house rents average approximately US$400 per month, which parolees are obligated to pay (Colorado Department of Corrections Parole Officer, personal communication, February 20, 2014). Many of our study participants who resided in halfway houses did not find employment for months, which meant that when they did find jobs, they owed several months back rent. The majority of jobs parolees secure pay minimum or close to minimum wage and often are not full time. If they do finally find work, much of their income goes to the halfway house to pay the back rent and they may find themselves no better off than they were when unemployed. As one parolee related, his stay in the halfway house did not ease his return to the community.

I think I was there (the halfway house) about a month and a half before I found work. My checks were going straight to the halfway house. I didn't even get money for the bus or any funds for anything from my payments. The halfway house took my whole check and didn't give me any of it. I'm still paying them off, actually.

Offenders are often paroled to a halfway house as part of their initial parole plan developed prior to their release from prison. Approximately 25 % of our sample was parolees who were required to live in halfway houses upon release. These individuals may suffer the greatest financial burden when compared to other ex-prisoners who reside with their families or those who end up staying in homeless shelters. An important point to note is that if halfway house residents do not pay all of the rent monies owed, they have violated the conditions of their parole and can be returned to prison on a technical violation for nonpayment. Many of our study participants who had paroled to halfway houses spoke of a fear of returning to prison because they had accumulated large debts which they were having difficulty paying.

In many instances, the courts include restitution payments as part of the felony sentence. Restitution technically is not "punishment," but, rather, a requirement that offenders reimburse their victims for the victims' financial losses. The restitution obligation follows individuals during their time in prison and payment of restitution is attached as a condition for parole. The determination of the monthly amount of money paid to the victim by the offender is usually set by the parole officer. Payments can vary depending on the parolee's employment status and amount of income earned and may increase over time if the ex-offender earns a higher salary in the future.

Payments for restitution, charges for mandatory drug and alcohol testing, supervision fees, and mandatory treatment expenses may all be conditions of parole. The total number of required payments was succinctly summed up by one participant.

> It's not that I don't like my job. It's an alright job. I mean, it's not something I want to spend the rest of my life at, that's for sure. Nobody wants to work at Wendy's forever. I get, like 18-25 hours a week. I have bills to pay. I've got restitution payments, supervision fees, child support, [and] I've got to live. I've got UAs (tests for drug use), SAs. I get like $300 a paycheck, and that's for two weeks. A person can't live off that.

Another study participant described the difficulty of meeting the financial obligations for parole.

> I have restitution, which is $152 every month. And then I have three UAs a month, so that's $45 a month and a $10 parole supervision fee, so that's about $207 a month.

This parolee was fortunate to not have to make payments to a halfway house since, unlike the majority of our respondents, he lived with his parents and did not have to pay rent. Despite this advantage, he was struggling to meet his financial obligations in order to remain compliant with his parole conditions since the only work he could find was part-time minimum-wage work. In addition, like many in our study, he was not eligible to receive benefits, such as health insurance, sick pay, or retirement, due to his part-time employee status.

Many of our research participants were unclear about the restitution they were required to pay. Unlike other states that do not rely as heavily on restitution, Colorado makes extensive use of restitution and many persons leaving prison do so with significant debts owed to their victims. The majority of offenders do not have the assets to repay their victims prior to leaving prison and few of them obtain employment that provides sufficient income to repay their victims in a timely manner. None of the interviewed parolees knew if they were obligated to pay the entire amount of their restitution. However, they had been told that being discharged from parole was not contingent on a full repayment of their restitution. Even parole agents we spoke with informally were unclear as to what happens to restitution requirements once the other conditions of parole had been fulfilled. When a parolee is discharged from parole, there is no mechanism for ensuring that restitution payments continue. The remaining restitution balance may be sent to collection, which further damages the credit of an individual attempting to make a clean start.

Financial obligations external to parole. Besides parole-required payments, additional financial obligations such as child support and other prior debt may create problems for persons leaving prison. In some cases, prior liabilities may affect family members on the outside. One participant described how his child support debt affected his wife after he went to prison.

> Schooling is very important to me, but right now I need money. We are homeowners and we have bills. I had an issue; they took my wife's income because of my past obligations when I was in prison. I owed back child support; they took all of her income tax refund, $6,800, to pay for it.

He and his wife were not able to start over debt free, which, according to this respondent, would have allowed him to change his life by pursuing an education when he left prison.

Parole Success

A few participants related more positive economic situations. One woman planned for her release from prison by not using the savings she had prior to being sentenced. Another female respondent described her careful use of money while in prison.

I had just saved it. I basically used it very minimally. I only used what I needed. I wasn't greedy. When I got out I had enough money to get my own place. It's not the best. It's a little two bedroom.

She also was employed and, unlike many of the research participants, she stated that between her job and her prior savings, she had no trouble paying for her parole-mandated programs.

One respondent described how an unexpected income tax return helped him become less reliant on his parents.

I was living with my parents and I would borrow money from them. On my birthday I got an income tax return for the last year I was out, and that helped a lot. That really kind of covered my expenses that I had to pay for, UAs and everything. Really, I was just lucky.

Inmates who were able to plan for their release and who had the ability to leave prison with some financial resources identified themselves as lucky to be able to meet the mandated expenses required of parole. These individuals appeared to be much less likely to run into problems with technical violations of parole related to nonpayment of mandated parole expenses than their "unlucky" counterparts who left prison with little money, who paroled to halfway houses, who had extreme difficulty in finding employment, and who had multiple financial obligations they had little hope of being able to pay.

Parole Failure

Between interviews with parolees, we casually spoke with parole officers and supervisors about the financial mandates for parole. From these conversations, we learned that it was not uncommon for parolees to abscond or return to criminal activity because they felt overwhelmed by the payments they were unable to make. This was especially true for halfway house residents who were in debt for large sums of money and had no legitimate way to make payments. Study participants who paroled to halfway houses spoke of the dilemma they faced: fearing a return to prison for failing to pay a debt they felt was impossible to overcome or making a decision to abscond because they felt that a return to prison was inevitable.

In addition to the difficulty in paying off halfway house debt, the inability to pay for mandated parole programs, such as required treatment and urine analysis (UA), can result in a technical violation and a potential return to prison. Respondents explained that if one shows up for a UA and is unable to pay, the company giving the test for drug use counts the parolee as a no-show. Two or more missed UAs are grounds for a technical parole violation. One unemployed parolee described his decision to abscond because he was not able to pay for his required UAs and group counseling sessions and was in danger of being returned to prison for a technical violation.

> The first time I absconded for nine months so they caught me. The second time I missed four UAs and four group sessions because I didn't have a job. The place that I took the UAs at told me I couldn't take them anymore.

This offender's explanation for absconding was not unique. In short, parolees' inability to pay for parole mandates that require access to money they do not have may push them to abscond and into parole failure.

Ex-offenders on parole who have difficulty in finding employment also suffer frustrations from their inability to find work and, as the following account demonstrates, these frustrations can lead to negative consequences.

> It's most stressful. Either you go out and get a job right away, or you're looking and looking. And because you have so much time on your hands, you go back to your old life, relapse, or go back and hang out with the homies.

Not only can unemployment and associating with felons be violations of parole, reconnecting with criminal associates and living the "old life" can also result in a return to prison for committing new crimes.

Discussion

Our focus for this study was on financial problems encountered by people leaving prison. As such, this article does not address additional collateral problems, such as mental illness, poor health, drug use, lack of housing and transportation, and other reentry challenges, that many offenders face upon their release from prison and return to their communities (Petersilia 2003; Pogrebin, Dodge, and Katsampes 2001). We also did not address racial/ethnic, gender, or age differences because we did not find significant differences between these groups in our sample. However, the median length of time on parole in our sample was 18 months and we likely did not have a good representation of individuals who failed quickly on parole, where racial/ethnic, gender, and age differences may be more apparent. Rather, the stark contrast in our sample appeared to be between those who had access to housing and/or employment help as they left prison and those who were trying to "make it" on their own. Despite the length of time many of our research participants had been out of prison and on parole, the problems they emphasized more than any others related to the financial challenges awaiting them upon release and that subsequently continued and often increased throughout their time on parole.

Parolees often must turn to family members for help, which can be humiliating. One participant described his primary focus as "Getting a job . . . paying for my parole, my UAs, and all that stuff.

[So] I won't have to ask people to help me with money. It must be understood that our study consisted of adults and not juveniles. Not having enough money to pay the mandated parole requirements and having to depend on others can place adult ex-inmates in childlike and dependent situations where they may be perceived by others as the same irresponsible individuals they were before they were convicted and imprisoned.

Those who are not able to achieve long-term and legitimate successes are often viewed by the wider society as possessing individual deficits that result in their economic failure. Without the necessary social capital via economic capital that is so highly regarded in American society, ex-prisoners confront nearly insurmountable odds against becoming productive and accepted citizens in this nation, even if they have a desire to do so. This is a greater challenge for offenders of color, who represent a disproportionate number of imprisoned persons. Not only do they suffer from the pains of societal and institutional discrimination (Western 2006) but also are competing with many other ex-offenders who are very much like them: individuals who are poorly educated, have minimal legitimate employment histories, and are returning to impoverished communities that offer few chances for legal employment that pay wages sufficient for the basic necessities of life, let alone the additional payments required for successful parole completion.

As researchers in the area of corrections, we are knowledgeable of the literature on reentry problems as ex-offenders return to their communities. We were expecting to find our participants referencing difficulty in finding employment upon release. However, we were not expecting to hear the consistent claim that the most persistent overall problem was other financial obligations that contributed to their financial instability over a lengthy parole period. Without employment, they were doomed to fail. But employment alone was not enough to ensure financial success, since even permanent employment did not appear to resolve the ongoing and often mounting debt associated with parole mandates.

A large percentage of formerly incarcerated men and women may be free from their inmate status but may later find themselves trapped by insurmountable challenges of a different nature: the longevity of stigma and discrimination in a capitalist social structure which places great emphasis on economic success. It is little wonder that reentry so often fails, since for the vast majority of returning felons the odds of attaining legitimate economic stability is almost nil, given the extremely limited financial opportunities available to them. Failure is a realistic consequence of the inability to progress economically in the short term. However, equally concerning is the foreshadowing of a future characterized by persistent failure to succeed. When one cannot succeed economically immediately upon release from prison, when debts incurred related to incarceration and to mandated parole expenses cannot be paid off, and when the future appears bleak for being able to economically succeed, it is understandable why a large percentage of parolees re-offend, abscond, or violate parole rules and return to prison.

In a 5-year-follow-up study of inmates released in 30 states in 2005, the Bureau of Justice Statistics reported that 67.8 % of ex-prisoners were rearrested within 3 years of their release and 76.6 % were rearrested within 5 years (U.S. Department of Justice 2014). While many look at these discouraging numbers and attribute reentry failure to personal failings for individuals leaving prison, it may be appropriate to explore whether the low rate of parole success may partially be attributable to various financial challenges placed upon reentering offenders as they return to their communities. The parole system, originally designed to not only provide supervision of individuals leaving prison but to also provide support during the difficult transition from prison to life on the outside, may be playing a significant role in parole failure through the often unrealistic financial expectations that persons recently released from prison have little hope of meeting.

Our study participants' accounts were filled with frustration and hopelessness. As Wanberg et al. (2005) noted, the inability to achieve even a small piece of the American dream has detrimental effects that can lead to poor self-concepts and bleak futures. The heavy toll of repeated rejection can create a stigma that results in discrimination (Branscombe et al. 1999) and a negative self-concept (Goffman 1963), added burdens on ex-offenders as they attempt to return to society. If, as LeBel et al. (2008) argue, feeling stigmatized is a predictor for reimprisonment, and if hope and self-efficacy are necessary but not sufficient to desist from crime, current parole practices do little to reduce the well-known barriers to successful reentry and may create nearly impossible financial burdens, which give Colorado parolees little reason to hope that they will succeed.

Conclusion

The tremendous increase in the prison population since the 1980s required that the majority of state correctional budgets be spent on the construction of new prisons to house the growing number of inmates.

This building boom, combined with the downturn of the economy, has left few financial resources for states to spend on reentry and other correctional programs designed to assist offenders in making successful transitions from prison to the community. High reentry failure rates and a continued lack of resources to adequately address prisoner reentry problems suggest that many parolees will be unable to overcome imposing reentry barriers and will continue to present society with numerous economic and social challenges.

Too many ex-prisoners on parole, as we have attempted to illustrate, are unable to acquire any type of sustainable employment and seem to be on their own as their debts mount. The system itself appears to bear some responsibility for the large amount of debt many parolees incur within a few months after they are released. If parolees encounter nearly insurmountable barriers to obtaining employment that pays enough to meet their financial obligations, if inmates are unable to accumulate "nest eggs" during the imprisonment that could help to offset some of the initial required parole expenses, and if they view parole failure and returning to prison as the likely result of parole, we should not be surprised that so many parolees are unable to successfully reenter society. The privatization of halfway houses and the use of vendors who provide fee-based UA testing, anger management groups, sex offender therapy, and other mandated fee-for-service programs appear to have added to the punitive nature of the parole system while creating barriers that many offenders simply cannot overcome. All play an important role in the "pay or fail" parole-mandated programs, where obligations related to parole place the unemployed, underemployed, and those who suffer from overwhelming financial burdens at a distinct disadvantage. Their path back to a society that cares little and understands less about the challenges these individuals face is not easy. What others see as an uphill climb may be, for many, an insurmountable mountain.

Of course, the results of our study cannot be generalized to other persons leaving prison. Unlike many states, the vast majority of individuals convicted of violent and property crimes in Colorado have restitution orders to repay their victims, an understandable debt that follows individuals as they leave prison. State requirements regarding parole vary significantly and not all inmates reentering society do so under mandatory parole conditions, as do almost all persons who leave prison in Colorado. Colorado is also highly dependent upon private vendors to provide halfway house or other transitional housing, counseling and substance abuse treatment, and other mandated parole requirements. Many of these services are provided by for-profit or nonprofit organizations, but the expenses associated with these parole mandates are paid for by parolees. Colorado also does not pay inmate workers enough for them to set aside any savings to prepare for release and; unless inmates had savings prior to their incarceration or they have family members who can help them financially, they leave prison with little besides prison-issued street clothes and a small "gate check."

It is little wonder that our research participants all spoke of the financial challenges they were facing and most described feelings of frustration and desperation that they would not be able to "make it" on the outside. Although future research is certainly needed not only in Colorado but also in other states to try to understand the full effect of financial limitations on parole success, there is little doubt that returning ex-offenders confront tremendous challenges in finding legitimate employment that allows for self-sufficiency. However, if there are additional structural barriers, such as those in Colorado, that create even more financial difficulties for individuals leaving prison, future research to examine alternative approaches for parole mandates could help to identify whether or not parole outcomes may be related to the economic requirements placed upon persons leaving prison.

Improving reentry outcomes over the last decade has been a major focus for both correctional researchers and practitioners. Practices such as the use of transitional housing and ongoing treatment to help with the change from prison existence to life in a community have been encouraged. However, if the costs of such practices are assigned to individuals who have little ability to pay for these requirements and if a threat of a return to prison for nonpayment of these debts hangs over parolees' heads, attempts to improve reentry outcomes may be making reentry for many persons leaving prison even more difficult. Finding ways to ease the mandated obligations related to parole may help many persons leaving prison overcome some of the economic challenges they face, which, in turn, may also allow them to believe that a path to economic stability through the legitimate workforce may be more than an impossible dream.

Declaration of Conflicting Interests

The authors declared no potential conflicts of interest with respect to the research, authorship, and/or publication of this article.

Funding

The authors received no financial support for the research, authorship, and/or publication of this article.

References

Bannon, A., Nagrecha, M., Diller, R. (2010). *Criminal justice debt: A barrier to reentlJ'*. New York, NY: Brennen Center for Justice, New York University School of Law. http://www.brennancenterorglsites/defaultifiles/1egacy/Fees%20and%20Fines%20FINAL.pdf

Becker, G. (1968). Crime and punishment: An economic approach. *Journal of Political Economy, 76*, 169–217. doi:10.1086/259394

Branscombe, N., Schmitt, M., Harvey, R. (1999). Perceiving pervasive discrimination among African Americans: Implications for group identification and wellbeing. *Journal of Personality and Social Psychology, 77*, 135–149. doi:10.1037/0022-3514.77.1.135

Colorado Department of Corrections. (1999). *Statistical report: Fiscal year 1998*. Colorado Springs, CO.

Colorado Department of Corrections. (2013). *Statistical report for fiscal year 2013*. Colorado Springs, CO.

Cobbina, J. (2009). *From prison to home: Women's pathways in and out of crime.* http://vvww.ncjrs.gov/pdffi1es1/nij/grants/226812.pdf

Freeman, R. (1992). Crime and unemployment of disadvantaged youths. In G. Peterson & W. Vroman (Eds.), *Urban labor markets and job opportunity* (pp. 68–83). Washington, DC: Urban Institute Press.

Glaser, B., & Strauss, A (1967). *The discovery of grounded theory: Strategies for qualitative research.* Chicago, IL: Aldine.

Goffman, E. (1963), *Stigma: Notes on the management of spoiled identity.* Englewood Cliffs, NJ: Prentice Hall.

Griswold, E. A., & Pearson, J. (2005). Turning offenders into responsible parents and child support payers. *Family Court Review, 43*, 358–371. doi:10.1111/j.1744-1617.2005.00039.x

Grogger, J. (1995). The effects of arrests on the employment and earnings of young men. *Quarterly Journal of Economics, 110*, 51–71. doi:10.2307/2118510

Hagan, J. (1993). The social embeddedness of crime and unemployment. *Criminology, 31*, 465–491.

Harding, D. (2003). Jean Valjean's dilemma: The management of ex-convict identity in the search for employment. *Deviant Behavior, 24*, 571–595. doi:10.1080/713840275

Holzer, H., Raphael, S., Stoll, M. (2007). The effects of an applicant's criminal history on employer hiring decisions and screening practices: Evidence from Los Angeles. In S. Bushway, M. Stoll, D. Weiman (Eds.), *Barriers to reentry: The labor market for released prisoners in post-industrial America* (pp. 117–150). New York, NY: Russell Sage.

Kling, J. (2006). Incarceration length, employment, and earnings. *American Economic Review, 96*, 863–876. doi:10.1257/aer.96.3.863

Kushel, M., Hahn, J., Evans, D., Bangsberg, D., Moss, A. (2005). Revolving doors: Imprisonment amongst the homeless and marginally housed population. *American Journal of Public Health, 95*, 1747–1752. doi:10.2105/AJPH.2005.065094

LaVigne, N., Visher, C., Castro, J. (2004). *Chicago prisoners' experiences returning home.* Washington, DC: The Urban Institute.

LeBel, T. (2012). Invisible stripes? Formerly incarcerated persons' perceptions of stigma. *Deviant Behavior, 33*, 89–107. doi:10.1080/01639625.2010.538365

LeBel, T., Burnett, R., Mamna, S., Bushway, S. (2008). The "chicken and egg" of subjective and social factors in desistence from crime. *European Journal of Criminology, 5*, 131–159. doi:10.1177/1477370807087640

Linn, R. (1997). Soldier's narratives of selective moral resistance. In A. Lieblich & A. Josselson (Eds.), *The nan-alive study of lives* (pp. 95–112). Thousand Oaks, CA: Sage.

Lyons, C., & Petit, B. (2011). Compounded disadvantage: Race, incarceration and wage growth. *Social Problems, 58*, 257–280. doi:10.1525/sp.2011.58.2.257

Mallik-Kane, K., & Visher, C. (2008). *Health and prisoner reently: How physical, mental and substance abuse conditions shade the process of reintegration.* Washington, DC: The Urban Institute.

Naser, R., & LaVigne, N. (2006). Family support in the prisoner reentry process: Expectations and realities. *Journal of Offender Rehabilitation*, *43*, 93–106. doi:10.1300/J076v43n01_05

Nelson, M., Dees, P., Allen, C. (1999). The first month out post incarceration experiences in New York City. *Federal Sentencing Reporter*, *24*, 70–71. doi:10.1525/fsr.2011.24.1.72

Ostermann, M. (2011). Recidivism and the propensity *to* forgo parole release. *Justice Quarterly*, *29*, 596–618. doi:10.1080/07418825.2011.570362

Pager, D. (2003). The mark of a criminal record. *American Journal of Sociology*, *108*, 937-975. doi:10.1086/374403

Petersilia, J. (2003). *When prisoners come home: Parole and prisoner reentry*. New York, NY: Oxford University Press.

Pew Center on the States. (2011). *State of recidivism: The revolving door of America's prisons*. Washington, DC: The Pew Charitable Trusts.

Pogrebin, M., Dodge, M., Katsampes, P. (2001). Collateral costs of short-tetmjail incarceration. *Corrections Management Quarterly*, *5*, 64–69.

Ragin, C. (1994). *Constructing social research*. Thousand Oaks, CA: Pine Forge Press.

Richards, S., & Jones, R. (2004). Beating the perpetual incarceration machine: Overcoming structural impediments to re-entry. In S. Maruna & R. Immarigcon (Eds.), *After crime and punishment: Pathways to offender reintegration* (pp. 201–232). Collompton, UK: Willan Publishing.

Seidman, T. (1998). *Interviewing as qualitative research: A guide for researching in education and social sciences*. New York, NY: Teachers College Press.

Travis, J., & Petersilia, J. (2001). Reentry reconsidered: A new look at an old question. *Crime and Delinquency*, *47*, 291–313. doi:10.1177/0011128701047003001

Travis, L., & Stacey, J. (2010). A half century of parole rules: Conditions of parole in the United States, 2008. *Journal of Criminal Justice*, *38*, 604–608.

U.S. Department of Justice, Bureau of Justice Statistics. (1982). *Prisoners in 1981* (NCJ 82262). http://www.bjs.gov/index.cfm?typbdetaii&iid3366

U.S. Department of Justice, Bureau of Justice Statistics. (2002). *Recidivism of prisoners released in 1994* (NCJ 193427). http://www.bjs.gov/index.cfm?typbdetail&iid1134

U.S. Department of Justice, Bureau of Justice Statistics. (2003). *Education and correctional populations* (NCJ 195670). http://www.bjs.gov/index.cfm?typbdetail&iid814

U.S. Department of Justice, Bureau of Justice Statistics. (2011). *Prisoners in 2009* (NCJ 231675). http://www.bjs.gov/index.cfm?typbdetaii&iid2232

U.S. Department of Justice, Bureau of Justice Statistics. (2012a). *Correctional populations in the United States,* 2011 (NCJ 239972). http://www.bjs.gov/index.cfm?typbdetail&iid4537

U.S. Department of Justice, Bureau of Justice Statistics. (2012b). *Prisoners in 2011* (NCJ 239808). http://www.bjs.gov/index.cfm?typbdetail&iid4538

U.S. Department of Justice, Bureau of Justice Statistics. (2012c). *Probation and parole in the United States, 2011* (NCJ 239686). http://www.bjs.gov/index.cfm?typbdetail&iid4538

U.S. Department of Justice, Bureau of Justice Statistics. (2013). *Probation and parole in the United States, 2012* (NCJ 243826). http://www.bjs.gov/content!pub/pdf/ppus12.pdf

U.S. Department of Justice, Bureau of Justice Statistics. (2014). *Recidivism of prisoners released in 30 states in 2005: Patterns from 2005 to 2010* (NCJ 244205). http://www.bjs.gov/contentlpub/pdf/rprts05p0510.pdf

Visher, C., Debus-Sherrill, S., Yahner, J. (2008). Employment after prison: A longitudinal study of former prisoners. *Justice Quarterly, 28,* 698–718. doi:10.1080/074I8825.2010.535553

Visher, C., & Kachnowski, V. (2007). Finding work on the outside: Results from returning home project in Chicago. In S. Bushway, M. Stoli, D. Weiman (Eds.), *Barriers to reentry? The labor market for returned prisons in post industrial America* (pp. 80–113). New York, NY: Russell Sage.

Wanberg, C., Glomb, T., Song, A., Sorenson, S. (2005). Job-search persistence during unemployment: A 10-wave lougitudinal study. *Journal of Applied Psychology, 9,* 411–430. doi:10.1037/0021-9010.90.3.411

Western, B. (2006). *Punishment and inequality in America.* New York, NY: Russell Sage Foundation.

Western, B., Kling, J., Weiman, D. (2001). The labor consequences of incarceration. *Crime and Delinquency, 47,* 410–427. doi:10.1177/001112870 I 047003007

Mark Pogrebin is Professor of Criminal Justice in the School of Public Affairs at the University of Colorado Denver. He has authored and co-authored six books, the most recent ones are *Voices from Criminal Justice: Thinking and Reflecting on the System* and *Guns, Violence and Criminal Behavior: The Offender's Perspective.* In addition, he has published numerous journal articles and has 48 articles published in various anthologies. He is a field researcher and his past studies all have used qualitative methods.

Mary West-Smith is an Assistant Professor of Criminology and Criminal Justice at the University of Northern Colorado. She holds a PhD from the University of Colorado Denver. Her research and teaching interests include corrections, victimization, problem-solving approaches within the criminal justice system, qualitative research methods. In addition to her academic work, she has conducted research for the U.S. Department of Justice on crime problems and prisoner reentry in Colorado and has worked with non-profit organizations that provide services to crime victims.

Alexandra Walker has over 18 years of experience working with offender populations in corrections. In addition, she has spent the last 10 years working with correctional and reentry professionals to develop and hone their skills through training and coaching on effective interventions, core correctional practices, and implementation science. She is currently pursuing her PhD in Sociology at Colorado State University and working on a statewide implementation project in community corrections.

N. Prabha Unnithan is a professor in the Department of Sociology at Colorado State University where he directed the Center for the Study of Crime and Justice from 2008 through 2015. He edited the *Journal of Criminal Justice Education* between 2000 and 2002 and the *Social Science Journal* from 2006 to 2011. Unnithan's research focuses on the antecedents and consequences of various forms of violence and on criminal justice policy analysis and program evaluation. His latest book was the edited collection *Crime and Justice in India* (2013). He recently completed a 3-year stint as Secretary of the Academy of Criminal Justice Sciences.

Epilogue

Stan Stojkovic

Robert Rubin (2016), former Treasury Secretary from 1995 to 1999 and current cochairman of the Council on Foreign Relations, recently wrote an editorial in the *New York Times* on what society needs to do to help former inmates thrive upon release from prison. He offered the following quote from an inmate in San Quentin prison in California: "I don't understand why over the 18-year period of my incarceration, over $900,000 was paid to keep me in prison. But when I was paroled, I was given $200.00 and told 'good luck.'" Herein lies the ongoing disjuncture between the costs and expenses of a mass incarceration strategy and the promise of prisoner reentry efforts within communities. Prisons are real and so are their costs. Prisoner reentry is real as well, and so are its costs, but we have not had the national resolve and the political will to move away from the mass incarceration strategy to an approach that recognizes the importance of prisoner reentry.

S. Stojkovic (✉)
Helen Bader School of Social Welfare, University of Wisconsin-Milwaukee, Milwaukee, Wisconsin, USA
e-mail: stojkovi@uwm.edu

© The Author(s) 2017
S. Stojkovic (ed.), *Prisoner Reentry*,
DOI 10.1057/978-1-137-57929-4_8

This latter point is clearly debatable, since as noted throughout this volume, the federal government and state governments have poured millions of dollars into prisoner reentry programs over the past 15 years. Yet, at the end of the day, we have too many prisoners and not enough funding for reentry efforts, and even the programming we have represents a patch work quilt of funding models and approaches to prisoner reentry. The number and quality of these programs is suspect by even the casual observer of corrections. What is needed is some general and first-order principles of prisoner reentry programming that is rooted in the scientific literature and offers clear directions to politicians, communities, citizens, and working correctional professionals on how best to proceed to have the most long-term impact on both released offenders and the communities in which they reside. So, what have the chapters in this volume provided to improve prisoner reentry efforts? I believe the following aphorisms can be gleaned from the chapters in this volume.

Prisoner reentry programming requires a firm delineation of theory and scientific evidence from which the program is based.

All of the chapters in this volume highlighted the importance and relevance of scientific evidence in assessing and evaluating prisoner reentry programs. We noted in the various chapters that we know much about effective correctional treatment, how offenders respond to treatment, and the importance of offender risk, needs, and responsivity to building effective correctional interventions. Additionally, the volume has offered a plethora of citations and research support for the views provided. The volume has the best science available in assessing prisoner reentry initiatives. Academicians, correctional practitioners, community agencies, and even prisoners themselves understand the necessity of doing things differently in corrections. We can make choices to offer programming to offenders, both inside of prisons and in reentry efforts in the community, that reflect the best practices supported by the best science. We have the technical skill to do so. We know much about effective prisoner reentry programming. We now need the political will to move the discussion forward such that better programming is provided to the thousands of prisoners that leave prison every year. We owe it to them and to the communities they return.

Families matter in the prisoner reentry process. We need to recognize the importance of families to the successful reentry of the formerly incarcerated.

Research is clear on the importance of recognizing family dynamics to the reentry process of people leaving prisons. Yes, it is true that for many offenders the idea of some type of family reunification is highly problematic and difficult to imagine. Yet, the research provided in this volume shows the importance of families to assisting correctional agencies in the reentry process. The research has shown how families are not only disrupted due to the incarceration of family members, but they can also be the foundation upon which solid prisoner reentry efforts can be built. In this way, the family works with correctional professionals and others to improve the adjustment of the offender once back into the community. The community benefits as well, since the threat released offenders pose is significant if they are not successfully reunited with their families.

In fact, we know that without family support effective prisoner reentry is problematic. Moreover, we need to recognize that any measures that strengthen families provides more support for the former prisoner. The analysis provided in this volume demonstrates how fragile family dynamics are and how they are tested when someone leaves the family due to incarceration, but also when they come back to the family after being in prison. The fragility of the family dynamic, along with the positive supports healthy families provide former prison offenders, cannot be neglected in our programming efforts.

In many cases, successful prisoner reentry hinges on how well the family dynamic is supported both immediately subsequent to incarceration of the family member, during the incarceration experience, and in the post-incarceration period where the offender is the most vulnerable to become reacquainted with the criminal lifestyle. Maintaining relationships with families of the incarcerated, both during the incarceration experience and subsequent to prison release, is an area that requires further examination. Our initial read of the literature suggests that family dynamics and prisoner reentry success are connected. Future research and future correctional efforts must recognize the importance and relevance of supporting families to provide both hope and direction to offenders once released into their communities.

Employment for offenders may not matter as much as we think in the prisoner reentry process.

We have documented the problems that many former offenders experience once released back into their communities. The intuitive appeal to simply finding a job for a former offender is overshadowed by the realities of poor financial decisions that were made prior to being incarcerated, while incarcerated, and after release from prison. Having employment opportunities is generally good for former offenders, but employment by itself is no panacea solution to post-release adjustment in the community for many offenders. With the overwhelming debt many former offenders carry, it is only reasonable to view employment as a small part of the solution to offender problems. Offenders simply need more than employment.

As noted in this volume, employment by itself will not address the financial problems offenders face when released from prison; this is because employment does not address possibly the underlying conditions and thought processes that direct offenders' behaviors to make poor financial and personal decisions. Analyses offered in this volume suggest that there still must be recognition of how offenders think when making decisions and the ways they think about their choices before making decisions, for example, impulsive thinking versus purposive thinking. There is something to be said about the role of poor decision-making in offender readjustment to the community. As stated in Chapter 5, "Most employment programs help offenders develop a resume and find a job position, but they fail to address offenders' attitudes toward work, their poor problem-solving skills, or poor coping skills."

At the crux of the matter is a recognition that employment by itself must be understood as part of a constellation of factors that affect prisoner readjustment in the community. We do not suggest that employment is not a key factor to successful prisoner readjustment to the community. We must ask further questions, however, such as this: How does employment facilitate or hinder the readjustment of offenders back into the community, and more importantly, as only one factor in the reentry process what is its salience vis-a-vis other relevant factors in the post-release adjustment process for offenders, such as family relations, treating drug and/or alcohol addiction, educational programming, etc.? Moreover, is employment more important for some offenders and less relevant for other types of offenders in the reentry adjustment process? Future research will have to address these questions to show the relevance and importance of employment as a factor to successful postprison readjustment among offenders in the community.

Offenders vary as to their receptivity to the post-release adjustment process and not all communities are singularly receptive to them once released back into the community.

As noted in this volume, there is considerable variability in behaviors among offenders once placed back into the community. Some offenders, for example, sex offenders, are very problematic and difficult to place back into communities. Special attention has to be made for these offenders. Generally, the more problematic the offender, the more detail to attention has to be made by correctional agencies in the supervision process. This can create many problems for offenders as they transition back to the community from prison. Nevertheless, problematic offenders can be successfully reintegrated back into communities, but the challenge is significant.

Chapters in this volume have indicated how best to deal with difficult offenders, but we would be remiss if we did not talk about the political problems of placing some offenders back into their communities. Often times for offenders, the daily problems of adjustment are enough to stall successful reintegration, yet what is most problematic are communities where there is either indifference or a lack of tolerance for offenders transitioning back. We have highlighted in this volume the difficulties prisoners face when coming back to their communities. We have also shown that problems in prisoner adjustment can be addressed through good supervision practices rooted in what we know works for varied prisoner populations.

Some of these problems, for example, adequate funding, community acceptance of former offenders, housing, employment opportunities, to mention a few, also require that there are significant and dedicated stakeholders within the community that are supportive of offender readjustment and will show their support through the political process. This involves grass roots commitment and political support that returning offenders from prison are, to some degree, welcomed back to their communities. We need not be overly optimistic that communities will receive offenders openly, and we have documented the opposite is true, especially with some offender populations, yet it is reasonable to assume that communities can see prisoner reentry as both an opportunity to promote effective change among offenders and a better, more effective, and efficient way to spend finite tax dollars. If anything financial interests and government accountability regarding offender supervision and management in the community can be compelling reasons to offer scientifically based prisoner reentry programs. We know what works better with what offenders in postprison release supervision. Now is the time to implement what we know to maximize successful reintegration of offenders back into their communities and do it in a way that enhances the investments made by taxpayers.

There are many successful and unsuccessful prisoner reentry programs across the country. We need to document them and share their experiences with others.

We need to know what governmental agencies, nonprofit organizations, private vendors, and individual citizens are doing to make sure offenders succeed once back into the community. The chapters in this volume have highlighted what works and what does not work with returning offenders in the reentry process. We know very little, however, of successful prisoner reentry programs. We described one successful agency in the state of California, and we noted the enormity of successful reentry efforts in one state. We also described the type of barriers that exist in doing prisoner reentry work. We would expect that opportunities, successes, and barriers vary considerably across the country.

No two states are alike on just about anything. We would expect the same to be true when it comes to prisoner reentry programming. We have made some good progress in documenting these entities. We, for example, have mentioned the work of the Council on State Governments and the work of the Justice Center in documenting prisoner reentry programs across the country and providing assistance to communities. We need for these efforts to continue, but we need more rigorous scientific research to answer some theoretical and program implementation questions, as well as offer some grounded process evaluations on what seems to work and what seems not to work among prisoner reentry programs.

By creating and implementing prisoner reentry programs that are rooted in best practices, or at least minimally driven by the tenets of the scientific method, we have the best chances of creating and implementing programs that will succeed with prisoners in the reentry process. Without scientific adequacy in design and implementation, we will continue to walk down a road where results are suspect and communities ultimately less safe. We can no longer afford unscientific programs that do not meet minimum standards of scientific adequacy. At the end of the day, programs either succeed or fail; offenders either succeed or fail. We need to know which type of program works best with which type of offender. We can only arrive at answering this question through the application of the scientific method when evaluating prisoner entry programs. For those programs that do meet the minimum standards of scientific inquiry and offer the most promising applications, we need to document and support them as we learn more about effective and ineffective prisoner reentry programs.

Prisoners' views on the reentry process must be incorporated into our understanding and operations of reentry programs.

As reentry "consumers," we must not ignore what is learned by those most intimately involved in the reentry process: offenders themselves. We can learn a lot from offenders, both good and bad things, regarding the prisoner reentry process by listening and observing them as they live the reentry lifestyle. No one knows something as well as he who has experienced it. Yes, offenders may be biased, but their thoughts, opinions, experiences can be a treasure trove of material on what works and what does not work in the reentry process. They are the people who have the most knowledge regarding their readjustment back into the community. We can design mechanisms that respect offender views, but also control for them as we evaluate and assess prisoner reentry efforts. In the end, offenders "live" the reentry program. We would be rather shortsighted if we did not respect and at least listen to their concerns and suggestions regarding a reentry program. As we have suggested in this volume, the offenders' views often times do not vary much from what the lay public expects. All of us believe that we should put forward the best possible reentry program that is affordable, practical, and works to transitions offenders from jail or prison to the community. Offenders' views can assist us to design and construct programs that work toward this end.

As we conclude this volume, we would like to note that prisoner reentry efforts will become central in how department of corrections transition offenders back into the community. We know that the federal government and state governments have made a significant change in their correctional operations due to the burgeoning prison populations and an inability to run them, either from a fiscal point of view or a legal point of view. The sea change in corrections is occurring. More and more offenders are heading back to communities without the direction and guidance needed to succeed. The challenge that we face is best summarized by the quote at the beginning of this epilogue: Do we as a society have the will to alter our current ways of doing business such that we invest more dollars on prisoner reentry efforts and less on prisons. This is not only an operational discussion but it is also a philosophical, political, and moral discussion best described by Schlager (2013):

> Only when we attach the same level of importance to prison release as we do to prison admission will we affect any real change. Our collective moral failure may be our continued insistence to glorify and publicize punishment while fostering and promoting ignorance and silence surrounding the reentry process and the human beings that engage in this herculean task.

References

Rubin, R.E. (2016). How to help former inmates thrive. *Op-Ed Piece*, 3 June 2016. New York: *New York Times*

Schlager, M. (2013). *Rethinking the reentry paradigm: A blueprint for action.* North Carolina: Carolina Academic Press.

Index

© The Author(s) 2017
S. Stojkovic (ed.), *Prisoner Reentry*,
DOI 10.1057/978-1-137-57929-4

CPSIA information can be obtained
at www.ICGtesting.com
Printed in the USA
LVHW081834131019
634069LV00011B/271/P